This is the second and final volume of manuscripts by or relating to Thomas Robert Malthus (1766-1834) that are now held at Kanto Gakuen University in Japan. Volume I, published in 1997, contains 75 items of correspondence. Volume II, now published, contains transcriptions of further original manuscripts, including: four of Malthus' sermons; his diary of a tour of the Lake District; an extensive set of calculations in the bullion trade, suggesting that at one stage he was giving serious thought to becoming a bullion trader on his own account; lecture notes on European history from the fifth to the tenth century; his wife's diary of their holiday in Scotland in 1826; an essay on foreign trade; and brief notes on other economic matters. These previously unknown and unpublished manuscripts promise insights into his intellectual development and the events and circumstances of his life, as well as glimpses of the lifestyle of his wider family and contemporaries.

T. R. MALTHUS:
THE UNPUBLISHED PAPERS IN THE COLLECTION OF KANTO GAKUEN UNIVERSITY

VOLUME II

T. R. MALTHUS:
THE UNPUBLISHED PAPERS IN THE COLLECTION OF KANTO GAKUEN UNIVERSITY

VOLUME II

edited by

JOHN PULLEN

University of New England

and

TREVOR HUGHES PARRY

Kanto Gakuen University

FOR THE ROYAL ECONOMIC SOCIETY

CAMBRIDGE
UNIVERSITY PRESS

CAMBRIDGE UNIVERSITY PRESS
Cambridge, New York, Melbourne, Madrid, Cape Town, Singapore,
São Paulo, Delhi, Dubai, Tokyo, Mexico City

Cambridge University Press
The Edinburgh Building, Cambridge CB2 8RU, UK

Published in the United States of America by Cambridge University Press, New York

www.cambridge.org
Information on this title: www.cambridge.org/9780521184106

First published 2004
First paperback edition 2010

A catalogue record for this publication is available from the British Library

ISBN 978-0-521-58871-3 Hardback
ISBN 978-0-521-18410-6 Paperback

Contents

Preface *x*
Editorial procedures *xii*
List of abbreviations *xv*
Acknowledgements *xvii*

1 Sermons *1*

1. Sermon on the text Matthew 7.12 4
2. Sermon on the text Job 27.6 8
3. Sermon on the text 1 John 4.10 12
4. Sermon on the text Deuteronomy 29.29 19

2 Malthus' diary of a tour of the Lake District *25*

3 Bullion trade transactions *56*

Explanatory notes and definitions 60

A. Trade with Amsterdam
1. Conversion of guilders per marc into schellings per ounce 64
2. Conversion of schellings per ounce to shillings per ounce 67
3. Calculation of the par of exchange between England and Holland 73
4. Table I: Calculation of the par of exchange when the price of gold in England is at its mint price and when the price of gold in Holland varies from its mint price 78
5. Table I and Table II: Calculation of the par of exchange when both the price of gold in England and the price of gold in Holland vary from their mint prices 80
6. Calculation of the direction of the bullion trade between London and Amsterdam: A general statement of procedure and a series of worked examples 82
7. Effect of changes in the price of silver in London on the exchange rate between the English pound and Flemish schellings 98
8. Calculation of profit on trade in silver 102

B. Trade with Hamburg

1. Ricardo's table for Hamburg 104
2. An adjustment to Ricardo's table to take account of variations in the value of gold in London from the mint price of £3.17.10½ per ounce 110
3. Calculation of the profit on exporting gold from London to Hamburg 111
4. Conversion of the value of a ducat in stivers to the value of an ounce of gold in stivers after adjusting for the difference in gold content between Hamburg gold and London gold 118
5. Effect of an increase in the value of a ducat on the exchange rate between English pounds and Flemish schellings 121
6. Effect of an increase in the value of a ducat expressed in stivers on the value of an ounce of gold expressed in schellings 125

C. Statistics

1. Exchange rates and bullion prices, 1811–1813 129
2. Exchange rates, bullion prices and commodity prices 131

D. Other brief items

1. Expenses in converting coin to bullion 132
2. Groots expressed as percentages of schellings 133
3. A note on the value of a ducat 134

E. Items in Other Hands

1. A diagrammatic method of comparing exchange rates between London, Amsterdam and Paris 134
2. Calculation of the direction and profit of the bullion trade 136

4 An essay on foreign trade *141*

5 Essays and notes on Charles I and Mary, Queen of Scots *159*

1. Essay on Charles I 160
2. Essay on Mary, Queen of Scots 162

6 Questions and answers on early European history *166*

1. Lecture I 171
2. Lecture II 181
3. Lecture III 192
4. Lecture IV 201

7 Harriet Malthus' diary of a family tour of Scotland in 1826	*212*
8 Letters to Harriet Malthus from her mother, Catherine Eckersall	*242*
1. Letter 1	246
2. Letter 2	251
3. Letter 3	258
4. Letter 4	263
5. Letter 5	269
9 Eight brief miscellaneous items	*275*
1. An essay on the advantages of colonies	275
2. Notes on taxation	277
3. An extract from a draft letter to an unnamed correspondent on saving and spending	278
4. Whether to pay for imports by exporting either precious metals or commodities	280
5. Redundancy of currency	281
6. Agricultural protection	283
7. Notes on foreign trade and the Bullion Report	283
8. Four book titles	284
Appendix A Additional material not reproduced	*285*
Appendix B Letters to David Ricardo	*292*
Bibliography	*303*
Kanto Gakuen Catalogue	*322*
Index	*327*

Preface

This is the second and final volume of the work entitled *T. R. Malthus: The Unpublished Papers in the Collection of Kanto Gakuen University*.

Kanto Gakuen University acquired in March 1991 a set of original manuscripts by Malthus and his associates, and decided to publish a typed transcript in a two-volume book. Volume I was edited by John Pullen and Trevor Hughes Parry, and published for the Royal Economic Society by Cambridge University Press in 1997. Volume II is edited and published by the same team.

The history of the University's sponsorship of this undertaking was explained in the preface to the first volume, and is not repeated here.

The contents of Volume II vary widely, exhibiting the extensive range of Malthus' intellectual interests. On religion, it contains four sermons on Biblical themes. On economics, there is an essay on foreign trade and a lengthy analysis of how to make profits from arbitrage transactions in the bullion trade. The latter suggests that Malthus may have had not only a theoretical but also a commercial interest in bullion trading, possibly incited by his association with David Ricardo, successful stockbroker and famous economist. On history, Malthus' questions and answers on early European history indicate that, during at least one period of his life, he had a keen interest in the events of that period and had prepared detailed notes for lectures.

Volume II also contains Malthus' diary of his tour of the Lake District, and the diary kept by his wife (Harriet) during a family holiday tour of Scotland. The Scottish diary provides us with interesting insights into the life of the intellectual community to which Malthus belonged. Together, the two volumes shed new and important light on his personal life, and on the development of his doctrines.

There can be no doubt that successful completion of this undertaking, spanning more than ten years, would not have been possible without the dedicated work of the many people involved. Their contributions have been duly acknowledged by the editors in the two volumes. Now, at the completion of the second volume, I wish to acknowledge again specifically two scholars' contributions: Mr Trevor Hughes Parry (M.A., Cantab.), for the strenuous and painstaking efforts he has exerted over many hours in scrutinising, deciphering and transcribing, with textual annotations, the often cramped and faded writing of the manuscripts; and Professor John Pullen of the University of New England, who provided the introductions to the chapters and the footnote commentaries. I, as President of Kanto Gakuen University, wish to express on behalf of the university and members of the Board of Management of this institution our deep gratitude to them for their professional work and dedication.

Hirofumi Shibata (Ph.D., Columbia)
Ota, Japan
24 April 2003

Editorial procedures

Our aim in transcribing the manuscripts has been to create texts which are as accessible and readable as possible while being faithful to the complexity of the originals. Although the University is happy to welcome visits from scholars with an interest in Malthus, it recognises that the relative inaccessibility of Japan will render such visits difficult for many. Their knowledge of the manuscripts will therefore depend upon the accuracy of the transcription, which must be capable of serving as a substitute for a personal visit. For this reason, we decided to record not merely the final intentions of the various writers, but also all their prior deletions and corrections. This has meant a proliferation of footnotes in some instances – especially in the case of draft letters – which might not be of great interest to the general reader, but which will provide for the more specialist reader an authentic account of each writer's process of composition.

The following editorial procedures have been adopted:

- All deletions and insertions in the manuscripts are recorded in footnotes within single inverted commas, followed by the words: *is del.* or *is ins.*

- In the event of additional alterations being superimposed on a prior alteration in the same context, the prior alteration is indicated within brackets; for example, the footnote *'in a different [way] manner' is del.* indicates that initially the word 'way' was replaced by 'manner' and that later the complete phrase 'in a different manner' was deleted.

- As a general rule, the punctuation, spelling, abbreviations and capitalisations have been transcribed exactly as they appear in the manuscripts. Thus, for example, we have not altered the contemporary use of a dash (–) instead of a full stop at the end of a sentence. And missing apostrophes in the manuscripts have not been added – for example, on p. 255 'some Bishops influence', on p. 29 'dont'. However, diphthongs have been transcribed as separate letters, and capitals have been given to the first words of sentences where they are lacking in MS.

- When the original spelling is either obsolete, or archaic (e.g. 'shewn' for 'shown'), or a misspelling (e.g. 'Heroditus' for 'Herodotus'), or an orthographic error, we have usually added a star (*) to the right of the relevant word to indicate that the transcribed form repeats the original manuscript form and is not a transcription error. The star (*) is equivalent to the more usual '[sic]', but given the large number of spelling errors, the star (*) was thought to be less visually intrusive and less disturbing for the reader.

- But, in a few instances, in order to avoid confusion and to facilitate the reading of the text, we have corrected the original instead of adding a star (*), showing the correction within brackets – for example, on p. 259, 'pri[n]cipal' has been substituted for 'pricipal'; on p. 54, 'look[ed]' for 'look'; on p. 271, 'eve[ry]' for 'eve'.

- Also, errors in the original punctuation have been corrected in cases where failure to correct would have caused confusion. For example, when a full stop does not appear at the end of a sentence in the manuscript, but when the context clearly indicates that the sentence has ended – because of the sense of the words, and/or because the following word begins with a capital letter indicating the start of a new sentence – then the missing full stop has been added to the transcript. In these cases we have thought it unnecessary and cumbersome to encase the added punctuation in brackets.

- We have not altered abbreviations, or adjusted their punctuation, even though some of the abbreviations are not commonly used today; for example,

  cou'd, cd, c'd
  wou'd, wd, w'd
  yrself
  y^{r}
  w^{ch} (for 'which')
  y (for 'the')
  ser^{t} (for 'servant')
  D^{r}, d^{r} (for 'dear), as well as the more usual D^{r} (for 'Doctor')
  Comps (for 'Compliments')

- However, where an uncorrected abbreviation (e.g. 'woud', 'coud') might be interpreted as a proof-reading error in the transcription, a star (*) has been added to indicate that it is thus in the manuscript.

- The manuscript letters are not accompanied by envelopes. Letters of the period were usually not inserted in envelopes, but folded to form a self-closed packet. The address and postmark were placed on sections of the page left free of the written text for that purpose. Thus, when we refer to a postmark being 'on the back', we mean on the back of the folded letter, not on the back of an envelope.

- There are a number of instances where parts of the original text are missing because the manuscript has been damaged, or where a word or words have been obliterated by the seal. The location of the missing word(s) is indicated in the transcript by an ellipsis, and (if possible) by a footnote suggesting what the missing word(s) might have been.

- An ellipsis is also used in situations where decipherment is difficult, with an accompanying footnote suggesting a possible reading.

- The original grammar has been retained, even if it is currently unacceptable – e.g. on page 54, 'If I had not determined to stay in the North, I *must have gone* post haste to some place'; on page 255, 'Friday 12 was showery – hitherto the rain had not *prevented us on any excursion* but falling in the morn^{g}. derang'd all our plans.' It was not thought necessary to signal these archaic grammatical usages by the insertion of a star (*).

- Watermark dates in the manuscripts have been noted, but they occur only infrequently.

- We have adjusted the layout of the writing to conform to modern practice. For example, all new paragraphs are indented in the transcript despite their sometimes beginning flush with the left margin in the manuscript; and the writer's address at the start of the letter has been positioned on the customary right side.

Abbreviations

AT	Latin translations provided by Dr Alan Treloar, Honorary Fellow, Department of Classics and Ancient History, University of New England, Armidale, Australia.
BLG	*Burke's Landed Gentry*, 18th edn, 1972, Burke's Peerage Limited, London.
BLGI	*Burke's Landed Gentry of Ireland*, 1912, Revised Edition. London: Harrison & Son.
DNB	*Dictionary of National Biography from the Earliest Times to 1900*, ed. L. Stephen and S. Lee, Oxford University Press, 1937–8.
EB	*Encyclopaedia Britannica*, various editions.
Foster	Joseph Foster, *Alumni Oxonienses: The Members of the University of Oxford, 1715–1886*, Kraus reprint, 1968.
GEC	G. E. C., *The Complete Peerage of England Scotland Ireland Great Britain and the United Kingdom*, St Catherine Press, London, 1910–59.
Malthus	The name 'Malthus' is used when referring to Thomas Robert Malthus. When referring to other persons with the surname 'Malthus', one or more first names are added – e.g. 'Daniel Malthus', 'Sydenham Malthus', 'Marianna Georgina Malthus'.
Malthus Library	The library now housed at Jesus College, Cambridge, consisting of items acquired by Malthus, his father, and other members of the family.

Malthus Library (Dalton Hill)	Items known to have been in the Malthus Library when it was at the house of Malthus' great-nephew, Sydenham Malthus (1831–1916), at Dalton Hill, Albury; but not now in the Malthus Library at Jesus College.
OCEL	*Oxford Companion to English Literature*, ed. Sir Paul Harvey, 4th edn, rev. D. Eagle, Clarendon Press, Oxford, 1967.
OED	*Oxford English Dictionary*, 2nd edn, Clarendon Press, Oxford, 1989.
Venn	J. A. Venn, *Alumni Cantabrigienses. Part II. From 1752 to 1900*, Cambridge University Press, 1944.

Acknowledgements

The great range of subject matter contained in these two volumes has left us deeply indebted to those who responded to our importunate pleas for help. We are very grateful to:

- *Eric Acheson*, University of New England, for very generous assistance with early European History.
- *Michael Ball*, National Army Museum, for information on Major Thomas Moody.
- *Helen Boothroyd*, Assistant Archivist, Lambeth Palace Library, for information on Bishop Euseby Cleaver.
- *R. Geoffrey Bowling*, Acting Local Studies Librarian, York Library, for information on the Yorkshire Musical Festivals in the 1820s.
- *Jeremy Bruhl*, University of New England, for assistance in identifying the plants and trees referred to by Malthus.
- *Frits Diehl*, University of New England, for advice on nineteenth-century Dutch currency and for translations from Dutch.
- *A.V. Grimstone*, Curator, Pembroke College, for details of the 'Great Sphere' of Dr Roger Long.
- *James Hogg*, Library Officer, Central Library, Edinburgh, for copious notes and photocopied extracts dealing with persons and places mentioned in Harriet Malthus' diary of the Scottish tour in 1826.
- *Andrew Johnson*, Manager, Camera Obscura, Edinburgh, for a history and explanation of the Camera Obscura.
- *Colin Johnston*, Archivist, Bath & North East Somerset, for information on the village of St Catherine near Bath, and on St Catherine's Court and St Catherine's Lodge.
- *Joost Jonker*, Amsterdam, for many helpful comments on Malthus' bullion calculations.

- *Herbert Kaplan*, Philadelphia, also for assistance in understanding the bullion calculations.
- *Beverley Kerr*, Humanities Reference Service, British Library, for advice on early nineteenth-century literature on foreign exchange.
- *Charles Kidd*, editor, Debrett's Peerage Limited, for searching for Malthus' missing pamphlet, 'The Crisis'.
- *Patrick Laplagne*, University of New England, for assistance in deciphering the letter of César Moreau.
- *Ian MacGregor*, Archive Information Manager, and *Lisa Alexander*, Climate Research Scientist, UK Met Office, for information about Lake District rainfall in the late 1700s.
- *Shona McEachern*, Librarian, Royal Observatory, Edinburgh, for information on the history of the Royal Observatory.
- *Norman Reid*, Keeper of Manuscripts, St Andrews University Library, for biographical details of Professor Jackson.
- *Anne Rowe*, Assistant County Archivist, Cumbria Record Office, for detailed information on places visited by Malthus in the Lake District, and on the circumstances of Malthus' confirmation.
- *Joyce Scobie*, Sedburgh District Historical Society, for information on the Duke of Cumberland Inn and Cautley Spout.
- *Noel Starr, Judith Starr,* and *Alice Jones*, without whose intimate knowledge of the Lake District, many place names would have remained undeciphered, or misspelt, or not located.
- *Alan Treloar*, University of New England, for decipherment and translation of Latin and Greek quotations, for identification of their sources, and for explanatory notes.
- *Donald Winch*, Publications Secretary, Royal Economic Society, for continued support, encouragement and advice.

1 Sermons

INTRODUCTION[1]

The following four sermons were written at various times between 1798 and 1832. They are the only sermons by Malthus known to have survived. As far as we are aware, no mention of their existence has ever appeared in the secondary literature on Malthus.

On the first three sermons Malthus added a number of dates – presumably the dates on which he delivered them – although it is not impossible that he repeated them on other occasions without noting the dates – and alongside some of the dates he wrote place names, presumably the places where they were delivered. No dates or places are added to the fourth sermon, and the manuscript is incomplete, ending in mid-sentence. This suggests either that part of the sermon has been lost, or that the sermon was never completed and never delivered. The large number of insertions and deletions in the fourth sermon suggests an unfinished draft.

Another feature of the sermons is a number of diagonal marks inserted in the manuscripts. If, as seems likely, their purpose was to indicate pauses, they showed that Malthus took as much care with the delivery as with the content.

The first sermon had as its text the Gospel according to St Matthew, Chapter 7, Verse 12, from the Sermon on the Mount: 'All things whatsoever ye would that men shoud* do unto you, do ye even so to them; for this is the law & the prophets'. It was delivered on nine occasions between 1789 and 1800. The first occasion, 19 July 1789, at Oakwood, could have been his very first sermon – as he had been ordained deacon and licensed to the curacy of Oakwood Chapel on 7 June 1789. The second sermon used as its text the Book of Job, Chapter 27, Verse 6: 'My heart shall not reproach me so long as I live'. Six delivery dates are listed between 1789 and 1798. The third sermon has as its text the Epistle of St John, Chapter 4, Verse 10: 'Herein is love, not that we loved God, but that

[1] These introductory comments are reprinted, with some alterations and additions, from Pullen 1998.

he loved us and sent his son to be the propitiation for our sins'. It was delivered at the East India College on Good Friday in 1827 and 1832. The fourth sermon has as its text Deuteronomy, Chapter 29, Verse 29: 'The secret things belong unto the Lord our God; but those things which are revealed belong unto us and to our children for ever, that we may do all the words of this law'.

It has been suggested by some commentators that even if Malthus was sincerely interested in his religious duties in his early years, his interest waned in later years. And the fact that when referring to metaphysical matters he usually appealed to natural theology – i.e. to what can be known by natural reason – rather than to revelation, has been interpreted as indicating that his religion was not of the biblical kind.

These four sermons indicate the contrary. The earnestness and thoughtfulness of their content – they are not merely an assemblage of hackneyed clerical phrases – and the fact that sermon no. 3 was delivered in 1832, at age 66, just two years before his death, suggest no late weakening of his commitment to the ministry. Unless he was a consummate actor and cynically duplicitous – as some critics, contemporary and modern, have implied – these four sermons confirm the views of his friend, William Otter, and his colleague at the East India College, William Empson, that Malthus was imbued with the spirit of the Gospel and with the doctrines of Christianity and that in the performance of his clerical duties he was conscientious, devout and pious. Otter's statement that Malthus read prayers and preached regularly in the chapel of the East India College is supported by the words 'One of the late sermons' in another hand at the start of the third sermon. According to Otter, his sermons became more earnest and edifying over the years (Otter 1968, p.liii; Empson 1837, p.481).

The four sermons also show that it is quite incorrect to say that he was guilty of a deistic rejection of revelation in favour of natural reason. As well as the four biblical texts that introduce the sermons, the sermons contain numerous biblical quotations and allusions. In all, there are twenty-two specific quotations – five from the Old Testament, five from the Gospels (Matthew, Luke and John), and twelve from the Epistles (eight from Paul, three from John, and one from Peter). It is also significant that, although the four leading texts are quoted accurately (apart from punctuation), all but one of the other eighteen quotations are inaccurate – not so inaccurate as to be unrecognisable or misleading, but inaccurate enough to suggest that their errors would not have been copying slips, and that the quotations were more likely to have been made from memory, indicating not a perfect but a close familiarity with the Bible. His statement in the first sermon that we should act 'agreeably to reason and to the social state of our nature as well as to the injunctions of the Gospel' indicates that he believed we should have recourse to both natural reason and revelation, and that the conclusions of reason and the injunctions of revelation would be mutually supporting.

Another interesting feature of the sermons is the further insights they provide into Malthus' views on the existence of Hell and on annihilationism. Malthus in the last two chapters of the first edition of the *Essay on Population* argued that eternal punishment in Hell is inconsistent with the notion of a benevolent Deity, and that immortality is not of the essence of human nature; it is a conditional, performance-related, acquired attribute. (See Vol. I, p.74, n.6). Unfortunately, however, the implicit and explicit statements on these matters in the four sermons are not unambiguous. Some statements imply that Hell, conceived as a place of future punishment, exists, and therefore that the souls of the wicked are not annihilated. For example, the second sermon states that the virtuous in this life can 'look forward to the next without terror' – which implies that the wicked can expect terror in the hereafter. Unless this 'terror' is interpreted, not in the sense of positive torment, but in the negative sense of the fear of non-existence, the statement must be regarded as a re-affirmation of the existence of Hell, even though the words were delivered in November 1798, soon after the publication of the *Essay* in which the existence of Hell had been rejected. The same could be said of the reference in the fourth sermon – for which the last recorded delivery was Good Friday, 1832 – to our 'escaping future punishment'.

On the other hand, other statements imply that only the good attain immortality, and that therefore the wicked are totally annihilated. The second sermon states that the righteous are 'supported ... by hopes full of immortality'; and the fourth sermon states that without 'holiness and purity of conduct ... the immortal prize is absolutely unattainable' and refers to 'the gift of eternal life' – all of which imply that immortality is not an essential part of human nature, but is a gift bestowed on those who lead a virtuous life. These statements in isolation would indicate that, although the last two chapters of the first edition of the *Essay* containing the annihilationalist passages were removed from later editions, Malthus continued to hold to the doctrine of annihilationism to at least Good Friday 1832. Perhaps the only conclusion to be drawn from the conflicting evidence is either that Malthus inconsistently continued to hold both the conventional Christian teaching and the heretical doctrine of annihilationism, or that not wishing to disturb the religious sensibilities of parishioners and young students, he refrained from explicitly expressing a rejection of conventional Christian beliefs (such as original sin and Hell) while at the same time giving some intimation of his views on conditional immortality and annihilationism.

Theologians and biblical scholars will probably have much to say about the content of the four sermons and about Malthus' interpretation of and commentary on the biblical texts.

1. SERMON ON THE TEXT MATTHEW 7.12

Matthew 7th. 12th.[2]

All things whatsoever ye would that men shoud* do unto you, do ye even so to them; for this is the law & the prophets. –

Among many other excellent laws & precepts contained in the system of Christian duties this in the text, from the high character our Lord has given it, – from its extensive utility & from the foundation it has in equity & reason, seems in a peculiar manner to claim attention. In considering the true import & extent of this precept, we shall find that the intention of it is not to constitute our inclinations & desires the rule of our actions or the standard of right & wrong, but to instruct us, to treat each other in all circumstances, according to reason & equity; & to observe in all cases that behaviour to others, which on similar occasions we coud* with justice & reason expect to receive from them.[3] This precept does not lay down any new injunction, or prescribe any new law, but it is meant to regulate the practise* of all the known social duties, to prescribe the proportion & ascertain the measure of justice, mercy & benevolence which we ought to mete out to others upon all occasions and to make that principle of self love,[4] which is the general occasion of injustice, fraud, oppression & iniquity, the means of pointing out & prompting us to acts of honesty, humanity & justice. For tho it is easy from our natural sentiments of justice & equity, to discern how far actions are right or wrong when their consequences are indifferent to us; yet where ideas of interest interfere, where there is the remotest consideration of self connected with the point before us; it is no easy task to disengage the mind from that connection. Our passions and inclinations are called in as counsellors, & thus have an imperceptable* influence even upon the best minds. They are

[2] Gospel according to St Matthew, Chapter 7, Verse 12; from the Sermon on the Mount.

[3] 'It' is del. and 'This precept' is ins.

[4] This denigration of the principle of self-love is in contrast with the support later given by Malthus to Adam Smith's principle of the invisible hand, according to which we promote the interests of others by pursuing our own interests; and suggests that at the time of writing this sermon, Malthus had either not read or not accepted Smith's view. However, as the dates at the end of the sermon indicate, he continued to give this sermon as late as September 1800, by which time he was certainly familiar with Smith's views, having referred to him a number of times in the *Essay on Population*, 1798.

ever ready to offer some flattering pretext, some favourable circumstance, to justify & approve in ourselves what we woud* disapprove & censure in another. It is to check that partiality then, so apt to give its determination in our favour, that we are directed to make it the rule of our behaviour to do to others what we should think it reasonable they shoud* do to us. [5] By this means we are put in a capacity of judeging* impartially between ourselves & others and, as far as may be, of feeling for them as for ourselves. It makes us in imagination change conditions with them, & places us in a situation where we may have the same equal discernment of their rights & claims as of our own.

[6] To do to others what we would that they shoud* do to us is so clearly just and reasonable,[7] that it requires no proof or illustration. The mind assents to it as soon as it is proposed; everyones conscience naturally acquiesces in it; & all sects & distinctions of men are unanimous in subscribing to the equity of it. The reasonableness of this rule in all cases of social intercourse is apparent. [8] We wish that others should treat us with benevolence & candour, that they should offer no unprovoked injuries or insults, nor refuse the good offices that friendship & humanity call for. All this every man thinks perfectly reasonable in his own case, and it is equally so in the case of all.

Should interest, humour or passion then at any time, as too often they do, prompt us to an injurious or unkind action, ought we not to suspend our compliance, till we have consulted & asked our heart, whether we shoud* think it reasonable to suffer that injustice [9] or unkindness ourselves which we are meditating against another? And every picture of behaviour, which in this light appears full of horror & deformity, should be an occasion of dissuading us from those actions which woud* bring the same disagreeable representation to the mind of our neighbour. Do we not desire that others in all transactions with us shoud* adhere to honesty, integrity & truth? If they ensnare us by fraudulent declarations, ambiguous expressions, or fallacious promises, do we not think it just to exclaim against such injurious treatment? & do we not suppose that our complaints will be thought well grounded and that the publick* voice will concur with our own in condemning it? How unreasonable then woud* it be to have recourse to the same[10] insidious methods which we condemn in others, or to exercise those arts of fraud which we so much resent when practised upon ourselves? If again we [11] have been surprised into some misbehaviour by passion, mistake or inadvertance,* do we not think a kind construction of it reasonable?

[5] 'This precept puts us' is del. and 'By this means we are put' is ins.

[6] At this point a diagonal mark (/) – possibly signifying a place to pause in delivery – has been inserted in pencil.

[7] The letters 'on' in 'reasonable' are repeated and del. [8] Diagonal mark. [9] '&' is del.

[10] 'same' is ins. [11] 'shoud'* is ins. and del.

& do we not wish to be forgiven? We cannot then think it equitable to refuse the same favourable construction, & the same forgiveness to others in similar circumstances. [12]

In order therefore to act agreeably to reason & to the social state of our nature as well as to the injunctions of the Gospel, we shoud* make our Saviours rule the subject of our frequent meditation. Whatsoever ye woud* that men shoud* do unto you, do ye even so to them; – a rule which all the divine revelations of mankind in the law & the prophets tended ultimately to establish. [13]

[14] And in order to enforce the observance of this rule among the different ranks & orders of men, the highest as well as the lowest, let it be considered that how wide soever the distance may appear which birth, fortune or station may have made between one person & another; however different & unequal the lots assigned; yet that these distinctions are merely accidental, that the whole race of mankind are of one stock, the workmanship of the same hands, formed with the same immortal souls, impressed with the same divine image, & alike related to God, the equal father of all: and that as all men are by nature thus equal, they are alike subject to every moral obligation, & have all an equal right to the same equitable treatment. Let it also be further considered how uncertain & precarious is the possession of those distinctions, which elevate one person above another; & how often those who are by nature equal are reduced to an equality of condition. What security have the great & fortunate, that they shall not[15] one day be numbered among the least & lowest of mankind? Such is the fluctuation of human affairs, so many surprising revolutions often happen, that it is [16] very possible that tomorrow's Sun may find him eating the bread of affliction[17] who has hitherto fared sumtuously* every day. This uncertainty may furnish a prudential motive to conduct ourselves with that equity & benevolence to our fellow creatures in one station of life, which we woud* desire & expect from them in another.

The utility & excellence of the rule prescribed in the text appears, from its being so well adapted to general use & suited to all capacities. Most other rules of conduct are more complex, & may require attention & discernment to determine when & to what degree they are binding: but the simplicity of this rule renders the application of it intelligible to all. Let us but consult this oracle & the way lies plain before us: the rule of righteousness is clear as the light & the measure of just dealing as the noon day. Another instance of the utility of

[12] Diagonal mark. [13] Diagonal mark. [14] Diagonal mark. [15] 'not' is ins. [16] 'the' is del.

[17] The first Book of the Kings, Chapter 22, Verse 27: 'And say, Thus saith the king, Put this fellow in the prison, and feed him with bread of affliction and with water of affliction, until I return in peace'. Also, Second Book of the Chronicles 18.26; Deuteronomy 16.3.

this precept is, that it is applicable to all circumstances; is a full, adequate and complete rule of behaviour. [18]

Our Saviour was the first who taught this comprehensive precept[19] worthy of a divine teacher, which comprises in it the whole duty of man to man, & is of more avail in the commerce of life than all the lectures of heathen morality. It may direct our whole social conduct so that no case can happen in which it will not determine. It will inform us what is due on[20] every occasion & in all circumstances to superiors, equals & inferiors. It is as applicable to lesser matters of civility & decency as to more consequential moral duties; and extends to all ranks & denominations of men, to the rich & the poor, the prosperous & the unfortunate, the master and the servant, the monarch & the subject.

If in all our intercourse with others we invert the case & place ourselves in our neighbours situation, & consider him in ours, our own heart will always be able to point out a right & proper conduct.

Let us then attend to this important and comprehensive rule of behaviour, & keep it ever in view, that we may form our whole conduct by it; that we may check the impulses of unfriendly passions, correct the partiality of self love, & act on all occasions as reason & equity direct. Were but this one precept duely* attended to, & adopted into general practise,* how would it change the scene of human life! What large additions woud* it make to the publick* happiness! It woud* introduce so much peace, order, harmony & virtue into the world, as woud* render it the image of heaven, or make it like itself at its creation when everything was pronounced good. We shoud* then see no injustice & hear no complaining in our streets. Injuries & oppressions woud* not then invade the quiet of private life; nor would ambitious power violate the rights of nations, & extend desolation thro the world. In every station men by acting up to their respective obligations, & by maintaining a commerce[21] of mutual good offices, woud* concur in fixing, & establishing the general happiness upon the most solid basis, – that of publick* virtue.

Let it also be remembered that we must all one day appear at the awful tribunal of heaven to render an account of our obedience to this law; where the judge of all the earth will reward every man according to his works, & act by us as we have done to each other. If we have forgiven others their trespasses he will forgive ours;[22] if we have had compassion on our fellow servants he will have compassion on us. If then we woud* act as reasonable beings, if we woud* attend to what is not only the substance of the law & the prophets, but the spirit

[18] Diagonal mark. [19] 'rule' is del. and 'precept' is ins.

[20] 'in' is altered to 'on'. [21] Spelling corrected in MS.

[22] 'For if ye forgive men their trespasses, your heavenly Father will also forgive you.' Matthew, Chapter 6, Verse 14.

of the Gospel: if we desire to add to the common happiness of mankind in this world & to secure our own in the next; – we must inscribe this short abstract of duty upon our hearts – Whatsoever ye would that men[23] shoud* do unto you, do ye even so to them.[24]

July 19th.89 Oakwood
Feby 7th. 90 Oakwood
Augt 25th. 1791 Cranley[25]
Decemr 2nd. –92 Oakwood
Octr 20th. 1793 Cranley
Dec. 21. 93 Ockley[26] once
Jany 18 95
Sepr 98
Sepr 1800[27]

2. SERMON ON THE TEXT JOB 27.6

Oakwood, Novr 8th 89
Septembr – 91
Octr 28 – 92
October 93.[28]

Job: 27.6
My heart shall not reproach me so long as I live.[29]

We are by nature formed with a power or faculty, which funishes* us with such impressions of moral good an[d] evil, that we must necessarily give our approbation to the one, and withhold it from the other. A sense of virtue and vice

23 'men' is ins.

24 The following nine dates are presumably the dates on which Malthus gave this sermon, although it is of course possible that he repeated it on other occasions without noting the dates. The dates were written randomly but have been rearranged chronologically here. The earliest of the nine dates – 19 July 1789 Oakwood – could have been the occasion on which Malthus gave his very first sermon. He was ordained deacon and licensed to the curacy of Oakwood (or Okewood) Chapel in the parish of Wotton in Surrey on 7 June 1789.

25 Cranley (or Cranleigh) is about five miles south of Albury and eight miles south-east of Guildford.

26 Ockley is about two miles north-east of Oakwood and about six miles north of Horsham. As there is no record of Malthus having been appointed curate at Ockley or Cranley, he was presumably officiating as a visitor on these dates.

27 The last three dates are written in pencil.

28 Three more dates are written at the end of the letter.

29 The Book of Job, Chapter 27, verse 6.

is so closely interwoven in our frame, that our being must be extinguished before that sense can be totally lost. It is this principle, this internal sense, to which Job in the text expresses his regard, and in conformity to which he determines to act. My heart shall reproach[30] me so long as I live.

By the heart is here meant that moral principle distinguished generally by the name of conscience, which points out the distinctions of good and evil, and exhibits to our view the law of our nature in plain and intelligible characters. It gives us a quick, immediate perception of our duty and of the rectitude or iniquity of our conduct; approves & prompts us to good actions, disapproves and dissuades us from others.

That there is such a directing principle within us is evident beyond a question. Every man must be conscious, not only of a power in common with the inferior creation of complying with the sollicitations* of passion or appetite; but also of a superior faculty or power, not possessed by other creatures, that of[31] suppressing the inclinations of a hurtful appetite, of opposing the impulses of a wrong passion, and of forming and regulating his whole conduct by certain laws. Every action is accompanied with a certain consciousness of right or wrong, whereby we become self approved or self condemned. This moral principle seems disigned* by the author of our being to be to the [32] mind what the eye is to the body; and it is its office to direct us[33] in the way in which we shoud* walk; to admonish us of every diviation* from it; and bring us back, whenever we turn aside to the right hand or to the left. It justifies and applauds when we do right, reproaches and condemns when we act amiss; and gives [34] secret intimations, that we shall accordingly be justified or condemned at a future tribunal where we must all one day appear. This principle is indeed in particular persons[35] more or less active and vigorous, according as they have established or reduced its influence by an habitual attention to its admonitions, or by constant efforts to silence and suppress them. If we attend to its suggestions and follow it as the guide of life, it will lead us on to piety and virtue; if we endeavour to oppose or evade its counsels, its power may be gradually diminished but never totally lost. There are seasons in which this principle in spite of all arts and efforts [36] to suppress it will recover its power, as when the passions have been subdued and broken by adversity and are succeeded by serious reflection. Conscience will then resume its authority and execute its office in laying the obligations of duty before us; and in severe accusations for having departed from them.

The testimony of the heart in our favour is a secret intimation suggested by nature that the judge of the whole earth will concur with such testimony, and

[30] Should be 'shall not reproach'. [31] 'of' is ins. [32] 'eye' is del. [33] 'us' is ins.
[34] 'secret' is del. and repeated. [35] 'persons' is ins. [36] 'will' is del.

confirm the judgement which our heart has formed. If our heart condemn us not, we may have confidence towards God. The approbation of our heart not only opens to us the prospect of a distant felicity, and gives us an assurance of the future favor* of heaven, but also diffuses thro the mind a present serenity and satisfaction. Nothing can be more pleasurable to the mind than to reflect that our conduct has been such as reason and conscience have approved; that we have acted in conformity to the laws of our maker, and have lived up to the design of our creation. If upon a just scrutiny into our actions, we find that as far as human infirmity permits we have endeavoured to be faithful in our duty to God; if we find that integrity, equity, fidelity and benevolence have been the rules of our behaviour to our fellow creatures; and that our passions have been if not always, yet generally under due government; if such is the result of our enquiry, we need not labour to work in ourselves a conviction that we have acted right; for peace and complacency will spontaniously* spring up from it. Our nature is so framed that it is impossible not to receive self congratulations from the consciousness of such behaviour.

This consciousness affords a most lasting and secure satisfaction, which is not like other pleasures limited to certain seasons, does not change with circumstances, nor grow old with time, but has this peculiar advantage that it may be enjoyed in the highest perfection when we can enjoy nothing else,[37] – when the body sickens and its senses languish and decay. Which leads me to observe that the satisfaction of a self approving heart is most sensibly felt, at the most awful period of our lives, at a time when all other pleasures forsake us – at the approach of our dissolution. If in that situation we can recall the transactions of former days, & of the years that are past, & suffer them to appear in review before us; and can observe that our deportment has upon the whole, been formed and regulated by the monitions of conscience; that no corrupt passions have been attend[ed] to in spite of its counsels; that our habitual care has been to know and to do the will of our maker; to consult his honour, the good of our fellow creatures, and our own eternal filicity;* that whatever particular failings and infirmities we may have been subject to, yet that the general and uniform course of our life has been conducted with uprightness and integrity; – we must doubtless receive a peculiar satisfaction, a deepfelt joy, – a joy which cannot be described, and which the heart of the virtuous and good alone can conceive: we shall not then be afraid to encounter the last enemy of our nature – death; which will be disarmed of its terrors and no longer formidable. The grave we shall consider as the gate to immortality, as introductory to that state where conscious integrity gives the best grounded hopes, of the approbation

[37] 'else' is ins.

and favour of our maker. And what can our conceptions form to us more desireable* than to have consolation minister'd to us in that hour of distress when nature most needs it, to have secret infusions of joy pour'd in upon the soul, and to have relief supplied from within when all outward assistance is vain? How inexpressible must be the satisfaction to have no guilty fears at that time to fix a sting in our bosom! to have the pains of disease mitigated by an internal composure! to be able to look back upon this world without remorse and to look forward to the next without terror! to have confidence towards God; a confidence that that all gracious being whose laws it has been our habitual care to obey, whose favour has been the first object of our desire, is about to reward our obedience with joys unspeakable and full of glory and that he who has been our patron and protector in life, will be our guide and guardian, thro the vale of death, and an inseperable* friend and father to us thro all eternity. Who then would not wish to live the life of the righteous that his last end may be like his, perplexed by no unrepented sins, disturbed by no painful reproaches, distracted by no guilty apprehensions; but supported by conscious goodness, by hopes full of immortality, and by such anticipations of the heavenly filicity* as are next to the possession of it?

From what has been offered, it may[38] appear, that the moral principle which we call conscience, and is in the text styled the heart, was given us to be the guide of our conduct, and to lead us to an obedience to the laws of God, with which our own happiness is inseperably* connected. Be it then our first and principle* care to be ever attentive to the friendly voice of this domestic monitor, this faithful guide within us. Let us ever obey its dictates. Let it be our equal endeavour to inform ourselves of the duties required from us; and to live suitably to our informations. Such a conduct will secure us the approbation of our heart, will diffuse a lasting serenity thro our whole life; will supply us with the happiest consolations at the hour of death; will recommend us to the approbation of the divine being; and will procure the most inestimable of all blessings – a gracious sentence at the final judgement.

Novem^{r}. 10th.[39] –94
Sep^{r}. –97
Nov –98

[38] 'may' is ins. [39] '10' is changed from '26'.

3. SERMON ON THE TEXT 1 JOHN 4.10[40]

One of the late sermons[41]
1. Epis. G[l] of S[t] John. 4.10[42]

Herein is love, not that we loved God, but that he loved
us and sent his son to be the propitiation for our sins.

The propitiation for the sins of the world made by the death [43] of our blessed Saviour, as it is a subject never improper to be insisted upon, so it is more especially seasonable on this day,[44] which the Christian Church has for many ages set apart for the solemn commemoration of it. This next after the Lords day which was kept by the apostles as a weekly commemoration of the resurrection, [45] brings before us the greatest and most important event to mankind recorded in the Scriptures.

In considering this momentous subject as we are especially called upon to do, at this season, I shall endeavour to shew;* First, the light in which it is placed by the inspired writers; Secondly, the impressions[46] which it is naturally calculated to produce and ought to produce[47] on those who seriously reflect on it: [48]

And First, in reading with attention the [49] various passages in the Apostolic writings, which allude to the death of Christ, and giving them[50] their most natural and obvious interpretation, it is impossible not to allow, that they declare an efficacy in what Christ did and suffered for us additional to, and beyond, mere instruction, example and government. They declare indeed in a great variety of expressions that the satisfaction made by him was of a vicarious and propitiatory nature.

S[t] Matthew, [51] in recording the institution of the holy supper by our Lord, [52] describes him as giving the cup to his disciples, desiring them all to drink of it, and then adding these memorable words. "For this is my blood of

[40] Watermarked 1824. [41] These five words possibly in a different hand.
[42] The First Epistle General of John, Chapter 4, Verse 10. [43] 'and passion' is del.
[44] i.e. Good Friday, as indicated by the dates at the end of the sermon.
[45] 'is the' is del. [46] 'effects' is del. and 'impressions' is ins. [47] 'and ought to produce' is ins.
[48] 'and, Thirdly the very precarious and dangerous state we are in, if we find ourselves insensible to these impressions and Fourthly, the best remedy in our power.' is del.
[49] 'different' is del. [50] 'and according to' is del. and 'and giving them' is ins.
[51] 'describing the holy supper instituted by our Lord' is del. [52] 'says that' is del.

the new testament which is shed for many for the remission of Sins."[53] The language of St Mark and St Luke in recording also[54] what fell from our Saviour on this solemn occasion is almost exactly the same,[55] implying the efficacy of [56] his approaching death in the remission of sins. St John in an early part of his gospel describes John the Baptist as seeing Jesus coming unto him, [57] and in his appropriate character of a witness to the light which was come into the world, exclaiming "Behold the Lamb of God which taketh away the sin of the world",[58] obviously referring to that great sacrifice about to be offered up, of which the sacrifices ordained by the Law of Moses were but the shadows.

The same Apostle in his Epistles says. "If any man sin, we have an advocate with the father Jesus Christ the Righteous; and he is the propitiation for our Sins, and not for ours only, but also for the sins of the whole world."[59]

Both St Matthew and St Mark describe the son of man as coming to give his life a ransom for many;[60] and St Paul in his first Epistle to Timothy uses the same expressive term. He calls Christ the one mediator between God and man, "who gave his life a ransom for all, to be testified in due time."[61]

But the Epistles of St Paul generally, and most particularly the epistle to the Hebrews, absolutely abound in passages which represent the death of Christ as an expiatory sacrifice, similar in kind to those [62] of the Mosaic Law, though infinitely exalted in degree, and intended entirely to supersede them. [63] The language of the inspired writers then[64] is, "that Christ suffered for our[65]

[53] The Gospel According to St Matthew, Chapter 26, Verse 28. [54] 'also' is ins.

[55] The Gospel According to St Mark, Chapter 14, Verse 24: 'This is my blood of the new testament, which is shed for many.'
The Gospel According to St Luke, Chapter 22, Verse 20: 'This cup *is* the new testament in my blood, which is shed for you.'

[56] 'of' is repeated. [57] 'and crying out' is del.

[58] The Gospel According to St John, Chapter 1, Verse 29.

[59] The First Epistle General of John, Chapter 2, Verses 1–2.

[60] The Gospel According to St Matthew, Chapter 20, Verse 28: 'Even as the Son of man came not to be ministered unto, but to minister, and to give his life a ransom for many.'
The Gospel According to St Mark, Chapter 10, Verse 45: 'For even the Son of man came not to be ministered unto, but to minister, and to give his life a ransom for many.'

[61] The First Epistle of Paul the Apostle to Timothy, Chapter 2, Verse 6: 'Who gave himself a ransom for all, to be testified in due time.'

[62] 'appo' is del.

[63] 'The doctrine of this epistle plainly is that the legal sacrifices were allusions to the great and final atonement to be made by the blood of Christ.' is del.

[64] 'then' is ins. [65] 'our' is ins.

sins, the just for the unjust",[66] that he gave [67] himself as[68] a ransom; [69] that he redeemed us by his blood, redeemed us from the curse of the law, being made a curse for us; that he is our advocate, intercessor and propitiation; that he was made perfect through sufferings, and being made perfect became the author of eternal salvation unto all them that obey him.

Sacrifices of expiation were commanded by the Jewish Law, and[70] prevailed in some form or other among most heathen nations. They were continually repeated both [71] occasionally, and at the returns of stated times, and made up a great part of the external religion of mankind. But now, once in the end of the world (as St Paul says in his Epistle to the Hebrews) Christ appeared to put away sin by the sacrifice of himself.[72]

On the efficacy of sacrifice to obtain the pardon of sin, Bishop Butler has the following [73] observations. "How, and in what particular way, it had this efficacy, there are not wanting persons who have endeavoured to explain; but I do not find that the scripture has explained it. We seem to be very much in the Dark concerning the manner in which the Ancients understood atonement to be made, that is, pardon to be obtained by sacrifices. And if the Scripture has, as it surely has, left this matter of the satisfaction of Christ mysterious, left somewhat in it unrevealed, all conjectures about it must be, if not evidently absurd, yet[74] at least uncertain. Nor has any one reason to complain for want of further information, unless he can shew* his claim to it."[75]

These are most just, wise and pious observations. [76] After we have clearly ascertained it to be the doctrine of Scripture that we are put into a capacity of escaping future punishment and obtaining future happiness by the mediation and death of Christ, it is certainly[77] our wisdom and our[78] duty [79] thankfully to accept the benefit, by performing the conditions on which it is offered on our part, without disputing *how* it was procured on his.

I shall proceed therefore, [80] to consider the impressions, which this great atonement is naturally calculated to produce and ought to produce[81] on

[66] The First Epistle of Peter, Chapter 3, Verse 18: 'For Christ also hath once suffered for sins, the just for the unjust …'

[67] 'his life' is del. [68] 'as' is ins. [69] 'that we are bought, bought with a price,' is del.

[70] 'They' is del. and 'and' is ins. [71] 'at stated times' is del.

[72] The Epistle of Paul the Apostle to the Hebrews, Chapter 9, Verse 26: 'but now once in the end of the world hath he appeared to put away sin by the sacrifice of himself'.

[73] 'most just and wise' is del. [74] 'yet' is ins.

[75] Joseph Butler, *The Analogy of Religion, Natural and Revealed, to the Constitution and Course of Nature* [1736], 1906, J.M. Dent, London, p.175. The Malthus Library has an 1820 edition by S. Halifax.

[76] 'And' is del. [77] 'certainly' is ins. [78] 'our' is ins.

[79] 'as stated by the same authority' is ins., then del. [80] 'secondly' is del.

[81] 'and ought to produce' is ins.

those who seriously reflect upon it; And perhaps if any light can be thrown on the reasons for the institution of sacrifice, and particularly for the great atonement appointed to be made by the son of God, it will arise *rather* from considering the effect which it [82] is calculated to produce upon feeble man, than upon Almighty God.

It cannot certainly be denied that an expiatory sacrifice has in its nature a tendency to draw the attention of mankind to their offences.[83] In an unimproved and unspiritual state of Society, if nothing were done or suffered publickly* in consequence of disobedience to the real or supposed commands of a ruling Deity, there is reason to think that such offences would be forgotten almost as soon as committed. But if expiatory sacrifices before the time of our Saviour, which we know from History were greatly liable to abuse, might be supposed to have had *some* effect in restraining men from sin, it is impossible not to believe that the great and final sacrifice, infinitely exalted as it was in its character, and incapable from its nature of being abused, must have a great and permanently beneficial effect on human conduct. It seems to be *especially* calculated to produce in our minds a deep impression of[84] the heinousness of Sin, and to connect it constantly with suffering; while the conditions necessary to be fulfilled in order to render *even* this great atonement available to our salvation, are such, that the immortal prize is absolutely unattainable without such an improvement in our hearts and dispositions, such a degree of holiness and purity of conduct, as will make us fit for the presence of the Lord. It is not easy to conceive in what manner the attention of mankind could be so strongly [85] and so[86] constantly directed to the evil of sin and disobedience as by the conviction[87] that the almighty God [88] has thought it necessary that his only begotten Son, should take our nature upon him, and suffer death upon the Cross, in order to avert those consequences which would otherwise naturally and unavoidably have[89] followed as the wages of sin. Nor can we readily imagine that the gift of eternal life could have been offered to us, while we were yet sinners in any other way so little calculated to make us think lightly of our offences; and so well fitted to make us[90] appreciate [91] highly the loving mercy of God.

The method of our redemption actually chosen [92] by the Almighty has often [93] and justly been defended by divines, on account of its tendency to

[82] 'likewise' is del.

[83] 'which they have committed against God and Society and to prevent them from being forgotten almost immediately after they were committed.' is del.

[84] 'of' is repeated. [85] 'directed,' is del. [86] 'so' is del., then ins.

[87] 'as by the conviction' is ins. [88] 'should' is del. [89] 'have' is ins.

[90] 'so well fitted to make us' is ins. [91] 'more' is del. [92] 'appointed' is del. and 'chosen' is ins.

[93] 'been defended' is del.

vindicate the authority of Gods laws; [94] but there is another effect of it, not often adverted to, which appears to me to [95] afford an additional, and very powerful argument in its defence.

Taking man as he is, and it is of no use to take him as he is not, we find from experience that the cool decisions of reason have a much more feeble effect upon human conduct than the impulses of feeling.[96] Nothing great and arduous in action,[97] nothing amiable and delightful in conduct, was ever accomplished without the aid of the passions and affections.

And this is[98] eminently true in regard to religion. It must necessarily be more a matter of feeling than of mere[99] reasoning. To love the Lord our God with all our heart, and with all our mind, and with all our strength, and our neighbours as ourselves,[100] are commandments which the soundest human reason must approve but which reason *alone* can never make us execute as we ought.[101]

[102] Man in [103] this life is placed in a situation in which he is constantly exposed to excitements which are awakening all his passions and affections.[104] To convince his reason that it will be of infinitely more importance to him [105] to direct his main attention to the concerns of futurity, is by no means sufficient to give him the *power* of doing it. The arms of the combatants are much too unequal to afford any chance of success to the right cause; and unless similar weapons can be engaged in[106] it, unless we can accomplish the great object of enlisting our feelings and affections on the [107] side of Religion and virtue, defeat and discomfiture may be considered as almost certain.

But if this be so, [108] the appointed means of salvation seem even to our conceptions to be preeminently fitted to accomplish this great object. It would

[94] ', and deter his creatures from sin' is del. [95] 'be deserving of the' is del.

[96] 'the feelings and affections' is del. and 'feeling' is ins.

[97] 'conduct and action, was ever accomplished by human beings without the aid of inlisting* the human passions in the cause' is del. and 'action' is ins.

[98] 'is' is ins. [99] 'mere' is ins.

[100] The Gospel According to St Luke, Chapter 10, Verse 27: 'Thou shalt love the Lord thy God with all thy heart, and with all thy soul, and with all thy strength, and with all thy mind; and thy neighbour as thyself'. Also Matthew 22: 37–9; Mark 12: 30–1.

[101] 'Whoever habitually with earnestness and sincerity performs these duties has accomplished the most desireable* of all objects, that of inlisting* his feelings and affections in the cause of religion and virtue' is del.

[102] 'If it seems therefore absolutely necessary in order to be religious that our' and 'in order to counteract' are del.

[103] 'his ordinary situation in' is del.

[104] '[his feelings and affections] his most powerful propensities' is del. and 'his passions and affections' is ins.

[105] 'finally' is del. [106] 'in' is ins. [107] 'cause' is del. [108] 'it would' is del.

be difficult to conceive [109] by what means our feelings and affections could be so powerfully awakened and engaged, as by the circumstances connected with the death of Christ. There is first the love of God transcendently shewn* by a[110] special interference with his [111] general laws for the purpose of removing the greatest of all evils, [112] the natural and necessary consequences of sin, and conferring the greatest of all benefits, eternal life. "In this was manifested the love of God towards us; because that God sent his only begotten Son into the world, that we might live through him."[113] It is perfectly true that we are endebted* to God for our first creation, our daily preservation, and all the blessings of this life; [114] and we ought to receive them with constant thankfulness. But we know from experience the effect of habit. [115] They appear to come to us according to the ordinary course of Gods laws; and it cannot be denied that our feelings of love and gratitude are more likely to be awakend* by [116] a suspension of these laws for the especial purpose of giving us the means of grace and the hope of glory.

We have next to reflect on the exceeding great love of our master and only Saviour,[117] Jesus Christ, who did humble himself *even* to the death upon *the cross*[118] for us [119] miserable sinners, who lay in darkness and the shadow of death,[120] that he might make us the children of God and exalt us to everlasting life. The *Son* of God [121] loved [122] us, and gave himself for us with a love which he himself compares to that of human friendship; and this *transcendent* act of compassion[123] and mercy [124] in a being so exalted, is brought home to our bosoms by his having taken upon him o[u]r nature, by our being able to dwell upon the details of his life and death in[125] his human character, to hail his advent into the world,[126] to trace his history up to manhood, to accompany him in his ministry, to be lost in wonder at his miracles; [127] to feel the truth and beauty of his doctrines, to admire his patience and inexhaustible compassion, to sympathize with his sufferings, to shudder at his agony and death and to rejoice with an exceeding great joy at his resurrection, the earnest and pledge of our own.

[109] 'any' and 'in what' are del. [110] 'the' is del. and 'a' is ins. [111] Second 'his' is del.

[112] 'and conferring' is del. [113] The First Epistle General of John, Chapter 4, Verse 9.

[114] 'but as they come to us in wh' is del. [115] 'and' is del. [116] Second 'by' is del.

[117] 'dying for us' is del.

[118] The Epistle of Paul the Apostle to the Philippians, Chapter 2, Verse 8: 'And being found in fashion as a man, he humbled himself, and became obedient unto death, even the death of the cross.'

[119] 'vile and' is del.

[120] Psalm 107, Verses 9–10: 'For he satisfieth the longing soul, and filleth the hungry soul with goodness. Such as sit in darkness and in the shadow of death …'

[121] 'so' is del. [122] 'the world' is del. [123] 'love' is del. and 'compassion' is ins.

[124] 'is brought' is del. [125] 'in' is repeated.

[126] 'rejoice at his berth'* is del. and 'hail his advent into the world' is ins.

[127] 'to acknowledge the source of his powers,' is del.

Who will venture to say that the same effect could have been produced upon the human heart in any other way? If [128] to draw our attention[129] in a sufficient degree from present[130] objects which are continually exciting our feelings and passions, it is absolutely necessary to interest our hearts and affections in the concerns of futurity, it is scarcely possible to imagine[131] any thing so especially fitted for the purpose as the stupendous and yet touching event to which we have referred.

Such indeed is the apathy of the great mass of mankind in regard to objects which they consider as distant, and involved in some degree of obscurity, that even the history of the death of our Saviour, an event the most important in its consequences and the most affecting in all its circumstances that the world ever saw, is often[132] heard or read with comparative indifference.

For this however we have been prepared by the language of scripture, which too clearly informs us that there will be [133] many who will not lay hold of the means of salvation offered to them.

Excited almost exclusively by the daily intercourse with those around them, and by the prospect of worldly pleasures and advantages,[134] their[135] hopes and fears, their affections and passions have but one direction, and are comparatively dead in regard to their eternal interests. That some among the many who now experience this apathy, will[136] at a future period be awakened to more salutary fears, and more elevated hopes, may without presumption be expected. To each individual it is a matter of the very deepest interest that he should be of that number. But[137] if he allows himself [138] time to reflect on the subject with the seriousness and earnestness to which it is entitled, he must be compelled to acknowledge that he is in the greatest possible danger of [139] *not* being of that number while he continues to hear the account of Christ's[140] sufferings and death, without feelings of love and gratitude to his Redeemer,[141] and an earnest desire and resolution to commence a better obedience to his laws. In this state it is the extreme of rashness not to seek all the [142] means which offer themselves of being awakened to such[143] feelings and resolutions.

Of all these means[144] there is none so [145] peculiarly fitted to excite them

[128] 'in order' is del. [129] 'the human mind' is del. and 'our attention' is ins.

[130] 'worldly' is del. and 'present' is ins. [131] 'conceive' is del. and 'imagine' is ins.

[132] 'often' is ins. [133] 'very' is del.

[134] 'Interested only, or at least too exclusively, by what they daily see and feel and by their worldly preoccupations' is del. and 'Excited almost exclusively ... pleasures and advantages' is ins.

[135] 'their' is ins. [136] 'may' is del. and 'will' is ins. [137] 'And' is del. and 'But' is ins.

[138] 'but' is del. [139] 'that' is del. [140] 'his Redeemer's' is del. and 'Christ's' is ins.

[141] 'to his Redeemer' is ins. [142] 'the' is repeated. [143] 'these' is del. and 'such' is ins.

[144] 'external services of our holy religion' is del. and 'means' is ins. [145] 'powerfully' is del.

as the Sacrament of the Lords supper. An opportunity of receiving this sacrament is near approaching. Let us then make it our earnest prayer to Almighty God so to dispose and fit us to receive this precious memorial of the sacrifice made to save us, that it may sink deep into our hearts, and be effectual to our eternal salvation.

EIC.[146] Good Friday 1827.
G^{d}. Friday 1832.

4. SERMON ON THE TEXT DEUTERONOMY 29.29

[147] Deut^{y} XXIX. verse 29.[148]

The Secret things belong unto the Lord our God: But those things which are revealed belong unto us and to our children for ever, that we may do all the words of this Law.

These words contain a very interesting and instructive doctrine – [149] which if it had been duly attended to in the different ages of the [150] Gospel would have turned the zeal of men for *opinions* into a zeal for *godliness*, and left Christian faith and charity upon their primitive and proper foundations.

The desire of knowledge is [151] natural to the mind of man and was doubtless planted there by God for the most[152] important purposes, and chiefly as it is the great incitement[153] to that advancement of our reasonable faculties, which is so suitable to our nature, so necessary to our present condition, and will constitute in all probability so considerable a part of our future everlasting happiness.

[154] On these accounts it should seem at first sight that the spirit of inquiry, being of a tendency so evidently[155] beneficial can never be pursued too far.

This [156] conclusion however, is not to be admitted but under certain restrictions. And what those restrictions are, we learn in general from the words before us: where such matters as may[157] present themselves to our inquiry

[146] i.e. East India College. [147] Watermarked 1811.
[148] The Fifth Book of Moses, called Deuteronomy, Chapter 29, Verse 29.
[149] 'a doctrine in which Christians are concerned as much as Jews: and' is del.
[150] 'world' is del. [151] 'indeed' is del. [152] 'valuable and' is del. and 'the most' is ins.
[153] 'spur' is del. and 'incitement' is ins. [154] 'And' is del.
[155] 'manifestly' is del. and 'evidently' is ins. [156] 'specious' is del.
[157] 'naturally' is del. and 'may' is ins.

are distinguished under the several heads of *secret* things, and things that are *revealed*: and our researches are expressly[158] restrained to the *latter*.

Now the principal points of doctrine contained in these words are two, namely, – 1. That all our inquiries in matters of religious[159] speculation are to be regulated and governed by the manifest designs of Providence in the provision it hath actually made for our information. – And[160] That [161] 2ndly. The great end and scope of all religious information, whether by nature or revelation, – the purpose for which our *reason* was given us at *first*, or any particular manifestation of the divine will *afterwards* – for which "God spake in times *past*, unto our fathers by the prophets, and in these latter days, unto us by the Son"[162] – In a word the great drift and design of the Law, the Prophets and the Gospel was [163] – "that we might do all the words of his Law".[164]

[165]

That the intention of God wherever it *can* be known ought to be a perpetual rule of action to all his creatures, is a truth not likely to be disputed: [166] The only question is how we shall know what God intended in this respect; And this, as I have intimated already is only to be collected from the provision actually made for our information.

Now we may observe, [167] that our abilities of every kind are greatly circumscribed. The objects within our notice are, comparatively but few: and our apprehension of those few *imperfect*. Natural causes of every kind, and final causes for the most part, that is, the modes by which[168] nature operates[169] in every instance, and its destinations in most, are utterly unknown to us: and ignorant as we are of the *whole* designs of Providence, particular events in the

[158] 'inquiry itself is' is del. and 'researches are expressly' is ins.

[159] 'religious' is ins. [160] 'And' is ins. [161] 'however' is del.

[162] The Epistle of Paul the Apostle to the Hebrews, Chapter 1, Verses 1–2: 'God, who at sundry times and in diverse manners spake in time past unto the fathers by the prophets, Hath in these last days spoken unto us by *his* Son ...'

[163] '*practice* – the practice of solid and substantial *virtue*' is del.

[164] The Second Book of the Kings, Chapter 23, Verse 24: 'that he might perform the words of the law'. The following is del.: 'or in the language of the Apostle, – "that the man of God might be perfect" according to his present capacity, "thoroughly furnished unto all good works".' (See the Second Epistle of Paul the Apostle to Timothy, Chapter 3, Verse 17: 'That the man of God may be perfect, throughly* furnished unto all good works'.)

[165] 'First then – all our inquiries in matters of speculation are to be regulated by the manifest designs of Providence in the provision it hath actually made for our information.' is del.

[166] 'because he who aims at more than it was [manifestly] designed he should attain to, must stand self convicted of the most palpable folly and arrogance that can well be imagined.' is del. Three vertical lines precede this deletion.

[167] 'what every exertion of them indeed must convince us of,' is del.

[168] 'operations of' is del. and 'modes by which' is ins. [169] 'operates' is ins.

course and conduct of things must necessarily confound and puzzle us. Now when such is the condition of our nature, what is the part we are to take? – Shall we complain[170] that our all-wise Creator hath not made us more perfect than we are? and that we are unable to comprehend all the vast designs of his infinite mind? Shall we, in the folly and arrogance of our hearts grasp at what we can never attain to? and attempt to unravel what must even remain inexplicable to us? Shall we[171] leave the plain dictates of our reason to follow the wild suggestions of our fancy? that is, quit the road that is marked out to us, and the guide that will conduct us safely in it, as far as we have occasion to go, to wander in pathless tracts without either light or footing? [172] Shall we not[173] rather be thankful that our rational powers are as extensive as we find them to be,[174] pursue those truths that are within our reach: and cultivate the knowledge which we are[175] capable of attaining to. Thus much will in gratitude to God and justice to ourselves be expected of us; and common prudence [176] will require that we go no further. This therefore is the [177] rule to be observed by us [178] that we aim not at the knowledge of things which in their nature are beyond our comprehension: because that very circumstance of their being beyond our comprehension is a plain proof that they were intended to be kept from us:[179] and that they are of the number of those "secret things which belong unto the Lord our God".[180]

It is true indeed that the same revelation which imparted to us the means of grace, became also the means of farther knowledge to us, and brought us acquainted with truths of which[181] we must naturally have remained for ever ignorant. [182] – But here also we must keep our rule in sight: and where the means of knowledge fail us, stop short also in our inquiries. For as with respect to natural truths we ought not to indulge groundless conjectures where we have no principles to proceed upon; so neither, with respect to revealed, are we[183] to be wise, "above that which is written".[184] Where [185] reason is dumb and revelation hath been silent, where nature cannot give, and God hath not vouchsafed us information, all our pursuits of, and all our pretences to knowledge are equally [186] presumptuous, and unwarrantable.

[170] 'take it amiss' is del. and 'complain' is ins. [171] 'Shall we' is ins.

[172] 'No surely [?] ! We' is del. [173] 'we not' is ins. [174] 'to be' is ins.

[175] 'we find them' is del. and 'which we are' is ins. [176] 'and modesty' is del. [177] 'great' is del.

[178] 'on this head, namely' is del. [179] 'our knowledge' is del. and 'us' is ins.

[180] Deuteronomy, Chapter 29, Verse 29: 'The secret things belong unto the Lord our God'.

[181] 'of which' is ins. [182] 'of' is del. [183] 'are we' is ins.

[184] The First Epistle of Paul the Apostle to the Corinthians, Chapter 4, Verse 6: 'that ye might learn in us not to think of men above that which is written, that no one of you be puffed up for one against another'.

[185] 'is' is del. [186] 'absurd,' is del.

And of this sort, there are many particulars in the constitution of nature, in[187] the divine economy; and in the course of Gods providential government, the knowledge of which is "too wonderful and excellent for us"; and such as in our present state and circumstances we "cannot attain to".[188]

Of this kind are questions relating to the [189] essence of the divine nature, the general decrees and counsels of God – the secret and particular designs of providence, whether they respect the present administration of things or the[190] future. [191] These and such as these[192] are the impenitrable* secrets which belong only unto the Lord our God, – which he keeps from our knowledge because we have[193] no concern in them; or as is certainly the case in many instances, because such knowledge would but prove a snare and a burden to us.

Accordingly our Saviour, as we may collect from different passages of his history, made it a constant rule to discourage inquiries of this kind, come from whom they would. If a question was put to him at any time which related to mens practice and the conduct of their lives; in the solution of which their duty or happiness was concerned, he made no delay to give a full and explicit answer. But when curiosity led them to seek for information where information was not likely to make them either wiser or better, he always discountenanced it – either gently reproving and pointing out the impropriety of it, or improving the opportunity it gave him of conveying some *useful* lesson to his hearers.

Thus, was he asked at any time what a man should do that he might inherit eternal life? The question being material, and what every man was concerned in, he gave an immediate and explicit answer. But when one of his hearers was curious enough to enquire about the number of those that should enjoy this blessing, instead of satisfying him in a point which it did not import him to know, he took occasion to give him a useful lesson of instruction, by saying generally[194] "Strive [195] to enter in at the straight gate",[196] intimating that[197] whether the number of those that shall be able to enter in, [198] be greater or less, your concern is to[199] take [200] care, that you are[201] *one* of that number.

[187] 'in' is ins.

[188] The Book of Psalms, Psalm 139, Verse 6: 'Such knowledge is too wonderful for me; it is high, I cannot attain unto it.'

[189] 'div' is del. [190] 'the' is ins. [191] 'events of any kind' is del.

[192] 'like' is del. and 'as these' is ins. [193] 'have' is repeated. [194] 'by saying generally' is ins.

[195] 'you' is del.

[196] Matthew, Chapter 7, Verses 13–14: 'Enter ye in at the strait gate ... Because strait is the gate, and narrow is the way, which leadeth unto life, and few there be that find it.'

[197] 'says he.' is del. and 'intimating that' is ins. [198] 'of those that shall be saved,' is del.

[199] 'your concern is to' is ins. [200] 'your' is del.

[201] 'by your sincerity and diligence to be' is del. and 'that you are' is ins.

In like manner though he gave his disciples[202] all possible assurance concerning the general fact of his second coming, and of such circumstances also of that event as it was of any consequence for them to be acquainted with; yet when they[203] were curious enough to inquire, *when* these things should be, and what should be the sign of his coming, and of the end of the world, he checked this spirit of inquisitiveness, and directed them rather to the use they ought to make of the information he had already given them, telling them that it was not for them to know the times and the seasons, which the father had put in his own power, and reserved in his own knowledge only; but that for the very reason[204] that they *knew not* what hour their Lord should come, they ought to[205] live in continual readiness to receive him.

[206]

We learn from Scripture that[207] there is no method [208] by which a reasonable creature can attain to happiness but that of conforming himself to the will of his maker by a holy and virtuous conduct.[209] *Every* manifestation of himself therefore[210] which God has vouchsafed may be concluded to have this object is view. [211]

[212] This indeed is [213] distinctly affirmed[214] by St Paul, who in his Epistle to Titus[215] speaking [216] of "the Grace of God which bringeth salvation," gives this as the general reason for which it was manifested, namely "to teach us that denying ungodliness and worldly lusts we should live soberly, righteously and Godlily* in this present world: Looking for that blessed hope, and the glorious

[202] 'them' is del. and 'his disciples' is ins. [203] 'his disciples' is del. and 'they' is ins.

[204] 'since, on that very consideration' is del. and 'for the very reason' is ins.

[205] 'should' is del. and 'ought to' is ins.

[206] The following is del.: '2ndly. The great end and design of all religion is *practice*: the practice of solid and substantial virtue, "that we may do all the words of this law".' It is replaced by the following alternative version which is also del.: 'The great design of God in all his transactions with mankind, as far as men themselves are concerned seems to be to make them happy; and to do this by such *methods*, as are suitable to their nature and capacities. Now as'.

[207] 'We learn from Scripture that' is ins. [208] 'perhaps' is del.

[209] Three diagonal marks at this point. [210] 'therefore' is ins.

[211] 'And that this was in particular the avowed design with which the *Gospel* of Christ was published, will always become more apparent the more its principles are studied, and the better they are understood.' is del.

[212] 'And' is del.

[213] 'the account given of it' is del.

[214] 'the account given of it' is del. and 'distinctly affirmed' is ins.

[215] 'in his Epistle to Titus' is ins. The Epistle of Paul to Titus (Chapter 2, Verses 11–14), reads: 'For the grace of God that bringeth salvation hath appeared to all men. Teaching us that, denying ungodliness and worldly lusts, we should live soberly, righteously, and godly, in this present world'; and thence to 'zealous of good works', as quoted by Malthus.

[216] 'of this dispensation under the title of' is del.

appearing of the great God and our saviour Jesus Christ; who gave himself for us, that he might redeem us from all iniquity, and purify unto himself a peculiar people, zealous of Good works."[217]

The Great and useful truths then suggested in [the] text are,[218] that since we are placed in a state where much of what is going on in the great business of Providence is purposely kept out of our sight, we *content* ourselves with that kind of knowledge which is suited to our natures, and that measure and degree of it which is attainable with our present powers. The knowledge of God is infinite, but all other beings however exalted in their stations, are in this as in every other respect greatly circumscribed. The higher their condition indeed is,[219] the greater we may suppose are their capacities, and the more enlarged their prospects. And the time will come when those of *us* who have made a right use of their present powers,[220] shall find those very powers[221] proportionably improved, [222] shall share with those blessed spirits in a nearer contemplation of the ways and works of Providence, and be able to comprehend "with all saints what is the breadth and length and depth and height"[223] of those several acts of *infinite* power and wisdom which are now either wholly hidden from our eyes, or at best but very imperfectly discerned. But then our progress in knowledge as in happiness must be by gradual advances, and we must be contented to make those advances by such steps and in such methods, as God in his wisdom hath appointed. We must be thankful for what it is given us to know though it be but in part; and that we are enabled to see what we *do* see, [224]

[217] 'And lest any man should deceive himself with a groundless expectation of being accepted on any other [terms] conditions than these, they are expressly declared not only to be the principal but the sole end of its publication: – All hopes of happiness, but what are founded on purity of heart, and obedience of practice, being everywhere discouraged as what must and will terminate at last in disappointment.' is del. and from 'Looking for' to 'Good works.' is ins.

[218] 'chiefly two. 1st' is del. [219] 'is' is ins. [220] 'talents' is del. and 'powers' is ins.

[221] 'talents' is del. and 'powers' is ins. [222] 'to them in weight and number' is del.

[223] The Epistle of Paul the Apostle to the Ephesians, Chapter 3, Verse 18: 'May be able to comprehend with all the saints what is the breadth, and length, and depth, and height'.

[224] The manuscript of this sermon ends here.

2 *Malthus' diary of a tour of the Lake District*

INTRODUCTION

This diary was kept by Malthus during a summer tour of the English Lake District. The diary entries cover a 26-day period, from 4 July to 29 July. The entry for the first day is not dated, but the entry for the second day is dated 'July 5th. Sunday'.

The year is not stated, but internal evidence indicates that it was almost certainly 1795. 5 July fell on a Sunday in 1789, 1795, 1801 and 1807. The first year (1789) is ruled out because he was delivering a sermon at Oakwood on 19 July 1789 (see Chapter 1, Sermon 1, above). The tour would not have been before 1789 (the year of Malthus' ordination): the following passage in the diary entry of 16 July (concerning a gentleman met at Grasmere) – 'I rather fancy he was a brother of the trade, & travel'd in the black cloth way, but I was unwilling to ask him any questions that might lead to a discovery' – implies that Malthus was at that time an ordained minister. Also, the statement on 10 July 'Saw Calgarth the new house that the Bishop [Watson] has built' dates the diary after 1789 – according to *DNB*, the year in which Calgarth was built. The last year (1807) is ruled out because by then Malthus was married with two children – Henry aged one and Emily aged two – and a third expected (Lucy, born December 1807). It is unlikely that he would have undertaken a month's summer holiday without his family and without once referring to them in his diary. The third year (1801) is also unlikely, because as the author of the *Essay on Population* (1798) he would probably have included many more details of population and living conditions, as he did in the diary of his tour to Scandinavia and Russia in 1799. The reference to the 'bill for the better security of Club money' (n.115) adds weight to 1795 as the probable date of the diary. This Bill was first enacted in 1793 and enlarged in May 1795. The reference implies that the Bill had been only recently enacted.

Further evidence pointing to 1795 as the date of the diary is found in the entry for 18 July, where Malthus recorded his visit to the museum of a Mr Crosthwaite in Keswick (See below, n.203). However, for the year to have been 1795, the statement regarding Mr Pitt in the diary entry for 19 July could not have been intended to be numerically precise (see below, n.209).

The entries for the first four days, 4–7 July, were not made until 8 July. The entry for 8 July states that the 'journal book' was bought in Kendal on 7 July. This suggests that at the time of setting out on the tour Malthus had not intended to keep a diary. It would also explain why there are no entries before 4 July describing the journey from his parents' home at Albury (where he is believed to have been living at the time) to the Lake District. As noted below (n.290) his tour to the north of England continued beyond 29 July, and raises the possibility that there might have been an additional diary.

His tour of the Lakes does not add to our knowledge of Malthus' political economy, but it does provide interesting insights into his personality. It reveals him as an ardent pursuer of the sublime and the picturesque, searching tirelessly for the most satisfying views of the mountains, lakes and waterfalls. He referred constantly to his guide book for advice on the best vantage points, adding his own comments and suggesting better alternatives. On one occasion he enhanced the aesthetic experience with readings from James Thomson's poem, *The Seasons*. Other reading during his tour included Shakespeare, and Philip Thicknesse's *Memoirs and Anecdotes*.

As well as commenting on the beauties of nature, the 29-year old bachelor shows that he was also a keen observer of other kinds of beauty. We are told that at Sedburgh, the innkeeper's daughter was 'a remarkably pretty girl about sixteen'. At Buttermere, his hostess' daughter had 'a most profuse head of hair', and near Loweswater we find him looking 'wistfully' at 'a very pretty girl in the window'.[1]

In addition to these aesthetic and gender-related matters, the diary notes the state of the crops, and records details of wages, rates, food prices and rents. Although there is as yet no formal economic theory, there is obvious concern for the economic condition of the country and the people.

Perhaps the most interesting biographical detail to emerge from the diary is the fact that, although he was 29 years old and an ordained minister of the Church of England, he had never been confirmed. After receiving a letter at Penrith from his brother-in-law, presumably with information about an appointment for which confirmation was a prerequisite, he was obliged to interrupt his northward progress and hastily proceed south again to Kendal to be confirmed (see n.274 below).

[1] See Pullen 1998.

TEXT

A Tour to the Lakes made by a gentleman & his mare.[2]

Much pleased with Hackfall. The only fa[u]lt – one of the rocky hills rising from the river (Eure*) is cover'd with an underwood that is almost perfectly smooth. A remarkably dull gardener – grudged my 2 shillings. The falls are very little affected by rains.[3]

Dined at Masham[4] – the first white town: A large square, with grass growing between the pavement looking a little deserted. Houses low & small.

Slept at Midlam.*[5] 10 miles. Prettily situated on a hill. The abbey[6] & white houses at a little distance give it an elegant appearance, which vanishes upon entring* it. Houses very small – great appearance of poverty, but not of misery. All grassland round. From 15s. to £2:10s. an acre. Wages from 16 to 18 pence. Many labourers keep [7] a cow. No bookseller of any kind, & no account of the Abbey to be had.

July 5th.Sunday. Breakfasted at Asgarth*[8] – lost my way twice in getting to it – the people of the country direct by the points of the compass & alway[s] begin by *well.* Pray which is the way to Askrig?*[9] – Well, you must take the first turning on your right, which will carry[10] you thro a little town. Thro the town you bear rather Eastward & at the end of it you turn thro a large pasture to the north, & keep on till you come to a gate & then you turn directly west, & go right across a large common.

Got at last down a very steep hill by "indirect crooked paths" into Wenslydale*[11] to Asgarth* – breakfasted at a small alehouse, & pass'd two or

[2] Written on the front page of the diary. The next three pages are blank.

[3] According to *The Place-Names of the West Riding of Yorkshire*, 1961–63, Part V, p.207, there is a sharp bend and a rocky twisting channel at Hackfall on the River Ure, but no waterfall. The name comes from the Old English haca ('hook'), sometimes used of the sharp bend in a river, and (ge)fall ('a place where trees have been felled'). We are grateful to Anne Rowe, Assistant County Archivist, Cumbria Record Office, Kendal, for this information.

[4] Eight miles north-west of Ripon. [5] Middleham, which is about ten miles north-west of Masham.

[6] Presumably the remains of Jervaulx Abbey, a twelfth-century Cistercian monastic house, above the river Ure, about three miles south-east of Middleham.

[7] 'cows' is del.

[8] Aysgarth, five miles west of Middleham. Malthus' difficulty in finding Aysgarth suggests that he rode across country from Middleham, instead of proceeding north via Leyburn on the main road.

[9] Askrigg, four miles north-west of Aysgarth.

[10] 'take' is del. and 'carry' is ins. [11] Wensleydale.

three hours very pleasantly in seeing the force,[12] & reading Thomson.[13] A close warm day with a few drops of rain. The rocks of Asgarth* force are broken so regularly as to look almost like art. The scenery round very pretty. The small falls above the bridge are perhaps more picturesque than the great one.

Dined at Askrig* – a town of the same kind as Midlam.* Saw a very pretty waterfall about half a mile from the town before dinner. The fall & immediate situation remarkably well adapted for a drawing. At Harthrow*[14] about five miles from Askrig* saw another fall of about the same quantity of water six & thirty yards quite perpendicular, higher & more curious, but not so picturesque as that at Askrig.* Obliged to go on 22 miles from Askrig*[15] over a very stony road to Sedburgh*[16] for a bed. Much pleased upon the whole with Wenslydale* – in the southern part the bottoms of the hills are rich – towards Sedburgh* bare. In much of[17] the west riding of yorkshire the crops of grass are very heavy. [18] In Wenslydale* they are but thin at present for want of warmth; & [19] Swaledale I was told lies[20] still colder. Hardly any grass cut.

Fell in with a man midwife about five miles short of Sedberg,* with whom[21] I rode the rest of the way. He was much struck with the beauty of my mare. Told me of a fall [22] among the hills 5 miles from Sedberg* 50 y^{ds} perpendicular – thought the situation not very pretty by his account, & was not tempted to go & see it. The latter part of the dale which appears to be a continuation of Wenslydale* has another name[23] which I forget. I observed that when any person lived in a part of the country that had a particular name such as Wenslydale,* Swaledale &c: he always talked of Yorkshire as of another country.

On the hills about 7 or 8 miles short of Sedberg* I understood there was capital grouse shooting. The manor[24] is either purchased or rented by a number of farmers; & the privilege of shooting & preserving, let to a Lancashire gentleman, who comes for two or three days & kills about 25 brace a day.

[12] i.e. the waterfall (Aysgarth Force), or Aysgarth Falls on the River Ure, one mile east of Aysgarth. The waterfall descends in a series of rock steps.

[13] Probably, James Thomson (1700–1748), poet. 'His "Seasons" first challenged the artificiality of English poetry, and inaugurated a new era by their sentiment for nature' (*OCEL*). See James Thomson, *The Seasons*, ed. James Sambrook, Clarendon Press, Oxford, 1981.

[14] Probably Hardrow Force, about five miles east of Askrigg.

[15] 'from Askrig' is ins. [16] Sedbergh. [17] 'all' is del. and 'much of' is ins. [18] Second 'heavy' is del.

[19] 'in' is del. [20] 'they' is del. and 'lies' changed from 'lie'. [21] 'whom' is ins.

[22] 'ab' is del. This waterfall was probably Cautley Spout, about six miles north-east of Sedbergh and a mile to the west off the Cautley Road leading to Kirkby Stephen. We are grateful for information on Cautley Spout and on the Duke of Cumberland Inn in Sedbergh to Mrs Joyce Scobie, Secretary, Sedbergh and District History Society.

[23] Garsdale. [24] 'was' is del.

Was recommended by my friend the man midwife to the Duke of Cumberland,[25] whose first born was a remarkably pretty girl about sixteen. She mistook me for a fine gentleman at first & came up to wait upon me, but upon my asking her some question about the market place by way of introducing myself, & upon finding when the lights came that I had no powder, she deserted me as one of the swinish multitude.

July [6th].[26] Fine & fair – warm. Breakfasted & past* the morning at the Duke's. Sedbergh is a small white town with narrow streets, & no good houses surrounded by bare & chiefly green mountains. Set off for Kendal[27] about half past 12. First part of the road pretty. After mounting the hills dreary tho in some points of view grand. Observed the false shadows on the sides of the hills, that Gilpin[28] speaks of as a great interruption to the painter.

On coming to the top of the last hill above Kendal, was much struck with the surrounding country. An arm of the sea to the south;[29] & the western & northern horizon finely mishapen* by the Westmoreland & Cumberland mountains. Kendal with its slated houses has a very pretty appearance from the hill. Got [30] there about 3. – portmanteau not come. [31] No chance till wednesday. Showers in the afternoon, warm. Walked about the town – neat houses, for the most part & two good streets – the women all standing at their doors knitting coarse worsted stockings – very little beauty or smartness [32] amongst them. In the evening talked to three girls who were knitting by the river side. They said if they worked hard they coud* knit a pair of stokings* a day, for which they got 7 pence; but that it was poor work, & that Kendal was a poor place – poor Kendal all the world over. Some people coming by, after they were passed* the girls said something to one another – I ask'd what – why sir there'll be some scandal at our talking with you – your cloth is too fine – no gentleman here ever stops to talk to poor girls; but for my part I dont heed much what they say. Perceiving however that I might be the cause, of their unsullied reputation's being tainted by the breath of scandal, I gave them a shilling with which they were much pleased, & walked away.

[25] The Duke of Cumberland Inn (popularly known as the 'Duke's Head') was situated on the north side of Main Street, Sedbergh.

[26] Malthus wrote 'July 7th' but presumably meant 'July 6th', as the preceding entry is for July 5th and the subsequent is for July 7th.

[27] About nine miles west of Sedbergh.

[28] William Gilpin, *Observations, Relative Chiefly to Picturesque Beauty, in Several Parts of England, Particularly the Mountains and Lakes of Cumberland and Westmoreland*, 2 vols., 1786.

[29] Morecambe Bay. [30] 'to Kendal' is del. [31] 'was' is del. [32] 'prevalent' is del.

July 7th. Fine & fair & very warm. Saw the Church, the castle & the pyramid[33] sacred to liberty erected in 1788, in commemoration of the revolution of 1688. [34]

Grass cutting; saw one load in. The scythes have no bend in their handles, & the blades are rather longer than ours[35] – the mower stoops more & takes a longer & much slower strike than in the South – The crops are very good near the Town – on the sides of the[36] hills thin, for want of warmth. I observed the same kind of strait handled scythe at Sedbergh. In Wensly dale* I did not see above two fields cut. They hoped for a tolerable crop [37] by waiting for some warm weather. By the by the cottages at the farther end of Wensly dale* have very few of their windows towards the road, which gives them a very miserable appearance.

In the afternoon took a very pretty walk to Livens,*[38] five miles, all the way by the side of the river Kent, which runs in a very rocky channel with here & there some pretty falls. – was rather belated & coud* not see all the park. Coming home, overtook near the Town a party of about 8 or ten girls who were romping with a couple of men. They appeared to approach very near in [39] blackguardism to the suburbians of london – Modest bitch & maid, seemd* to be the[40] terms of[41] greatest reproach among them. They however only used these insulting expressions to one, & to her, they appeared to me to be applied[42] with the greatest possible injustice. Tho I gave them no manner of applause,[43] they were so good as to sport around me all the way into the town & to say truth I felt rather ashamed at making my entrèe* so attended.

July 8 fine – hot. Pass'd the morning in reading anecdotes of Philip Thicknesse[44] which I got at a library, & in writing in this same[45] journal book which I purchased

[33] The pyramid is a limestone obelisk, 36 feet high, on Castle Har (or Castle How Hill), the site of a motte and bailey castle. It carries the inscription 'SACRED TO LIBERTY, this obelisk was erected in the year 1788, in memory of THE REVOLUTION IN 1688'. The following words, now obliterated, are said to have been engraved on a corner stone: 'That no foreign prince or potentate has, or ought to have, any power, civil or ecclesiastical, within these realms' (J.F. Curwen, *Kirkbie-Kendall*, 1900, pp.85–6). We are grateful to Anne Rowe, Cumbria Record Office, for this information.

[34] 'Some little Sun – yet saw only one load in, & much cutting' is del.

[35] 'than ours' is ins. [36] 'sides of the' is ins. [37] 'if they' is del. [38] Levens.

[39] 'blas' is del. [40] 'the' is ins. [41] 'the' is del. [42] 'used' is del. and 'applied' is ins.

[43] To 'applaud' in this context was probably intended in the sense of 'To express approval of in any way; to approve of, praise' (*OED*).

[44] Philip Thicknesse (1719–1792), *Memoirs and Anecdotes of Philip Thicknesse*, London, 1788. This book of over 400 pages, described by the author as 'this trifling publication' (Thicknesse 1790, p.112), recounts the adventures of his military career in Georgia and Jamaica, together with a curious collection of unrelated anecdotes, some humorous, some lacking in propriety.

[45] 'my' is del. and 'this same' is ins.

yesterday. Went afterwards to see fishhooks[46] made. – Capital rods at 8 shillings, & flies with guts to them 1 shilling a dozen. 3 o clock. The Skipton[47] waggon is come in without my portmanteau. My heart sinks within me as I write this – but I am determind* to go on this evening to Low wood or Amble side,* tho without my guide[48] & only one shirt.
Lowwood Inn.[49]

Set out from Kendal a little after six – a very pleasant ride & delightful evening. Upon first coming in sight of winandermeer*[50] it appears like a river. – The hills towards the bottom of the lake not high; about the head, very fine, & being involved in a little obscurity by the setting sun were scarcely to be distinguished from heavy clouds in alpine shapes. Got to Low wood a little before nine much pleased with my ride, particularly the first & last part. – drank some tea, & push'd immediately out upon the lake, greatly rejoicing.[51] The mountains had the same blue cast, but did not look near so high as in descending the hill. The water was beautiful. In seeing mountains from a hill one is very apt to fancy that they will look higher when you get into the vale; but that is scarcely ever the case, only perhaps when you approach very near them. On a hill the opposite mountain subtends a larger angle at the[52] eye, & if this is the true reason, a mountain, ceteris paribus with regard to distance &c: will appear the highest when seen from an opposite hill of half the[53] height.[54] The man with the boat observed that the hills look'd very low, which he interpreted as a sure sign of fine weather.

[46] 'fishhooks' changed from 'the fishhook man'.

[47] Skipton is south-east of Kendal, but the diary does not state that he passed through Skipton. It shows that the route he took from Masham (the first-mentioned town) to Kendal was not the direct route from Skipton to Kendal. The reason why his portmanteau should be on the Skipton waggon is therefore not evident.

[48] Presumably his guide book, which was in his missing portmanteau, with his other shirts.

[49] Low Wood (or Lowwood) on the eastern shore of Windermere, about 10 miles north-west of Kendal. Of Low Wood Inn Wordsworth said: 'Low-wood Inn, a mile from the head of Windermere, is a most pleasant halting-place; no inn in the whole district is so agreeably situated for water views and excursions; and the fields above it, and the lane that leads to Troutbeck, present beautiful views towards each extremity of the Lake' (Wordsworth [1835] 1977, p.6). According to Parson and White ([1829] 1976, pp.66, 678): 'Many visiters* make this excellent inn their quarters for some time'. We are indebted to Anne Rowe, Cumbria Record Office, for assistance in identifying Low Wood Inn.

[50] Windermere, the largest lake in England, formerly called Wynandermere.

[51] 'at being able to get upon a fine expanse of water' is del.

[52] 'your' is del. and 'the' is ins. [53] 'the' is repeated.

[54] It can be shown geometrically that when a mountain and an opposite hill rise from the same ground level, the angle subtended by the mountain at the top of the hill is greatest when the hill is exactly half the height of the mountain. It is not clear from the diary whether Malthus reached this conclusion intuitively or geometrically.

July 9th. Fine & fair. In the morning a coolish easterly breeze, mountains clear; at noon hot & a slight haze. Breakfasted at Ambleside.[55] Walked up to Stockgill fall[56] above the inn & was tempted by its beauty to spend some time there*. Admired the[57] walk thro the copse & the views back upon the village of Ambleside. [58] Was much struck with the first appearance of the fall, tho not full of water. Got afterwards down, & sate* upon a rock in the channel. – saw the lower part of the fall to advantage but coud* see little of the upper part – Had a most beautiful view of the distant mountain Langdale Pike,[59] thro the narrow rocky & woody vista of the dell. It look'd beyond comparison higher than from the lake or the valley: & the wood of the dell concealing in part the low grounds; left the imagination to come in aid of the principles of optics, & to form the valley deeper, & the mountains higher than they really were. "Omne ignotum pro mirifico"[60] has certainly some truth in it. Our imaginations when once warmed by the sportive features of nature, woud* soon make too bold advances, if we[61] were not sometimes seasonably check'd by her modesty, & forbid* to transgress those chaste laws which she holds sacred & inviolable. There are many other views from different parts of the glen that take in a larger field, where the mountains appear to great advantage. – in short I thought it upon the whole a most enchanting spot. Returned to Ambleside & walk'd to Rydal Hall.[62] All the neat houses are rough cast & white wash'd; the stone [63] of the country is dark & used very rough. The few cottages that are not wash'd, tho not unpicturesque have no air of comfort or cheerfulness. Sir Michael Fleming's is certainly a very fine situation, commanding the view down the lake[64] (tho perhaps I shoud* say not quite near enough) & surrounded by noble

[55] Near the head (or northern end) of Windermere, about 1½ miles north of Lowwood.

[56] Stockgill Force ('Stockhill' was altered to 'Stockgill'), said by Wordsworth ([1835] 1977, p.10) to be 'one of the sights of the neighbourhood', and described thus by Parson and White: 'a combination of four falls in one; the water is divided into two streams, and, after a moment's rest in the middle of a rock, is finally precipitated into the deep shaded channel below' (Parson and White [1829] 1976, p.74). Also spelt 'Stock Ghyll'.

[57] 'The' is del. and 'Admired the' is ins. [58] 'very pretty' is del.

[59] Langdale Pikes, to the west of Ambleside.

[60] 'Everything unknown is considered marvellous' (Tacitus, *Agricola*, Ch. 30). Tacitus' original reads 'magnifico', not 'mirifico' (AT).

[61] 'we' is ins.

[62] The seat of Sir Michael le Fleming, fourth baronet of Rydal. *DNB* states (see under his great-uncle, Sir George Fleming, bishop of Carlisle, second baronet of Rydal) that 'Michael, the fourth baronet – "the brilliant baronet"' was 'incidentally noticed for his social and literary gifts by Sir W. Scott', and that 'the prefix "le", which had dropped out of the family name since the time of Edward IV, was revived at [his] baptism'. Sir Michael's great-great-uncle, Sir Daniel Fleming, had 'inherited considerable estates in the neighbourhood of Rydal' (*DNB*).

[63] 'used' is del.

[64] Rydal Water, a small lake on the river Rothay, half a mile east of Grasmere and two miles north-west of Ambleside.

hills. – Saw the two falls[65] – the lower one very pretty on a small scale. – The upper one tho it had about the same quantity of water as Stockgill fall, seem'd to shew* the want of it more – the rocks are fine & the situation good, but not in my opinion equal to Stockgill: – the walk for the accommodation of the ladies petticoats has not improvd* it. – Pursuing the water course[66] there are some wild pretty parts of the stream[67] above, among the hills & some fine views of the lake. Descending the hill on the other side of the stream I observ'd a neat white house[68] that appeared to have one of the most advantageous views of the lake that I had seen. Upon enquiry I found it was Sir Michaels – who lived there, while the other was repairing.[69] It was not above two hundred y[ds] from the hall but from one of the fells forming a better[70] ground, [71] I prefer'd it, tho not nearer the lake. Rydal park has plenty of fine wood. There are some very favourable views of it from among the trees on the banks of the river that runs to the lake. Some grass cut, saw no forks used in spreading it – all done by the hands. – Different accounts of the crops. The landlord at Ambleside & some labourers there, said they woud* be tolerably good; but my Landlord at Low wood who is a farmer & seems to be an intelligent man, said that they were in general very thin, owing to a want of rain from the middle of April to nearly the middle of June, during which time they had cold winds without any rain that coud* benefit them. He said that a rainy may was absolutely necessary for good crops in that country: that the soil was dry & gravelly; & that they very seldom had enough rain for it. I express'd my surprise & said I had always understood that it was a rainy country. He thought it quite a mistaken notion, & believd* the contrary to be the fact. He had heard it supposed that the hills attracted & [72] broke the clouds, but he did not[73] conceive they were high enough for that purpose. In short the effect of rain was produced much less frequently than was wanted. Very little corn grown in the country, not near enough for its consumption. What there is, chiefly oats, according to my Lanlord,* looks remarkably well. He says that the people of the country prefer oaten cakes to the best wheat bread, but thinks they are very little cheaper. He is of opinion that if he maintained his family which consists of fourteen servants all the year

[65] Rydal Waterfalls, described as 'magnificent cascades' (Parson and White [1829] 1976, p.617).

[66] 'stream' is del. and 'water course' is ins.

[67] 'situations' is del. and 'parts of the stream' is ins. [68] 'house' is ins.

[69] Rydal Hall 'is a large ancient building, which was greatly improved by the late Sir Michael le Fleming, Bart. whose taste and liberal spirit contributed much towards the perfection of those beauties which nature has so lavishly scattered round this sequestered vale' (Parson and White [1829] 1976, p.617).

[70] 'its situation with regard to two high fells which provide a fore' is del. and 'one of the fells forming a better' is ins.

[71] 'near its side' is del. [72] 'attracted &' is ins. [73] 'not' is ins.

round upon the finest flower,* it woud* not cost him five pounds more than[74] it does at present. He hires two women twice a week merely to bake the oaten cakes. He surprised me by affirming that the wages of a good labourer for the common works of husbandry were 2 shillings a day. In harvest they earn 3 & 6 pence[75] & 4 shillings; & yet the poor rates have risen very much lately, owing, as he thinks, to the carding Jennies[76] being so generally adopted. Almost every farmer & labourer is a weaver. The only large [77] work house is at Kendal & held in the usual detestation by the poor. Rates 3 & 6 pence in the pound. After dinner took to the water – went over the lake by myself, & saw Mr Law's, & a house that the Bishop of Llandaff,[78] had for 3 years – the breeze freshen'd; – had a hardish pull back – cool in the evening – wind more northerly. I prefer Low wood to Ambleside on account of its immediate proximity to one of[79] the finest parts of the Lake.

July 10th. Morning fine – hot. Mountains clear. Walked up under Low wood; but coud* not get a good view of the[80] north end of the lake with [81] Langdale pike, [82] Hard knot[83] &c: as I expected. Breeze rose after breakfast – Sail'd down the lake & visited all the celebrated stations[84] – prefer upon the whole the first that is mentioned in the guide.[85] The rocky hill[86] immediately on the left gives it an advantage, but Mr Youngs takes in [87] Langdale Pikes, which has a finer shape than any of the other mountains. Dined upon cold veal pye & oat cakes at the Ferry house.[88] – [89] Breeze freshend.* Had to tack [90] all the way back with

[74] 'than' changed from 'that'. [75] i.e. three shillings and six pence.

[76] A 'carding jenny', or carding machine, is 'a machine for combing or cleansing wool or cotton' (*OED*).

[77] 'poor' is del.

[78] Richard Watson (1737–1816), bishop of Llandaff (1782–1816): 'few men have done greater honour to the county of Westmorland' (Parson and White [1829] 1976, pp.56, 622, 677).

[79] 'one of' is ins. [80] 'the' is ins. [81] 'the' is del.

[82] 'Gable' is del. [83] Hardknott Pass.

[84] 'station' in this sense is 'A point at which one stands or may stand to obtain a view' (*OED*).

[85] From comments later in the diary (see n.110, below) it seems that Malthus was carrying with him on his tour the guide book by Thomas West, *A Guide to the Lakes*, first published 1778. Further editions, entitled *A Guide to the Lakes in Cumberland, Westmorland and Lancashire*, appeared in 1780, 1784, 1793, etc. It is not known which edition Malthus was using on this tour. Our references are to the 7th edn, 1799. See pp.55–60 for West's 'Station I' in his description of Windermere.

[86] 'hill' is ins.

[87] 'the' is del. Arthur Young (1741–1820) published his *Six Months' Tour Through the North of England*, 4 vols., in 1770.

[88] A ferry crossed Windermere near the middle of the lake, forming a link in the road from Kendal in the east to Hawkshead in the west.

[89] 'had' is del. [90] 'alway' is del.

not a very good sailing boat. – Did not get to Lowwood till past ten. Evening cold. Saw Calgarth the new house that the Bishop has built – The grounds are not yet finish'd – did not land at it, but from what I coud* see did not think the situation particularly eligible.[91] Mr Curwen's Island[92] is laid out in the common garden style of walk & shrubbery round the banks. Some of the middle part is still in grass. From the station above the Ferry & Mr Youngs station the Island does not appear spoilt; but from above Harrow farm house it does.

Examined the boatman & Mr Curwen's gardener (a Scotchman) in order to verify my landlord's accounts. – Found them upon the whole pretty just. The Bishop only gives 16 pence the winter half year, & 18^{d}. the summer: but he gets only the inferior labourers, & even these often leave him in Summer. The gardiner* has given as much as 2 & 3 pence, for an odd day or two. 4 shillings a week wet or dry. He says the people of the country are in general remarkably good labourers. He thinks the strait* shafts to the scythes an advantage – they take a larger stroke – in light grass a yrd forward at a time. He talks of their being able some times to mow two acres a day; & the common price of an acre is 3 shillings.

The poor people eat meat every day. 3^{s} & 3^{s}.6^{d} a week their butchers bill. To be sure he says they dont mind what they wear much. In scotland he himself has earnd* only 4^{s}.6^{d} a week, & lived like a gentleman upon it, but without the luxury of meat. He thinks that oat bread is not so much eat* in Westmoreland* as it was; & that wheat flower* begins to be prefer'd. In the evening Rydal head & Fairfield[93] were cover'd with heavy clouds.

Got back to my inn cold hungry & tired.

July 11th. Woke at four & saw from my window the sun gilding the tops of the opposite mountains, but as the wind blew fresh, & I felt very lazy, was tempted to take another nap. Determined after breakfast to rest my body & eyes, by spending

[91] Bishop Richard Watson, born in Heversham and buried in Bowness in Westmorland, resided first at Dallam Tower (near Beetham), then at Calgarth Park on the shore of Windermere where he built a house (1789) and 'devoted himself to extensive plantations and improvements of waste lands' (*DNB*). Watson records that in 1805 and 1806 he planted 322,500 larches on 'two high and barren mountains, called Berkfell and Gomershaw, situated near the foot of Winandermere' (Watson 1817, p.436).

[92] i.e. Belle Isle, the largest island in Windermere. West, noting that Arthur Young spoke 'in rapture' of the 'great island' of Windermere, added that the island is 'no more to be seen in that beautiful unaffected state', because of a formal garden established by the present owner (West, 1799, p.59). A footnote in the seventh edition states that the island later became the property of John Christian Curwen who 'demolished the garden, laid the whole out in pleasure-grounds, in the modern style, suitable to the place, and made it one of the sweetest places that can be imagined' (West, 1799, p.60). Malthus, however, thought the island spoilt by Curwen's development when seen from 'Harrow farm house'. John Christian (d.1828) married Isabella, only daughter and heiress of Henry Curwen (d.1790), and assumed the surname 'Curwen' following the death of his father-in-law (Mannix and Whellan [1847] 1974, p.426).

[93] A mountain of 2863 feet, north of Ambleside, two miles south-east of Helvellyn.

most of the morning within doors. About 2 hours before dinner walk'd up the wood beyond the house thro some very obscure paths in search of a particular view that I wanted. – Chiefly high thick copse wood without any openings. Got at last upon a dark slaty rock rather too high up the hill; – The mountains however look'd [94] grand, but the situation did not take in enough of the lake from being too near the end of it. The fells beyond the north west [95] corner of the lake are toss'd about in fine alpine disorder. Day fine, wind North, & rather fresh – a slight haze. After dinner, [96] intended to have gone up to Low pike[97] for a distant view, & to see the sun set, but was deter'd by advice of my Landlord on account of the haze – Rode to Troutbeck[98] instead, a pretty village scatterd* along the side of a high[99] hill opposite to the ridge that is crown'd by hill* Bell[100] At half past six, the sun was set to almost all the houses. Soon after I turnd* out[101] of the high road from Low wood, winding up the hill, I was particularly struck, on looking back, with the extraordinary height of the fells; seen thro trees on each side of the road, & assisted by the Haze. It was the very view that I had been looking for, tho perhaps not quite so much of the lake was seen as one coud* wish. Wind in the evening high & cold. Sunset cross'd with clouds.

July 12th. Woke at three, but found the clouds too low for a view from the pike. Wind North, & rather fresh. Rode before breakfast [102] across the head of the lake & along the banks of the Brathay,[103] which runs for some way smooth & placid between green meadows – one of them cut & carried – apparently a light crop. Turn'd afterwards up by Roughrig*[104] with a little lake at the bottom; pass'd Elterwater,[105] & a white house of a Mr ...[106] at the [107] head call'd Elterwater

[94] 'very fine' is del. [95] 'end' is del. and 'corner' is ins. [96] 'too' is del.

[97] Low Pike, a smaller mountain, about two miles north of Ambleside.

[98] Troutbeck village, south-east of Ambleside, takes its name from the Troutbeck river that flows into Windermere. The valley of the Troutbeck is 'distinguished by the mountains at its head – by picturesque remains of cottage architecture; and, towards the lower part, by bold foregrounds formed by the steep and winding banks of the river' (Wordsworth [1835] 1977, p.9).

[99] 'high' is repeated. [100] Ill Bell, a mountain north-east of Ambleside.

[101] 'out' is repeated. [102] 'along' is del.

[103] The river Brathay has its source in Langdale, west of Windermere. It is one of the two main feeders of Windermere, the other being the river Rothay, whose source is in Grasmere, north of Windermere.

[104] Loughrigg lies between the rivers Brathay and Rothay, south of Grasmere, and west of Ambleside. The land 'rises boldly into a lofty and romantic fell' [Loughrigg Fell] (Parson and White [1829] 1976, p.617). The 'little lake at the bottom' is Loughrigg Tarn, said by Wordsworth to be 'the most beautiful example' of a tarn (Wordsworth [1835] 1977, p.40) and described as 'round, clear, and bright as heaven' in his 1811 poem Epistle to Sir George Beaumont; but in a later note he added that it had lost much of its beauty through tree felling (Wordsworth [1835] 1977, pp.40, 177–8; an 1811 illustration of the tarn is reproduced facing p.178).

[105] Elterwater (or Elter Water), a small lake or tarn, 2–3 miles west of Ambleside, on the river Brathay.

[106] Name unclear, possibly Begsons or Byrons. Elterwater Hall was later occupied by David Huddleston who started (1823–24) a gunpowder mill near the village of Elterwater.

[107] 'top' is del.

hall. Came upon Grasmere[108] – the opposite situation to that which Mr Gray[109] describes, & which Mr West[110] prefers. The lake answers the beautiful description given of it. Wound by a rough path down the hill to the edge of Rydalwater[111] & return'd much pleased with my ride. Wind almost sunk – Day cloudy & rather warm. Before dinner, went on the water round the head of the lake, & a little way up the Brathay – endeavour'd to punt round the shores, but found the bottom too uneven.

In the evening, walked up to the top of the hill behind the house, which tho not dignified with the name of mountain, I found to be a walk of an hour[112] and a half. I reached what I conceived to be the summit 4 times, before I really got to it. Hills heap'd on hills.[113] Had a fine view of the mountains, some bright with gleams of sun, others coverd* with dark clouds. Saw the sea by the Lancaster sands & Ingleborough*.[114] Evening cloudy with a few drops of rain. Wind rather high & cool. A note to say that my portmanteau has not reach'd Kendal. Determine to go tomorrow to make enquiries & leave directions.

The bill for the better security of Club money[115] has effected the destruction of almost all the societies in the North. The people were greatly enraged & thought it a trick of government to get the money. Most of the clubs dissolved themselves, & divided their capital in proportion to the time that each person had been a member, without regard to whether they had had occasion to draw from the fund or not. The contribution was generally only 6 pence [116] a month, & some of the clubs were very rich. They lent out their money on mortgage. My Landlord thinks that it was the intention of [the] ministry to

[108] One of the most picturesque lakes, being completely encircled by mountains. The town of Grasmere, at the head of the lake, is about 3½ miles north-west of Ambleside.

[109] Thomas Gray, *Journal in the Lakes*, 1775. Thomas Gray (1716–71), poet, made a journey through the English Lake District in 1749, and his *Journal* recording the journey was published in 1775. It is regarded as his most finished prose work (*OCEL*). West's *Guide* includes quotations from Gray's *Journal* and reproduces the full text of Gray's *Journal* in an Appendix (pp.199–223 in West, 1799).

[110] On pp.79–80 West quotes Gray's description of Grasmere, and on p.80 states: 'Mr Gray's description is taken from the road descending from Dunmail-raise. But the more advantageous station, to view this romantic vale from, is on the south end of the western side', i.e. from Dearbought Hill (Parson and White [1829] 1976, p.67).

[111] Rydal Water, a small lake, about half a mile east of Grasmere, and about two miles north-west of Ambleside.

[112] 'hour' is ins.

[113] Probably an allusion to West's 'mountains heaped upon mountains' (West, 1799, p.53).

[114] Pennine mountain, in North Yorkshire, about 35 miles south-east of Ambleside.

[115] Probably 'A Bill for the Encouragement and Relief of Friendly Societies', presented by Sir George Rose, ordered to be printed 25 April 1793, enacted 33 Geo. III, c. 54, the provisions of which were enlarged in 1795 by another bill presented by Sir George Rose, ordered to be printed 8 May 1795, enacted 35 Geo. III. c.111.

[116] 'a ye' is del.

destroy the clubs, from an idea that they assisted the dissemination of republican principles. He believes there might be some little foundation for the supposition, but thinks that the bill had a much worse effect of the same kind.

About four or five years ago Sir Michael Fleming & the Bishop[117] sent out notices to all the Farmers not to shoot. The people were so enraged that in the course of two years there was hardly a partridge or a hare in the country which before had been[118] extraordinarily well stock'd. The gentlemen perceived their mistake, & the game now increases again rapidly.

July 13. Morning cloudy. Set off at five. Seeing the mountains clear rode round by Bowness,[119] to take Mr Young's station,[120] as is recommended, in the morning. Found that I had not gone high enough before. It is certainly a good situation & takes in all the beauties of the lake at one view.

Breakfasted at Bowness with an intent to go on the lake to take my leave, but the wind increasing, & there being no sailing boat, rode to Kendal instead.

Kendal. After much enquiry, found that my portmanteau had gone by an opportunity, & had been lying at a by place in[121] Kendal since wednesday. –Reflected upon the fatal uses to which opportunities are sometimes put. Middle of the day fine, wind lower. Rode in the afternoon to Newby Bridge[122] very prettily situated on the river about half a mile from the end of winder mere.* Had a distant view of my old friends the fells at the head of the lake looking purple with the rays of the setting sun. Beautiful evening, wind sunk. Never once saw windermeer* perfectly smooth. Hay very generally about, at Kendal, but a good deal uncut yet. Crops not so good as expected. Never slept in a more agreeable, or cheaper house. Charges, 8 pence for myself, & 19 pence my mare, three quarters of corn. –

July 14th. Beautiful morning; set of* six for Ulverston.[123] Had a very pleasant ride thro an agreeable country. After breakfasting & getting my mare shod, went to

117 Presumably Bishop Richard Watson. 118 'been' is ins.

119 Near the middle of the eastern shore of Windermere, about 6 miles south of Ambleside – and 8½ miles north-west of Kendal.

120 Arthur Young's description of Windermere as seen from the vicinity of Bowness was quoted by West (1799, pp.59, 65–9) from Vol. III, p.176 of Young's *Six Months' Tour*. Young's description is West's 'Station V' in his guide to Windermere.

121 'at' is del. and 'in' is ins.

122 'Newby Bridge, a hamlet, charmingly situated at the foot of Windermere ... 9 miles NE by N of Ulverston' (Parson and White [1829] 1976, p.702).

123 About 18 miles south-west of Kendal.

see Furness Abbey.[124] Took the iron mines at Whitrigs*[125] in my way. Shaft about 60 y[rds]. Now it is so deep, they can raise only 16 tons in the 12 hours. The men earn only 2 shillings a day. Their faces & hands are like burnish'd copper. The ore when it first comes up is very moist & butteraceous.*[126] Some of the hard lumps appear as heavy as so much solid iron – They are reckon'd the richest parts, but are more difficult to smelt. The ore is carried away in small one horse carts, [127] & the dust of the roads they travel is stained almost pink.

Furness Abbey is prettily, but not finely situated; & the ruins are I think inferior to Fountains[128] or Netley[129]. The stone is red, but the exposed parts cover'd with the white kind of[130] moss. Day fine, [131] hot.

Walk'd in the afternoon to Conishead priory.[132] Did not think it quite answer'd the brilliant description given of it; but the horizon was hazy & I did not see it to advantage. Evening rather cloudy, no sun setting. Wind N by W. Good deal of hay carrying – all in one horse carts – Crops good.

July 15. Grey morning. Set of* at six for Coniston.[133] The ride from the end of the lake to water head[134] very beautiful. Observ'd the two first stations mentioned,[135] but prefer some further on. The [136] mountains being nearer take up more of the picture than in any of the views on windermere.

[124] Furness Abbey, a mediaeval abbey, 'whose interesting and magnificent remains ought to be seen by every visiter* to the Lakes' (Parson and White [1829] 1976, p.709), is about six miles south-west of Ulverston near the town of Dalton, and about two miles north-east of Barrow-in-Furness.

[125] Whitriggs, about half a mile west of Lindal-in-Furness, north-north-east of Dalton-in-Furness. The iron mines at Whitriggs, now disused, were called 'the Peru of Furness'.

[126] 'butteraceous', altered by Malthus from 'buttersaceous', is a nonce-word for 'butyraceous', meaning 'of the nature of butter, buttery' (*OED*).

[127] 'which' is del. [128] Fountains Abbey, near Ripon, North Yorkshire.

[129] Netley Abbey, the remains of a thirteenth-century abbey, near Southampton, Hampshire.

[130] 'of' is repeated. [131] 'warm' is del.

[132] Conishead Priory, about two miles south of Ulverston, was described by West as 'the paradise of Furness ... so wonderfully pretty a place, to which nature has been so profuse in noble gifts, and where art has lent its best assistance, under the regulation of an elegant fancy, and a refined taste' (West, 1799, pp.42, 44).

[133] About 13 miles north of Ulverston, near the head (north end) of Coniston Water, and about six miles south-west of Ambleside.

[134] i.e. the village of Waterhead at the head of Coniston Water.

[135] See West, 1799, pp.46–9; 'Station I' and 'Station II'.

[136] 'high' is del.

After breakfast, took a fatiguing but very amusing walk to [137] Coniston Old man[138] "up among the loose disjointed cliffs, & fractured mountains wild".[139] It is the highest fell in the country; & its open side[140] answers very exactly Thomsons description. It fully satisfied me as a mountain excursion. Near the top there are some of the finest slate quarries of any in the country. Stopt* to see the process of riving[141] which is rather curious. The men earn according to the nature of their work from 2 & 8 pence to 2 shillings. The rive'r whose work requires most skill has 2 & 8 pence. There are some coppermines, not very[142] rich, on the side of the hill that are not work'd just at present.

Down the rocky clefts of the mountain roll some rapid streams. They are [143] now very low in water but from the appearance of their beds they must be thundering torrents when full. From the summit there is a very extensive sea view, but the horizon was not clear. Of the mass of mountains to the North some were finely illumined by the sun, others cover'd with dark clouds. Helvellyn was bright, but Skiddaw had a cap.[144] It was warm & almost perfectly calm, so I sate* myself down by the old man & beg'd half an hour of his company. He was a tall venerable looking personage with hard features very much weather beaten. [145] I coud hardly make a guess at his age; for tho his cheeks were deeply furrow'd, he appeared [146] healthy & strong, & had very few marks of decay about him. He must have seen much of the world tho he had not the air of a traveller; for his views of nature were enlarged & comprehensive, but I was sorry to remark in a character in many respects so independent too great an attention as I thought to rank; for he seem'd as if he woud* look down upon all who were not in very high situations. This mark of pride together with his air which was particularly stiff, made me wonder that I felt so little embarrassment in his presence; however he shewd* no signs of being offended at the liberty I had taken of setting myself down by[147] him: but all my efforts to draw him into

[137] 'up' is del. and 'to' is ins.

[138] The mountain known as The Old Man of Coniston is the highest point of Coniston Fell, about two miles west of Coniston Water.

[139] 'And up among the loose disjointed Cliffs, / And fractur'd Mountains wild, the brawling Brook / And Cave, presageful, send a hollow Moan, / Resounding long in Fancy's Ear' (Thomson, *Seasons*, 'Winter', lines 68–71).

[140] 'side' changed from 'sides'. [141] i.e., the process of splitting or cleaving.

[142] 'very' is repeated. [143] 'at pre' is del.

[144] The third and fourth highest mountains of the Lake District.

[145] 'He appear'd to have seen a good deal of the world, tho he had not at all the air of a traveller. I shoud* judge him to be a man of enlarged & comprehensive views, & tho apparently without pride, he coud* hardly help looking down' is del.

[146] 'very' is del.

[147] 'near' is del. and 'by' is ins.

chat were vain, & I was obliged to have recourse to Lavater's principles,[148] & to form my ideas of his character, more from his countenance than conversation. I shoud* say upon the whole that he was superior in appearance[149] to any man I had ever met with. He had [150] the steadiness & experience, without any of the weaknesses of age; & of all the old people I ever was in company with, he was the least inclined to be narrative. When I got up to take my leave he did not move but look'd very grave, & what I thought rather extraordinary after the cold[151] manner in which he had received me, he appear'd more offended at my going than at my coming; for shortly after I left him, upon turning round I saw a cloud over his brow, & he appeard* to frown more, to look darker than I had ever seen him. Upon getting to the village I enquired his character among the people of the country. I find that he lives very much alone. Few like to visit him for he has always had the character of being very high & difficult of access, & some think him[152] a little crazy; [153] for in changeable & cloudy weather, his head is very evidently affected, & he appears at those times quite lost.

After dinner took a walk to the side of the lake, but coud* get no boat. The best views are from [the] eastern side of the water. The hill opposite the village is not high & very strait* at top.[154] The village is [155] prettily scatter'd under the mountain, & looks very picturesque from the opposite shore. Fell in with an old schoolmaster, the oracle of the place, & guide to Tourists, a great mathematician & natural philosopher, & a little bit of a democrat.

They complain at Coniston of a scarcity of grass owing to the cold spring – a great deal not begun to be cut.

July 16. Clouds very low, but sun at intervals. Call'd upon my friend the philosopher, who shew'd* me some maps of his son, who is with the famous Boulton,[156] very neatly done, & a table of the heights of all the mountains in the country. Went afterwards with him to a famous station at the North end of the lake,[157] but did not like it so well as some on the eastern side. The old man was in the clouds. My day & night at the publick* house at coniston cost me 7 shillings, the cheapest I have had yet. Rode to breakfast at Hawshead.*[158]

[148] Johann Kaspar Lavater (1741–1801), Swiss poet and mystic, exponent of physiognomy, according to which character can be inferred from appearances.

[149] 'in appearance' is ins. [150] 'all' is del. [151] 'the' is del. and 'the cold' is ins.

[152] 'him' is del. and 'think him' is ins. [153] 'at top' is del.

[154] 'at top' changed from 'atop'. [155] 'very' is del.

[156] Matthew Boulton (1728–1809), engineer and manufacturer, the business partner of James Watt.

[157] Presumably the 'charming scene' described by West (1799, p.51) at the upper end of Coniston Water.

[158] Hawkshead, about three miles east of Coniston, at the head of Esthwaite Water, a lake about two miles west of Windermere.

Nothing much worth seeing in Esthwaite water.

Dined at Ambleside.[159] Rode afterwards to Lowwood. Disappointed in finding no letter from Charlotte.[160] Went from thence to Grasmere,[161] a neat publick* house at the further end of the Lake near the church, which receiv'd me very comfortably. I imagine[162] it is the same house that Mrs Montgomery lived in, & being the [163] best in the place, when she left it, was let for an Inn. Clouds very low. Small rain at times. W.N.[164] & rather high. After I had drunk tea, a gentleman with bags was introduced. Found him an agreeable man. He came from Wales & was going to Carlisle. I rather fancy he was a brother of the trade, & travel'd in the black cloth way, but I was unwilling to ask him any questions that might lead to a discovery.

July 17th. Some little rain in the night & in the morning. Clouds very low. After breakfast it cleared up a little & I walkd* round the lake to Mr Wests[165] Station again, that I might have it in my mind when I saw Mr Gray's in my way to Keswick. There are some pretty views of the lake among some scrubby thorns & shrubs some way down the diclivity* immediately below Mr Wests point; [166] a situation might be chosen here, that woud* not be too high for a drawing.

My landlord at Grasmere has a very good crop of hay & a very promising one of oats. He says the farmers generally find their men in victuals & drink, & then the common price is a shilling in summer & 10 pence in winter; eighteen pence in harvest. Chickens are 6 pence & 7 pence a piece – a fat fowl ten pence. Small chickens to put up 4 pence. This is the only article that I have observ'd to be very much cheaper than in the South: & on this account you may have what appears a very handsome dinner for almost[167] as little money as a shabby one. At Ambleside I had a roasted fowl with slices of cold ham, cold beef, salad, & tarts for 1^s.9^d. At Ulverston I had a dish of Salmon, a fine [168] fowl, & a whole cold tongue, a dish of peas, tart &c: for 1^s.6^d. At Kendal & Low wood, they charged me 2 shillings whether I had a beef steak or fish & fowl.

Set off at half past 12 for Keswick. A small driving rain came on, & I saw [169] Mr Grays view to great disadvantage; but as far as I coud* judge, I prefer the views from the other side.[170] In coming from Keswick the little paradise as

[159] About five miles north-east of Hawkshead.

[160] Malthus' sister, Mary Catherine Charlotte (1764–1821).

[161] A village about 4½ miles north-west of Low Wood, at the head of the lake of that name.

[162] 'understand' is del. and 'imagine' is ins.

[163] Second 'the' is del. [164] i.e., Wind. North. [165] 'Wests' is ins. [166] '& much' is del.

[167] 'almost' is ins. [168] '& peas' is del. [169] 'my' is del.

[170] Gray's description was taken from the north end of Grasmere, looking south. West believed that the more advantageous station is the south end of the western side, looking north (West, 1799, pp.79–81).

Mr Gray calls it[171] is more unsuspected, as the road runs for some way between two barren mountains, & this circumstance might make the beauty of the first opening to the view strike him more strongly. By the by, Rydal water with its two wooded islands[172] when seen from the shore opposite to Rydal crag, [173] which is a rocky & finely shaped hill wooded at the bottom, has a good deal of beauty: but both Grasmere & Rydal now they are low in water are a little defaced with reeds near their heads.

Leathes water[174] runs for some way by the side of the road, which skirts Helvellyn. It is a respectable lake; & some fine rocks rise from it. I shoud* think the best views were from the other side, where there is one house seemingly well situated. Almost immediately upon losing sight of Leathes water, I enter'd Agberthwaite,*[175] which struck me as a most picturesque little vale, tho I believe it is the same that Mr Gray speaks rather disrespectfully of.[176] There is one house by the stream situated under a wooded rock (which I take to be St John)[177] that upon looking round, I thought woud* make as pretty a picture as any view that I had seen.[178] The stream & bridge were in front, a high dark rock to the right, & Helvellyn in the back ground to the left. How long the inhabitants see the sun in a day, I cant pretend to say. There was grass cut a little further on, tho I did [not] see any just about the village. I fancy indeed that Old Helvellyn warms himself for some time in a morning at their expence,* particularly in winter. When I reach'd the top of the last hill I mistook Bassenthwaite[179] for Derwent,[180] & was a good deal disappointed. In proceeding I hardly thought I saw the view that M^r

171 'Not a single red tile, no flaring gentleman's house, or garden walls, break in upon the repose of this little unsuspected paradise; but all is peace, rusticity, and happy poverty, in its neatest, most becoming attire' (Gray, 1775, p.211; quoted in West, 1799, p.80, where 'garden walls' is given as 'garden wall').

172 Heron Island and Little Isle; 'with its two wooded islands' is ins. at this point.

173 Possibly the hill now known as Nab Scar, north of Rydal Water, above Nab Cottage; 'has a goo' is del. at this point.

174 i.e., Thirlmere – 'often called LEATHES WATER, from the family to whose estate it belongs; and sometimes WYTHBURN WATER, from the valley in which it is partly situated' (Parson and White [1829] 1976, p.72).

175 Legburthwaite.

176 'The vale you go in has little breadth; the mountains are vast and rocky, the fields little and poor, and the inhabitants are now making hay, and see not the sun by two hours in a day so long as at Keswick' (Gray, 1775, p.210).

177 West (1799, p.84) referred to 'the romantic, castle-like rock of St. John' terminating the narrow green vale of 'Legberthwaite'. This might be the rock now known as Castle Rock, just north of Legburthwaite, above St John's Beck, at the entry to St John's in the Vale.

178 'seen' is ins. 179 Bassenthwaite Lake, about 3½ miles north-west of Keswick.

180 Derwent Water, just south of Keswick.

Gray was so enchanted with as he left Keswick;[181] but the mountains were all coverd* & the day so gloomy that I coud* [182] see nothing to advantage.

Found my portmanteau at Keswick – rejoiced thereat.

In the evening, walked down to the lake[183] in a misty rain. Coud* see little but that Esquire Pocklington,[184] with his staring[185] house, forts & batteries had spoilt his island.

July 18 Clouds very low with small rain at times. After breakfast it cleard* up a little & I walked all round the lake. First to Crow Park which has not now even the Stumps of the old trees remaining[186] – It [187] certainly [188] commands a very fine general view of the lake. Pursuing the line of the shore I got wrong for Cockshut hill,[189] so I left that for another opportunity & proceeded to M^r^

[181] 'about two miles from the town [Keswick] mounted an eminence called *Castle-Rigg*, and the sun breaking out discovered the most enchanting view I have yet seen of the whole valley behind me, the two lakes, the river, the mountains all in their glory' (Gray, 1775, p.210). Wordsworth was similarly inspired by Derwent Water: 'Derwent is distinguished from all the other lakes by being *surrounded* with sublimity: the fantastic mountains of Borrowdale to the south, the solitary majesty of Skiddaw to the north, the bold steeps of Wallow-crag and Lodore to the east, and to the west the clustering mountains of New-lands' (Wordsworth [1835] 1977, p.97n).

[182] Second 'that I coud*' is del.

[183] i.e., Derwent Water.

[184] 'Mr. Pocklington, a native of Nottinghamshire, ... played strange pranks by his buildings and plantations upon Vicar's Island, in Derwentwater, which his admiration, such as it was, of the country, and probably a wish to be a leader in a new fashion, had tempted him to purchase' (Wordsworth, [1835] 1977, p.150; facing p.166 there is a reproduction of a contemporary illustration of 'Pocklington's or Vicar's Island'). Further details of Pocklington's buildings are given in the entries for 18 July and 24 July. The island and its buildings presented a more favourable impression to Parson and White in 1829: '*The Vicar's Isle* contains 5½ acres, beautifully laid out in pleasure grounds, interspersed with a variety of trees, and crowned with a neat house in the centre. It is the property of General Peachey, but formerly belonged to the Pocklingtons' (Parson and White [1829] 1976, p.72).

[185] The expression 'staring house' seems to be a misreading by Malthus of 'flaring gentleman's house' in Gray's statement quoted in n.171 above. The use by Gray and West of the long 's' apparently misled Malthus into reading 'flaring' as 'staring'. In this context, 'to flare' would mean 'to open or spread outwards, as the sides of a bowl, the mouth of a horn', or 'to spread out to view, display' (*OED*). Wordsworth, quoting Gray, read the word as 'flaring' (Wordsworth [1835] 1977, p.162).

[186] 'Crow-Park' is West's 'Station II' in his account of Keswick. He described it as 'a gentle eminence, not too high, on the very margin of the lake, which it commands in all its extent, and looks full into the craggy pass of Borrowdale', a paraphrase of Gray's description. Gray (1775, p.207), quoted by West (1799, p.87), stated that it was 'once a glade of ancient oaks, whose large roots still remain in the ground'. Crow Park is on the eastern shore of Derwent Water, close to the centre of Keswick.

[187] 'has' is del.

[188] 'a very fine view' is del.

[189] West's 'Station I': 'Cockshutt-Hill is remarkable for a general view ... has an easy ascent to the top, and from it the lake appears in great beauty' (West, 1799, p.86). On the following day, 19 July, Malthus walked to 'Cockshutt Hill' – probably the hillock now known as Castlehead Wood, a National Trust viewpoint, above Cockshot Wood, about half a mile south of Keswick – but was disappointed with the view.

Wests 3rd station[190] under Wallow Crag.*[191] I think it inferior to Crow Park, tho in the northern view Skiddaw looks well in the back ground. Went on to the 'rough rocks of dread Lowdore*',[192] & little else was to be seen, for the torrent [193] was dwindled to a small stream, almost entirely conceal'd by the promenent* rockiness of the channel. It must be a noble fall when full. The situation is beautiful. The village of Grange[194] is prettily situated on the[195] Derwent[196] among some fine craggy hills, but a small rain came on & I coud* see only the entrance of Borrowdale[197] which is very fine.

Returned on the western side of the lake chiefly thro shady lanes with plenty of hedge roses & woodbines, here & there catching a beautiful partial view of the lake. Walked in my way through Lord William Gordon['s] place,[198] the house & grounds of which are very pretty. From the end of a promontory in the park that pushes far into the lake, on a black rock under a small oak, there appeard* to me to be a very favourable view of the lake, as far as I coud* judge in so obscure a day: Skiddaw was more than half hid; but it only raind* at intervals, was calm & rather warm. I found it a longer walk than I expected, & as[199] I had loitered a good deal, & not look'd at my watch, I was rather surprised[200] to find the people of the country wishing me a good night before I had ordered my dinner.

As for Mr Pocklington & his Island, it woud* be a good thing for the lake, if they were both to sink into it some afternoon. [201] Nothing but his coming to some violent end can prevent his doing more mischief. He has already two Guwgaw*[202] houses besides the one on the Island, not to mention a church, & forts & summerhouses without number, & yet I understand his appetite for building is not yet satiated. He has red cornerstones to most of his houses, & I am afraid he has introduced the fashion for I observe some more in the same style.

The flies are most uncommonly troublesome in this country. There is

[190] See West (1799, p.88): 'Here all that is great and pleasing on the lake, all that is grand and sublime in the environs, lie before you in a beautiful order, and natural disposition'.

[191] Walla Crag, a ridge about 400 yards high, and about 1½ miles south of Keswick.

[192] Lodore Falls, a cascade on Watendlath Beck, near the southern end of Derwent Water.

[193] 'alass' is del.

[194] 'Grange, a hamlet in Borrowdale, 4 miles s. by w. of Keswick where ... the surrounding mountains form an awful amphitheatre' (Parson and White [1829] 1976, p.329).

[195] 'the' is ins. [196] River Derwent.

[197] The valley – at the head (or south end) of Derwent Water – through which the river Derwent flows.

[198] 'property' is del. and 'Lord William Gordon['s] place' is ins.

[199] 'as' is ins. [200] 'alarm'd' is del. and 'surprised' is ins. [201] 'as a whole example' is del.

[202] A 'gewgaw' is 'A gaudy trifle, plaything, or ornament, a pretty thing of little value, a toy or bauble', or 'A paltry thing of no account, a trifle' (*OED*).

no keeping them out of one's eyes & mouth. They seem determined to make all they can of those that come to see the lakes, & like the innkeepers they consider the season for Tourists as their great harvest. South country flesh is probably reckoned more delicious amongst them, as being better done.

Afternoon clouds very low, but without rain. Went to see Mr Crosthwaite's museum. He keeps an accurate journal of the weather, & of the height of the Thermometer, the Barometer, the rain gage,* & the clouds, together with the state of the wind as to the quarter it blows from, & its velocity, from observations made three times a day. In looking at his book I observed 5 or 6 inches of rain in some of the months, & ask'd for the quantity that had fallen last year, which to my great surprise was 71. – the year before 59, almost 60. I dont know whether his reports are to be depended upon. Some of them I understand have been printed in a meteorological journal published by a Mr Dalton.[203]

Walked in the evening to the lake. W. SW.

July 19th. Clouds very low. Walk'd before breakfast to Cockshut hill, but the plantation is now grown so high that [a] great part of the view is intercepted. After breakfast, as the day mended, went round the lake in a boat; at times all the hills but Skiddaw were free from clouds, & the air pretty clear. There was hardly [204] wind for sailing, but the water was not smooth enough to see the reflection of the rocks.[205] The views from a boat are perhaps not upon the whole so favourable as from the shores. The head of the lake & parts of the margin are a little defaced with [206] reeds & the meadows near are very spongy & rushy, particularly in front of Lowdore* house. The boatman was the guide who had conducted Mr West & all the great Tourists about the country. He wish'd to persuade me that I coud* do nothing without him, & that I coud* not[207] go up

[203] Mr Ian MacGregor, Archive Information Manager, National Meteorological Archive, has kindly provided rainfall data prepared by 'P. Crossthwaite' at Keswick in the 1790s. They show that the rainfall at Keswick was 71.77 inches in 1794 and 59.69 inches in 1793. This would appear to be compelling evidence that Malthus' diary of his tour of the Lake District was written in 1795.

Further research reveals that Peter Crosthwaite was a close friend of John Dalton (1766–1844), originator of the atomic theory, and regarded as the father of chemistry. They were keen and assiduous collectors of precipitation data. Dalton, based at Kendal, made 200,000 observations over 57 years in his meteorological journal, and engaged Crosthwaite to make simultaneous observations at Keswick (*DNB*: John Dalton). Crosthwaite set up his museum in Keswick in 1780. Dalton published rainfall data for Keswick up to 1792 in his *Meteorological Observations and Essays*, 1793.

[204] 'enough' is del.

[205] Malthus was apparently hoping to view the following scene described by West (1799, p.110): 'The transparent beauty of the lake is only seen in the boat, and it is very surprising. The bottom resembles a mosaic pavement of party*-coloured [i.e. variegated] stone. The fragments of spar at the depth of seven yards, either shine like diamonds, or glitter in diversity of colour ...'

[206] 'rushes' is del. [207] 'not' is ins.

Borrowdale to Buttermere[208] with my own horse; but I determined to make the experiment. In these degenerate days there are no eagles in Borrowdale. None have been seen for these seven or eight years, ever since Mr Pitt came in:[209] except indeed about two years ago an odd pair of Golden eagles had a nest somewhere about Langdale Pikes or Pavey Ark,[210] & the guide got one of the young ones, which he kept alive for 3 or 4 months, & now has stuffed.[211]

In the afternoon, rode some way on the western side of Bassenthwaite; but a thick mist & small rain came on at times, & I coud* see very little. From what I coud* judge, there is nothing very fine in the situation of this water. The low grounds between the two lakes seem to be rather swampy.[212] W. S.W.

July 20th. Morning bright, calm. Rode by the eastern side of the Lake to Borrowdale, thro Grange & to the foot of Castle crag.[213] Tied my mare to a tree, & got with some difficulty up a slate path to the top. The view is certainly very fine both to the north & south.[214] The lake was just ruffled in places: as I rode along the shore it had been quite smooth & transparent. Cross'd the Derwent by a ford & got to a small alehouse at Rosthwaite,[215] a picturesque little village in the middle of Borrowdale to breakfast. After breakfast pass'd two hours in wandering about the dale. [216] The rocky hills are for the most part well clothed with wood at their bottoms, – oak, ash, & birch. The flat parts by the Derwent are divided into small grass inclosures,* & the villagers being about their hay I shoud* not have said that the characteristic of the dale was terror.[217] Walkd* up

[208] The town of Buttermere, near the foot of the lake of that name, is about eight miles south-west of Keswick.

[209] William Pitt (1759–1806) became prime minister in 1783. If the statement 'for these seven or eight years, ever since Mr Pitt came in' was intended to be numerically precise, the date of Malthus' tour would be 1790 or 1791; but that would be inconsistent with the evidence cited in the introduction to this chapter. However, the context suggests that the link between the coming of Mr Pitt and the disappearance of the eagles was intended rather as a humorous correlation. Golden eagles are again nesting in the Lake District, under protection.

[210] Langdale Pikes are mountains west of Grasmere. Pavey Ark is a crag near Langdale Pikes.

[211] Gray (1775, p.206) describes the attempts of the farmers of Borrowdale to get rid of the eagles.

[212] i.e., between Derwent Water and Bassenthwaite (cf. Parson and White [1829] 1976, p.71: when heavy rains fall in Borrowdale the level of Derwent Water rises, and 'the meadows from here to Bassenthwaite are overflowed').

[213] A hill in Borrowdale, about one mile south of Grange.

[214] 'From the top of Castle-crag in Borrowdale there is a most astonishing view of the lake and vale of Keswick, spread out to the north in the most picturesque manner ... From the summit of this rock, the views are so singularly great and pleasing, that they ought never to be omitted ... Castle-crag, in Borrowdale, stands first of all the forest of embattled rocks, whose forked heads, reared to the sky, shine in the sun like spears of burnished steel ... the grand pyramidal Castle-Crag commands the whole' (West, 1799, pp.93, 94, 105, 109).

[215] Six miles south of Keswick. [216] '& river' is del.

[217] West referred to 'the most horrid, romantic mountains' of Borrowdale, its 'sublimely terrible' scenes, and its 'solemn horror' (West, 1799, pp.94, 95, 114). Gray referred to the 'awful amphitheatre' (Gray, 1775, p.205).

a rocky valley between Height knot,[218] & a part of Glanamara;*[219] sat for some time upon Knot Howe[220] where I thought I had a finer view of this dale than from Castle crag; Skiddaw compleated* the circle of fells very handsomely; but the lake appeared too small. The people that you meet have an odd kind of pleasant familiarity. Pray what kind of crop have you? Well, I'll tell you what, it is but light. Set off about 12. for Buttermere. Went over a[221] high fell, [222] a most stony horse way, by the side of a brawling beck with some fine views back upon Borrowdale.[223] From the summit discended* into a very deep narrow valley with a rocky mountain to the right & the most tremendous perpendicular crag I have yet seen to the left. I observd* soon after I began to descend, that [224] a distant fell seen thro the narrow valley gave me the most mountainous idea I had yet had. I certainly shoud* not take any body to the bottom of Skiddaw to give them a notion of mountains. The scenery from Honistar* crag[225] to Buttermere is quite of the terrific kind. The huge masses are here thrown about in all the wild forms of convulsed nature, as the man says in the book.[226] High Steel*[227] is a fine craggy alpine looking fell, & from its perpendicularity appears the highest that I have seen yet. I asked some men about it who said they believed it was as high as any in the country except Skiddaw & great Gavel[228] which [229] is a mountain further to the West.

My hostess, a little tight old woman very much like dame Tucky, was baking oat cakes, which is perform'd upon a large flat iron on the fire. She brought in some of them to me as a treat [230] after dinner, & I found that with a great deal of fine flavour'd butter they were excellent. In the afternoon walked down to the two lakes Buttermere & Crummock[231] – They are very well worth seeing. The margins of the lakes want richness, but the mountains[232] rise so

[218] Possibly High Knott.

[219] Glaramara, one of the mountains that enclose Borrowdale, described by West as 'a mountain of perpendicular naked rock, immense in height, and much broken' (West, 1799, p.96).

[220] Possibly Low Buck How.

[221] 'a very' is del. and 'a' is ins. [222] 'by' is del.

[223] 'with some fine views back upon Borrowdale' is ins.

[224] 'fell' is del. [225] Honister Hause.

[226] Possibly a reference to West's description of the mountains around Honister Crag and Buttermere – 'all the horrors of cloven rock, broken cliff, and mountain streams tumbling headlong ... the most extraordinary amphitheatre of mountainous rocks that ever eye beheld' (West, 1799, pp.132, 133).

[227] High Stile, on the west side of Buttermere.

[228] Great Gable, or Great Gavel, 'so called from its shape' (Parson and White [1829] 1976, p.81), is south-south-east of Buttermere.

[229] 'I found by this description of its situation to be Helvellyn, tho they did not know it by that name.' is del. and 'is a mountain further to the west' is ins.

[230] 'for' is del. [231] Crummock Water, less than one mile north-west of Buttermere.

[232] 'The margins of the lakes want richness, but the mountains' is changed from 'The mountains want richness at bottom, but they'.

bold & abrupt, that where you can get a tolerable foreground the views are[233] grand & beautiful. Crummock is a fine lake with hardly a single rush, & from the lower end of it looking up towards Buttermere are some of the best views. Mine hostess's daughter returned in the evening from market, & brought with her a most profuse head of hair. Cockermouth[234] is reckoned a cheaper market than Keswick, [235] & is as much frequented by the buttermerians tho it is two miles further off. Wind N. & NE.

July 21st. Morning bright, warm. Walk'd before breakfast to a celebrated fall[236] about two miles off, 52 y^rds^ quite perpendicular in a dark chasm of solid rock overhung near the top by birch & mountain ash. [237] When the stream is full it falls clear of the rock, but now it is low, it runs down it. In its present state however it is very beautiful, & highly worth seeing from its extraordinary situation. I found it a very welcome retreat after a hot walk. I question if the lower parts of the cleft ever see the sun.

Before dinner rode by the side of Crummock with an intent of seeing Lowes water,[238] but miss'd my way & got beyond it. I coud see no soul to ask; hallow'd for sometime at a farm house to know if I was right for Lowes water, heard a kind of assenting aye & went on; but seeing no probability of coming to a lake I returnd,* & found that the person who had given me my information was a house lamb. At last I came to a smart house with a very pretty girl in the window, who seeing me look wistfully at her came out, & was kind enough

233 'they appear very' is del. and 'the views are' is ins.

234 The town of Cockermouth is about ten miles north of Buttermere.

235 'but it is two miles further from Buttermere' is del.

236 i.e., Scale Force, described as follows by Parson and White ([1829] 1976, pp.74–5): 'SCALE FORCE, on the western side of Crummock Lake, about two miles W. by N. of Buttermere, is the deepest cataract in all the region of the lakes, the water being precipitated in one grand fall to the depth of 156 feet, besides a smaller fall below. The water sinks into a tremendous chasm, between two mural rocks of sienite, beautifully overhung with trees, which have fixed their roots in the crevices; whilst the sides are clad with a profusion of plants, which glitter with the spray, caused by the falling water. Visiters* generally enter from below into this stupendous chasm, where the air, filled with moisture and shaded from the sun, is cold and damp. Passing the lower, they may proceed towards the foot of the principal fall, till the more copious sprinkling of the spray compels them to return.' This was probably the waterfall that West said 'exceeds the boasted Lowdore, in height of rock, and unity of fall' (West, 1799, p.104).

237 'The water' is del.

238 Loweswater, a small lake about two miles west of Crummock Water. Malthus' view that it is 'not worth seeing' differs from that of Parson and White who assert that, in one direction, 'it exhibits a sweet rural landscape, the cultivated slopes being ornamented with neat farm-houses', and, in the opposite direction, the lake makes a middle distance, to a combination of mountains scarcely to be equalled' (Parson and White [1829] 1976, p.68). And in Wordsworth's opinion 'Lowes-water is tame at the head, but towards its outlet has a magnificent assemblage of mountains' (Wordsworth [1835] 1977, p.97n).

to send me all the way[239] back; [240] & I found myself at dinner without having seen Lowes water: but I comforted myself with the reflection, that I certainly shoud* not have miss'd it in so extraordinary a manner, if it had not been very small & not worth seeing. The country about Crummock & buttermere [241] is certainly much more mountainous than near any of the other lakes. Grasmire*[242] & Mellbreak[243] & on the eastern & western side of Crummock; the craggy fell to the west of[244] buttermere from which rise the[245] points of high steel,* red pike[246] &c with Honistar* crag; green Gavel,[247] [248] Fleetwith[249] & many others to the [250] South & west form altogether a fine range of mountains.

Returned in the evening thro Newlandvale[251] to Keswick – was caught in a slight thunder shower; & observd* that High Steel* seen in the rain thro the vista of two fells on each side appeared of very great height. Newland vale is worth seeing. Rocky channels down which mountain torrents have roared are to be met with on the sides of almost every fell.

Butter at buttermere 8 pence a pound. Hay very generally about. The men who work in the quarries at Honistar* crag earn only 20 pence or 22 pence a day, & have five miles to walk to it. W. NE. a little haziness at noon.

July 22. Morning cloudy with small rain, which continued with harder showers at times till near one.

Walk'd before dinner up the side of Latrig,*[252] which is one of Mr West['s] stations & commands a fine view of the lake & vale. The mountains were clear & had some fine lights upon them. A good deal of hay carried about Keswick. Beef & lamb five pence. Mutton 4 pence & 4 pence ½. Veal 3 pence & 3 pence ½. In the afternoon made an attempt to go up Skiddaw, but some rain came on & the clouds got low, & I was obliged to return. W.S.W.

July 23rd. A good deal of rain in the night, & small rain most of the morning – betook myself to Shakspear.* Went before dinner to see Mr Hutton[253] the guide's museum. His eagle, tho only six months old when he died, is a fine specimen.

[239] 'all the way' is ins. [240] 'the way I came' is del. [241] 'lakes' is del.

[242] Grasmoor, a mountain on the eastern side of Crummock Water, 3½ miles north of Buttermere.

[243] Mellbreak, a mountain about half-a-mile from the western side of Crummock Water.

[244] 'of' is repeated. [245] 'the' is repeated.

[246] Red Pike, about ½ mile high, and about ⅔ mile north-west of High Stile.

[247] Green Gable, about ⅓ mile north-east of Great Gable.

[248] '& many' is del. [249] Fleetwith Pike. [250] 'west &' is del. [251] Vale of Newlands.

[252] Latrigg, 1160 feet, a spur of Skiddaw to the north of Keswick, described by West as 'Station VII ... a soft green hill, that interposes between the town and Skiddaw' (West, 1799, p.104).

[253] Possibly the boatman/guide mentioned on 19 July.

It was caught in a fox trap at two months old. No golden eagles were ever before known to breed in the country. Walk'd to Crow park to see if the rain had affected Lowdore* fall, but did not perceive much difference. Afternoon rainy – took the opportunity of having my hair cut. W. W.

July 24. Rain in the night, & morning, Rode as soon as it held up to Lowdore.*[254] Overtook a man who advised me [255] to call at Mr Pocklingtons, Barrow house in my way & see his fall,[256] which I did, & was very much pleased with it. It consists of two descents which from the bottom appear as one of above 60 feet in height & 7 or 8 in breadth. The situation is very pretty, & it makes a good shew* with a moderate quantity of water. M^r P has built a vile kind of summer house or rather seat at top [257] painted red on the inside, with two high white horns, which are seen all over the country except fortunately from the bottom of the fall. Lowdore* had increased in water, but not sufficiently to make much figure: the bed is so large & rocky, that an absolute torrent is required to cover it. The Rain had fallen much heavier [258] Skiddaw way than about Borrowdale, contrary I understand to the general custom. There was a temporary torrent from Skiddaw, & the guide said that if the same quantity of rain had fallen at Barrowside, there woud* not have been a rock of Lowdore* to be seen.

Got an early dinner of cold meat, & set off at ½ past one, to go over the fells to Ulswater.*[259] Gave eighteenpence [260] for a guide who conducted me very safely some way along a turnpike road: – as for the foggy mountain he said he was[261] pretty sure that I shoud* be able to find my way over that without his assistance, & so we parted. It is true I did find my way, & did not get bog'd; but I think[262] I coud* have got along the turnpike road with as little danger & difficulty. Came down by a village call'd Matterdale into Gobarrow* Park[263] – saw a very fine fall there,[264] but I think inferior to Mr Pocklingtons. I almost

[254] The cataract or cascade of Lodore is near the south-east corner of Derwent Water, about four miles south of Keswick. 'It is a very considerable stream, rushing through an immense chasm, and bounding with great fury over and among the huge blocks of stone with which the channel is filled' (Parson and White [1829] 1976, p.74). West described it as 'the renowned cataract of Lowdore* ... the Niagara of the Lake' (West, 1799, p.91).

[255] 'first' is del. [256] Barrow Cascade, two miles south of Keswick.

[257] 'with' is del. [258] 'on' is del.

[259] Ullswater, to the east of Derwent Water, is the second largest lake in the Lake District.

[260] 'to the' is del. [261] 'was' is ins. [262] 'am pretty sure that' is del. and 'think' is ins.

[263] Gowbarrow Park, now a National Trust property.

[264] Aira Force, a 60-foot-high waterfall, on the northern side of Ullswater, in Gowbarrow Park, about six miles south-west of Pooley Bridge. 'The water, compressed between two cheeks of rock, rushes forth with great violence, and dashing from rock to rock, forms a spray, which, with the run in a favourable direction, exhibits all the colours of the rainbow' (Parson and White [1829] 1976, p.75).

wonder that the lakes are so clear, for after a little fresh of rain all the falls are very much discolour'd. The road winds down just opposite the southern extremity of Place fell.[265] The clouds cleared away, & the afternoon became bright & warm. Tied up my mare & walk'd about the park which commands some of the finest views of the lake. The water is a little in the shape of an S. The first reach from Patterdale,[266] the head, is the most mountainous. Gobarrow* Park sees two reaches. Rode afterwards six miles along the shore to Pooley Bridge.[267] Towards the end of the second reach where the road rises there are some fine views looking back to the south. The broadest part of the water is opposite to a white house of a Mr Robinson, near the beginning of the last reach & it is there about a mile over. The margins seem to be free from rushes, & in size & beauty as a lake it yields only to Windermere. I prefer the character of a very magnificent river to that of a lake, & I dont think it a particular recommendation of Derwent, that seen from whatever point, it always retains its shape as a lake.

After tea walk'd up Dunmallet[268] from which the last bend looks very broad & magnificent, but the two southern are not seen. W.SE.

July 25. Morning fine & fair. Walk'd before breakfast up the eastern side of the lake; but the horizon was not clear, & the mountains at the head of water hardly to be distinguish'd. About 12. took a walk on the western side, up a high green hill. The mountains were pretty clear. Set off about 2. for Penrith, the first town with any red houses that I had seen for some time. Some are brick, some a red freestone, & some white wash'd. Fine warm, W.N.E.

Walk'd in the evening some way out of the town to a hill where there is a kind of pyramid.[269] Saw the range of fells over which Cross Fell[270] presides. It is the custom [271] I understand of some gentlemen in the town to go every year on midsummer day to dine in the Snow, which has very seldom left its summit at that time. W.N.E.

July 26th. Fine. Waited till eleven for the Post. Received a letter from Godschall, which threw me into the greatest doubt [272] & uncertainty. Resolved however to proceed by Hawswater[273] to Kendal, & if possible to get confirm'd, by a man

[265] Place Fell, a mountain on the eastern side of Ullswater.

[266] A village just south of the head (or southern end) of Ullswater.

[267] At the foot, or north end, of Ullswater, about five miles south-west of Penrith. The bridge crosses the river Eamont, flowing out of the lake.

[268] A conical hill near Pooley Bridge.

[269] Presumably Beacon Hill (937 feet), just north-east of Penrith, with a square building erected after the rebellion of 1715.

[270] A mountain of 2930 feet at the summit of the Pennine Range, east-north-east of Penrith.

[271] 'of' is del. [272] Second '& doubt' is del. [273] Hawes Water, now a reservoir.

of great repute for knowledge, tho not a bishop.[274] Dined at Bamston*[275] or something like it two miles short of Hawswater.* I was told at Penrith that I coud* not possibly get over the fells to Kendal without a guide; was told here that I coud* not miss the way – the last information I found nearest the truth.[276] Had a long stage of 19 miles after dinner, but no difficulty in finding the road. Rode for about 3 miles along the water, & thought it a pretty lake, tho the fells except at the head are not high. As I was passing some houses under the fells at the head of the lake, a good natured farmers wife asked me if I woud* drink with them. She said there was no publick house, & she often gave travellers to drink. "Sometimes grand gentlemen come here, & ladies with high feathers from London & some years back an old gentleman was here, who ask'd about everything & the name of every fell & he afterwards put out some books". I

[274] We can only speculate on the reason that Malthus, after receiving at Penrith on 26 July the letter from Samuel Godschall (his brother-in-law), was thrown into 'the greatest doubt and uncertainty' and hurried down to Kendal to be confirmed the next day, returning to Penrith on 29 July. Presumably, Godschall had advised him of a position for which confirmation was a prerequisite. The fact that the letter came from Godschall – rather than, say, from Malthus' father – suggests that it was an appointment over which Godschall had some influence.

It is interesting to note that Malthus had not previously been confirmed, even though he was now 29 years of age (assuming that the date of this diary is July 1795) and an ordained priest. It is possible that during the course of his unorthodox education – first at Richard Graves' school near Bath, then at the Dissenting Academy in Warrington, and finally as a private pupil in the home of Gilbert Wakefield near Nottingham – his confirmation at the normal age had been overlooked.

The phrase 'by a man of great repute for knowledge, tho not a bishop' is puzzling. At first sight it could be interpreted to mean that Malthus intended to be confirmed by someone who was not a bishop. But he surely would have been aware that in the Church of England it would be most unusual, and perhaps not even permissible, for confirmation to be administered by anyone other than a bishop. A more probable interpretation of the above phrase is 'by a bishop who has a great repute for knowledge, though not a great repute as a bishop'.

Anne Rowe (Cumbria Record Office) has kindly advised that Kendal at that time was in the diocese of Chester, and that the bishop of Chester from 1788 to 1800 was William Cleaver (1742–1815). The vicar of Kendal from 1789 to 1806 was Henry Robinson, fellow of Trinity College, Cambridge, who had a library of 12,000 volumes. However, she also advised that no note or entry has been located in the parish register or the churchwardens' accounts for the period 1795–98 to indicate that a confirmation had taken place in the parish church. Although Revd Henry Robinson's extensive library suggests 'a man of great repute for knowledge', it is more likely that Malthus was confirmed by Bishop William Cleaver. His many publications indicate that he enjoyed a great repute for knowledge; and his constant absence from his diocese – he was principal of Brasenose College, Oxford, from 1785 to 1809, and preferred to reside there – might have contributed to his not having repute as a bishop. It has been said of him: 'As a bishop he is commended for benevolence, for discrimination in the exercise of patronage, and for encouraging among his clergy, by the erection of parsonage houses, that residence of which he did not set the example' (*DNB*).

It would be interesting to know whether Malthus, at the time of his confirmation, had already formed the heterodox theological opinions which he included three years later in the final two chapters of his *Essay on Population*; and, if so, whether Bishop Cleaver was aware of them.

William Cleaver was the brother of Euseby Cleaver (1746–1819), bishop of Ferns and Leighlin (1789–1809), archbishop of Dublin (1809–19), with whom Catherine and Henry Wynne stayed in London in April 1796. See Vol. I, Ch. 2, letter 43, p.63, n.7.

[275] Bampton, about seven miles south of Penrith. [276] 'Rode' is del.

ask'd if his name was West, & she said yes. I then mounted a fell up a most stony zigzag road, which made my mare sweat like a fox chace.* In going down on the other side I look[ed] anxiously for Mr Wests torrent of 100y^{ds}. perpendicular,[277] but [278] coud* not see it. I shoud* imagine it only exists in flood times. There were some furrows in the rocks nearly perpendicular that might be of that height. The mountain road which was[279] altogether about three miles brought me at last to a pretty good one in a sweet little narrow valley call'd long Sleddel[280] or as I shoud* suppose it might be spelt Long Slate Dale from the slate that is brought from the head of it. The bottom thro which a stream ran, that had accompanied me down the fell, was divided[281] into small grass inclosures,* most of which were cut & carried, & look'd particularly green. The brows & bottoms of the hills on each side, were wooded & their summits rocky, & here & there were scattered in the prettiest situations neat white farm houses, so as to make the dale look particularly cheerful & habitable. I mistook the church, or rather chapel, for a small farm house, till I saw upon nearer inspection half a rood of churchyard annex'd to it. The Road continued along the valley 7 or 8 miles & then left the stream & brought me onto the turnpike road about 4 miles short of Kendal. W.NW.

July 27. Rain from between 6 & 7, the whole day, small in the evening. Got confirm'd but not time enough for the [282] mail. In a predicament about money; cant get a draught changed. If I had not determined to stay in the North, I must have gone post haste to some place where I was known & have lived[283] upon bread & water all the way, or have been obliged to stop five or six days, [284] till my draught was received. W.S.W.

July 28. Few slight showers, rather warm. Rode to Kirby Steven*[285] to dinner, 24 miles, to enquire about moor game – heard tolerable accounts about Stainmoor*[286] ten miles further on, reckon'd the best: [287] Spital House a famous place of resort. Proceeded in the evening to Appleby[288] ten miles, prettily situated

[277] West described the torrent in 'Long-Sledale' thus: 'Over a most tremendous wall of rock, a mountain torrent, in one unbroken sheet, leaps headlong one hundred yards and more' (West, 1799, p.162).

[278] 'behold I' is del. [279] 'might be' is del. and 'was' is ins. [280] Longsleddale.

[281] 'cut' is del. and 'divided' is ins. [282] Word del.

[283] Several words are del. and 'to some place where I was known & have lived' is ins.

[284] 'in some place or other' is del. [285] Kirkby Stephen, on the river Eden.

[286] Stainmore. [287] 'Rode' is del. [288] About 12 miles south-east of Penrith.

on the side of a hill by the river Eden. The Castle, a good deal of wood[289] about it. The Town consists chiefly of one broad street that runs up to the castle; the houses of which are of all sizes & colours, some brick some redstone, some white turn'd up with red & some blue pointed with white &c: but altogether it has a clean & cheerful appearance. W.S.W.

July 29th. Before breakfast walk'd about the Town & its environs. Most of the hay got in. The rain on the 27th came very unseasonably, as it did for the hay at Kendal. Rode to dinner to Penrith. Fine & fair, warm.[290]

[291] A man may judge in some degree of the passions of others, from what passes in his own breast, but he can make no inference of the same kind from his [292] tastes. Tastes tho they certainly in some cases influence the passions, are indefinitely more various & uncertain. They are more the children of accident & education than nature.

A play strictly moral & tending to one certain end has generally this fault, that you see the author putting men of straw in the way of his horse to the end that they may be knocked down, either by argument or otherwise. One of the great beauties of Shakspear* to a person fond of character, is that he seems always to put himself in the place of the speaker, & to say, & do the best that the character & situation will allow of. This sometimes divides our interest, particularly in the historical plays, but from its just representation of nature, has a great effect.

[289] Malthus' expression 'a good deal of wood' in 1795 could be compared with the description given by Parson and White in 1829: 'Appleby Castle ... a large edifice, ... on the lofty summit of the western bank of the Eden, the steep declivity of which is thickly clothed with wood; indeed the castle is ornamented on every side by fine groves and shady avenues' (Parson and White [1829] 1976, p.521).

[290] It would seem that, although the last entry in this diary is for 29 July, Malthus' tour in the north of England continued beyond that date. The entry for 27 July indicates that he had 'determined to stay in the North', and the entries for 28 and 29 July show that, after proceeding south to Kendal to be confirmed, he did not continue southwards to his home in Albury, but returned north via Kirkby Stephen and Appleby to Penrith, either to explore the Lake District further – in which case there might have been an additional diary – or for other reasons.

[291] The following two paragraphs are written on the final two pages of the diary, separated from the last diary entry (29 July) by three blank pages. The diary had been inverted, so that the two paragraphs appear upside down.

[292] 'own' is del.

3 *Bullion trade transactions*

INTRODUCTION

These 40 pages of manuscript are concerned with the trade in bullion between London and other European centres – in particular, with Amsterdam and Hamburg. Their main aim appears to have been to show under what conditions (of prices and exchange rates) profits could be made by buying gold or silver in one centre and selling it in another. They include not only general instructions on how to calculate profits in the bullion trade, but also many calculations using hypothetical or historical data.

It is not known whether Malthus prepared these notes out of academic interest or with a view to engaging in the bullion trade. His academic interest in the bullion trade is evident in the following question that he set in an examination paper at the East India College in 1808 – 'What are the causes which tend to raise the Market Price of Bullion above the Mint Price?' An academic interest in commercial matters is also implied by the terms of his appointment to the East India College. Although his title was later changed to 'Professor of History and Political Economy', his letter of acceptance of 10 July 1805 shows that he was initially appointed to the 'Professorship of General History, Politics, Commerce and Finance'. The question posed at the end of Section C.1 below – viz. 'which best represents the state of the currency – the exchange or the price of gold?' – has implications for the practising bullion trader, but it also suggests an academic research interest that might have been the motivational force behind all the calculations in this chapter. However, the detailed and intricate nature of the calculations means that it is unlikely that they would have been the subject matter of his lectures at the East India College.

It is not possible to set a precise date on when these bullion notes were assembled. Many are on pages watermarked 1813. One of the sheets must have been written on or soon after 14 December 1813: it states 'Gold coming in at present at the rate of above ten per cent. December 14th 1813'. A number of other calculations also use dates from the beginning of December 1813, and statistical tables include dates up to 6 July 1816.

Some of Malthus' calculations refer to two tables sent to him by Ricardo in letters dated 30 December 1813 and 1 January 1814. The first letter begins: 'I have been amusing myself for one or two evenings in calculating the exchanges, price of gold, &c, – at Amsterdam, and I enclose the result of my labours. I have every reason to believe that my calculations are correct.' He enclosed an extensive table of twelve columns showing under what conditions it would be profitable to buy gold and silver in Amsterdam and sell it in London, or vice versa. The second letter begins: 'Having finished a table for the Hamburgh exchanges, similar to that which I have already sent you for Holland, I thought you might like to have a copy of it.'[1] In the commentary below, we refer to Ricardo's two tables as the Amsterdam table and the Hamburgh table.

The calculations which specifically refer to these two tables must therefore be dated after the end of December 1813. However, the tone of the opening sentence of the letter of 30 December 1813 suggests that the bullion trade had been a topic of discussion between Ricardo and Malthus before that date. It is unlikely that Ricardo would have sent Malthus two complicated tables relating to the bullion trade if the topic had not been addressed beforehand, either in conversation or in letters that have been lost. It is possible, therefore, that some of Malthus' calculations might have preceded the receipt of Ricardo's two tables.

An unfortunate feature of these bullion notes is the fact that many of the numerical calculations are not accompanied in the manuscript by titles or explanations. This has meant that, in many cases, the nature and purpose of the calculations has had to be inferred from the numerals involved. The interpretation has been made more difficult by Malthus' inconsistent use, or non-use, of decimals, and by a number of arithmetical errors, some of which he corrected, some of which he left uncorrected.

When the bullion notes were acquired by Kanto Gakuen University, they did not appear to be arranged in any particular order. We have thought the following arrangement, and the accompanying headings, to be the most appropriate, but with the reservation that it may not have been the one preferred by Malthus.

[1] Ricardo, *Works*, Vol. VI, 1952, pp. 97–101. The two tables are reproduced below.

1 Price of Gold at Amsterdam p^{m} on *f* 335 p^{r} marc	2 Value of a marc in Current Guilders	3 Corresponding price of an oz of stand^{d} gold in London*	4 Correspon^{g} price of an oz of stand^{d} silver in London	5 Value of an oz of stand^{d} gold in Flemish current Shillings	6 Value of an oz of standard gold in Flemish Banco Shill^{gs} †Agio 3 pc^{t}	7 Real par of Exch^{ge} in Flemish Current Shillings p^{r} £ ster^{g} in gold.	8 Real par of Exch^{ge} in Flemish Banco Shillings p^{r} £ ster^{g} in Gold. Agio 3 pc^{t}	9 When the price of gold in London in Bank notes is p^{r} oz.	10 The bullion Par must be multiplied by	11 Price of standard silver in London in Bank notes p^{r} oz.	12 Par of exch^{ge} with Amsterdam in Banco (Agio 3 pc^{t})
			Pence					£4. –	.973	5/2	37.48
Par *f* 355	*f* 355		68.00	137	133	35.20	34.17	4. 1	.961	5/3	36.88
1 p.c. P^{m}	358.55		67.32	138.4	134.3	35.55	34.51	4. 2	.949	5/4	36.30
2	362.10		66.67	139.8	135.7	35.90	34.85	4. 3	.938	5/5	35.75
3	365.65		66.02	141.3	137.2	36.25	35.19	4. 4	.927	5/6	35.21
4	369.20		65.38	142.5	138.6	36.61	35.54	4. 5	.916	5/7	34.68
5	372.75		64.76	143.9	139.8	36.95	35.87	4. 6	.905	5/8	34.17
6	376.30		64.15	145.3	141.1	37.31	36.22	4. 7	.895	5/9	33.67
7	379.85		63.55	146.6	142.5	37.66	36.56	4. 8	.885	5/10	33.19
8	383.40		62.96	148	143.9	38.01	36.90	4. 9	.875	5/11	32.72
9	386.95		62.39	149.3	145.3	38.36	37.24	4.10	.865	6/–	32.27
	389.37	£3.17.10½	62.00	150.3	146.0	38.61	37.48	4.11	.856	6/1	31.84
10	390.50	3.18. 1		150.7	146.3	38.71	37.58	4.13	.838	6/2	31.42
11	394.05	3.18.10		152.1	147.6	39.06	37.92	4.15	.820	6/3	30.98
12	397.60	3.19. 6½		153.5	149.0	39.62	38.27	4.17	.803	6/4	30.58
13	401.15	4. –. 3		154.8	150.3	39.77	38.62	4.19	.786	6/5	30.17
14	404.70	4. –.11½		156.2	151.7	40.12	38.96	5. –	.779	6/6	29.79
15	408.25	4. 1. 8		157.5	152.9	40.48	39.30	5. 2	.764	6/7	29.41
16	411.80	4. 2. 4½		158.9	154.3	40.83	39.64	5. 4	.749	6/8	29.04
17	415.35	4. 3. ½		160.3	155.6	41.18	39.98	5. 6	.735	6/9	28.69
18	418.90	4. 3. 9		161.7	157.0	41.54	40.32	5. 8	.721	6/10	28.33
19	422.45	4. 4. 5½		163.1	158.3	41.89	40.67	5.10	.708	6/11	27.99
20	426	4. 5. 2		164.5	159.6	42.24	41.02			7/–	27.66
21	429.55	4. 5.10½		165.8	161.0	42.59	41.36			7/1	27.32
										7/2	27.02
										7/3	26.71
										7/4	26.40
										7/5	26.11
										7/6	25.82

* When the price of gold in Holland is above 10 pc^{t} P^{m} and the mint in England is open to the public silver will be the standard in London consequently its market and mint prices will agree and gold will be above the mint price. When under 10 pc^{t} silver will be above the mint price and gold will be the standard.

When the price of gold in Holland was above 9 pc^{t} p^{m} the english £ ster^{g} would be estimated in silver and therefore the par of exchange would invariably continue 38.61 currency; and 37.48 Banco if the agio were 3 pc^{t}

† The agio is variable but is supposed to be constant in this table for the purpose of calculation.

A marc weight = 3798 grains troy.
A marc is divided into 5120 assen. 200 assen of pure silver in a guilder. Gold and silver are sold by the marc in Holland perfectly pure.

British standard { Gold – 11 fine, 1 alloy; Silver 11. 2 fine, 18 dwts. alloy }

Columns 11 and 12 will shew on inspection whether silver be passing from London to Amsterdam, or fom Amsterdam to London. Suppose the price of silver in London to be 6/7 and the exch^{ge} with Amsterdam 28/– Against 6/7 in Col. 11, the par of exch^{ge} is 29/41 in Col. 12 consequently being at 28 it is unfavorable to Amsterdam and silver can be exported from Amsterdam to London with a profit of 5 pc^{t} If under the same circumstances the exch^{ge} had been 31 silver could have been exported to Amsterdam with a profit of 5 pc^{t}

Col. 8, 9 and 10 will shew from which country gold may be profitably exported. Suppose the price of gold in Amsterdam to be 16 pc^{t} p^{m}, the agio 3 pc^{t}, the exch^{ge} with London 31 and the price of gold in London £5.10; from which country would gold be exported and with what profit?

Against 16 pc^{t} in Col. 1, the par of exch^{ge} in Col. 8 is 39.64 and against £5.10 the price of gold in London in Col. 9, the multiplier .708 stands in Col. 10. 39.64 multiplied by .708 gives 28.06 as the par for Bank notes, therefore when the exch^{ge} is at 31 it is unfavorable to Holland and gold may be imported from thence with a profit of 10½ pc^{t} nearly. Or thus [.] An oz of standard gold when the marc could be bought at 16 pc^{t} p^{m} at Amsterdam would cost 154.3 flemish Shillings Banco when the agio was 3 pc^{t}, which reduced into English money at 31 shillings per £ sterling will give £4.19.6¾, but it will sell in London for £5.10 which is a profit of 10½ pc^{t} nearly.

Hamburgh

Price of a ducat or 53 grains of fine gold in marks Banco	Price of an oz of standard gold in flemish Shillings Banco	Par of Exch^{ge} with London in flemish shillings Banco p^{r} £ ster^{g} of gold	Corresponding price of an oz of standard silver in London in Pence	Corresponding price of an oz of standard gold in London in £ &c^{a}	When the price of gold in London in Bank notes is p^{r} oz	The bullion par of exch^{ge} must be multiplied by	When the price of dollars in London is p^{r} oz	The par of exch^{ge} in silver is
							s. d	
5.39	119.33	30.60	70.79		£4	.973	4.11½	35.08
5.45	120.66	30.94	70.19		4. 1	.961	5. 1	34.22
5.51	121.99	31.28	69.43		4. 2	.949	5. 2½	33.39
5.57	123.32	31.63	68.68		4. 3	.938	5. 4	32.61
5.63	124.65	31.97	67.95		4. 4	.927	5. 5½	31.87
5.69	125.98	32.33	67.23		4. 5	.916	5. 7	31.15
5.75	127.31	32.68	66.53		4. 6	.905	5. 8½	30.47
5.81	128.64	33.03	65.84		4. 7	.895	5.10	29.82
5.87	129.96	33.37	65.17		4. 8	.885	5.11½	29.19
5.93	131.29	33.72	64.51		4. 9	.875	6. 1	28.59
5.99	132.62	34.07	63.86		4.10	.865	6. 2½	28.02
6.05	133.95	34.42	62.23		4.11	.856	6. 4	27.46
6.11	135.28	34.76	62.61		4.13	.838	6. 5½	26.93
6.17	136.61	35.08	62. –	3.893	4.15	.820	6. 7	26.42
6.23	137.92	35.42		3.931	4.17	.803	6. 8½	25.93
6.29	139.25	35.76		3.968	4.19	.796	6.10	25.46
6.35	140.57	36.11		4.005	5	.779	6.11½	25
6.41	141.89	36.45		4.043	5. 2	.764	7. 1	24.55
6.47	143.21	36.79		4.081	5. 4	.749	7. 2	24.13
6.53	144.54	37.14		4.119	5. 6	.735		
6.59	145.86	37.48		4.157	5. 8	.721		
6.65	147.19	37.83		4.195	5.10.–	.708		
6.71	148.51	38.18		4.233				
6.77	149.84	38.52		4.270				
6.83	151.17	38.87		4.308				
6.89	152.50	39.22		4.346				

When dollars are 4/11½, standard is 2½ Pence more
When 6/1 3 Pence more
When 7/– 3½ Pence more

N.B 3 marks are equal to 8 flemish shillings Banco

EXPLANATORY NOTES AND DEFINITIONS

Bank money (or banco) and current money (or currency)
Banco is 'A term used to indicate the bank money of account in certain places, as distinguished from the current money or currency, when the latter had been depreciated from the earlier value retained by bankers in calculating exchanges with foreign countries' (*OED*).

Bank money was the standard money of a country, as distinct from its worn or depreciated currency. The distinction between bank money and currency existed in Amsterdam, Hamburg and some other places.

Agio
The charge made by a bank for the conversion of currency into bank money, or the premium paid for banco money over specie or current money.

Weights

English (Troy system)

1 pound (lb.)	=	12 ounces (oz.)
1 oz.	=	20 pennyweight (dwt.)
1 dwt.	=	24 grains
1 oz.	=	480 grains
1 lb.	=	5760 grains

Flemish[2]

1 marc[3]	=	5120 assen
	=	160 engels

Comparison of Flemish and English weights

1 marc	=	3798 grains	=	3780 ÷ 480 ounces
			=	7.9125 ounces
2 marcs	=	7595 grains		
1 ounce	=	1 ÷ 7.9125 marcs	=	0.12638 marc

[2] The adjective 'Flemish' was used by Malthus – and by the writers of the pages below that are not in Malthus' hand – when referring to the currency of The Netherlands. In our commentary we follow this usage, even though the correct adjective today would be 'Dutch'.

[3] Malthus sometimes used the English version 'mark' of the Flemish 'mark', but at other times used 'marc'. In our editorial notes we use 'marc'.

Currencies

English

1 pound (£1)	=	20 shillings (20s. or 20/-)
	=	240 pence (240d.)
1 guinea	=	21 shillings

Flemish

1 guilder (or florin)(fl)	=	3⅓ schellings[4]		
	=	20 stivers	=	40 groots
1 schelling	=	6 stivers	=	12 groots
1 stiver	=	16 pennings		
1 guilder	=	320 pennings		

Hamburg

ducat – a gold coin weighing 57½ grains. As 1 ounce (or 480 grains) of standard gold had a mint value of £3.17.10½ (or 934½ pence), the value of a ducat in English currency was:

934½ ÷ 480 × 57½	=	111.9 pence
	=	9.32 shillings
	=	9 shillings 4 pence

Standard gold and fine gold

Standard gold (as distinct from fine or pure gold), according to the English Mint proportions, was an alloy of fine gold (11/12, or 91.67%, or approx. 92%) and copper (1/12, or 8.33%, or approx. 8%). It was the gold used in gold coins. The purity of gold is measured in carats. Fine gold is said to be of 24 carats. Standard gold is 22-carat gold. One unit by weight of fine gold contains as much fine gold, and is therefore of the same value, as 12/11 or 1.0908 units by weight of standard gold (1.0908 × 0.9167 = 1).

In English weights, one ounce of fine gold has the same value as

[4] Malthus generally used the Flemish spelling 'schellings' but occasionally used 'schillings', 'shillings', 'shellings', or 'scellings'. In transcribing Malthus' text we have inserted an asterisk (*) after these alternative spellings of 'schellings'. In our editorial commentary, we use 'schellings' when referring to Flemish currency; 'shillings' refers to English currency.

1.0908 ounces of standard gold; or, 480 grains of fine gold have the same value as 480 × 1.0908 = 523.6 grains of standard gold.

In Flemish weights, one marc of fine gold has the same value as 1.0908 marcs of standard gold. Converting to English weights, one marc (= 7.9125 ounces, or 3798 grains) of fine gold has the same value as 7.9125 × 1.0908 = 8.63 ounces, or 3798 × 1.0908 = 4143 grains, of standard gold.

If the mint proportions are taken approximately as 92% fine gold and 8% copper, one unit of fine gold has the same value as 1.086 units of standard gold (1.086 × 0.92 = 1).

Mint value of gold

England

44½ guinea coins were coined from 1 lb. (Troy weight) of standard gold. Each guinea coin thus contained 12 ounces ÷ 44½ = 0.2697 ounces of standard gold. A guinea was defined by law as equivalent in value to 21 shillings. Therefore, 0.2697 ounces of standard gold have a value of 21 shillings. Hence, one ounce of standard gold is worth 21 ÷ 0.2697 shillings = 77.875 shillings = £3.17.10½ or 934½ pence. As one ounce of fine gold contains 12/11 times the amount of gold contained in one ounce of standard gold, the value of one ounce of fine gold is 12/11 × £3.17.10½ = £4.4.11½.

Holland

Gold prices in Holland are usually quoted with reference to fine gold, not standard gold. The value of one marc of fine gold is equal to the value of 15.21 marcs (or 15.21 × 5120 = 77875.2 assen) of fine silver. One guilder (banco) is equal in value to 200 assen of fine silver. Thus, one marc of fine gold is worth 77875.2 ÷ 200 = 389.376 = 389⅜ guilders.

One marc of standard gold is worth 389⅜ × 11/12 = approx. 355 guilders.

Converting to English weights (1 marc = 7.9125 ounces), one ounce of standard gold in Holland is worth 355 ÷ 7.9125 = 44.87 guilders = 148.1 schellings.

Current or market value of gold

The current or market values of standard and fine gold can differ from their mint values.

Malthus expressed the current value of fine gold in Holland as a certain percentage of the mint value that standard gold would have in Holland, despite the fact that gold prices in Holland are quoted with reference to fine gold. Thus the expression ‘Gold at 15 per cent in Holland’ meant that the current value of fine gold in Holland is 15 per cent above 355 guilders per marc, i.e. 15 per cent above the mint value that standard gold would have in Holland. It would perhaps have been simpler to express the current value of fine gold in Holland as a percentage of the mint value of fine gold in Holland. Malthus was presumably following the conventional practice used by Ricardo and by bullion traders generally.

Par of exchange
'the recognized value of the currency of one country in terms of that of another' (*OED*).

'the intrinsic value of the money of one country, compared with that of another country ... estimated by the weight and purity of the gold or silver which they respectively contain' (Carey 1818, p.351).

To calculate the par of exchange between English pounds and Flemish schellings:

> One ounce of standard gold in England has a value of £3.17.10½ or 934½ pence.
>
> One ounce of standard gold in Holland has a value of 149.59 schellings.
>
> The par of exchange is therefore:

934½ pence	=	149.59 schellings
or, £1	=	240 pence
	=	149.59 ÷ 934½ × 240 schellings
	=	38.42 schellings

A. Trade with Amsterdam

1. Conversion of guilders per marc into schellings per ounce

TEXT

```
The Par of a Mark of pure gold in which the price of gold is quoted in Amsterdam is according to our Mint proportions, as found by Mr Ricardo[5] 389⅜ guilders. The grains Troy of Pure Gold in a Mark = 3798 = 4143 Standard grains. Therefore 383¾* = 4143 Standard grains.[6]

        Convert the guilders into groots by multiplying by 20 to turn them into Stivers,[7] and then by[8] 2 to turn them into groots. And then 4143 the Standard grains in a Mark[9] [will] be worth 15575 groots, the groots in 389⅜ guilders; 480 grains, the grains in an ounce, will be worth 1805 very nearly, which reduced to flemish shellings* will be equal to 150/5 150 schillings.* 5 groots.
```

COMMENTARY

The above two paragraphs show how the price of gold in Amsterdam expressed in guilders per marc can be converted into an equivalent price in Flemish schellings per English ounce. The steps are:

1 marc of fine gold in Amsterdam is worth 389⅜ guilders
1 marc has the same weight as 3798 English troy grains
1 troy grain of fine gold is equal in value to 1.0908 grains of standard gold
∴ 3798 troy grains of fine gold are equal in value to 3798 × 1.0908 = 4143 grains of standard gold (i.e. 4143 standard grains)
∴ 1 marc of fine gold has the same value as 4143 grains of standard gold

If 1 marc of fine gold is worth 389⅜ guilders, then 4143 grains of standard gold are worth 389⅜ guilders = 389⅜ × 40 groots = 15575 groots, ∴ 1 grain of standard gold is worth 15575 ÷ 4143 groots

And 1 ounce (= 480 grains) of standard gold is worth
15575 ÷ 4143 × 480 groots
= 1805 groots = 150 schellings 5 groots

[5] Ricardo's Amsterdam table shows that a value of 389.37 guilders per marc for fine gold (in Amsterdam) is equivalent to a value of £3.17.10½ per ounce for standard gold (in London).

[6] 'And As 389¾ : 4143 :: 480 The grains in an Ounce' is del.; 389¾ should be 389⅜.

[7] Malthus used the English version 'stivers' of the Flemish 'stuivers'.

[8] 'to' is del. [9] 'will be' is del.

The process of converting guilders per marc into schellings per ounce is illustrated by several worked examples:

TEXT

```
4143 : 389.7½ :: 480
       20
       -----
       7787½
         480
       -----
      622960
     31148
     -------
     3737760
         240    ½ × 480
     -------
4143 / 3738000 / 902.2
     37287
     -----
        9380
        8286
        ----
         9940
```

COMMENTARY

The most likely interpretation of the problem being addressed here is: if one marc (= 4143 grains) of gold is worth 389 guilders 7½ stivers, what is the price (in schellings and groots) of 480 grains (or one ounce) of gold?

Malthus converted 389 guilders 7½ stivers to 7787½ stivers (1 guilder = 20 stivers).

To calculate the value of 480 grains of gold in stivers he multiplied 7787 by 480, and multiplied ½ by 480, added the two results together, and divided by 4143, reaching an answer of 902.2 stivers.

Some of the figures in the division have been altered in MS, but they are still incorrect and should read:

```
4143 / 3738000 / 900.2
       37287
       -----
          9300
          8286
          ----
          1014
```

6 / 902[10] / 150.4 groots Therefore 150 schellings 4 groots is the par for the ounce of gold standard.	902 stivers are then converted into schellings and groots, giving 150 schellings 2 stivers, or 150 schellings 4 groots (1 schelling = 6 stivers 1 stiver = 2 groots) On these assumptions, one ounce of gold is worth 150 schellings 4 groots.
389⅜ : 390 150/4 389.4 : 390 :: 150.3 390 ----- 135270 4509 ------ 3894 / 586170 / 150.5 3894 ----- 19677 19470 ----- 20700 19470	Having established that, when the price of a marc of gold is 389 guilders 7½ stivers (= 389⅜ guilders = 389.4 guilders), the price for an ounce of gold is 150 schellings 4 groots (= 150.3 schellings), Malthus calculated what the price for an ounce will be if the price of a marc is 390 guilders. After several revisions, indicated by superimposed numbers, his answer was 150.5 schellings = 150 schellings 6 groots.
389.4 : 391 :: 150.3	A third problem of the same kind was presented, but not solved.

[10] The numbers 2 12 24 are written vertically under 902; and the numbers 6 / 9022 / 150 are written to the left of this line.

```
389 : 390 :: 350[11]
               390
              ----
             31500
            1050
            ------
      389 / 136500 /

               150
                390
              ----
             13500
             450
             -----
    389 / 58500 / 150.4
             389
             ----
             1960
             1945
             ----
               1500
```

For some unexplained reason, Malthus repeated the calculation using simplified figures. He assumed that the price of gold is 389 guilders per marc (instead of 389 guilders 7½ stivers per marc), and assumed that a price of 389 guilders per marc is equal to 150 schellings per ounce (instead of 150.3 schellings per ounce). On these assumptions he then asked what the price will be in schellings per ounce if the price in guilders per marc is 390 rather than 389. He began the calculations by mistakenly writing 350 instead of 150 and completed the next four lines before realising the mistake. Starting again with 150, he multiplied by 390 and divided by 389 to get a result of 150.4 schellings per ounce. Because of the simplification of the figures, this differs slightly from the 150.5 schellings previously obtained.

2. Conversion of schellings per ounce to shillings per ounce

TEXT	COMMENTARY
Having found the par according to the English mint proportions of the mark of gold in guilders, find also the par of an ounce of standard gold in Flemish shillings* and then the Par in gulders* will be to the actual price in guilders as the par in flemish to the actual price in flemish.	The first paragraph appears to be saying merely that the ratio of the par to the actual price will be the same whether expressed in guilders or in Flemish schellings.

[11] '1' is superimposed on '3', presumably after Malthus realised the error.

Having obtained the actual price of the ounce of standard gold in schellings flemish current,[12] look at the exchange and the agio, and having [13] reduced banco to currency by the addition of the agio, say -

As the actual exchange in Current schellings[14] is to 20 shillings, so is the actual price of the ounce of gold in schillings* flemish to the price in English currency, and according as the actual price is more or less than the market price in England, gold will be exported to or imported from Holland

This paragraph appears to be saying merely that the ratio of the price of gold in schellings per ounce to the price of gold in shillings per ounce will be equal to the ratio of schellings to shillings (i.e. the rate of exchange).

Thus, for example, if the actual exchange rate is 32 schellings = 20 shillings, and the actual price in Flemish currency of an ounce of gold is 160 schellings, then the actual price in English currency of an ounce of gold will be 100 shillings (32 : 20 :: 160 : 100).

This procedure for converting Flemish prices (schellings per ounce) to English prices (shillings per ounce) is illustrated by a number of calculations.

[12] 'current' is ins. [13] 'redu' is del.

[14] 'guilders' is del. and 'schellings' is ins.

[15]

```
   38  7      150  2
   12          12
   --         ---
  456        1802


463 : 20 :: 1802
                20
            ----
      463 / 36040 / 77
            3241
            ----
             3630
             3241
             ----
              389
               12[16]
             ----
       463 / 4668 / 10
             463
             ---
               30[17]
```

In this first calculation, the exchange rate is given as £1 = 38 schellings 7 groots = 463 groots. The Flemish price of an ounce of gold is given as 150 schellings 2 groots = 1802 groots. If 463 groots are worth 20 shillings, 1802 groots will be worth

$1802 \div 463 \times 20$
$= 77$ shillings 10 pence
$= £3/17/10$

[15] The calculations that follow are written upside down at the foot of the page.
[16] The remainder (389 shillings) is converted to pence by multiplying by 12.
[17] Should be ‘38’.

```
            1804
              20
           -----
463 / 36080 / 77
            3241
           -----
            3670
            3241
            ----
             429
              12
            ----
 463 / 5148 / 11
            463
            ---
             518
```

The calculation is repeated using 1804 groots instead of 1802 groots as the standard price of gold, giving £3.17.11 the English price of an ounce of gold.

This second calculation – using 1804 instead of 1802 groots – was probably intended to show that, given an exchange rate of £1 = 38 schellings 7 groots, the price of gold in Flemish schellings that is equivalent to the English mint price of £3.17.10½ per ounce, will be between 1802 and 1804 groots per ounce.

```
2825 : 20 :: 1529
               20
             ----
    2825 / 30580 / 108[18]
             2825
             ----
              23300
              19775
```

The calculation shows that if the exchange rate is 20 English shillings = 28.25 Flemish schellings, then 152.9 schellings (the decimal points are, as usual, missing in MS) are equal to 108 shillings. The figure ‘152.9’ presumably referred to the price of an ounce of gold in schellings. The aim of the calculation was to change the price in Flemish schellings to a price in English shillings. The calculation is written at the foot of a page, below a line, and is deleted. The reason for deleting it is not clear.

[18] Malthus initially gave the quotient incorrectly as 107, and then replaced it by 108. The figure 19775 is del. To the side are the figures 23300 and 22600.

The next six examples refer to trade with Hamburg but the gold price in Hamburg is expressed in Flemish currency (schellings per ounce), not in stivers per ducat.

```
Hamburgh[19] March 1810.
Gold 101. Exchange 29
Gold 101  Ounce = 140.4

29 : 20 :: 1404
              20
            ----
      29 / 28080 / 97
           261
           ---
            198
            203

Gold in Hamburgh in English
currency 4.17
```

In the first of these six Hamburg examples, the price of gold in Hamburg is given as 140.4 schellings per ounce. Using an exchange rate of 20 shillings = 29 schellings, this is converted into English currency at 97 shillings or £4.17.0.

```
          1405
             20
           ----
     29 / 28100 / 97
          261
          ---
           200
           203
```

The calculation is repeated for a gold price of 140.5 schellings per ounce with the same exchange rate. The answer (to the nearest unit) remains the same, viz. £4.17.0 per ounce.

[19] Malthus' spelling of 'Hamburgh' is reproduced in this transcription.

```
Sepr 1809. Gold 104.
Exchange 28/1
Ounce of standard 144.6

281 : 20 :: 1446
               20
             ----
      281 / 28920 / 103
            281
            ---
              820
              841
```

The calculation is then repeated for a gold price of 144.6 schellings per ounce, and an exchange rate of £1 = 28 schellings 1 groot (or 28.1 schellings). The price of gold in Hamburg is then found to be 103 shillings (= £5.3.0) per ounce.

```
90 : 103 :: 100

90 / 10300 / 114 4/9
```

This price of 103 shillings per ounce is compared to a price of 90 shillings per ounce, and shown to be $14\frac{4}{9}$% higher. This presumably was meant to show the profit that would be made by buying gold at £4.10.0 (= 90 shillings) per ounce in London and selling it in Hamburg at £5.3.0 (= 103 shillings) per ounce.

```
Hamburgh Jany. Gold 100½
Exchange 28    Ounce of gold
139.2

28 : 20      139.2
                20
             -----
        28 / 27840 / 992
             252
              260
              252
              ---
                80

Gold at Hamburgh £4.19.2½.
```

When the price of gold at Hamburg is 139.2 schellings per ounce, and the exchange rate is 28 schellings = 20 shillings, the Hamburg price is equivalent to 99.2 shillings = £4.19.2½.

```
Hamburgh Jany 1809
Gold 103⅞ Exchange 30/8
Ounce of standard gold 1446

30.7  20 :: 1446
              20
            ----
      307 / 28920 / 94.2
            2763
            ----
             1290
             1228
             ----
               620
               614

Gold at Hamburgh in English
Currency £4.14.2½
```

Here the price of gold at Hamburg is 144.6 schellings per ounce, and the exchange rate is 30 schellings 8 groots (or 30.7 schellings) = 20 shillings, giving a price in English currency of 94.2 shillings or £4.14.2½.

3. Calculation of the par of exchange between England and Holland

COMMENTARY

Malthus here shows how to calculate the par of exchange, i.e. the exchange rate between English pounds and Flemish schellings that would make the price of gold in Amsterdam just equal to the price of gold in London. When the actual exchange rate (or, 'the course of exchange') equals this par of exchange, there would be no advantage in buying gold in one country and selling in the other; but when the two rates are different, it might be possible to make a profit by trading in gold.[20]

[20] Transaction costs such as transport, insurance, and fees to agents would of course have to be taken into consideration.

TEXT

One Dutch Mark weight is equal to 3798 grains troy. 3798 grains troy pure gold = 4143 grains standard. 4143 grains standard gold at £3.17.10½ or 934½ Pence per ounce = 80659[21] Pence = 130.1 ounces of standard silver or 120.34 oz pure silver = 57763.2 grains troy = 15.21 marks weight. ∴ 1 mark of pure gold = 15.21 pure silver. 1 mark = 5120 Assen.[22] 200 assen of pure silver are contained in 1 guilder.
778.75.2[23] assen = 15.21 marks. ∴ 1 mark = 389⅜ guilders. 80659[24] Pence = 77875.2[25] assen of pure silver. ∴ 240 Pence or £1 sterling = f11..11.8 or 38/7 currency which reckoning the agio at 5pc. is equal to 36/8. Banco. When the mark of gold sold in Amsterdam for 389⅜ guilders, & the exchange was at 36/8 no advantage could be made in Holland either by the exportation or the importation of gold bullion whilst gold was at its standard price in England.

COMMENTARY

The argument runs:

1 marc is equal in weight to 3798 grains. ∴ 1 marc of fine gold is equal in value to 3798 grains of fine gold, or 4143 grains of standard gold (because 1.0908 grains of standard gold contain one grain of fine gold; 3798 × 1.0908 = 4143).

The mint value of standard gold is 934½ pence per ounce (i.e. per 480 grains). ∴ 4143 grains of standard gold are worth 4143 ÷ 480 × 934½ = 8065.9 pence; i.e. one marc of fine gold is worth 8065.9 pence.[26] The value (unstated)

[21] i.e. 8065.9. Here and below the decimal point is omitted in MS.

[22] Malthus used the English version 'Ass' (plural 'Assen') of the Flemish terms 'Aas' and 'Azen'.

[23] i.e. 77875.2. [24] i.e. 8065.9. [25] MS has 778.52.

[26] If the value of gold in Amsterdam is taken as 389⅜ guilders per marc, it would be possible at this point in the argument to proceed directly to the calculation of the par of exchange (without converting the value of gold into an equivalent value of silver):
1 marc of gold is worth 8065.9 pence and 389⅜ guilders.
∴ 8065.9 pence = 389⅜ guilders
∴ 240 pence = 389.375 ÷ 8065.9 × 240 × 10 ÷ 3
= 38.6 schellings.

of silver is 67 pence per ounce fine, and 62 pence per ounce standard. ∴ 1 marc of fine gold is worth 8065.9 ÷ 67 = 120.34 ounces of fine silver = 120.34 × 480 grains of fine silver

= 57763.2 grains of fine silver
= (57763.2 ÷ 3798) marcs (one marc weighs 3798 grains)
= 15.21 marcs of fine silver
= (15.21 × 5120) assen. (1 marc weighs 5120 assen)
= 77875.2 assen of fine silver
= (77875.2 ÷ 200) guilders
(1 guilder is worth 200 assen of fine silver)
= 389.376 guilders (or 389.375 approx.)

To calculate the par of exchange, the value of a marc of fine gold in pence is equated with its value in guilders:

i.e. 8065.9 pence = 389.376 guilders

∴ 240 pence (or £1) = 389.376 ÷ 8065.9 × 240 guilders
= 11.5858 guilders
= 11.5858 × 10 ÷ 3 schellings
= 38.62 schellings
= 38 schellings 7 groots

The par of exchange is thus

£1, or 20 shillings = 38 schellings 7 groots

Deducting 5% for agio, this becomes

20 shillings = 38.62 × 0.95 schellings
= 36.689 schellings
= 36 schellings 8 groots

Thus, if the actual values of a marc of fine gold in London and Amsterdam are the same as the mint values, viz. 8065.9 pence and 389⅜ guilders, and the actual exchange rate is 20 shillings = 36 schellings 8 groots, no profit could be made by exporting or importing gold.

TEXT	COMMENTARY
[27] The Ounce of Standard Gold at Par according to the English mint Proportions is 137 flemish scellings* = £3.17.10½	The apparent purpose of this exercise is to show how to calculate the par of exchange between English pounds and Flemish schellings, based on the mint values of an ounce of gold in both countries. In England, the mint value of an ounce of standard gold is £3.17.10½. In Holland, the mint value of gold is said by Malthus to be 137 schellings[29] [per ounce].
Reduce to hal[f]pence. 77 12 -- 934[28] the pence in £3.17.10	Malthus then converted £3.17.10, omitting the final halfpenny, into 1868 halfpence.
Multiply by 2 for the halfpence 934 2 --- 1868	

[27] This passage is preceded by the words 'To estimate the Hamburgh', written as if it were a title, but as that phrase bears no relation to what follows, it seems that Malthus changed his intentions at this point.

[28] In this one operation, Malthus has multiplied 77 shillings by 12 (= 924) to reduce shillings to pence, and then added the 10 pence (= 934).

[29] In stating that the value of an ounce of standard gold in Holland is 137 schellings [per ounce] Malthus appears to have made an error. He appears to have taken the value of standard gold in Holland as 355 guilders (= 1183.3 schellings) per marc, and calculated the value in schellings per ounce by dividing 1183.3 by 8.63 to give 137 schellings. But the divisor should have been 7.9125, not 8.63. The figure of 7.9125 is the number of ounces that are equivalent in *weight* to one marc. The figure of 8.63 is the number of ounces of standard gold that are equivalent *in value* to 1 marc (or 7.9125 ounces) of fine gold (7.9125 × 12 ÷ 11 = 8.63). The correct figure for the value in schellings of one ounce of standard gold is therefore 1183.3 ÷ 7.9125 = 149.5. The ensuing calculations would have to be adjusted:
149.5 × 480 ÷ 1868 = 38.4 i.e. the par of exchange is £1 = 38.4 schellings.

```
The halfpence in a poun[d]
          24
           20
          ---
          480
```

```
If 1868 halfpence be worth 137
schillings,* how many will 480
be worth

        137
         480
       -----
       10960
       548
       -----
1868 / 65760 / 35.2
       5604
       ----
        9720
        9340
        ----
         3800
         3736
         ----
           64
```

If an ounce of gold is worth 137 schellings in Holland and 1868 halfpence in England, the par of exchange is therefore:
£1 (or 480 halfpence)
$= 137 \div 1868 \times 480$
$= 35.2$ schellings

```
Remainder in schellings

         380
          12
         ---
 1868 / 4560 / 2 groots
        3736
        ----
         724[30]
```

In converting 0.2 schellings into groots, he could have simply multiplied 0.2 by 12 to obtain 2.4 groots; but he adopted the unnecessary complication of converting the remainder (380 schellings) into 4560 groots and dividing the latter by 1868.

[30] Should be '824'.

4. Table I: Calculation of the par of exchange when the price of gold in England is at its mint price and when the price of gold in Holland varies from its mint price

Table I

TEXT

	Price of gold in Holland	Par of exchange whilst gold was at its mint price in England
1791	f 390.10	36/9
	378.1	35/7
1790	396.14	36/10
1794	408	38/5
	415	39/-
	419	39/5
1809	426	40/1
	372	35
	374	35/3
	376	35/5
	378	35/7
	380	35/9
	382	35/10
	384	36/1
	386	36/4
	388	36/7
	390	36/9
	392	36/11
	394	37/2
	396	37/4
	398	37/6
	400	37/8
	402	37/10
	404	38/-
	406	38/3
	408	38/5
	410	38/7
	412	38/9

COMMENTARY

Table I above does not correspond to Ricardo's Amsterdam table that was included in his letter of 30 December 1813 to Malthus. There is nothing in MS to indicate whether Table I was calculated by Malthus, or whether it was supplied to him by Ricardo in another (now missing) letter, or whether Malthus obtained it from another source.

Table I shows the par of exchange between English pounds and Flemish schellings, i.e. the exchange rate that will make the price of gold in England (quoted at its mint price of £3.17.10½ per ounce of standard gold) equal to the price of gold in Holland (quoted in guilders per marc of fine gold), and so render the exportation or importation of gold between the two countries unprofitable. Thus, the first entry indicates that, if the price of standard gold in England is £3.17.10½ per ounce, and the price of fine gold in Holland is 390.10 guilders per marc,[31] then the prices of gold in the two countries will be equal if the exchange rate is £1 = 36 schellings 9 groots after adjusting for agio, and there will be no advantage in buying gold in one country and selling it in the other.

The steps involved in constructing this table appear to have been as follows, taking the first entry as an example:

The current price of fine gold in Holland is 390.10 guilders per marc.
The mint price of standard gold in England is £3.17.10½ (= 934.5 pence) per ounce.
Convert the Holland price from guilders per marc to schellings per marc (3 guilders = 10 schellings).
390.10 guilders = 390.1 × 10 ÷ 3 = 1300.3 schellings
Convert the Holland price from schellings per marc of fine gold to schellings per ounce of standard gold:
1 marc of fine gold is worth 1300.3 schellings
1 marc of fine gold has the same amount of fine gold as 8.63 ounces of standard gold.
∴ 8.63 ounces of standard gold are worth 1300.3 schellings.
∴ 1 ounce of standard gold is worth 1300.3 ÷ 8.63 = 150.68 schellings.

31 The symbol 'f' in the first line of the table stands for florins, i.e. guilders.

The par of exchange is the exchange rate that will make 150.68 schellings equal to 934.5 pence.

If 150.68 schellings	= 934.5 pence,
then £1 (or 240 pence)	$= 150.68 \div 934.5 \times 240$
	= 38.7 schellings
The par of exchange is thus: £1	= 38.7 schellings.

Adjust for agio. The agio used in this table is not stated, but the calculations indicate 5%.

$38.7 \times .95 = 36.77$ schellings = 36 schellings 9 groots.

The second entry in the table can be established in a similar manner. When the price of fine gold in Holland is 378.1 guilders per marc, the par of exchange is found thus:

$378.1 \times 10 \div 3 \div 8.63 \div 934.5 \times 240 \times .95$

= 35.63 schellings = 35 schellings 7.6 groots

i.e. the par of exchange is 20 shillings = 35 schellings 7 groots (approximately).

5. Table I and Table II: Calculation of the par of exchange when both the price of gold in England and the price of gold in Holland vary from their mint prices

COMMENTARY

The following table was extracted by Malthus from the Amsterdam table contained in the letter sent from Ricardo to Malthus on 30 December 1813. It shows the multipliers to be used in calculating the par of exchange between England and Holland when the price of gold in England increases from its mint price (£3.17.10½ per ounce) to £4, £4.1.0, £4.2.0, ... £5.10.0. The left-hand column here is column 9 in the Amsterdam table, and the right-hand column here is column 10. Column 9 is headed 'When the price of gold in London in Bank notes is p^{r}. oz.' Column 10 is headed 'The bullion Par must be multiplied by'. The first entries in columns 9 and 10, viz. '£4' and '.973', were not copied by Malthus into the table. The rest of Malthus' copy is the same as in Ricardo's table. Columns 9 and 10 in the Amsterdam table are repeated in the (un-numbered) columns 6 and 7 in the Hamburg table.

Table II. An Extract from Ricardo's Amsterdam Table

TEXT

	[£4.0]	[.973]
When at	£4.1	by .961
	4.2	.949
	4.3	.938
	4.4	.927
	4.5	.916
	4.6	.905
	4.7	.895
	4.8	.885
	4.9	.875
	4.10	.865
	4.11	.856
	4.13	.838
	4.15	.820
	4.17	.803
	4.19	.786
	5	.779
	5.2	.764
	5.4	.749
	5.6	.735
	5.8	.721
	5.10	.708

When the price of Gold in England in £4.- p^{r} oz the par of exchange, as above, for £3.17.10½, must be multiplied by .973 to obtain the true par for £4, because as

£4 : £3.17.10½ :: 100 : .973.[32]

COMMENTARY

The first entry in Table I shows that when the current price of fine gold in Holland in 390.10 guilders per marc, a par of exchange of 20 shillings = 36 guilders 9 groots will make the Holland price equivalent to the English mint price of £3.17.10½ per ounce of standard gold. But if the current English price is £4.0.0 per ounce of standard gold, the previous par of exchange (36 guilders 9 groots) has to be reduced by multiplying it by a factor of .973 (because £3.17.10½ ÷ £4 = 934½ pence ÷ 960 pence = .973).

[32] Should be '1:.973' or '1000:973'.

Thus, when the price of fine gold in Holland is 390.10 guilders per marc and the price of standard gold in England is £4 per ounce, the adjusted or 'true' par of exchange is found by multiplying 36 schellings 9 groots by .973.

= 36.75 × .973 = 35.76 schellings

i.e. the adjusted par is 20 shillings = 35 schellings 9 groots. Thus, for any current price of gold in England, a multiplier can be found and used to convert the par of exchange as shown in the right-hand column of Table I into the adjusted or 'true' par of exchange.

To take another example, if the current price of fine gold in Holland is 390.10 guilders per marc and the current price of standard gold in England is £4.1.0 per ounce, the adjusted par of exchange is found by taking the entry in the right-hand column of the first line of Table I, viz. 36 schellings 9 groots, and multiplying it by a factor of .961 – because

£3.17.10½ ÷ £4.1.0 = 934½ pence ÷ 972 pence
= .961

The adjusted par is therefore

20 shillings = 36.75 × .961 = 35.32 = 35 schellings 4 groots

Table II lists the multipliers corresponding to current English gold prices from £4.1.0 to £5.10.0 per ounce.

6. Calculation of the direction of the bullion trade between London and Amsterdam: A general statement of procedure and a series of worked examples.

TEXT

To find which way gold is moving – whether it is advantageous to export it or import it.

Amsterdam

Having found the par according to the English mint proportions of the mark of gold[33] in Dutch guilders; find also the par of an ounce of Standard gold in Flemish schellings current. And then – the Par in guilders will be to quoted[34] price in guilders[35] as the par in flemish current to the actual price in flemish current.

[33] 'as quoted' is deleted. [34] 'natural' is del. And 'quoted' is ins. [35] 'to the' is del.

Having obtained the actual price of the ounce stand[d] of gold in schellings flemish current look at the quoted agio and exchange, and having converted banco to currency by the addition of the agio say.

As the actual exchange in current schellings is to 20 shillings English, so is the actual price of the ounce of gold in schillings* flemish to the price of the ounce of Standard gold at Amsterdam in English currency; And according as this price is more or less than the market price in England, gold will be exported to or imported from Holland.

By the foregoing table it is easy to see from which country gold is passing, if the price of gold in the two countries and the rate of exchange is known.

Thus suppose the exchange to be 28/-,[36] the price of gold in Holland 10pc : p[m] or 390.5[37] & the price in England £5.10 - for standard. By the first table the par against 390.5 is 36/9[38] or 441 grotes*,[39] which multiplied by .708 the multiplier against £5.10 [in Table II] gives 312 grotes* or 26/-[40], but the exchange is 28/- therefore gold can be exported to Holland with a profit of 7½ pc[m].[41]

COMMENTARY

If the gold prices in the two countries are known and the current exchange rate is also known, it is 'easy to see from which country gold is passing'; or in other words, it is easy to see whether it will be profitable to buy gold in Holland and sell it in England, or buy gold in England and sell it in Holland.

For example, taking the first entries in Table I and Table II, if the fine gold price in Holland is 390.1 guilders per ounce and the standard gold price in England is £4.1.0 per ounce, the true par is (as shown above) 20 shillings = 36.75 × .961 = 35 schellings 4 groots.

If the actual exchange rate is higher, say 20 shillings = 38 schellings, then a profit can be made by buying gold in England and selling it in Holland, because every pound spent on gold in England will buy gold to the value of

36 i.e. 20 shillings = 28 schellings.

37 i.e. 10% above the mint price of 355 guilders per marc, or 390.5 guilders per marc.

38 Table I as shown in this MS does not have an entry for 390.5. Malthus either was using a more detailed table or used the entry for 390 as an approximation.

39 Malthus generally wrote 'groots'. 36 schellings 9 groots = 441 groots.

40 i.e. 26 schellings.

41 i.e. 7½ per cent. A profit of 2 schellings on 26 schellings is 7.69%.

35 schellings 4 groots, which when sold in Holland will yield 38 schellings.

But if the actual exchange rate is lower than the adjusted par, say 20 shillings = 30 schellings, then a profit will be made by buying gold in Holland and selling it in England, because every pound spent in Holland will buy gold to the value of 30 schellings, which when sold in England will yield 35 schellings 4 groots.

Malthus then added further worked examples showing how to determine the direction of the bullion trade between London and Amsterdam – i.e. whether it is profitable to export gold and/or silver from London to Amsterdam, or from Amsterdam to London – and how to calculate the rate of profit on that trade. The examples are based on either hypothetical or historical data for bullion prices in the two countries and for the rate of exchange between the two currencies.

The first example shows that when fine gold is worth 408.25 guilders per marc in Holland and standard gold is worth £5.10.0 per ounce in London, and the rate of exchange is £1 = 28.25 schellings, a profit of 1.55% can be obtained by transferring gold from Amsterdam to London.

TEXT	COMMENTARY
Amsterdam 25 Sep[r] Exchange 28/3 Gold 15 per cent Gold at 15 per cent in Holland par banco 39.3 Price of gold in london £5.10 Multiplier .708 39.3 .708 ---- 3144 2751 ------- 27.8244 Par therefore 27.82 and gold is at its mint price (£3.17.10½ per ounce) in London	The rate of exchange is given as 20 English shillings equal to 28 Flemish schellings 3 groots, i.e. 28.25 schellings. In Ricardo's Amsterdam table, the statement 'Gold at 15 per cent' means that the price of fine gold in Amsterdam is 15% above the mint price of a marc of standard gold, i.e. 355 × 1.15 = 408.25 guilders. Ricardo's Amsterdam table shows that when the price of fine gold in Holland is 408.25 guilders per marc, the real par of exchange in Flemish banco schellings per pound sterling (with an agio of 3%) is £1 = 39.30 schellings. This is calculated as follows:

Convert guilders per marc to schellings per marc:
408.25 × 10 ÷ 3 = 1360.83
Convert schellings per marc of fine gold to schellings per ounce of standard gold:
1360.83 ÷ 8.63 = 157.68
Adjust for agio of 3%:
157.68 × .97 = 152.96
To establish the par of exchange, let 152.96 schellings = £3.17.10 ½ = 934.5 pence
∴ £1 = 240 pence = 152.96 ÷ 934.5 × 240
= 39.3 schellings

Table II shows that when the price of gold in London is £5.10.0. per ounce, the par of exchange (39.3) has to be multiplied by .708, giving a par of 27.82 schellings.

```
Actual exchange
28/3 groots = 28.25
              27.82
              difference 00.43
              -----
      27.82 : 28.25 :: 100
                100
              -----
       2782 / 282500 / 10.1[42]
              2782
              ----
                4300[43]
                2782[44]
```

As the actual exchange rate is £1 = 28 schellings 3 groots
= 28.25 schellings, there must be a profit of 28.25 – 27.82 = .43 schellings when gold is bought in Amsterdam and sold in London.

The percentage profit is 28.25 ÷ 27.82 × 100 = 101.55 or 1.55%
which Malthus declared to be 'about 2 per cent'.

```
Coming in at rate of[45] about 2
per cent
```

[42] '10.5' is del. [43] '14300' is del. [44] '13901' is del. [45] '5 per cent of' is del.

`28.25 : 43 : 100`
 	
`/ 4300`
	These two lines suggest that Malthus had started to recalculate the percentage profit by expressing the profit (.43 schellings) as a percentage of the selling price in London.

`Price of gold in Holland 16 per cent`
`Exchange with London 31`
`Price of Gold in London 5.10.0`
`Value of an ounce of Gold in Flemish schellings banco 154.3`
	This example shows that, when gold prices in London and Amsterdam and the exchange rate between London and Amsterdam are at the stated levels, a profit of 10.55% can be made by transferring gold from Amsterdam to London. The price of one marc of gold in Holland is given as 16 per cent. As shown in Ricardo's Amsterdam table, this means 16% above the mint price for standard gold of 355 guilders per marc,
	= 355 × 1.16 guilders
	= 411.8 guilders
	= 411.8 × 10 ÷ 3 schellings
	= 1372.67 schellings
	
	Deducting 3% agio
	= 1372.67 × .97
	= 1331.49 schellings
	
	One marc of fine gold has the same value as 8.63 ounces of standard gold,
	i.e. 8.63 ounces are worth 1331.49 schellings.
	∴ 1 ounce is worth 1331.49 ÷ 8.63
	= 154.3 schellings

```
31 : 20 :: 154.3
              20
              --
        31 / 30860 / 99.5
              279
              ---
               296
               279
               ---
                170
                155
```

154.3 schellings are converted into 99.5 English shillings by multiplying by 20 and dividing by 31. (The exchange rate is given as £1 or 20 English shillings equal to 31 Flemish schellings.)[46]

Thus, one ounce of gold can be bought in Holland for 99.5 English shillings, and sold in London for £5.10.0 or 110 English shillings.

```
99.5 : 110 :: 100
         100
         ---
99.5 / 11000 / 110.55
        995
        ---
        1050
         995
         ---
          5500
          4975
           ---
           5250
           4975
```

The percentage profit on the transaction can then be calculated: $110 \div 99.5 \times 100 = 110.55$ i.e. a profit of 10.55%.

```
Gold coming in at the rate of
10.55 per cent.
```

[46] This particular calculation occurs also in another part of MS where the text reads: 'Price of the ounce of gold in Flemish shillings* is 154.3. This reduced to English currency at an exchange of 31' followed by the same calculations, with one more step in the division, leading to an answer of 99.55.

COMMENTARY

The next example uses the same data for gold prices and the exchange rate as the previous one, but calculates the rate of profit on importing gold into London by a different method, viz. by calculating the percentage difference between the actual rate of exchange and the adjusted par of exchange.

TEXT	COMMENTARY
Against 16 per cent stand 39.64 And against 5.10 .708 3964 708 ---- 31712 27748 ------- 2806512 Par	Ricardo's Amsterdam table shows that when the price of gold in Amsterdam is 16% above 355 guilders per marc, i.e. 411.8 guilders, the par of exchange is 20 shillings = 39.64 schellings. This assumes the price of gold in London is £3.17.10½ per ounce. But when the price in London is £5.10.0 per ounce, Ricardo's Amsterdam table shows that the par of 39.64 must be multiplied by .708. (See the extract from Ricardo's Amsterdam table in Table II above.) In this calculation Malthus shows that the adjusted par is 39.64 × .708 = 28.06.
28 : 31 :: 100 28 / 3100 / 1107 28 --	Malthus then calculated the percentage difference between the actual exchange rate (£1 = 31 schellings)[47] and the adjusted par of exchange.
30 28 -- 200 196	If the latter is rounded to 28 schellings, the profit is 31 ÷ 28 × 100 = 110.7 or 10.7%.
	Thus, gold can be bought in Amsterdam at the rate of £1 = 28 schellings and sold in London at £1 = 31 schellings, yielding a profit of 10.7%.

[47] The information supplied with this example does not specifically state the exchange rate. But the figure '31' in this calculation indicates that the exchange rate being used is £1 = 31 schellings.

```
With the Decimal

2806 : 31 :: 100

2806 / 3100 / 110.5[48]
       2806
       ----
        2940
        2806
        ----
         13400
         11224
         -----
          2176

10½ per cent nearly
Gold coming in at present
at the rate of above ten per
cent.
Decemr 14th 1813
```

If the par of exchange is stated 'with the decimal', i.e. 28.06, the profit is 31 ÷ 28.06 × 100 = 110.47 or '10½ per cent nearly'.

This result obtained by use of the tables could also have been obtained by comparing the Amsterdam price (99.55 shillings per ounce) – as calculated above – with the London price, said to be £5.10.0 per ounce: 110 ÷ 99.5 × 100 = 110.55, or 10½% nearly.

COMMENTARY

The above calculation occurs again in another part of MS, in a slightly different format, thus:

TEXT

```
Opposite 16 per cent par
39.64
Opposite 5.10
Multiplier 708
           39.64
            .708
           -----
           31712
            27748
            --------
            28.06512
```

[48] '110.4' is altered to '110.5'.

```
        28 : 31 :: 100

        28 / 3100 / 110.7
             28
             --
              30
              28
              --
               200
               196

        Gold coming in at 10.7
per cent.
```

COMMENTARY

The following calculation appears to refer to a situation where the price of standard gold in Amsterdam is 93.5 shillings per ounce and its price in London is £5.10.0 = 110 shillings per ounce.

TEXT

```
Exchange 33. The price of gold
at Amsterdam would be 93.5

93.5 : 110 :: 110

93.5 / 11000 / 117.6
        935
       ----
        1650
         935
        ----
         7150
         6545
         ----
          605

Gold coming in at the rate of
17.6 per cent
```

COMMENTARY

Malthus shows that the profit obtained by buying gold in Amsterdam and selling it in London would be 110 ÷ 93.5 × 199 = 117.6, or 17.6%.

COMMENTARY

In the following example, Malthus calculated the profit rate using an Amsterdam gold price of 411.8 guilders per marc, a London gold price of £5.8.0 per ounce, and an exchange rate of £1 = 27 schellings 8 groots.

TEXT	COMMENTARY
Amsterdam 24th Novr. Exchange 27/8 Price of gold 16 Opposite 16. Banco par 39.64 Gold London £5.8 Multiplier .721	In this example the price of gold in Amsterdam is said to be 16% above 355 guilders per marc, i.e. 355 × 1.16 = 411.8 guilders per marc. According to Ricardo's Amsterdam table, this price of gold corresponds to a par of exchange of 39.64.
396 72 --- 792 2772[49] ------ 28.512[50] Par of gold therefore 28.5[51]	As the price of gold in London is £5.8.0 per ounce, Ricardo's Amsterdam table (as seen in the extract in Table II above) shows that the par of 39.64 has to be multiplied by .721, giving an adjusted or true par of 28.58. Malthus simplified the calculation by dropping the final digits (i.e. 39.6 × .72) and arrived at an adjusted par of 28.51, or 28.5.
Actual exchange 27 8 grotes* 27⅔ = balance against London[52]	As the actual exchange rate is given as 27/8, i.e. £1 = 27 schellings 8 groots = 27.67 schellings, the balance is against London. It would be profitable to buy gold in London at £1 = 27.67 schellings and sell it in Amsterdam at £1 = 28.5 (or 28.58) schellings.

49 '2672' is altered to '2772'. 50 '27.512' is altered to '28.512'. 51 '27.5' is altered to '28.5'.
52 'slight balance in favour of London' is altered to 'balance against London'.

```
Silver 6s 6d
Par to 6s 6d          29.79
Actual Exchange       27.8

Silver going out at a
considerable advantage

Silver
27.7 :: 29.7 :: 100

277 / 29700 / 107
      277
      ---
       2000
       1939
```

Ricardo's Amsterdam table stated (columns 11 and 12) that when silver is worth 6 shillings 6 pence per ounce in London, the par of exchange is £1 = 29.79 schellings.

If the actual exchange rate is £1 = 27 schellings 8 groots (or 27.7 schellings), Malthus calculated that there would be a 7% profit in buying silver in London at £1 = 27.67 schellings and selling it in Amsterdam at £1 = 29.79 schellings.

COMMENTARY

The following calculation shows how the price of gold expressed in guilders per marc can be converted into schellings per marc, and then into schellings per ounce, and finally into shillings per ounce.

TEXT

```
The Gold 16 per cent
154.3 value of an ounce of
Standard Gold in schellings
flemish banco.
Reduced to English shgs
53

2⅞  : 20 : 1543
              20
            ----
277  277 / 30860 / 110[54]
           277
           ---
            310[55]
            277
            ---
             33
```

COMMENTARY

Ricardo's Amsterdam table shows that when the price of fine gold in Amsterdam is 16% above 355 guilders per marc (i.e. 411.8 guilders per marc), the equivalent price of standard gold is 154.3 schellings per ounce. The conversion of the price of fine gold in guilders to the price of standard gold in schellings is done as follows:

Convert guilders per marc to schellings per marc:

$411.8 \times 10 \div 3$

$= 1372.7$ schellings per marc

Convert marcs of fine gold to ounces of standard gold:

$1372.7 \div 8.63$

$= 159.05$ schellings per ounce

(There is 1 marc of fine gold in 8.63 ounces of standard gold.)

Deduct 3% for agio:

$159.05 \times .97$

$= 154.3$ schellings per ounce

In this example Malthus converts 154.3 schellings into 111 shillings using an exchange rate of 20 shillings = 27.7 schellings

(or 27 schellings 8 groots)

$154.3 \div 27.7 \times 20 = 111$ shillings

(Malthus incorrectly calculated it at 110 shillings.)

[53] At this point '1543.20' is del.

[54] Should be 111.

[55] The last three lines should be:

```
316
277
---
 39
```

COMMENTARY

The next example uses the same price data as in the previous example, but uses a different exchange rate, converting guilders per marc into shillings per ounce. It then calculates the profit obtainable by importing gold from Amsterdam into London.

TEXT	COMMENTARY
[56] Decembr 3rd 1813 The Exchange with Holland was 33. The price of gold in London £5.10. Let us suppose the price of Gold at Amsterdam 16 per cent or 411.80 which in shilling* banco flemish for the ounce of Standard gold will be 154.3	As in the previous example, the price of gold in Amsterdam is given as 16%, i.e. 411.8 guilders per marc, which is equivalent to 154.3 schellings per ounce.
154.3 at the exchange 33 33 : 20 :: 154.3 20 ----- 33 / 30860 / 93½ 297 --- 116 99 --- 17[57]	This price is then converted into English currency at an exchange rate of 20 shillings = 33 schellings: 154.3 ÷ 33 × 20 = 93.5 shillings = £4.13.6

[56] 'Jan' is del. [57] Altered from '27'.

The price of gold at Amsterdam in English Currency £4.13.6; in London £5.10.0	Malthus then took the difference between the Amsterdam price (93.5 English shillings) and the London price (110 English shillings) – viz. 16½ shillings – and calculated it as a percentage of the London selling price – i.e. 16½ ÷ 110 × 100 = 15%.
[58] 110 : 16½ :: 100 11.0 / 165.0 / 15 11 -- 55	
Gold may be imported at a profit of 15 per cent.	If the profit on importing gold were expressed as a percentage, not of the London selling price, but of the Amsterdam buying price, it would be: 16½ ÷ 93.5 × 100 = 17.6%.

COMMENTARY

The next example uses the same data for gold prices and exchange rate as the previous one, but uses a different method in calculating the profit obtainable by importing gold into England.

TEXT	COMMENTARY
Gold at Amsterdam 16 per cent or 411.80 Real Par in Flemish banco 39.54 Multiplier for £5.10 .708	In the preceding example the gold prices in Amsterdam and London are compared by converting them both to English shillings per ounce. This example makes use of the multiplier method.
39.54 708 ------- 31632 27678 ------- 27.99432 28	In Ricardo's Amsterdam table, the real par of exchange corresponding to a gold price of 411.80 guilders per ounce is said to be 39.64[59] i.e. £1 = 39.64 schellings.

[58] '5.10' is del. [59] Malthus seems to have misread this as 39.54.

Ricardo's Amsterdam table (as seen in the extract given in Table II above) shows that, when the price of gold in London is £5.10.0 per ounce, this figure of 39.64 must be multiplied by .708.

In this example Malthus found the adjusted par to be: 39.54 × .708 = 27.99, rounded off to 28. If he had begun with Ricardo's figure of 39.64, the adjusted par would be: 39.64 × .708 = 28.07.

```
28 : 33 :: 100

28 / 3300 / 117
     28
     --
      50
      28
      --
      220
      196
      ---
       24
```

The actual exchange rate is not specifically stated but the calculations show that it was taken as £1 = 33 schellings (as in the preceding example). Malthus showed that this is 17% higher than the adjusted par.

```
33 : 5 :: 100

33 / 500 / 15
     33
     --
     170
     165
```

Here Malthus took the difference between the actual exchange rate and the adjusted par of exchange, i.e. 33 – 28 = 5 schellings, and expressed it as a percentage of the actual exchange rate, viz. 5 ÷ 33 × 100 = 15%, showing a profit of 15% as in the previous example.

COMMENTARY

The following two examples of trade in silver appear in an insert on the same MS page as the previous example.

TEXT	COMMENTARY
Silver Same date 7[s] per oz. The Par of 7. 27.66 Actual exchange 33	Ricardo's Amsterdam table stated (columns 11 and 12) that when the price of standard silver in London is 7 shillings per ounce, the par of exchange with Amsterdam is £1 = 27.66 schellings.
Consequently Silver might be imported at premium of more than 15 per cent	Malthus states, without showing his calculations, that there would be profit of 'more than 15 per cent' on importing silver into England. The profit would be: (33 – 27.66) ÷ 33 × 100 = 16.2%.
Hamburgh Same date Dollars 7[s]. Exchange 29. When Dollars are 7[s] the par is 24.55.	Ricardo's Hamburg table shows that when the silver dollar is worth 7s 1d per ounce, the par of exchange is £1 = 24.55 schellings. (There is no entry in Ricardo's Hamburg table for 7s. Malthus seems to have misread 7s 1d as 7s.)
29 : 4.45 :: 100 29 / 44500 / 15 29 -- 155 145	In this calculation Malthus shows that, when the actual exchange rate is £1 = 29 schellings, importing dollars will give a profit of about 15%, i.e. (29 – 24.55) ÷ 29 × 100 = 15.34.

7. Effect of changes in the price of silver in London on the exchange rate between the English pound and Flemish schellings

TEXT

COMMENTARY

```
Par in Silver with Hamburgh
   62 : 422 :: 63
            63
           ---
          1266
         2532
         -----
62 / 26586 / 4288
         248
         ---
          178
          124
          ---
           546
           496
           ---
            500
            496
            ---
```

In this calculation Malthus took the price of silver in London as 62 pence per ounce,[60] and the exchange rate as 20 shillings = 422 groots. He calculated that an increase in the London price from 62 to 63 pence will mean an increase in the exchange rate from £1 = 422 groots (or 35 schellings 2 groots) to £1 = 428.8 groots (or 35 schellings 8.8 groots).

```
    62 : 422 :: 64
             64
            ---
           1688
          2532
          -----
  62 / 27008 / 435
          248
          ---
           220
           186
           ---
            348
            310
            ---
             38
```

He then repeated the exercise for the case where the London price rises from 62 pence to 64 pence per ounce, and concluded that the exchange rate rises to 435 groots to the pound.

[60] i.e. the mint price of standard silver.

[61]

```
s d
5/2    35/2
5/3    35.8[62]
5/4
```

These results are listed in this incomplete table.

```
63 : 62 :: 422
             62
            ---
            844
           2532
          -----
     63 / 26164 / 415.3
           252
           ---
            96
            63
            --
            334
            315
            ---
             190
             189

12 / 415 / 34.7
```

However, below a line drawn across the page, he then adopted a different method of calculation, probably realising that a rise in the English price of silver means a fall in the value of the English currency, and therefore a lower (not a higher) exchange rate.

Whereas previously he had multiplied 422 by 63 and divided by 62, now he multiplied by 62 and divided by 63, and concluded that a rise in the price of silver in London from 5/2 to 5/3 per ounce means a fall in the exchange rate from £1 = 422 groots to £1 = 415.3 groots (or 34 schellings 7.3 groots).

[61] At this point, MS has:

```
 35
 12
---
420
```

i.e. a conversion of 35 schellings into 420 groots. This is followed in MS by: 12/408/34 and 12/402/33, i.e. conversions of 408 and 402 groots into schellings but the relevance of these calculations to the context is not evident.

[62] Presumably intended to mean 35 schellings 8 groots, not 35.8 schellings, which would be 35 schellings 9.6 groots.

```
64 / 26164 / 408.8
     256
     ---
       564
       512
       ---
        520

65 / 26164 / 402.5
     260
     ---
       164
       130
       ---
        340
        325

66 / 26164 / 396.4
     198
     ---
      636
      594
      ---
       424
       396
       ---
        280
        594[63]
        ---
          6
```

The calculation was then repeated for silver prices of 64, 65, 66 and 67 pence, showing a movement in the exchange rate to £1 = 408.8, 402.5, 396.4 and 390.5 groots respectively (i.e. 34 schellings 1 groot, 33 schellings 6.5 groots, 33 schellings 4 groots, and 32 schellings 6.5 groots).

[63] Should be:

```
280
264
---
 16
```

```
67 / 26164 / 390.5
     201
     ---
      606
      603
      ---
        340
        335
```

```
70 / 26164 / 373.7
               31
```

A price of 70 pence is then stated, without the actual calculation being shown, to be equivalent to an exchange rate of £1 = 373.7 groots = 31 schellings 1.7 groots.

5.2	35/2[64]
5.3	34.7
5.4	34.1
5.5	33 6.5
5.6	33.4
5.7	32/6.5
5.8	32.0.7
5.9	31.7
5.10	31.1
5.11	30.8.5
6	30 3.3
6.1	29 10.4

The results are finally presented in tabular form, and include further results (for 5/8, 5/9, 5/11, 6/0, 6/1) for which the calculations are not shown.

[64] Three methods are used in this table to distinguish schellings and groots – forward slash, dot and space. The dot is also used to indicate a decimal. Thus '30.8.5' means 30 schellings 8.5 groots.

8. Calculation of profit on trade in silver

COMMENTARY

In the following three brief calculations Malthus argued that a profit can be made by exporting silver from Amsterdam to London. The text refers to a 'Table ii'. The figures are taken from columns 11 and 12 of Ricardo's Amsterdam table.

TEXT	COMMENTARY
Price of silver, same date[65] 7s.	Ricardo's Amsterdam table shows that when the price of standard silver in London is 7 shillings, the par of exchange with Amsterdam is £1 = 27.66 schellings. In this calculation, Malthus compared the actual rate of exchange (£1 = 31 schellings) to a par of exchange of £1 = 27.66 schellings, and concluded that the exportation of silver from Amsterdam to London would yield a profit of 12.8% – an error for 12.1%.
Opposite 7s in Table ii is 27.66 the par of silver.	
But the exchange is 31.	

```
2766 : 31 :: 100

2766 / 3100 / 112.8
       2766
       ----
        3540[66]
        2766
        ----
         7740
         5532
         ----
         22080
         22128

Silver coming in at the rate
12.8 per cent
```

[65] 'same date' is ins. The date (referred to in the preceding line of MS) was 14 December 1813.
[66] Should be '3340'. With the ensuing corrections, the quotient becomes 112.1.

```
March 1811

24 : 30 :: 100

24 / 3000 / 125
     24
     --
      60
      48
      --
      120
      120
```

As in the preceding example, the ratio of 24 : 30 presumably represents the ratio of the par of exchange for silver to the actual rate of exchange.

In that situation, the exportation of silver from Amsterdam to London would yield a profit of 25%.

```
23 : 29 / 2900

23 / 2900 / 126
     23
     --
      60
      46
      --
      140
      138

26 percent
```

The calculation is repeated for a ratio of 23 : 29, showing a profit of 26%.

B. Trade with Hamburg

1. Ricardo's table for Hamburg

COMMENTARY

In the following table, the three columns represent (reading from left to right) the price of a ducat (i.e. 57½ grains of gold) in Hamburg expressed in stivers, the price of gold in Hamburg in schellings per ounce, and the exchange rate between English pounds and Flemish schellings.

It shows the effect that successive increases of one stiver in the value of a ducat will have on the value of gold expressed in schellings per ounce, and on the exchange rate between English pounds and Flemish schellings.

Table III [67]

TEXT

Table for Hamburgh upon Mr R^{s} Plan[68]

98.46	137	35/2
99	137.7	35/4
100	139.1	35/8
101	140.5	36/1
102	141.9	36/5
103	143.3	36/9
104	144.7	37/1
105	146.1	37/6

COMMENTARY

In the first row, the entry (98.46) in the left-hand column is the value of a ducat in Hamburg expressed in stivers, after adjusting for the greater purity of gold

[67] To distinguish this table from the two previous tables we have named it 'Table III'. This name does not occur in MS.

[68] The table is presented twice in MS. The second presentation, which is the same as the first except that the middle column and the right-hand column are transposed, is not reproduced in this transcript. What Malthus meant when he said that this table is 'upon Mr R^{s} Plan' is not clear. Table III does not correspond to either of the two tables (the Amsterdam table and the Hamburg table) included in Ricardo's letters of 30 December 1813 or 1 January 1814 to Malthus. It is possibly an extract from another table that was sent by Ricardo but is now missing. The reference in the next section (B2) to 'the third column of M^{r} R['s] Table' suggests that Table III was in fact constructed by Ricardo. Alternatively, Table III might have been constructed by Malthus himself, following a method used by Ricardo in a missing table.

in England. In Hamburg the mint price of a ducat was 96 stivers, but the gold content of English gold in relation to the ducat was in the ratio 15.21 : 14.83. Adjusting for the purer gold content, 57½ grains of English gold would be worth $96 \times 15.21 \div 14.83 = 98.46$ stivers.

In the first row, the entry (137) in the middle column is the price of gold in Hamburg expressed in schellings per ounce. As the ducat contains 57.5 grains of gold and the ounce contains 480 grains, a value of 98.46 stivers is equal to
$98.46 \div 57.5 \times 480$ stivers per ounce
= 822 stivers per ounce
= 137 schellings per ounce.

In the first row, the entry (35/2) in the right-hand column is the exchange rate between pounds and schellings when gold in London is at its mint value of £3.17.10½ (or 934½ pence) per ounce, and the current value of gold in Amsterdam is 137 schellings per ounce
∴ 934½ pence = 137 schellings
£1 = 240 pence = 137 ÷ 934½ × 240 schellings
= 35.18 schellings
= 35 schellings 2 groots

The second row states that when the value of a ducat is 99 stivers, the value of gold will be
$99 \div 57.5 \times 480$ stivers per ounce
= 826.4 stivers per ounce
= 826.4 ÷ 6 schellings per ounce
= 137.7 schellings per ounce

When gold in London is at its mint value of 934½ pence per ounce and the current value of gold in Hamburg is 137.7 schellings per ounce, then 934½ pence will be equal to 137.7 schellings, and the exchange rate between pounds and schellings will be:
£1 = 137.7 ÷ 934½ × 240 = 35.36 schellings
= 35 schellings 4 groots.

TEXT

Hamburgh Table

According to the English mint Proportions, the Par of the Ducat is 98.46 Stivers, the Par of the ounce of gold is 137 schillings* flemish banco, and the Par of exchange is 35/2 flemish banco.

For each Stiver banco in the price of the Ducat, the par of the Ounce of Standard gold increases rather less than[69] 1.4 and the Par of the exchange increases 4 groots and nearly[70] three tenths

COMMENTARY

The opening sentence here is a statement of the first line of the Table for Hamburg (Table III).

There are no calculations in MS to support this conclusion. It is not clear therefore whether Malthus made the calculations himself, or whether he quoted them from another source.

The conclusion can be supported by calculation as follows:

When the value of a ducat increases from 99 to 100 stivers, the value of an ounce of gold will rise from
$99 \times 480 \div 57.5$
$= 826.43$ stivers
$= 137.74$ schellings
to $100 \times 480 \div 57.5$
$= 834.78$ stivers
$= 139.13$ schellings
i.e. an increase of 1.39 schellings (or 'rather less than 1.4').

For each successive increase of one stiver in the value of a ducat, the increase in the value of an ounce of gold will be
$480 \div 57.5 = 8.35$ stivers
$= 1.39$ schellings (or, 'rather less than 1.4').

[69] 'than' is ins. [70] 'one third' is del.

When the ducat increases from 99 to 100 stivers, the rate of exchange between English pounds and Flemish schellings will increase from
£1 = 99 × 480 ÷ 57.5 × 240 ÷ 934½ stivers, to
£1 = 100 × 480 ÷ 57.5 × 240 ÷ 934½ stivers, a difference of
480 ÷ 57.5 × 240 ÷ 934½
= 2.1439 stivers
= 4.2878 groots
(or '4 groots and nearly three tenths').

```
To try the Table more accurately - The most accurate Pars are 98.46 Stivers banco for the Ducat, and 137 flemish schillings banco for the ounce of gold Standard.
```

Malthus verified the accuracy of Table III in four other cases – viz. when the value of a ducat increases from 98.6 to 99, from 98.6 to 100, from 98.6 to 101, and 98.6 to 105 stivers.

```
                 137
98.46 : 137 :: 99
                 ---
                1233
               1233
               -----
    98.46 / 13563 / 137.7
                9846
                ----
                37170
                29538
                -----
                 76320
                 68922
                 -----
                  73980
                  68922
                  -----
                   5058
```

The first of the four calculations shows that when the value of the ducat increases from 98.46 to 99 stivers, the value of gold in schellings per ounce will increase from 137 to 137.7 – thus confirming the accuracy of the entry in the second column of the second row of Table III.

```
9846 : 137 :: 100

98.46 / 13700 / 1391
        9846
        ----
        38540
        29538
        -----
         90020
         88614
         -----
          14060
           9846
           ----
           4214


           137
9846 : 137  101
            ---
            137
          137
          -----
          13837

9846 / 13837 / 1405
        9846
       -----
        39910
        39384
        -----
          52600
          49230
          -----
           3370
```

He repeated the calculation for three further entries in the first column of Table III, viz. 100, 101 and 105 stivers.

In each case his calculations verify the accuracy of the corresponding entries in the middle column (the prices in schellings per ounce) viz. 137.7, 139.1, 140.5 and 146.1.

```
              137
9846 : 137 : 105
              ---
              685
             137
             -----
             14385

9846 / 14385 / 146
        9846
       -----
        45390
        39384
        -----
         60060
         59076
         -----
          9840
```

[71]

In proportion to each Stiver Banco from 99. The ounce of Standard increases rather less than 1.4

He concluded, as before, that for every increase of one stiver in the value of the ducat, the value in schellings per ounce will increase by 'rather less than 1.4'.

The conclusion could have been reached more simply, without lengthy multiplications and divisions, by showing that the increase in schellings per ounce corresponding to a one stiver increase in the value of the ducat (from n to n+1) would be:

$[137.7 \div 98.46 \times (n+1)] - [137.7 \div 98.46 \times n] = 137.7 \div 98.46 = 1.39$, or 'rather less than 4'.

[71] More accurately, 146.1.

2. An adjustment to Ricardo's table to take account of variations in the value of gold in London from the mint price of £3.17.10½ per ounce.

TEXT

A multiplier might be found to apply to the third column of M[r] R['s] Table and tell at once the price of gold in English currency at Hamburgh

```
£3.17.10½ : £4 :: 1

      77              80
      12              12
      --              --
     924             960
      10               2
      --             ---
     932½[72]        1920
      ×2
     ---
    1865

1865 : 1920 :: 1

1865 / 1920 / 1.029
       1865
       ----
         5500
         3730
         ----
         17700
         16785
         -----
           915
```

COMMENTARY

The 'Table for Hamburgh upon M[r] R[s] Plan' (Table III) is based on the assumption that gold in London is at its mint price of £3.17.10½ per ounce. In this calculation Malthus shows how the third (or right-hand) column in Table III can be adjusted to take account of movements in the actual price of gold in London away from its mint price.

If gold in London is £4 per ounce, he calculates that the figures in the third column of Table III have to be multiplied by a factor of £4 ÷ £3.17.10½. He proceeds by converting £3.17.10½ and £4 to halfpence, and derives a factor of 1.029, but a mistake in the calculations means that the multiplier should be 1.027.

[72] Should be '934½'. With the subsequent calculations adjusted accordingly, the multiplier becomes 1920 ÷ 1869 = 1.027.

3. Calculation of the profit on exporting gold from London to Hamburg

TEXT	COMMENTARY
March 1800 Gold 4.10 Exchange 29.11 Gold at Hamburgh 104. Opposite 104 The par 37/1 or 445 groots	In this example, gold is £4.10.0 per ounce in London and the value of a ducat in Hamburg is 104 stivers. Table III shows that when the price of gold at Hamburg is 104 stivers per ducat, the par of exchange will be 37/1, i.e. 20 shillings = 37 schellings 1 groot or 445 groots. This par of exchange will make the value of a ducat in Hamburg (104 stivers) equivalent to the mint price of gold in London (£3.17.10½ per ounce).
Opposite 4.10.0 the multiplier is 865 445 865 --- 2225 2670 3560 ------ 12 / 384.925 / 32	Table II above shows that when the value of gold in London is £4.10.0 per ounce, the par of 20 schellings = 445 groots must be multiplied by .865, giving an adjusted par of £1 = 384.925 groots or 32.077 schellings.
865 37 --- 6055 2595 ----- 31905[73]	In this next calculation, Malthus multiplied the par of £1 = 37 schellings by the multiplier .865, giving an adjusted par of 32.005 (incorrectly calculated at 31.905). The purpose of this calculation was presumably to show how the adjusted par would be affected if the par of £1 = 37 schellings 1 groot was altered to £1 = 37 schellings.

[73] Should be '32005'.

Par of gold 32. Actual exchange 29.11. Gold going out at the rate of nearly 7 per cent.

This statement of the profit to be made by exporting gold is not accompanied by an explanation. The explanation is as follows: If gold is bought in London at £1 = 29 schellings 11 groots = 29.92 schellings, and sold in Hamburg at £1 = 32 schellings, the profit will be 32 ÷ 29.92 × 100 = 106.95 or 6.95%.

Sep[r] 1809. Gold at Hamburgh 104. Exchange 28. Par 32. Gold going out at the rate of 14 per cent.

In this case, Malthus took the same value of the ducat in Hamburg as in the previous example, viz. 104 stivers, and the same price of gold in London, viz. £4.10.0 per ounce, but a different exchange rate, viz. £1 = 28 schellings instead of £1 = 29 schellings 11 groots. Table III shows that a price of 104 stivers per ducat corresponds to a par of exchange of 37 schellings 1 groot; and Table II shows that when gold in London is £4.10.0 per ounce, the appropriate multiplier is .865. The adjusted par of exchange is therefore:
37.1 × .865 = 32.09 (rounded to 32 schellings).

```
28 : 32 ::   : 100
                32
              ----
        28 / 3200 / 114[74]
             28
             --
              40
              28
              --
              120
```

There would thus be a 14% profit in buying gold in London at £1 = 28 schellings and selling it abroad at £1 = 32 schellings.

[74] '113$^{9}/_{7}$' is del.

```
Hamburgh Gold 101½
Exchange 27/8
Opposite 101½     36/3
Price in London 4.11.0
Multiplier 856
Par reduced to groots

36/3
  12  =  435
         856
         ---
        2610
       2175
      3480
      ------
 12 / 372360 / 31

Par 31
Actual exchange 27/8

27⅔   :  31 :: 100
277 / 3100 / 112
      277
      ---
       330
       277
       ---
        530
```
[75]

```
Gold going out at the rate of
11½ or 12 per cent.
```

This calculation is based on different gold prices and a different exchange rate. Malthus stated that, when the value of the ducat is 101½ stivers, the par of exchange is 30 schellings 3 groots. As Table III in MS does not contain an entry for 101½, Malthus must have been either quoting from a more detailed table or taking a mean between 36/1 (the par for 101) and 36/5 (the par for 102). Converting 36/3 to groots (435 groots) and using the multiplier .856 corresponding to a London price of £4.11.0 (as in Table II), the adjusted par is £1 = 31 schellings, which is 12% higher than the actual exchange rate of

£1 = 27 schellings 8 groots
= 27.7 schellings,

making it profitable to buy gold in London and sell it abroad.

[75] Final line unclear, presumably 554.

TEXT	COMMENTARY
In March 1809 The Price of gold at Hamburgh was 104 and the exchange 29.11. Opposite 104 is 144.3 schillings*	The value of the ducat in March 1809 in Hamburg is said to be 104 stivers. Misreading Table III, Malthus stated that this is equivalent to 144.3 schellings per ounce. The correct figure is 144.7. This can be verified: Convert the value of the ducat in stivers to the value of an ounce of gold in stivers: 104 × 480 ÷ 57½ = 868.2 stivers (1 ounce has 480 grains; 1 ducat has 57½ grains) Convert stivers per ounce to schellings per ounce: 868.2 ÷ 6 = 144.7
which reduced to English currency at 30. 30 : 20 :: 144[76] 20 --- 30 / 2880 / 96	The exchange rate is given as '29.11'. This was apparently intended to be read as 20 shillings = 29 schellings 11 groots or 29.92 schellings. Malthus simplified it as 20 shillings = 30 schellings. He also simplified the price of gold in Hamburg (144.3 schellings per ounce) as 144 schellings per ounce, and converted it into 96 shillings per ounce (144 × 20 ÷ 30), or £4.16.0 per ounce.

[76] Alongside these figures the text has: 'omit the fractions which about balance each other'.

```
Price of Gold at Hamburgh in
English Currency £4.16.0 an
ounce.
In England at the same time it
was £4.10.0. Gold was therefore
going out at a profit
90 : 96 :: 100
90 / 9600 / 107
of near 7 per cent
```

Therefore, gold bought in England at £4.10.0 per ounce and sold in Hamburg at £4.16.0 per ounce will yield a profit of 6.67% ('near 7 per cent').

```
Hamburgh March 1810
Price 101. Exchange 29
Opposite 101 the price of
an ounce of standard gold
is 140.1. Reduced to English
Currency at 29.
```

In the next calculation, he took a different Hamburg price – 101 stivers per ducat instead of 104 – and showed how this can be converted to shillings per ounce. Again misreading Table III he stated that 101 stivers per ducat is equivalent to 140.1 schellings per ounce. The correct figure is 140.5 schellings per ounce.

```
29 : 20 :: 1401
              20
            ----
      29 / 28020 / 966
           261
           ---
            192
            174
            ---
             180
             174
```

Using a new exchange rate of 20 shillings = 29 schellings, he showed that a price of 140.1 schellings per ounce is equivalent to 96.6 shillings (=£4.16.7) per ounce. But he did not, in this example, quote the English price of gold, and did not calculate the profit and direction of the bullion trade.

```
29 : 20 :: 1404
              20
            ----
     29 / 28080 / 96.82
          261
          ---
           198
           174
           ---
            240
            232
            ---
             80
```

The next calculation takes the Hamburg price as 140.4 schellings per ounce, and shows that (with the exchange rate of £1 = 29 schellings) this is equivalent to 96.6 shillings (= £4.16.7) per ounce. Again, he did not calculate the profit and direction of the bullion trade.

```
March 1811
Gold 4.13. Suppose gold at Par
in Hamburgh. one ounce will
the[re?] equal 137.
```

Malthus then repeated the exercise for a different date (March 1811), for different gold prices (98.46 stivers per ducat instead of 104 and £4.14.0 per ounce instead of £4.10.0), and a different exchange rate (£1 = 24 schellings instead of £1 = 29 schellings 11 groots).

Table III shows that the mint price of gold in Hamburg after adjusting for gold content – viz. 98.46 stivers per ducat – corresponds to a price of 137 schellings per ounce.

```
which reduced to English
currency at the rate of 24

24:20::137
         20
        ---
  24 / 2740 / 115 = £5.15
       24             English
       --
        34
        24
        --
        100
```

Malthus calculated that, if the exchange rate is 20 shillings = 24 schellings, then 137 schellings = 115 shillings or £5.15.0

```
Sold in London at 4.13.6[77]
                  4.14

94 : 115 :: 1000

94 / 11500 / 122
      94
      --
      210
      188
      ---
       220

Gold might be exported at 22
percent profit
```

He then calculated that if gold is bought in London at £4.14.0 (= 94 shillings) per ounce, and sold in Hamburg at 115 shillings per ounce, there will be a profit of 22%.

[77] Malthus appears to have intended at first to perform the calculation using a London price of either £4.13.0 or £4.13.6, before deciding to use £4.14.0.

4. Conversion of the value of a ducat in stivers to the value of an ounce of gold in stivers after adjusting for the difference in gold content between Hamburg gold and London gold.

TEXT	COMMENTARY
The Hamburgh Par of Gold for the Ducat is 96 Stivers banco. And this par will be to the English Par as the proportions of the two metals in each country as 14.83 to 15.21	The Hamburg par (1 ducat is worth 96 stivers) is converted to the English par by adjusting for the difference in the purity of the gold of the two countries. The gold content of English standard gold exceeds that of the ducat in the ratio 15.21 : 14.83.

```
  1483 : 1521 :: 96
              96
            ----
            9126
          13689
          ------
1483 / 146016 / 9846
          13347
          -----
           12546
           11864
           -----
             6820
             5932
             ----
              8880
              8898
```

The adjusted value of a ducat is thus:
$96 \div 14.83 \times 15.21$
$= 98.46$ stivers.

```
If 57.5 be worth

         98.46 ::what will 480
            480
          -----
         787680
        39384
        -------
  575 / 4726080 / 822
        4600
        ----
         1260
         1150
         ----
          1100
          1150

= 137 flemish schllings* banco.
```

Malthus then converted the price of a ducat expressed in stivers into the price of an ounce of gold expressed in stivers, by adjusting for the different weights of the ducat (57½ grains) and the ounce (480 grains). If 57.5 grains of gold are worth 98.46 stivers, then one ounce or 480 grains will be worth
$98.5 \times 480 \div 57.5 = 822.3$ stivers = 137 schellings.

COMMENTARY

The above calculations are repeated (in a slightly different format) in another part of MS:

TEXT	COMMENTARY

```
96 is the Hamburgh Par.
And the Par according to
our mint proportions will be
obtained by saying

As 1483 : 1521 :: 96 to 98.46
                        or 98.5
```

There are 57½ standard grains in a Ducat,[78] which is worth therefore in Stivers banco 98.5 very nearly. And
57.5 : 98.5 :: 480 the grains in an ounce to the value of an ounce of gold in stivers banco.

```
   575 : 985
          480
          ---
        78800
       3940
       ------
 575 / 472800 / 822.2 Stivers
       4600            banco
       ----
        1280
        1150
        ----
         1300
         1150
         ----
          1500
```

Reduce these to Flemish shillings* by dividing them by 6
[79] 6 / 822.2 / 137.0
Par of an ounce of gold in Flemish shillings*

[78] 'And is equating' is del.
[79] '6 / 8222 / 136.7' is del.

If the Pars be taken as 98.5 and 137: 985 : 137 :: 100 985 / 13700 / 139 985 --- 3850 2955 ---- 8950 8865 ---- 850	In this calculation Malthus appears to have taken the value of a ducat in Hamburg as 98.5 stivers and the Flemish price as 137 schellings per ounce. He then calculated that 137 is 39% greater than 98.5, but his reason for comparing the value of a ducat in stivers with the value of an ounce of gold in schellings is not obvious.

5. Effect of an increase in the value of a ducat on the exchange rate between English pounds and Flemish schellings.

TEXT	COMMENTARY
To try the Par of Exchange according to the price of gold. The two Pars are 98.46 and 35/2	The 'two Pars' referred to here are the value of a ducat in Hamburg expressed in stivers (98.46), and the exchange rate between the English pound and the Flemish schelling (£1 = 35 schellings 2 groots). As shown above, the exchange rate can be calculated from the value of gold in the two countries. The value of a ducat in stivers can be converted into the value of an ounce of gold in stivers by adjusting for the difference in weight between the ducat and the ounce (57.5 and 480 grains respectively)

i.e. 98.46 ÷ 57.5 × 480
= 821.9 stivers per ounce.
The price of gold in England is £3.17.10½ (or 934.5 pence) per ounce. The par of exchange is therefore:
934.5 pence = 821.9 stivers
£1 = 821.9 ÷ 934.5 × 240
= 211.08 stivers
= 35.18 schellings
= 35 schellings 2 groots
= 422 groots

```
9846 is to the groots in 35/2
(422) :: 99

               422
9846 : 422 :: 99
               ---
              3798
             3798
             -----
   98.46 / 41778 / 424.3
             39384
             -----
              23940
              19692
              -----
               42480
               39384
               -----
                30960
                29538
                -----
                 1422
```

Malthus then showed how an increase in the value of a ducat in Hamburg from 98.46 to 99, 100, 101 and 104 stivers will affect the exchange rate between the pound and the schelling. The question he addressed is:
If, when one ducat is worth 98.46 stivers, the exchange rate is £1 = 422 groots, what will the exchange rate be when the ducat is worth 99 stivers? The answer is 422 ÷ 98.46 × 99 = 424.3 groots and similarly when the value of a ducat is 100, 101 and 104 stivers.

```
98.46 : 422 :: 100

9846 / 42200 / 428.6
       39384
       -----
        28160
        19692
        -----
         84680
         78768
         -----
          59120
          59076

12 / 428.6 / 35[80]

                 422
98.46 : 422 :: 101
                 ---
                 422
               422
               -----
      9846 / 42622 / 432.9
             29384
             -----
              32380
              29538
              -----
               28420
               19692
               -----
                87280
                88614

12 / 432 / 36
```

[80] 428.6 groots are divided by 12 to convert them to (approx.) 35 schellings. The same approximate conversion is done in the two following cases.

```
                422
98.46 : 422 :: 104
                ---
               1688
              422
              -----
      9846 / 43888 / 445.7
              39384
              -----
               45040
               39384
               -----
                56560
                49230
                -----
                 73300
                 68922
                 -----
                  4378
```

```
12 / 445.7 / 37
```

```
For each stiver banco in the
price of the Ducat the Par
increases from 35/2  4 groots
and nearly ⅓ of a groot.
```

He concluded that for each stiver increase in the price of the ducat, the exchange rate (between pounds and schellings) increases by '4 groots and nearly ⅓ of a groot'.

The result could have been achieved more simply, as above, by showing that for any increase of one stiver in the value of a ducat (from n to n+1), the increase in the exchange rate would equal

$[422 \div 98.46 \times (n+1)] - [422 \div 98.46 \times n] = 422 \div 98.46 = 4.286$

i.e. an increase of 4.286 groots to the pound.[81]

[81] Malthus calculated that when the price of gold increases from 99 stivers per ducat to 100, 101 and 104 stivers, the par of exchange increases from 424.3 to 428.6, 432.9 and 445.7 groots, i.e. increases of 4.3, 4.3 and 12.8 (= 3 × 4.27) groots. To three places of decimals, these figures would be 424.314, 428.600, 432.886 (i.e. increases of 4.286) and 445.774 (= 3 × 4.286).

6. Effect of an increase in the value of a ducat expressed in stivers on the value of an ounce of gold expressed in schellings.

COMMENTARY

Here, Malthus performed a series of six calculations to show that each increase of one stiver in the value of a ducat corresponds to an increase of 1.4 schellings in the value of an ounce of gold.

TEXT	COMMENTARY
`In Hamburgh gold sold by the ducat in Stiver lub's banco. The Par according to the English mint proportions is 98.4. And at this price an ounce of Standard gold would be worth about 136.7 flemish banco. The proportions will be very nearly as 98 to 136. And a table may be easily formed by saying as 98 : 136 :: 99 to a fourth number.`	He began with the statement that the par of exchange between London and Hamburg (adjusted to the gold content used in the English mint) is 20 shillings per ounce = 98.4 stivers for the ducat, and that the corresponding Flemish price is about 136.7 schellings per ounce. Using 98 and 136 as approximations, presumably for ease of calculation, he calculated that if the value of the ducat increases to 99 stivers, the corresponding Flemish price will be $136 \times 99 \div 98 = 137.4$ schellings per ounce. Similar calculations are made for increases in the value of the ducat to 100, 101, 102, 103 and 104 stivers. 'Lubs' (or 'Lubish' or 'Lubesh') means 'of or belonging to Lubeck, a town of northern Germany'. The expressions 'stiver lubs', 'marks lubs', etc. refer to the money of account used at Lübeck, Hamburg, and extensively in northern Germany. (*OED*)

TEXT

```
 98 : 136
        99
       ---
      1224
     1224
     -----
98 / 13464 / 137.4
     98
     ---
      366
      294
      ---
       726[82]
       686
       ---
        400
```

```
  98 : 136 :: 100

98 / 13600 / 138.7
     98
     ---
     380
     294
     ---
      860
      784
      ---
       7601[83]
       686
       ---
        74
```

[82] Should be '724 − 686 = 38'.
[83] Should be '760'.

```
  98 : 136 :: 101
       101
       ---
       136
     136
     -----
98 / 13736 / 140.1
      98
     ---
      393
      392
      ---
        100
```

```
  98 : 136
       102
       ---
       272
     136
     -----
98 / 13872 / 141.5
      98
     ---
      407
      392
      ---
       152
        98
       ---
        540
        490
        ---
         50
```

```
  98 : 136
       103
       ---
       408
     136
     -----
98 / 14008 / 142.9
      98
     ---
      420
      392
      ---
       288
       196
       ---
        920
        882
        ---
         38
```

```
       136
       104
       ---
       544
     136
     -----
     14144

98 / 14144 / 144.3
      98
     ---
      434
      392
      ---
       420
       392
       ---
        280
```

TEXT		COMMENTARY
98.4	136.8[84]	The above results are then presented in table format, together with two further results for which the calculations are not shown; for some unexplained reason a deletion line is drawn through the whole table.
99	137.4	
100	138.8[85]	
101	140.1	
102	141.5	
103	142.9	
104	144.3	
105	145.7	
106	147.1	

An increase of 1.4[86] flemish schillings* for each Stiver banco.

Although he noted that the 'proportion will be very nearly as 98 to 136', Malthus apparently did not realise that for any two successive figures, n and n+1, in the left-hand column, the difference between the corresponding two figures in the right-hand column would be
$[136 \div 98 \times (n+1)] - [136 \div 98 \times n] = 136 \div 98 = 1.387755$, and that successive entries in the right-hand column could be found merely by adding 1.3877 to the previous entry, without the need for lengthy multiplications and divisions.

[84] A figure of 'about 136.7' was given at the start of this section.
[85] '138.7' is altered to '138.8' – a more accurate figure; 13600 ÷ 98 = 138.7755.
[86] 'each' is del.

C. Statistics

1. Exchange rates and bullion prices, 1811–1813

COMMENTARY

The bullion papers include three-and-a-half MS pages of statistics of exchange rates and bullion prices over four different intervals between April 1811 and July 1813, together with calculations of the percentage changes that have occurred. Exchange rates are quoted for Amsterdam, Hamburg, Paris, Cadiz and Lisbon. Bullion prices are quoted for Portugal gold and New Dollars. The four intervals are: 3 April 1812 to 18 September 1812; 17 January 1812 to 3 April 1812; 18 June 1813 to 27 July 1813; and April 1811 to September 1812.[87] Malthus noted that gold prices had not moved in the same proportion as silver prices, and that there had been instances where movements in bullion prices differed considerably from movements in exchange rates. He concluded with the question: 'Which best represents the state of the currency – the exchange or the price of gold?'

TEXT

Exchanges April 3rd 1812.

Amsterdam 31.4	Hamburgh 29.4	Paris 20.10
Cadiz effect. 47	Lisbon 67¾	

Portugal Gold 4.13.6   New dollars 6.1½

Exchanges Sepr 18 1812.

Amsterdam 31.0	Hamburgh 28.9	Paris 19.15
Cadiz effect 49	Lisbon 69½	

Portugal Gold £5.11.0   New dollars 6.8½

----

[87] The dates indicate that these notes were written after 27 July 1813. The reference to 'the present disturbed state of Europe' suggests that they were written before the Battle of Waterloo (11 June 1815). Malthus did not cite the source of these statistics, and therefore it cannot be reliably assumed that they are historically accurate. Also, as shown in the following footnotes, his calculations of the percentage changes in these prices were only intended to be approximate.

An instance of a rise in the price of Gold of near 19 per cent,[88] while none of the exchanges varied so much as 5 per cent.[89] And Silver during the same time[90] varied only a little above 9 per cent.[91]

Since Gold has cease to be our standard, it has evidently varied much more than silver. And this was to be expected in the present disturbed state of Europe.

Gold has varied from the standard 42 per cent and silver 31,[92] besides which the fluctuations in gold have been more sudden.

Jany 17th 1812	April 3rd 1812
Portugal Gold in Coin £4.19.0	Portugal Gold 4.13.6
New Dollars 6.1	New Dollars 6.1½

In this case Gold has fallen between 5 and six per cent,[93] and silver has risen ½ penny an ounce.

As there is much more silver in the commercial market than gold it is less likely to be affected in its price by sudden demand.

The great demand for gold from Russia in[94]

Exchanges [95] June 18. 1813		
Amsterdam 30.6	Hamburgh 26.6	Paris 19.15
Cadiz effect. 49½	Lisbon 76.0	
Prices of Gold & Silver		
Portugal Gold 5.3.0	New dollars 6.8½	

Exchanges July 27th [96]		
Amsterdam 30.6	Hamburgh 26.0	Paris 19.50
Cadiz effect. 51.0	Lisbon 77½	
Prices of Gold & Silver		
Portugal Gold 5.11.0	Last price of New dollars 6.10	

88 The price of gold rose from £4.13.6 to £5.11.0 per ounce, or 18.7%.

89 Of the five quoted exchange rates, the greatest variation was in Paris, a fall from 20.10 to 19.15, or 4.7%.

90 'seems to have' is del.

91 Silver (i.e. New Dollars) rose from 6/1½ to 6/8½ per ounce, a rise of 9.5%.

92 According to the prices cited above, gold had increased from its standard price of £3.17.10½ to £5.11.0 per ounce, an increase of 42.5%; and silver had increased from its standard price of 5/2 to 6/8½ per ounce, an increase of 29.8%.

93 A fall from £4.19.0 to £4.13.6, or 5.55%. 94 Phrase not completed in MS.

95 'Exchanges' is repeated. 96 The year is unstated in MS but was presumably 1813.

An instance of a rise of near 8 per cent[97] in Gold,[98] with Stationary exchanges on Amsterdam, Hamburgh[99] and Paris, and but a slight fall with Cadiz and Lisbon. At the same time a rise of only about 2 per cent in Silver.[100]

In April 1811 the exchange with Hamburgh was 23.6, and the price of gold[101] 5.0.10½ (Mushet).[102]

In September 1812, the Hamburgh exchange was 28.9, and the price of gold £5.11.0.

How are these facts to be reconciled? Which best represents the state of the currency - the exchange or the price of gold?

2. Exchange rates, bullion prices and commodity prices

The bullion papers also include five pages of detailed statistics, some of which appear to be in the hand of a copyist. They consist of:

- Three pages of manuscript (numbered 595–597 in the Kanto Gakuen Collection) giving information on exchange rates, the prices of gold and silver, and the prices of wheat and oats, for specified days over the period from 24 November 1811 to 10 December 1813, in five centres: Amsterdam, Paris, Hamburg, St Petersburg and Riga.

- A page of manuscript (p. 569) in a copyist's hand giving the prices for a variety of commodities – hemp, flax, tallow, ashes, bristles, wheat, linseed, logs, timber and deals – at St Petersburg for 20 June / 2 July 1816 and at Riga for 24 June / 6 July 1816. Two names, presumably the sources of the statistics, are appended, viz. 'Hill & Whishaw', and 'Hill & Flurit,* recommended by James Pierson'.

- Two MS pages (numbered 599 and 600 in the Kanto Gakuen Collection) containing statistics on bullion prices between 1800 and 1810. On page 599

[97] An increase from £5.3.0 to £5.11.0, or 7.77%. [98] 'of Gold' is ins.
[99] The figures show a slight change in the Hamburg rate of exchange.
[100] An increase from 6/8½ to 6/10, or 1.86%. [101] 'of gold' is ins. [102] Mushet 1811, p.113.

there is a table giving the prices of gold bars, silver and guineas for every month between January 1800 and December 1809, i.e. 360 entries in all. For example, the entry for August 1800 reads:

```
August
Gold bars 12¾ to 14
Silver 25.15 to 26
Guineas 12.6 to 9
```

On page 600 there is a table giving, in each of two years 1809 and 1810, the highest and lowest prices for seven items, viz. Gold in Bullion, Silver dit°, Spanish Dollˢ, Dutch Ducats, Guineas, Louis Old, D° New.

There is no indication of the sources of these statistics and no calculations are involved.

These five pages of statistics are not reproduced in this edition. Copies are obtainable on application to Kanto Gakuen University, quoting page numbers 569, 595–597, 599–600.

D. Other Brief Items

The following three small items occur at various points throughout the collection of bullion manuscripts, but do not appear to be directly related to what precedes or follows them.

1. Expenses in converting coin to bullion
2. Groots expressed as percentages of schellings
3. A note on the value of a ducat

1. Expenses in converting coin to bullion

TEXT

Gold Coin is commonly melted in[103] Bars, when the Standard can be better ascertained. The Expences* are for melting 4 Stivers per Mark.

The Assay 2 florins per Bar.

When Gold Coins are alloyed with Silver, it is seperated* from it, for which 28 Stivers per Mark are paid.

[103] 'in' is repeated.

Silver Coin is also melted in Bars. The expences* for melting 1½ Stivers per Mark.

The Assay is 12 Stivers per Bar. Besides the Assayer keeps the bit of Silver on which the Standard is ascertained. It may be calculated at 10 Engels per Bar. Of the Gold it is returned. When Silver is melted which contains gold, the seperation* costs 52 Stivers per mark. Petty Expences* on gold 1 to 3 florins per bar according to the size.

On Silver in bars ¼ per mille.

Commission ⅓ to ½ per cent. Brokerage ½ per mille.

19 marks Troy's fine gold in Amsterdam are equal to 164 ounces Standard Gold in London.[104]

10000 Asses*[105] Troys* are equal 7417 English Grains.

2. Groots expressed as percentages of schellings

TEXT	COMMENTARY
One schelling on 33 schellings[106] 4 groots is exactly 3 per [cent][107] and therefore 4 groots will exactly equal 1 per [cent].	One schelling = 12 groots. 33 schellings 4 groots = 400 groots. ∴ one schelling is 3% of 400 groots, and 4 groots are 1% of 400 groots.
One schelling on 25 groots[108] will exactly equal 4 per cent. An[d] consequently 3 groots on [25] schellings will exactly equal 1 percent.	

[104] 1 marc troy is the same weight as 7.9 ounces troy. It has the same value as 8.63 ounces of standard gold. 19 × 8.63 = 163.97.

[105] 1 marc = 5120 assen = 3798 (English) grains
∴ 10,000 assen = 3798 ÷ 5120 × 10,000 = 7417.97 grains.

[106] 'schellings' is ins. [107] MS is torn here and below. [108] This should be '25 schellings'.

3. A note on the value of a ducat

TEXT

```
70.6 ducats are coined from one mark, therefore a ducat when
gold is to silver as 15.21 to one, the English mint proportions,
a ducat is worth f5.11 nearly.
```

COMMENTARY

The mint value of 1 marc of standard gold is 355 guilders. If 70.6 ducats are coined from one marc of standard gold, the mint value of one ducat = 355 ÷ 70.6 = 5.11 guilders.

E. Items in Other Hands

1. A diagrammatic method of comparing exchange rates between London, Amsterdam and Paris

The bullion papers in the Kanto Gakuen collection include the following single sheet, not in Malthus' hand. There is no indication in the rest of the bullion papers that Malthus made use of this information.

TEXT

The Estimate of the Arbitration of Exchanges depends on a Compound Proposition.

E.g. if the Pound Sterling = 20 livres

& if 3 livres = 50 grotes* = $\frac{20\times50}{3\times12}$ Sh.Flem[109]

The Pound St^{g} = $\frac{20\times50}{3\times12}$ Sh.Flem, or $\frac{20\times50}{4\times9}$ — Any other two numbers, whose product is 36, may be taken in the denominator.

[109] i.e. Flemish schellings.

The Logarithm of £. S^g = log 20 - log 4 + log 50 - log 9.
In the figure below CB, GH, FE are perpendicular to AD; BE is drawn ad libitum;

G bisects AD $\therefore$ GH = $\frac{AB + DE}{2} = \frac{CB - CA + FE - FD}{2}$

Let CB, FE be the linear logarithms of the variable numbers (20 & 50 respectively)
... CA, FD ... ... constant numbers (4 & 9 respectively)

If the linear logarithms drawn on HG be in a scale the half of that used on the lines CB & FE, GH will represent CB - CA + FE - FD, or, returning to the natural numbers, will represent $\frac{CB \times FE}{CA \times FD} \ldots \frac{20 \times 50}{4 \times 9}$.

In the same manner may be drawn a scale for calculating any quantity depending on two other variable quantities. -

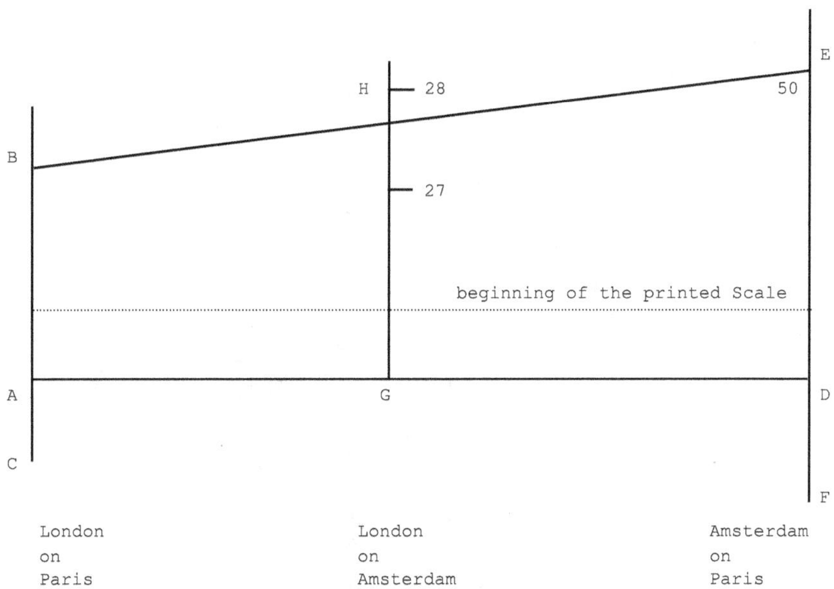

2. *Calculation of the direction and profit of the bullion trade.*

The collection of bullion manuscripts includes one sheet of instructions and calculations in another hand, showing how to calculate the profit obtainable from purchasing gold in Amsterdam and selling it in London. It was presumably prepared by someone who was advising Malthus on the transactions involved in the international trade in bullion. The fact that the calculations are not accompanied by a step-by-step written explanation, with the result that the chain of reasoning is not easy to follow, suggests that they were written as an adjunct to a verbal discussion.

Text

Question
What may be gained by purchasing Gold in Holland & selling it in London? (the prices & rates being as follows)
Portugal Gold in London £5.10 p^{r} oz; price of Gold in Amsterdam 16pc^{m}.[110] on 355 Curr^{y} Guilders for the Marc Weight pure Gold; Exchange 31; Agio 3pc^{m}.

Operation
What is the produce of <u>£1</u>

If £1	=	31^{s} B°. flem
if 10^{s} / B°. flem	=	3 Guilders B°.
if 100 Guild^{s}. B°.	=	103 D°. Curr^{t}.
if 116 D°. Curr^{y}.	=	100 D°. D°. (for Agio)[111]
if 355 D°. D°.	=	1 Marc fine Gold
if 22 M$^{cs.}$ Fine	=	24 M^{cs}. Portug. Stand^{d}
if 2 Marcs	=	7595 Grains Engl. Troy
if 480 Gr. Eng Tr.	=	1 Oz. D°. D°.
if 1 Oz. D°	=	5½£ Sterling

COMMENTARY

These nine equalities are the data or assumptions to be used in making the bullion calculations. Their explanation is as follows:

[110] i.e. 16 per centum.

[111] In MS, the words 'for Agio' are written alongside line 4; but as the agio was previously stated to be 3%, the words 'for Agio' were probably intended to be placed alongside line 3.

Line 1
The exchange rate between English pounds and Flemish schellings is £1 equals 31 Flemish schellings banco.

Line 2
10 Flemish schellings banco equal 3 guilders banco, i.e. 1 guilder banco is worth 3⅓ schellings banco.

Line 3
100 guilders banco equal 103 guilders currency (or current), i.e. a 3 per cent agio has to be paid to the bank (D° is an abbreviation for Ditto).

Line 4
The apparently contradictory statement that 116 guilders currency equal 100 guilders current was presumably intended to mean that the price of gold in Amsterdam was 16% above its mint price.

Line 5
The mint price of 1 marc of fine gold[112] in Amsterdam is 355 guilders current.

Line 6
As noted above, the purity of standard gold compared to the purity of fine gold is in the ratio of 11:12. Hence, 22 units (by weight) of fine gold are equal in value to 24 units (by weight) of standard gold.

Line 7
2 marcs are equal (in weight) to 7595 grains English troy; or 1 marc equals 3798 grains English troy.

Line 8
480 grains English troy equal one ounce English troy.

Line 9
One English troy ounce of standard gold is worth £5.10.0 sterling. This states that, although the mint price of standard gold in London was £3.17.10½ per ounce, its current price (or the price assumed for the purpose of the ensuing calculations) was £5.10.0 per ounce.

[112] This should read 'standard gold' rather than 'fine gold'. As noted in 'Explanatory Notes and Definitions' above, the mint price of one marc of fine gold in Amsterdam was 387⅜ guilders. One marc of standard gold would therefore be worth 387⅜ × 11/12 = 355 guilders (approx.).

In this set of nine equalities, diagonal lines have been drawn in MS. through the following entries:

line 3	100
line 6	22 and 24
line 7	2 and 7595
line 8	480 and Oz
line 9	Oz and 5½

The diagonal lines were probably intended to indicate not that the entries were incorrect and were to be deleted, but that the information had been progressively incorporated into the ensuing calculations.

TEXT

[113]

```
            355                                       1519
            116                                         31
           ----                                       ----
           2130                                       1519
           355                                       4557
          355                                        -----
          -----                                      47089
          41180                                        309 =(103×3)
             32                                      -----
          -----                                     423801
          82360                                    1412670
        123540                                     --------
        -------                                    14550501
  ×10 = 13177600
                                         13177600 / 14550501 / 1.104£
                                                    13177600    or £1.2.1
                                                    --------
                                                     13729010
                                                     13177600
                                                     --------
                                                       55141000
                                                       52710400
                                                       --------
                                                        2430600
```

[113] The following figures are written and largely deleted at this point:
322 11
2
204,16 1519

Therefore:
If a person purchases Gold in Holland, draws upon England for the Money he paid for the Gold, sends this Gold to England, & causes it to be sold there (the whole under the above conditions & supposing him to have been at no expense for[114] Commission, Freight & Insurance) he will obtain £1.2.1 for every £1: or £1104 for every £1000: so laid out, i.e.: he will gain nearly 10½ pc^{m}.

COMMENTARY

Explanation of the two columns

The left column is the cost of buying one marc of fine gold in Holland. The mint price of one marc of standard gold in Amsterdam is 355 guilders. The actual price of fine gold at the time is 16% above the mint price of standard gold. The actual price of fine gold is therefore 355 × 1.16 = 411.8 guilders. This is multiplied first by 32 and then by 10, thus converting 411.8 guilders into 131776 pennings (1 guilder = 320 pennings).

The right column shows the selling price of one marc of fine gold in London. One marc of fine gold has the same value as 8.63 ounces of standard gold. In this example, the price of standard gold is £5.10.0 per ounce. Therefore, the price of one marc of fine gold in London would be 8.63 × 5.5 = £47.5. The right column begins with an unexplained figure of 1519. It was possibly a mistaken calculation for 47.5 × 320 = 15200.[115] The amount of 1519 is multiplied by 31 (the exchange rate between pounds and schellings) and by 0.309. Multiplying by 0.3 converts schellings to guilders. Multiplying by 1.03 adds 3% for agio. These two operations are done together by multiplying by 0.309, giving 145505.01 pennings as the selling price in London.

An alternative procedure, giving a similar result, would have been:

Convert £47.5 to schellings:
47.5 × 31 = 1472.5 schellings
(the given exchange rate is £1 = 31 schellings)
Convert 1472.5 schellings to guilders:
1472.5 × 0.3 = 441.75 guilders

[114] 'excluding the considerations of' is written above the line, presumably intended to replace, or to be an alternative expression for, 'supposing him ... no expense for'.
[115] i.e. 47.5 pounds multiplied by the number of pennings (320) in a guilder.

Add 3% for agio:

$441.75 \times 1.03 = 455$ guilders

(In MS the previous two steps are combined:

$0.3 \times 1.03 = 0.309$)

Convert 455 guilders to pennings:

$455 \times 320 = 145600.8$ pennings

Thus: $47.5 \times 31 \times 0.309 \times 320 = 145600.8$ (which differs from the figure of 145505.01 in MS because of the use of 1519 instead of 1520).

Alternatively, schellings could have been converted directly into pennings (1 schelling = 96 pennings) instead of converting schellings into guilders and guilders into pennings:

$$47.5 \times 31 \times 96 \times 1.03 = 145600.8$$

Dividing the selling price (145505.01) by the cost price (131776) gives a ratio of 1.104. Every pound spent in buying gold in Amsterdam will therefore yield 1.104 pounds (or £1.2.1) when the gold is sold in London; a profit of about 10½%.

In summary, the result is derived in MS from the equation (ignoring the discrepancy between 1519 and 15200):

$$\frac{47.5 \times 320 \times 31 \times 0.309}{355 \times 1.16 \times 320} = 1.104$$

The calculations could have been simplified by not converting schellings into pennings:

$$\frac{47.5 \times 31 \times 0.309}{355 \times 1.16} = 1.104$$

4 An essay on foreign trade

INTRODUCTION

The following untitled draft was written by Malthus with the intention of publishing it in the *Edinburgh Review* in May 1811. This is evident from his use of the phrase 'in our last number' when referring to his review of the pamphlets of Ricardo and others in the *Edinburgh Review* of February 1811.

It is likely that the drafting of this article was a response to the letter of 2 April 1811 from Francis Jeffrey, editor of the *Edinburgh Review* (published in Vol. I, pp.114–15) in which Jeffrey strongly urged Malthus to 'do another article upon Bullion and paper'. Jeffrey was about to visit the East India College, and proposed to take Malthus' article back to Edinburgh on 12 May, and to publish it in the next number (Vol. XVIII, No. 35, May 1811) of the *Review*. Malthus replied to Jeffrey on 7 April 1811, stating that he had no leisure 'to go into the subject now', and that if, as Jeffrey suggested, he did not start the article until after the debates on the *Bullion Report* (due to start on 29 April) he might be prevented by 'College business' from being able to finish it in time for Jeffrey to take it back to Edinburgh on 12 May (James 1979, p.207).

The next number of the *Edinburgh Review* in May 1811 did not contain an article by Malthus. The subsequent number, August 1811, did contain an article by Malthus (see Malthus 1811b), but it did not include the material in this draft article. No other publication by Malthus, and no anonymous publication, has so far been found that includes this draft material.

Patricia James (1979, pp.270–1) has noted that a letter of 3 January 1815 to Malthus from his publisher, John Murray, referred to his 'two tracts on "Rent" and on "Bullion"'. James commented that Murray could not have been referring to Malthus' two articles on bullion in the *Edinburgh Review* (Malthus 1811a and 1811b), and that Murray's words seem to imply that a tract by Malthus on bullion had already been published. James concluded that 'the tract on Bullion is a complete mystery', and doubted 'if the matter can be cleared up until more documents came to light' (p.271).

James (1979, p.271) has also noted that, when Malthus wrote to John Murray on 5 October 1827 proposing a new edition of the *Principles of Political Economy* (1820), he indicated that the new edition would include new matter on 'the Level of the Previous Metals'. James asked whether this could be a revision of the undiscovered tract on bullion.

It is possible that the draft here published is part of the missing tract on bullion, and therefore would have been published if Murray had acceded in 1827 to Malthus' request for a second edition of the *Principles*. As it stands, the draft would not have been sufficiently extensive to be published as an article in the *Edinburgh Review*. It was perhaps intended as the opening portion. Jeffrey's letter to Malthus of 2 April 1811 suggested that Malthus' article could be submitted in instalments.

If this draft is indeed part of the mysterious bullion tract, we are left to wonder why it appears never to have been completed and published. One possible explanation is that 'College business' did in fact prevent Malthus from writing more than this introductory portion during the time suggested by Jeffrey – between the commencement of the Parliamentary debate on the *Bullion Report* on 29 April 1811 and Jeffrey's departure from the East India College on 12 May 1811 – and that afterwards Malthus never had the time or the inclination to complete it.

Another possible explanation is that Jeffrey, having criticised Malthus' first *Edinburgh Review* article (February 1811) because it was 'addressed almost exclusively to persons in some degree acquainted with the subject' (Vol. I, p.115), also found fault with this draft, and redirected Malthus' efforts along the lines that resulted in his second *Edinburgh Review* article in November 1811. Jeffrey in his letter of 2 April 1811, had asked Malthus for another article on 'Bullion and paper', but this draft paper is mainly concerned with the causes of 'the transit of the precious metals from one country to another' – whether it was caused by an unfavourable balance of trade and payments (as Malthus contended), or solely by a comparative redundancy of currency (a view that Malthus attributed to Ricardo); and additionally, whether the transit of precious metals was the effect of an unfavourable balance of trade, or its cause. It is possible that when Jeffrey spoke of a paper on 'Bullion and paper', he had in mind something more directly related to the *Bullion Report* – perhaps a more popular version of the February 1811 article (Malthus 1811a) – and was not prepared to accept an article on the more academic themes of this draft. The draft was essentially a rejoinder by Malthus to a criticism by Ricardo (in the Appendix to the fourth edition of the *High Price of Bullion*) of the comments by Malthus (in the *Edinburgh Review* of February 1811) on the views expressed by Ricardo in the first edition of the *High Price of Bullion* and in *Reply to M[r] Bosanquet's Observations*. It is understandable that Jeffrey might not have wanted this convoluted controversy to continue in the pages of the *Edinburgh Review*. In a letter to Ricardo on 14 August 1811, Malthus stated that the article he was then preparing for the *Edinburgh Review* of August 1811 (Malthus 1811b) 'will be quite of a general nature, and will have nothing to do with our controversy' which, he admitted, was 'too nice a question for the generality of readers to be interested about' (Ricardo, *Works*, Vol. VI, p.48).

However, the matters contained in this draft were discussed extensively in correspondence between Malthus and Ricardo in June and July 1811.[1]

In his first letter to Ricardo on 16 June 1811, Malthus expressed the hope that 'we might supersede the necessity of a long controversy in print respecting the points in which we differ, by an amicable discussion in private'.[2]

The reference to the fourth edition of Ricardo's *High Price of Bullion* indicates that the draft was written (or at least commenced) at some time after 7 April 1811. As Sraffa has noted,[3] the fourth edition was advertised in the *Monthly Literary Advertiser* for 10 April, and in the *Morning Chronicle* for 27 April, but on 7 April Malthus wrote to Francis Horner, referring to the Appendix (in the fourth edition) in which Ricardo commented on Malthus' article in the February 1811 number of the *Edinburgh Review*: 'I have this moment been reading M[r] Ricardo's observations on the Review, but remain quite unconvinced – indeed there is no point on which I feel more sure than of the incorrectness of attributing the variations of the exchange exclusively to redundancy or deficiency of currency'.[4]

TEXT[5]

Having now put the reader in possession of the chief[6] arguments which have been brought forwards, against the principles of the Bullion Report, and explained[7] at the same time as far as our limits would permit, the errors on which they appear to rest,[8] we shall take the present opportunity of adverting to a point of some

1 Ricardo, *Works*, Vol. VI, pp.21–42.

2 Ricardo, *Works*, Vol. VI, p.21. In a draft (dated 17 June) of a letter to Malthus, apparently written before he had received Malthus' letter of 16 June, Ricardo also expressed a preference for 'amicable discussion in private' (Ricardo, *Works*, Vol. VI, pp.23–4).

3 Sraffa, 'Note on the Bullion Essays', in Ricardo, *Works*, Vol. III, pp.11–12.

4 Quoted by Sraffa, in Ricardo, *Works*, Vol. III, p.12, from MSS in the possession of Lady Langman.

5 Watermark 1809.

6 'stated the principal' is del. and 'put the reader in possession of the chief' is ins.

7 'stated' is del. and 'explained' is ins.

8 Malthus was probably referring here to his article (Malthus 1811a) on 'Depreciation of Paper Currency' in the *Edinburgh Review*, February 1811, in which he reviewed six publications on the *Bullion Report* – by Robert Mushet, William Blake, William Huskisson, Charles Bosanquet, and two by David Ricardo.

importance on which a difference of opinion still[9] prevails among those who are perfectly agreed about the general question. We mean, the mode of explaining the doctrines of exchanges. The precise point under discussion is whether the transit of the precious metals from one country to another [10] takes place in consequence of what is called in the language of merchants an unfavourable balance of trade and payments, [11] originating sometimes in a redundancy of currency which raises prices, and sometimes in the varying wants of different societies [12] unconnected with the genera l[13] state of their currencies: Or whether [14] such transit originates[15] exclusively in a comparative redundancy of currency, and ought [16] to be considered as the cause of an unfavourable balance of trade and payments rather than the effect.

The latter doctrine has been chiefly & most distinctly[17] brought forwards by M[r] Ricardo, a gentleman whose authority is entitled to great[18] attention from the very able and important[19] part which he has taken in the present discussion on the depreciation of the currency. He stated it[20] very broadly, and applied it[21] to some strong [22] cases in his first pamphlet,[23] steadily adhered to it in his valuable[24] answer to M[r] Bosanquet,[25] and has lately endeavoured to confirm it in a new edition of his first publication, by additional arguments in answer to[26] some remarks in [27] an article of our last number.[28]

We are in general disposed to leave our criticisms to [29] produce that impression upon the public mind which they may appear to deserve, without thinking it necessary to reply to those who may still continue to differ from us in opinion: nor should [30] we make an exception in the present case, if it did not advantageously lead us to the explanation of a subject which has sometimes been considered as one of the most difficult in political economy; and afford us[31] an opportunity of attempting to correct the deviations of others[32] besides M[r] Ri[c]ardo, who while they have [33] most meritoriously exerted themselves to

[9] 'still' is ins. [10] 'really' is del. [11] 'or whether every instance of such transit' is del.

[12] 'quite' is del. [13] 'general' is ins. [14] 'every instance of' is del.

[15] 'ought to be resolved' is del. and 'originates' is ins. [16] 'to be therefore' is del.

[17] '& most distinctly' is ins. [18] 'very considerable' is del. and 'great' is ins.

[19] 'very singular and able' is altered to 'very able and important'.

[20] 'It was stated' is altered to 'He stated it'. [21] 'it' is ins. [22] 'instances' is del.

[23] Ricardo 1810. [24] 'valuable' is ins. [25] Ricardo 1811a.

[26] '[occasioned by] in reply' is del. and 'in answer to' is ins. [27] 'our las' is del.

[28] Ricardo 1811b. The 'additional arguments' are in the Appendix to the fourth edition of Ricardo's *High Price of Bullion.* This Appendix was also published as a separate pamphlet, *Observations on Some Passages in an Article in the Edinburgh Review on the Depreciation of Paper Currency* ..., London: John Murray, 1811. This Appendix was a reply to Malthus' article on 'Depreciation of Paper Currency' in the *Edinburgh Review,* Vol. XVII, February 1811 (Malthus 1811a) in which Malthus had reviewed Ricardo's *The High Price of Bullion,* 1810.

[29] 'the judgement of the public without' is del. [30] 'we have' is del. [31] 'us' is ins.

[32] 'some other famous friends' is altered to 'others'.

[33] 'properly distinguished them from the mercantile classes by the superior' is del.

correct [34] the confined and erroneous views of the mercantile classes, appear to us to have [35] rejected their received language without sufficient reason.

We [36] are by no means disposed to undervalue the advantage of a new nomenclature, when it is called for by the incorrectness or inconvenience of the old but we think it will be conceded that a change is always in itself a positive evil, and ought not therefore to be admitted without a very clear case being made out in favour of the new system, either[37] in point of superior correctness or[38] superior convenience. How far this is really done[39] in the present instance, it is for the reader to judge, and we are confident [40] he will agree with us, that without some obvious necessity,[41] it would be in every respect unwise to risk a wider seperation* than at present exists between the[42] great body of the mercantile classes, and those who have studied the subject scientifically.[43]

In our last number we clearly[44] admitted that the language which[45] M^{r} Ri[c]ardo had used to explain the[46] causes which operate upon the exchange was perfectly correct, and [47] unobjectionable, in reference to one large class of transactions, such as the distribution of the precious metals from the mines, the increase of currency from paper issues, and [48] the restoration of the level of the precious metals when it has[49] been temporarily disturbed. But that his language did not appear to us [50] to apply with any degree of propriety to another class of transactions originating in the unequal wants[51] of different nations, and occasionally producing [52] an unfavourable exchange and a balance of payments in bullion, [53] although previous to such inequality of [54] wants the precious metals might have been perfectly on a level. Among the latter class we adverted particularly[55] to the necessity of making large importations of corn in consequence of a bad harvest, or the obligation[56] of paying a large[57] subsidy to

[34] '[unprofessional laziness of their views and their knowledge of general principles, appear to us improperly to have quitted their received language] the confined views of' is del.
[35] 'quitted' is del. [36] 'should premise however that we' is del. [37] 'both' is del. and 'either' is ins.
[38] 'and' is del. and 'or' is ins. [39] 'made out' is del. and 'done' is ins. [40] 'that' is del.
[41] 'in thinking that' is del. and 'that without some obvious necessity,' is ins.
[42] '[to cause unnecessarily] to do anything that [might] would probably occasion a wider seperation* between the' is del. and 'to risk a wider seperation* than at present exists between the' is ins.
[43] 'than that which unfortunately at present exists.' is del.
[44] 'distinctly' is del. and 'clearly' is ins. [45] 'view which' is del. and 'language which' is ins.
[46] 'had taken of' is del. and 'had used to explain the' is ins. [47] 'his language quite' is del.
[48] 'those occasional and temporary inequalities in the general level of the precious metals which we supposed to be occasionally and temporarily disturbed by the unequal wants and unequal produce of different countries.' is del. and 'the restoration ... disturbed' is ins.
[49] 'whenever it may have' is altered to 'when it has'. [50] 'correctly' is del.
[51] 'where on account of the varying wants [and desires] and necessities' is del. and 'originating in the unequal wants' is ins.
[52] 'a balance of payments in the precious metals' is del. [53] 'unconnected with the' is del.
[54] 'desires' is del. [55] Malthus 1811a, p.344.
[56] 'and the necessity' is altered to 'or the obligation'. [57] 'large' is ins.

a foreign power[58] in consequence of a treaty to that effect – wants which it must be allowed may exist without any previous[59] redundancy [60] of currency.

Mr Ricardo however is of opinion that even in this class of transactions, whenever bullion passes, it [61] is still[62] resolvible* into [63] a comparative excess of currency[64] in the country from which it is[65] exported, and explains the particular case of the export of bullion to pay for large[66] imports of corn in consequence of a bad harvest in the following manner. He observes that though the currencies of the two countries in question might be supposed to be equal in value before the scarcity took place, yet that the [67] existence of such a scarcity would at once effect a change in [68] their relative proportions.[69] The country which had experienced an unfavourable season would have the mass of its commodities diminished; and not requiring of course so large [70] a quantity of currency to circulate a smaller quantity of commodities would have a comparative excess to export to the country from which it had imported the corn.

Now we would observe that supposing this to be a correct representation of what takes place,[71] still, the unfavourable exchange and the passage of bullion [72] cannot in this case[73] be considered as *originating* in[74] excess of currency.[75] Even according to this explanation, we were strictly correct in [76] saying in our last number that "whatever variations between the quantity of [77] currency and commodities [78] may be stated to take place subsequent to the commencement of these transactions, it cannot be for a moment doubted that the cause of them is to be found in the wants and desires of one of the two nations, and not in any *original*[79] redundancy or deficiency of currency in either of them."[80]

But we contend that this is not a correct representation of what takes place.[81] It is perfectly well known that in a scarce year of corn the whole of what is consumed, is sold for a greater sum [82] than in average years, and the distribution of it must therefore require an extended rather than a diminished currency. Part of the extended currency thus used for the distribution of[83] corn will of course be taken from the diminished price of other commodities, but in whatever degree this may take place, it is an absolute contradiction[84] to suppose

[58] 'to a foreign power' is ins. [59] 'reference to the question of' is del. and 'any previous' is ins.
[60] 'or deficiency' is del. [61] Word del. [62] 'always' is del. and 'still' is ins.
[63] 'an' is del. [64] 'the precious metals' is del. and 'currency' is ins.
[65] 'they are' is del. and 'it is' is ins. [66] Word del. [67] 'very' is del.
[68] 'the quantity of circulating medium required' is del.
[69] 'of each, and that' is del. [70] 'a circulating' is del.
[71] 'the transaction' is del. and 'what takes place' is ins. [72] 'must be' is del. [73] 'in this case' is ins.
[74] '*originally* caused by' is altered to '*originating* in'.
[75] 'and as we said in our former number, "whatever and' is del.
[76] 'in' is repeated. [77] 'commodities' is del. [78] 'which' is del. [79] '*original*' is ins.
[80] Malthus 1811a. p.345. [81] 'the fact' is del. and 'what takes place' is ins.
[82] 'of the currency' is del. [83] 'of' is ins.
[84] 'perfectly impossible' is del. and 'an absolute contradiction' is ins.

that the want of more[85] currency to circulate any particular set of commodities, should have the effect of making it[86] redundant in reference to the whole mass. And consequently if as M^r^. Ricardo distinctly admits [87] the exchange may be rendered unfavourable and some bullion may [88] be sent out of the country owing to a bad harvest, which would not have been sent out without such an event, it is quite clear that to attribute this unfavourable exchange and export of bullion to redundancy of currency, is not merely to make a useless change in the received language of merchants, but to convey an impression directly contrary to the truth.

What is it then that can send the bullion out of the country? Neither coffee, nor sugar, nor any other commodity could be exported under such circumstances; and if we maintain that bullion might, we [89] are accused of betraying that deep-rooted prejudice which still persists in considering coin and bullion as things essentially differing in their operations from other commodities. To this accusation we have no hesitation in fairly pleading guilty, [90] and we will give the reader our reasons for this opinion – an opinion however not adopted as a prejudice, but the result of the most[91] mature deliberation.

We will premise by observing that it does seem improbable *a priori*[92] that a commodity which performs such important functions with regard to all others as money, should in addition to those qualities which it has in common with others, have some which are peculiar to itself. Nor [93] would such peculiar and additional qualities, if they should be found to exist, appear to be necessarily inconsistent with the assertion [94] made in our last number that "every kind of circulating medium as well as every other kind of commodity is necessarily depreciated by excess and raised in value by deficiency compared with the demand; and that this doctrine follows immediately from the general principles of supply and demand which are unquestionably the foundation on which the whole superstructure of Political Economy is built."[95]

But the question now to be considered[96] is whether in point of fact bullion[97] is to be distinguished from other commodities by any peculiar qualities.

[85] 'an increased' is del. and 'more' is ins. [86] 'it' is ins. [87] 'some bullion may go abroad' is del.
[88] 'go abroad, owing to a bad har' is del. [89] 'betray that' is del.
[90] 'and one of the principal objects which we had in view in entering upon this discussion' is del.
[91] 'the most' is ins. [92] '*a priori*' is ins. [93] 'does it seem' is del.
[94] 'that money in common with all other commodities is subject to' is del.
[95] Malthus 1811a, p.341. Malthus did not quote himself with complete accuracy. In Malthus 1811a, 'compared with the demand' was followed by 'without reference either to confidence or intrinsic use', and there are other minor differences.
[96] 'then' is del. and 'now to be considered' is ins.
[97] 'there is any difference between bullion or money' is del. and 'bullion' is ins.

There are in our opinion four[98] essential points of difference.

In the first place bullion, or that commodity which is[99] used in society as the standard measure of value in exchange, though of great instrinsic* worth[100] itself, will admit of the substitution of a commodity entirely worthless in the performance of a considerable portion of its most important functions. This [101] we attributed in our last number to the circumstance of every person being a dealer in the medium of exchange, and there being no last purchaser for consumption, a quality which we believe [102] does not belong to any other commodity.

Secondly, it is generally agreed that the wants of society for the precious metals as[103] a circulating medium are entirely relative; and that with regard to the main [104] use to which they are applied, the world would be in no respect poorer if they were reduced in quantity to one half, one fourth or one tenth, provided they were still divided among the nations of the earth exactly in the same proportions as they are at present. This quality we confess appears to us to be quite peculiar to a medium of exchange.

Thirdly, the measure of value, whatever[105] it may be, has the striking peculiarity of [106] being incapable of measurement itself in any other way than by comparing it with the mass of other commodities. It has properly speaking no nominal price.[107] Every other[108] commodity is[109] compared with a common standard which renders[110] all its variations immediately obvious; but the variations of the measure of value are only to be distinguished through the medium of their influence on the prices of goods, and it is [111] more properly the dearness or cheapness of these goods that sets the precious metals in motion than the dearness or cheapness of the metals themselves. If coffee be comparatively plentiful in [112] any country, the primary[113] object of the merchant in exporting it is[114] to sell his [115] coffee at a better price;[116] but if the medium of exchange[117] be comparatively plentiful the primary object of the merchant is to buy goods at a cheaper market, and the metals are only set in motion in[118] consequence.

98 'three' is del. and 'four' is ins.
99 'whatever commodity may be' is altered to 'that commodity which is'.
100 'value' is del. and 'worth' is ins. 101 'quality' is del. 102 'is quite' is del.
103 'for the purpose of' is del. and 'as' is ins.
104 'purposes' is del. 105 Spelt 'whatatever'. 106 'knot' is del.
107 'and consequently the variations in its value, are vastly less obvious unlike those of all other commodities [are only seen through] which may be immediately compared with a particular standard;' is del.
108 From 'Every other' to 'measure of value' is ins. 109 'may be' is del. and 'is' is ins.
110 'will render' is altered to 'renders'. 111 'rath' is del. 112 'a partic' is del.
113 'specific' is del. and 'primary' is ins. 114 'will be' is del. and 'in exporting it is' is ins.
115 'cheap' is del. 116 'market' is del.
117 'the precious metals' is del. and 'the medium of exchange' is ins.
118 'as a' is altered to 'in'.

Fourthly, as all commodities are measured by and charged in the currencies of the countries from which they are exported, and as one or other of[119] the precious metals is[120] always convertible into these currencies at the expence* of coinage, there must necessarily be at all times and in every country[121] such a demand for the precious metal[122] which forms it[s] measure of value[123] as will prevent it[124] from ever being refused [125] when so converted in payment of debts.[126] No conceivable redundancy of silver[127] at Hamburgh could ever make a merchant think of refusing the number of *marcs banco* which he had charged for his goods. It is hardly possible[128] indeed under such circumstances that it should suit the purchaser to pay him by a remittance in silver,[129] but if it should suit him, the tender is legal and could not be refused.

The differences here enumerated between bullion and other commodities appear to us we confess to be amply sufficient to account for some differences in the laws by which they are governed; to explain[130] particularly [131] the occasional passage of bullion from one country to another without being forced by redundancy, and to shew* the reason why[132] the export of the precious metals [133] is the last step in mercantile transactions, and is invariably the [134] consequence of an unfavourable balance of trade or payments, and not the cause.

In explaining the case of a scarcity and[135] great imports of corn upon these principles, we should say that if any[136] bullion goes abroad in consequence of a scarcity which would not have gone otherwise, [137] it is unquestionably in payment of an unfavourable balance occasioned by the excess of imports; and bullion is chosen to discharge a part of this debt, not because there is any kind of comparative excess of it, the scarcity of corn[138] having rather increased than diminished the demand for it; but because according to the supposition, [139] an

[119] 'one or other of' is ins. [120] 'are' is altered to 'is'. [121] 'all countries' is altered to 'every country'.
[122] 'metals' is altered to 'metal'. [123] 'which forms it[s] measure of value' is ins.
[124] 'them' is del. and 'it' is ins.
[125] 'in payment of goods, at least after they have been converted into coin.' is del.
[126] 'goods' is del. and 'debts' is ins. [127] 'currency' is del. and 'silver' is ins.
[128] 'by no means probable' is del. and 'hardly possible' is ins.
[129] 'of bullion' is del. and 'in silver' is ins. [130] 'and' is del. and 'to explain' is ins. [131] 'fi' is del.
[132] 'for the circumstance of' is del. and 'to shew* the reason why' is ins.
[133] 'being invariably the consequence' is del. [134] Second 'the' is del.
[135] 'of' is del. and 'of a scarcity and' is ins. [136] 'any' is ins.
[137] 'it can only be to pay a debt contracted, in the currency of the commercial world, which cannot be paid at the required time, without loss, by goods. And though we thus distinctly acknowledge that the debt cannot be discharged at the appointed time so cheaply as by the export of bullion, and that it is precisely on account of its [cheapness] economy that this mode of payment is adopted, yet upon the supposition that there was no relative redundancy of currency in the country before, it is surely quite evident that as the scarcity rather increases than diminishes the demand for currency afterwards, to expect to resolve the export of bullion in this case into comparative redundancy of currency, is an absolute perversion of language and conveys a most incorrect impression.' is del.
[138] 'of corn' is ins. [139] 'the foreign market for our goods would be glutted by their exportation' is del.

additional quantity of our goods is not[140] in demand in the foreign market and could not therefore be exported without great loss; while[141] bullion, on account of its peculiar qualities as the[142] currency of the commercial world,[143] is[144] always in such demand as never to admit of a loss in the payment of a debt greater than the expence* of transport and coinage. And though we thus most willingly and distinctly admit that this mode of discharging the debt is adopted precisely[145] because it is the cheapest; yet to infer from this concession that bullion must be comparatively redundant, and [146] under the circumstances just described, [147] to resolve the export of bullion into this comparative redundancy of currency, appears to us we confess[148] a palpable abuse of language, and directly[149] contrary to the fact.

Nor can we[150] by any means agree with Mr Ricardo [151] in thinking that except in the case of a comparative redundancy, the precious metals "could not be exported without the most serious consequences". [152] We were indeed[153] particularly surprised to find him expressing this opinion, after having remarked[154] in his answer to Mr Bosanquet that "if the Continent should adopt the almost impossible, absurd policy of [155] wishing to buy more of that of which they had already too much (meaning bullion) what evil consequences would ensue to us even if our currency were reduced to the same level at which it stood before the discovery of America? Would it not be a national gain inasmuch as the circulation of the same commerce being carried on by a smaller amount of gold, the balance might be profitably employed in procuring a return of more useful and more productive commodities." [156]

[140] 'would be' is del. and 'is not' is ins.
[141] 'and' is del. and 'and could not therefore be exported without great loss; while' is ins.
[142] '[from] as the' is del. and 'on account of its peculiar qualities as the' is ins.
[143] 'world' is ins. [144] 'being' is del. and 'is' is ins. [145] 'precisely' is ins. [146] 'that' is del.
[147] 'it only this redundancy that causes it to be exported' [sic] is del.
[148] 'is surely' is del. and 'appears to us we confess' is ins.
[149] 'and calculated to convey an impression' is del. and 'and directly' is ins.
[150] 'we' is ins . [151] Ricardo 1811, p.74. Second 'agree with Mr Ricardo' is del.
[152] 'And' is del. [153] 'indeed' is ins. [154] 'observing' is del. and 'having remarked' is ins.
[155] 'whi' is del.
[156] A footnote 'Reply to Mr Bosanquet p. 89' obviously refers to this quotation, although no point of insertion is indicated in the text. See Ricardo 1811a, pp.89–90. The quotation is substantially accurate, but the words '(meaning bullion)' were added by Malthus.
The following passages are del.:

In this opinion we are much more inclined to agree with him than in that which he has substituted in his last publication.

The reader will understand, that we mean broadly and distinctly to assert that our account of the peculiar qualities above stated belonging to the precious metals as the currency of the commercial world, the laws which regulate their export and import are somewhat different from those which regulate the export and import of other commodities. Let us see how far this statement accords with fact.

If an additional quantity of cotton goods to the amount of a million sterling were thrown into the market, there can be no doubt.

The rigid level of currency, and the impossibility of forcing the exportation of it, when this level has been attained, on which M^r^ Ri[c]ardo so strongly insists, appears to us we confess to be a very fanciful doctrine, supported neither by just theory, nor by facts. When we talk of the level of the precious metals among the different countries of the commercial world we merely mean that state to which they are[157] always for very obvious reasons constantly tending, [158] and to which when disturbed, by temporary causes, they will certainly return.[159] But we know of no moveable levels that are not liable to such disturbances; nor is it any argument against the certainty of their[160] return (as intimated by Mr Ricardo) that the precise moment of the first retrograde movement can seldom be distinctly foreseen. When we give an impulse to a pendulum we seldom know how many inches and tenths of an inch it will go before it begins to turn, but we know to a certainty that it will turn a[s] soon as the projectile force is overcome by the force of gravity. In the same manner when the level of the precious metals has been disturbed by the necessity of paying debts, which could not at the appointed time have been discharged by [161] commodities, though we do not know how many months and days will elapse before they return, we may be quite sure that this movement will begin as soon as the [162] fall of prices in the country which has been deprived of a part of its currency, and the rise of prices in the country which has added to its currency, shall make the exports of the former exceed its imports.

In our last number [163] we noticed a passage in Mr Huskisson's pamphlet[164] which led us to remark that we considered the precious metals as performing a more important part in society and as more frequently called into action as a measure of value, than as a universal equivalent, or instrument of commerce.[165] In saying this we were aware how much their use as an instrument of commerce was superseded, [166] in the first place, by the admirable convention of[167] bills of exchange, and afterwards by the various modes [168] adopted, [169] in an improved state of commerce, of making payments by bills through different places, and speculating on the return of those exchanges which have deviated from their

[157] 'are' is ins. [158] 'nor do we know' is del. [159] 'return' is ins. [160] 'their' is ins.

[161] 'th' is del. [162] 'discouragement to impo' is del. [163] 'we stated in noticing' is del.

[164] Huskisson 1810; reviewed in Malthus 1811a.

[165] In his review of Huskisson's pamphlet Malthus said: 'One of the most important functions of the precious metals is that of acting as a measure of value in exchanges; ... We have no great objection to the term, *universal equivalent*, which Mr Huskisson considers as the quality which most pre-eminently distinguishes the precious metals from all other commodities; but we doubt whether it advantageously supplies the place of the term *medium of exchange*, or *instrument of commerce*; because it is precisely an account of their being adopted by the common consent of society as the general medium of exchange, that they are received as a universal equivalent' (Malthus 1811a, p.351; Malthus, *Works*, Vol. 7, p.33).

[166] 'by the' is del. [167] 'the admirable convention of' is ins. [168] 'of' is del. [169] 'of' is del.

usual par. But the doctrine of Mr Ricardo does not [170] merely imply a great[171] economy of the precious metals as a medium of exchange or instrument of commerce, [172] in which, consistently with the opinion above expressed, we should have readily agreed with him; but it implies their total disuse in this capacity – a doctrine which we can by no means assert for the following reasons.[173]

In the first place if there were[174] no commodity in the mercantile world which performed the part of a medium of exchange, and in consequence of its peculiar qualities as such was universally acceptable, it appears to us that a[175] merchant could not without the greatest risk come under a contract to pay for a quantity of goods [176] at a particular time. As things now stand, and with the currencies of different countries in their natural states, he [177] knows exactly what are the[178] limits of the loss to which he may be subjected under the most unfavourable circumstances; and as this is inconsiderable and very nearly fixed, he can enter into engagements with confidence. But if the commercial world had nothing which could be considered [179] in the capacity of a currency, [180] he might either be absolutely unable to discharge his[181] debt at the time appointed, or could only do it by the export of commodities at a very heavy loss. And if by sending bullion without a[182] comparative redundancy of it[183] the necessity of [184] its return after a certain interval is created; yet when the small expence* of exporting the precious metals, [185] and the very small proportion that such exports must bear to the mass of mercantile transactions are considered,[186] the whole expence* and trouble [187] occasioned in this way[188] will appear to be very cheaply purchased, by the confidence which is thus[189] given to merchants in entering into their engagements, and the power which they thus derive of fulfilling them under all circumstances, with steadiness and punctuality.

2^ndly^. Without the use of a medium of exchange or instrument of commerce, [190] nations would be unable with the same convenience [191] either to supply their[192] sudden wants, or to derive the proper advantage [193] from peculiarly favourable seasons. We have already adverted to the case of a scarcity of corn,

[170] 'go' is del. [171] 'to the' is del. and 'imply a great' is ins.
[172] 'but it implies their total disuse in this capacity' is del.
[173] 'the facts attending the mercantile commercial intercourse of nations appear to us clearly to contradict' is del. and 'we can by no means assert for the following reasons' is ins.
[174] 'the mercantile world had' is del. and 'there were' is ins. [175] 'a' is ins.
[176] 'which he had received' is del. [177] 'is quite sure of being able' is del. [178] 'the' is ins.
[179] 'as its currency' is del.
[180] 'as it [is] quite incredible that its bills for commodities should exactly balance out' is del.
[181] 'the' is del. and 'his' is ins. [182] '[the] when the inter' is del. and 'without a' is ins.
[183] 'of it' is ins. [184] 'a second journey' is del. [185] 'is considered,' is del. [186] 'are considered' is ins.
[187] 'then' is del. [188] 'in this way' is ins. [189] 'thus' is del., then ins. [190] 'woul' is del.
[191] 'without great inconvenience' is altered to 'with the same convenience'.
[192] 'their' is ins. [193] 'occas' is del.

which it is generally agreed [194] occasions some export of the precious metals to pay the debts of increased importation; although it is unquestionable, that on such an occasion[195] no currency can possibly be let loose and become redundant.[196] In the same manner, when a sudden opportunity occurs of laying in with advantage[197] a large stock of foreign[198] commodities on account of their peculiar cheapness,[199] it is surely of the utmost importance [200] to society that there should be a [201] medium of exchange capable of paying with certainty for that part of the price, which may not at the time be wanted in commodities. [202] Some bullion will in such cases almost always be sent out. Yet the cheapness in the foreign market may be peculiar to the particular commodities in question, and not[203] imply a dearness of the precious metals; and the[204] increased quantity of commodities in the home market in consequence of the increased[205] importations cannot certainly account for the export of bullion[206] upon the principle of redundancy.

The engagement to pay a subsidy to a foreign power is so generally acknowledged to have the effect of immediately turning the exchange against us, and occasioning a temporary exportation of the precious metals, that the Bank of England, it is said, exacted a promise from Mr Pitt [207] not to enter into any such[208] engagement without previously consulting them. Though we should by no means sympathize with the Bank as to the *evil* arising to the country from a temporary exportation of the precious metals, if its money affairs were properly conducted; [209] we cannot doubt the fact of its being generally necessary to export some bullion[210] on these occasions. And yet it will hardly be contended that such an engagement might not be made when all our exchanges were at par.
[211]

Upon the same principle a medium of exchange or, as Turgot calls [212] the precious metals, a universal representative of value, is equally necessary to enable a country to derive the proper advantage from peculiarly favourable

194 'in effect' is del.

195 'that the wants of [the] a society thus circumstanced for a circulating medium will be rather increased than diminished that' is del. and 'that on such an occasion' is ins.

196 'by such scarcity' is del. 197 'with advantage' is ins. 198 'particular' is del. and 'foreign' is ins.

199 'occasioned either by abundant seasons' is del. 200 'that there' is del.

201 'circulating m' is del.

202 'And in the case here alluded to the cheapness in the foreign' is del.

203 '[and by [by] no means] without' is del. and 'and not' is ins.

204 'the' is ins. 205 'increased' is ins. 206 'the precious metals' is del. and 'bullion' is ins.

207 'actually made Mr Pitt promise' is altered to 'exacted a promise from Mr Pitt'.

208 'such' is ins. 209 'yet' is del. 210 'of the precious metals' is del. and 'bullion' is ins.

211 'In all these cases it appears to us quite clear that a medium of exchange is necessary and that in point of fact the precious metals are really used in this capacity.' is del.

212 'it,' is del. In his *Réflexions*, 1788, Turgot referred to money as 'le gage universel de toutes les valeurs' (Section XLII, p.50).

seasons.[213] A country with an unusually abundant supply of[214] native commodities is not on that account likely to want an unusual supply of foreign commodities. Yet it will not surely be deterred from parting with its superfluous goods. What then will it[215] do?[216] It will unquestionably realize these goods in the precious metals, [217] in the universal representative of value, and this [218] representative [219] which does not spoil by keeping will enable it at a future time to purchase foreign [220] commodities when it has more need of them. "Tout homme, (says Turgot) qui a une denrée superflue, et qui n'a pas dans le moment besoin d'une autre denrée d'usage s'empressera de l'echanger contre de l'argent avec lequel il est plus sure qu'avec toute autre chose de se procurer la denrée qu'il voudra au moment[221] du besoin." [222] This passage appear[s] to us [223] to apply with no[224] less truth to a country than to an individual. We were much astonished therefore to find Mr Ricardo denying that a country under such circumstances would sell its superfluous goods for money⁺,[225] though he afterwards rather oddly seems to admit it, and to explain what would take place nearly as we should do.

Thirdly, although the different modes adopted in an improved state of commerce of economising the [226] use of the precious metals, so much, and so justly, insisted upon by Mr Ricardo, have unquestionably the effect of[227] greatly diminishing the frequency of the fall of the exchanges to that point which sets in motion the precious metals; yet as in fact, the fall of the exchanges to this point [228] and the consequent movement of the precious metals, is both a more frequent and a more sudden occurrence than [229] can be satisfactorily accounted for by the distribution of the precious metals from the mines and the issues of paper; the conclusion is,[230] that bullion moves for other purposes besides that of affecting the level of the precious metals. And this conclusion is most strongly confirmed by the fact that the quantity of the precious metals imported into,[231] and exported from the different countries of Europe very greatly exceeds the quantity used by these countries: and this in a degree, and in directions which do not admit of explanation from their being the channels of the distribution

[213] 'We were quite astonished we confess that Mr Ricardo after supposing the case of a nation possessed of a superabundance of corn.' is del.
[214] 'comm' is del. [215] 'it' is ins. [216] Second 'do' is del. [217] 'in the medium of exchange,' is del.
[218] 'universal' is del. [219] 'of value' is del. [220] 'goods' is del.
[221] 'au moment' is repeated, and first is del.
[222] 'Nor does' is del. In Turgot's *Réflexions*, 1788, this passage is in Section XLII, p.51; 'qui n'a pas dans le moment' should be 'qui n'a pas, au moment,'.
[223] 'in the present case' is del. [224] 'no' is ins.
[225] The footnote reads: '⁺, p. 75'. In the fourth edition of Ricardo's *High Price of Bullion*, this statement is on p.74.
[226] 'the' is repeated. [227] 'diminishing' is del.
[228] 'is a more frequent occurrence than can satisfactorily' is del. [229] 'be' is del.
[230] 'we consider it as a certain' is del. and 'the conclusion is' is ins. [231] 'into,' is ins.

of the precious metals from the mines. All the countries of Europe[232] cannot be such channels. And the character of oscillation backwards and forwards which the European exchanges so frequently assume, accords[233] exactly with the use of the precious metals as a medium of exchange, but not with their exclusive use as a measure of value.

On the grounds which we have here stated we cannot but conclude 1st that a medium of exchange, or universal representative of value is still necessary to carry on with convenience the mercantile transactions of the world, notwithstanding the various improvements which have been introduced to economize it. And 2ndly that in point of fact the precious metals are used[234] in this capacity in the present commercial intercourse of the civilized world.

But on every occasion where bullion is[235] put in motion as a medium of exchange or representative of value, and not for the express purpose of affecting the level of the precious metals, it is quite clear that the language of Mr Ricardo is [236] positively incorrect, and does not accord with the facts: while the received mercantile language which states that [237] bullion, or the currency of the commercial world is used in the payment of those balances or those debts of any kind[238] which at the time that they are required to be settled cannot be discharged without loss[239] by commodities, and that the export of it is the consequence not the cause of an unfavourable exchange[240] seems to be[241] unobjectionable, and to express what really takes place.

There is however a large class of transactions to which, as we before intimated, the language of Mr Ricardo will apply with sufficient correctness; but even here the peculiarities attending the operations of the precious metals, as distinguished from other commodities, prevent the necessity of a change in the language of merchants.

In the third point of difference which[242] we stated[243] between the precious metals and other commodities, we observed[244] that the measure of value was incapable of being measured itself, [245] in any other way than by comparing it with the mass of other commodities, and thro the medium of its influence on their prices; and that consequently it was more[246] properly the dearness or cheapness of these commodities which set the precious metals in motion, than the dearness or the cheapness of the metals themselves.

232 'fail' is del. 233 'suits' is del. and 'accords' is ins. 234 'are used' is ins.
235 'the precious metals are' is del. and 'bullion is' is ins. 236 'qui' is del. 237 'the' is del.
238 'or those debts of any kind' is ins. 239 'without [great] loss' is ins.
240 'and that ... unfavourable exchange' is ins. 241 'be' is repeated, and the first is del.
242 'which' is repeated. 243 'mentioned' is del. and 'stated' is ins.
244 'stated' is del. and 'observed' is ins. 245 'but by the mass of other commodities' is del.
246 'would be' is del. and 'was more' is ins.

Let us see what effect this difference will have in a particular instance.

Let us suppose, first, cotton goods to the amount of a million sterling to be thrown into the market. We cannot doubt that the fall in the price of these goods would become immediately obvious by comparing them with the standard measure of value, and that if trade were free[247] a very large portion of them would be without delay exported to the different [248] foreign markets where they still retained their [249] former value.

But what would happen, if instead of cotton goods, we were to suppose that[250] bullion to the amount of a million sterling were thrown into the market, supposing at the same time that the gold and silver were[251] in such proportions [252] as not to alter their relative values, that[253] the currency of the country was in[254] its natural state, and foreign exchanges at par. The first effect would probably be a very slight fall in the price of bullion compared with coin; but the moment that[255] this exceeded the [256] disadvantage [257] arising from the delay in converting it into coin, [258] nearly the whole would be taken to the mint. [259] This mode of disposing of it would be evidently preferred to exportation, because though the same value might [260] be had for it abroad, the expence,* risk and trouble of transport would materially reduce the [261] profit upon its foreign sale. When the coin had been brought from the mint there would be no standard measure with which it might be[262] compared, and which as in the case of the cotton would immediately shew* the fall in its price. Its diminished value would not appear till it had been absorbed into the circulation and had begun to raise the prices of commodities. When this however had taken place, it would[263] naturally [264] dispose our merchants to increase their [265] orders for goods[266] in the comparatively cheaper markets of Europe, while at the same time it[267] would indispose foreigners to continue the same[268] orders for British goods, now become dearer.[269] The effect of this state of things would evidently be to increase the imports and diminish the exports. And when[270] these unequal orders came round for payment, [271] the exchange would fall [272] below the expence* of transporting the precious metals,

[247] 'if trade were free' is ins. [248] 'market' is del. [249] 'value' is del.

[250] 'we were to suppose that' is ins.

[251] 'and' is del. and 'supposing at the same time that the gold and silver were' is ins.

[252] 'of gold and silver' is del. [253] 'supposing at the same time' is del. and 'that' is ins.

[254] 'in' is ins. [255] 'that' is ins. [256] 'delay' is del. [257] 'of' is del. [258] 'the whole or' is del.

[259] 'and' is del. [260] 'perhaps' is del. [261] 'value so obtained' is del. [262] 'be' is repeated.

[263] 'The effect of this rise of prices would' is del. and 'When this however had taken place, it would' is ins.

[264] 'be to' is del. [265] 'foreign' is del. [266] 'for goods' is ins. [267] 'foreign' is del. and 'it' is ins.

[268] 'diminish their' is del. and 'continue the same' is ins. [269] 'unusually dear' is altered to 'dearer'.

[270] 'it would not be till' is del. and 'when' is ins. [271] 'that' is del. [272] 'to such' is del.

and the assistance of the bullion merchant would be called in, to supply the deficiency of foreign bills. Part of the bullion which had been coined would then in probability be reconverted into bullion for exportation.

[273] And it should be further remarked that an exportation of the precious metals[274] would take place owing to[275] the increased orders of our merchants for foreign goods,[276] although the accession of bullion here supposed, were not sufficient to raise prices in general to the full amount of the expence* of transporting the precious metals.[277] If the prices of home and foreign exportable goods had been before as nearly as possible on a level, [278] a very inconsiderable rise [279] of home commodities would turn the balance of demand in favour of the continent: and [280] from the competition for foreign bills in consequence of this demand, the prices of these bills[281] would be raised in a greater degree than the prices of other commodities with which the increased currency would come in contact.

When we trace in this manner the different effects produced by [282] an increased supply of cottons and an increased supply of bullion, it may not perhaps appear to be a prejudice, to consider the laws which regulate the import and export of [283] money as somewhat different from those which regulate the import and export of other commodities.

The case which we have just contemplated is unquestionably a case where the original impulse is[284] given by redundancy of currency; [285] and yet even here the [286] export of the precious metals appears to be[287] consequential to and dependent upon, a previous trade in commodities. And we believe that this will be found to be true whenever the precious metals are put in motion.

Our[288] trade with India and China till within these few years might fairly be considered as a trade [289] where there was on one side an unquestionable redundancy of currency. But what was it that limited and regulated this trade? – not surely the indefinite wants of India and China for bullion; nor our indefinite desires to get rid of a redundant currency; but the definite wants of this country [290] for the manufactures and produce of India and China, [291] and our[292] inability

[273] 'It will hardly be denied we conceive that in the cases here considered when we then compare the manner in which bullion and other commodities are affected by an increased supply, some peculiarities will appear to belong to the former.' is del.

[274] 'bullion' is del. and 'the precious metals' is ins.

[275] 'in consequence of' is del. and 'owing to' is ins.

[276] 'and the consequent scarcity of foreign bills' is del. [277] 'metals' is ins. [278] 'an inconsi' is del.

[279] Word(s) del. [280] 'thes' is del. [281] 'these prices' is altered to 'the prices of these bills'.

[282] Second 'by' is del. [283] 'oth' is del. [284] 'movement was' is del. and 'impulse is' is ins.

[285] 'ye' is del. [286] 'redundancy of precious' is del. [287] 'was clearly' is del. and 'appears to be' is ins.

[288] 'The' is del. and 'Our' is ins. [289] 'between two nations' is del. [290] ', a fact' is del.

[291] '[or] combined with the necessity of making certain payments on account of [her] our eastern establishments,' is del.

[292] 'her' is del. and 'our' is ins.

to pay for these commodities[293] so conveniently and cheaply as in the currency of the commercial world of which compared with the countries in question we had[294] a redundancy.

The same may be said of our former trade with Portugal. It was evidently limited and regulated not by the indefinite[295] wants of Great Britain for gold, but by the definite[296] wants of the Portuguese for British manufactures or at least by their inclination to take[297] British bills. To such an extent and no further could the purchases of the British bullion merchant go,[298] and if he wanted more [299] he must purchase it elsewhere.

In all these cases it appears to us quite clear that the trade in the precious metals is entirely subsidiary to the trade in other commodities, that it is the last step in the completion of a set of mercantile transactions [300] the main body of which is of course conducted by barter; and that on this account, and in reference to the daily language applied to the use of the medium of exchange, it is [301] more properly as well as more conveniently distinguished by the name of payment, than by that of sale.

Nor ought we to allow ourselves to be deceived in a case of this kind [302] merely by the language and proceedings of the bullion merchant. He undoubtedly feels and acts as if he was carrying on a trade, in no respect to be distinguished from the trade in other commodities. He looks to the state of the exchange in different countries, as to the *Price current* and determines upon his exports and imports of bullion exactly upon the same grounds as he would determine upon the export and import of sugar; [303] but if upon attentively examining the causes which operate upon the exchange, we find that it never falls to that point at which it will answer to him to export the precious metals till there is an actual excess of payments to be made abroad, we are bound to consider the bullion dealer merely as an instrument and to designate the trade according to its real character.

[293] '[these debts or make these] debts, or make payments,' is del. and 'for these commodities' is ins.
[294] 'have' is altered to 'had'. [295] 'indefinite' is ins. [296] 'definite' is ins.
[297] 'accept' is del. and 'take' is ins. [298] 'go' is ins. [299] 'gold' is del. [300] 'for indiv' is del.
[301] 'with great propriety as well as great convenience that' is del.
[302] 'by' is del. [303] 'that is according as its price abroad' is del.

5 *Essays and notes on Charles I and Mary, Queen of Scots*

INTRODUCTION

These three items are found in different locations amongst the Malthus manuscripts, but are brought together here because of their broadly similar themes. The first is an untitled essay or lecture on Charles I, beginning with the phrase: 'Charles the first to be considered as more unfortunate than criminal'.

An examination paper entitled 'Questions in Modern History' set by Malthus in 1808 for his students at the East India College shows that Malthus lectured on Charles I. The paper (now in the Bodleian Library, Oxford) contains four questions (out of 24) on Charles I. The following question specifically concerns the subject matter of this essay: '12. What was the great fault in the character of Charles I, from which his misfortunes seemed chiefly to arise? And what may be considered as the most criminal period of his public conduct?'

However, the rather declamatory style of this essay – 'How low! How abject did our countrymen bow before the throne of the 8th Henry' – and its florid language – 'man blushes not to bend the knee to Despotism' – suggest that it might have been written, not as a lecture to students, but as a submission in a school or university essay competition. If the thoughts contained in the essay were Malthus' genuine views – and not merely contrived debating points – they provide an interesting insight into his political opinions at the time. They also provide a further illustration of his habit of adopting a middle ground – in this instance, between 'the unthinking clamours of the populace for freedom & liberty' and 'the cold unfeeling vindications of arbitrary power'. This search for the middle ground became the characteristic methodology of his political economy – a methodology that he named 'the doctrine of proportions'. (See Pullen 1982.)

The second item is an essay or lecture on Mary, Queen of Scots. It is untitled, but opens with the sentence: 'Mary, Queen of Scots was justly beheaded'. It was possibly written as a lecture for students at the East India College, but its rather declamatory and ornate style suggests that, like the essay on Charles I, it was more likely to have been an entry in an essay competition.

The third item, also dealing with Mary, Queen of Scots, consists of extracts from Lucy Hutchinson, *Memoirs of the Life of Colonel Hutchinson, Governor of Nottingham Castle and Town*, published by Rev. Julius Hutchinson, London, 1806. Lucy Hutchinson (b. 1620) was the wife of Colonel John Hutchinson (1615–64), one of the judges who signed the death sentence against Charles I (*DNB*). A copy of the 1806 edition is in the Malthus Library.

On the other side of this leaf there are some notes on the population of Batavia in 1796 and of Holland in 1732 and on the public debt of Ireland (see Appendix A below). The latter concludes with a reference to the *Monthly Magazine*, November 1807.

The date of the *Memoirs* (1806) and the date of the reference to the *Monthly Magazine* (1807) – assuming that the two sides of the leaf were written at about the same time – indicate that this third item was probably written about 1807. The more formal, non-declamatory style suggests lecture preparation.

The three items give us a glimpse of Malthus' opinions on these historical events, but do not constitute a serious contribution – and were probably not intended as a serious contribution – to historical research.

1. ESSAY ON CHARLES I

Charles the first to be considered as more unfortunate than criminal. –

In taking a view of a period in our history so peculiarly interesting to Englishmen, & forming a judgement of the character & conduct of that monarch who fatally experien'd their too daring spirit, we must equally avoid joining in the unthinking clamours of the populace for freedom & liberty, & the cold unfeeling vindications of arbitrary power.

On the one side every just exertion of regal authority is branded with the opprobrious terms – Tyrannic & oppressive; & on the other[1] every stretch of the Crown's[2] prerogative supported & admir'd.

When [3] a people, not generally esteem'd cruel & capricious, [4] insult that throne to which for ages they had bow'd submission, & embrew*[5] their sacriligious* hands in royal blood, we naturally conclude that their prince had

[1] 'other' is ins. [2] 'Crown's' is ins. [3] 'we see' is del.
[4] 'embrew* their sacriligious ha' is del. [5] 'embue' is altered to 'embrew'.

committed some black offence, some daring outrage against the laws of his country. If however we attentively consider the particular state of England at that time & the more particular situation of Charles himself, we may cease to be surpris'd that while many of his predecessors – cruel avaricious & oppressive – possess'd the throne unmolested, this unhappy prince distinguish'd for his virtue & piety shoud* meet with so severe & unexampled a fate.

While the shade of ignorance obscures the views & contracts the rising powers of the mind, Tyranny & oppression reign undisturb'd. Unconscious of the dignity of his nature, man blushes not to bend the knee to Despotism; & while the individual preserves his possessions entire, he submits his neck to the yoke[6] & enjoys an equal share of happiness under the iron reign of a lawless Tyrant & the smiling auspices of freedom & Liberty. How low! how abject did our countrymen[7] bow before the throne of the 8th Henry – Oppressed by an Arbitrary King, an avaricious Pope, & a revengeful favorite,* how patient did they bear their chains.

But the ungenial contracted sentiments of Barbarism were now to have an end. Error was no more to spread her baneful influence oer this happy Isle. – Commerce was introduced & in her train liberty.

The nation was[8] no longer blindly led[9] [by the] inte[re]sted voice[10] of some popular leader. Each individual began to think for himself, to search out the hidden rec[e]sses of truth & enquire into the inherent privileges of mankind. The result of these enquiries was fatal to the constitution. The people[11] felt their natural rights, & felt that the power in the Crown was inconsistent with them. Every spirit was impatient under the restraint, every eye look'd forward to a change, every heart beat high with the thought of Freedom. Thus warm'd in their imaginations – Thus panting to be free from the galling shackles of Monarchy, are we to be surpris'd that each action of their Prince was jealously scrutiniz'd, every failing magnified & even the execution of law considered as an infringement of their privileges?

Charles on the other hand mistook the disposition of his subjects – The principles of divine right & uncontrol'd authority had been instill'd into his youthful mind, & he was easily persuaded to rule by those maxims which were endear'd to him by early prejudice & sanctified by paternal authority. [12] The constitution of the country was built on arbitrary power. Charles in maintaining the dignity of his prerogative scarcely deviated[13] from the[14] law, never from precedent.

6 '[[feels] patiently submits] bends' is del. and 'submits his neck to the yoke' is ins.
7 'the nation' is del. and 'our countrymen' is ins. 8 'people' is del. and 'nation was' is ins.
9 'joined in the' is del. and 'led' is ins. 10 'views' is del. and 'voice' is ins.
11 'They' is altered to 'The people'. 12 'we forget by whose fall the never' is del.
13 'deviated' is ins. 14 'the' is ins.

2. ESSAY ON MARY, QUEEN OF SCOTS

Mary Queen of Scots was justly beheaded.

When we contemplate with a reflecting mind the history of illustrious characters, & examine unprejudiced[15] the general opinions of mankind in their favour, we may be surprised perhaps to find, how often a few agreeable qualities have stood in the place of virtues, how often in a decision[16] on their conduct, the understanding has been led away by the heart. We are as naturally inclined to excuse & gloss over the frailties of those who have gained our affection,[17] as to pry into & exaggerate the defects in the unfortunate objects of our hatred & disgust.[18] The history of every court & nation in Europe would furnish innumerable examples[19] of this propensity in mankind to be biass'd in their jud[g]ements.[20] We cannot however have a more striking[21] instance than that under contemplation.[22] No one has had more advocates for her conduct[23] than [Mary] queen of Scots, no one if that[24] conduct be strictly investigated will appear less to have deserved them. Decorated with all the graces of personal elegance, possessing a mind fraught[25] with every engaging accomplishment natural & acquired, endowed in a peculiar manner with the powers of pleasing, affable, insinuating, witty, by the charm of her address & conversation, she engaged the heart of every beholder & appeared to the world in the character of the most amiable of women. [26] Few coud* persuade themselves that under so bewitching an exterior there lurked a heart abandon'd by every principle of virtue & honour, few while they admired her accomplishments coud* believe that in her person they beheld[27] a murderer, an adulteress, a bigot[28] & a traitor.

[15] 'of those who have rendered themselves conspicuous either by their exalted situation or illustrious actions' is del. and 'of illustrious characters, & examine unprejudiced' is ins.

[16] 'judgement' is del. and 'decision' is ins.

[17] 'those whom we love' is del. and 'those who have [in agreeable ways] gained our affection' is ins.

[18] '[him] unapproved character' is del. and 'the unfortunate objects of our hatred & disgust' is ins.

[19] 'Innumerable instances' is del. and 'The history of every court & nation in Europe would furnish innumerable examples' is ins.

[20] 'might be brought from the history of every court in Europe' is del.

[21] 'a much stronger' is del. and 'a more striking' is ins.

[22] 'one before us' is del. and 'under contemplation' is ins.

[23] 'during a series of misfortunes ever met with so much pity & compassion as' is del. and 'has had more advocates for her conduct' is ins.

[24] 'her' is del. and 'that' is ins.

[25] 'fraught' is apparently used here in the sense of 'stored, supplied, furnished, filled, equipped with', rather than in the more usual and modern sense of 'distressed; distressing' or 'fraught with danger' (*OED*).

[26] 'Blinded by this bewitching exterior' is del.

[27] 'in the person of Mary they beheld an unprincipled profligate, an abandon'd sensualist & an ambitious bigot, to sum up the whole' is del. and 'under so bewitching ... they beheld' is ins.

[28] 'a bigot' is ins.

That these terms, however[29] harsh they may appear, are not the idle voice of calumny alone, proofs of the strongest nature[30] bear undeniable testimony. The circumstances attending the murder[31] of Darnly,*[32] her prior connection with Bothwell,[33] & her subsequent conduct, must bring a conviction of the most[34] atrocious guilt to every judgment capable of exerting its powers. Where indeed can we parallel so unheard of a piece of conduct. Admitting even her perfect innocence with regard to a murder[35] of which I am afraid [36] the proofs are too strong to be contrary: yet to marry a man who had a few days before been so scandalously divorced from his wife, to chuse* for her guardian & protector the reputed, and publickly* accused, assassinator of her husband, was so glaring a defiance to all decency, so inexplicable a neglect of reputation as [37] alone to consign her name to æternal infamy & disgrace. For[38] what plea of youth, imprudence, indiscretion or even passion coud* in any degree[39] palliate so gross a violation of every law human & divine, of every principle of virtue, honour & humanity.

[40] When at last her subjects, roused from the lethargy that had oppress'd them, compell'd her to seek a[41] refuge in the friendship of Elizabeth, we shall find the conduct of that princess towards her unfortunate kinswoman[42] in every respect such as the critical situation of her [43] affair demanded. [44]

Coud* she with any shew* of reason attempt[45] to reinstate her friend[46] in a throne while accused of such enormous crimes;[47] coud* she thus[48] patronize vice & murder, & sully the arms of England in so detestable a cause? The honour of the kingdom forbade. The glory of Elizabeth's name required at least some [49] degree of innocence & right on the part of her suppliant,[50] to authorize her first generous purpose [51] of exerting all her authority[52] to restore the fallen

[29] 'however' is repeated. [30] 'nature' is ins.
[31] 'the death of her husband' is del. and 'the murder' is ins. [32] Lord Darnley, her second husband.
[33] Earl of Bothwell, her third husband. [34] 'the most' is ins.
[35] 'to the death of her husband' is del. and 'to a murder ... to be contrary' is ins.
[36] 'the weight of strong' is del. [37] 'woud'* is del. [38] 'For' is ins.
[39] 'measure excuse' is del. and 'degree' is ins. [40] 'When Mary' is del. [41] 'a' is ins.
[42] 'her unfortunate kinswoman' is ins. [43] 'friends' is del.
[44] 'Activated by motives of pity & considering more her present distress'd situation, than her past misconduct, her first generous purpose was to employ all her authority & power to reinstate her in that throne from which her subjects had but too justly deposed her.' is del.
[45] 'or justice exert her authority ... [word unclear]' is del. and 'attempt' is ins.
[46] 'her friend' is del. and ins.
[47] 'which a woman whose enormous crimes had so foully disgraced' is del. and 'while accused of such enormous crimes' is ins.
[48] 'thus' is ins. [49] 'small' is del.
[50] '& right in her suppliant' is del. and 'on the part of her suppliant' is ins.
[51] 'in Mary's favour, of exerting every power to restore the Queen of Scots to the dignity from which she had fallen' is del.
[52] 'of exerting all her authority' is ins.: 'all her' is repeated.

queen to her former[53] dignity. When however there remained no longer the least possibility[54] of her innocence, when her own handwriting stood the indelible mark of her infamy; to protect her from the insolence of her enemies, & afford her a safe & honorable* ...[55] was surely as much as reason coud* justify, or the strict friendship demand. The ambitious & enterprizing spirit of Mary[56] rouz'd* rather[57] to resentment than broken by her misfortune rendered a slight confinement of her person absolutely necessary. To have permitted her retiring to France if we consider the affairs[58] of Europe at that time, the precarious state of the protestant religion, & her intimate connection with the house of Guise, those inveterate persecutors of it, woud* have been a measure so replete[59] with dangers to the peace & happiness of England, that policy coud* not allow it,[60] nor can I think [61] at such a juncture either justice or honour coud* demand it. Allowed therefore a secure retreat[62] she was treated with all the respect due to her former rank & dignity. Continual negotiations were carried in the kindest manner by Elizabeth to conciliate the differences between her & her scottish subjects but that proud & haughty princess refused every proposal that fell short [63] of restoring her to the absolute possession of that throne from which she had been so justly deposed. Disappointed therefore in her ambitious view, she turned her malice towards her guardian[64] & benefactor. By her address & entrigues* she fill'd the country that protected her with tumults & seditions. [65] Even persons well affected to the government were reduced by her insinuating behaviour & fallacious promises to engage themselves[66] in the most daring & horrid enterprizes.* The Duke of Norfolk, a peer[67] of the highest rank, honour & reputation, was drawn by her snares to engage in an attempt which in the end proved so fatal to that unhappy nobleman. We come now to that grand conspiracy the dreadfull* purpose of which was the assassination of Elizabeth, the promotion of Mary to the crown of England & the absolute submission of the protestant religion. While [we] look[68] upon so black & deep laid a scheme, can we hesitate to pronounce the promoter of it guilty of the most egnomenuous*

[53] 'the fallen queen to her former' is ins.

[54] '... [words unclear] against her' is del. and 'there remained no longer the least possibility' is ins.

[55] Word missing, possibly 'refuge'. [56] 'of Mary' is ins. [57] 'rather' is repeated.

[58] 'considering the state' is del. and 'if we consider the affairs' is ins.

[59] 'big' is del. and 'replete' is ins.

[60] 'utterly forbad* it' is del. and 'coud* not allow it' is ins. [61] 'that' is del.

[62] '[Confin'd therefore at a nobleman's house in the country] Allowed therefore a safe & honorable retirement at the Earl of Shrewsburys' is del. and 'Allowed therefore a secure retreat' is ins.

[63] ', that fell' is del. [64] 'protector' is del. and 'guardian' is ins.

[65] 'A Bull of the Pope was by her means issued out which excommunicated Elizabeth & absolved her subjects from their oaths of allegiance.' is del.

[66] 'to engage themselves' is ins. [67] 'nobleman' is del. and 'peer' is ins.

[68] 'Can we look without' is del. and 'While look' is ins.

death? Is any rank or dignity whatever either by the law of nature or nation exempted from the punishment due to such an atrocious crime?

When therefore the most incontestable evidence proved that the Queen of Scots, had encouraged [&] countenanced the conspiracy,[69] can we longer refuse to confess the justice of that sentence which her numerously repeated crimes had long before merited?

3. NOTES ON MARY, QUEEN OF SCOTS

M[rs]. Lucy Hutchinson in her life of Col[l]. Hutchinson speaking of the causes which led to the civil wars, says "The interest of the people which had been many years growing made an extraordinary progress in the days of King Henry 8th who returning the vast revenues of the church into the body of the people, cast the balance clear on their side and left them now only to expect an opportunity to resume their power into their own hands; and had not differences[70] in religion divided them among themselves and thereby prolonged the last gasps of expiring monarchy, they had long since exercised it in a free commonwealth." P 5 ...[71]

Speaking of the conduct of[72] Elizabeth to[73] Mary Queen of Scots whom she calls a wicked Queen of a bloody lustful temper,[74] she says[75] the Queen of England was very loth to execute this necessary justice; but the true hearted protestants of her councils,[76] foreseeing the sad effects that[77] might be expected if ever she arr[i]ved to [78] the [79] crown urged it on; and after the death of Queen Elizabeth, the wiser of them much opposed the admission of her son &c.

The editor justly remarks that this observation of M[rs]. Hutchinson may [80] be the true solution of the enigma respecting the signing and expediting of the warrant for the execution of Mary; and accounts for it more naturally than the mean jealosy* attributed to Elizabeth, which would in fact have[81] been a better reason for putting her to death many years sooner. P.58.

[69] '& supported with all her powers' is del. and 'the conspiracy' is ins.

[70] 'of' is del.

[71] The leaf has been trimmed, and a units digit of this page number seems to have been removed. In Hutchinson 1936, this information occurs on p.60.

[72] 'the conduct of' is ins. [73] 'and' is del. and 'to' is ins.

[74] 'About this time in the kingdom of Scotland there was a wicked queen, daughter of a mother that came out of the bloody house of Guise, and brought up in the popish religion, which she zealously persevered in, as most suitable to her bloody lustful temper; she being guilty of murders and adulteries ...' (Hutchinson 1936, p.58).

[75] From 'the Queen of England' to 'admission of her son' is a quotation from Hutchinson 1936, p.61. There are no quotation marks in MS.

[76] Hutchinson 1936, p.61 has 'council'. [77] 'that' is repeated in MS.

[78] 'at' is del. On the use of the expression 'arrived to' meaning 'to attain, gain, achieve', see *OED*.

[79] 'throne' is del. [80] 'the' is del [81] 'have' is repeated.

6 Questions and answers on early European history

INTRODUCTION

This is a book of 76 pages of manuscript dealing with European history from the fifth to the tenth century. The contents are divided into four sections, entitled 'Lecture i', 'Lecture ii', 'L iii' and 'L iv', but the material is in the form of questions and brief answers, rather than full-length lectures. In the original, the questions are written on the versos and their answers on the rectos (except in a few cases where the answers spill over into spare spaces on the versos); but for simplicity of presentation each answer in this transcription is placed immediately after its corresponding question, with the question in bold type.

The questions in MS are numbered, although as noted below the numbering sequence is broken at one point. There are 84 questions in all – 20 in the first lecture, 22 in the second, 22 in the third (incorrectly numbered '21' in MS), and 20 in the fourth. All of the questions have answers. In some cases the answers are in the form of brief notes and incomplete sentences, but generally they consist of formal statements, probably intended for lecture-room dictation. The method of presentation is similar to that used by Malthus in his lectures on political economy as seen in the Inverarity Manuscript (Pullen 1981; Hashimoto 1988), although the answers are expressed more fully and in a more formal style in these history lectures than in the political economy lectures.

In addition to the numbers i–iv for the four lectures and to the numbers (1–20, 1–22, 1–22, 1–20) for the questions within each of the four lectures, the numbers 1–24 are pencilled in the margins at regular intervals throughout the book. Within Lecture i there are the pencilled numbers 1–7; within Lecture ii, 8–13; within Lecture iii, 14–19; and within Lecture iv, 21–24.[1] A likely

[1] The sequence of these pencilled numbers is broken at several points; for example, '16' occurs twice, so that Lecture iii should have the numbers 14–20, not 14–19; and the first pencilled number in Lecture iv is (correctly) '21' but '21' is repeated, so that the final pencilled number in Lecture iv should be '25', not '24'.

possibility is that these pencilled numbers referred to successive teaching sessions or lessons. In this transcription the word 'Lesson' in square brackets has therefore been placed before each of the pencilled numbers.

The following table indicates the numbering system used by Malthus for the four lectures, the 25 lessons and the 84 questions, and gives a brief summary of the subject matter of each question and answer.

Lecture	[Lesson]	Question	Topics of Questions and Answers
i	1	1	Barbarian invasion of former Roman provinces
		2	Fall of Roman empire in the west
		3	People and government of the Roman provinces
	2	4	Principal barbarian nations at the end of the fifth century
		5	System of government of the Barbarian invaders
		6	Salic and Ripuarian laws
	3	7	Sources of the feudal system
		8	Main object of the feudal system
		9	Uniformity of the feudal system in different countries
	4	10	Land holding conditions under Barbarian rule
		11	Changes in land holding conditions
		12	Effect of former Roman provinces on the Barbarian system of government
		13	Reasons for Italy's independent states
	5	14	Clovis: founder of the French monarchy. Distinction of ranks
		15	Conversion of Clovis and the French to Christianity
		16	Division of France after the death of Clovis

		17	Condition of France under Clotaire II
	6	18	France: the change from a society of free men to a society of seigneurs and serfs
		19	Rise to power of the mayors: Pepin d'Heristal, Charles Martel, Pepin the Short. Salic Law versus Roman Law
	7[2]	20	Fall of the Merovingians and start of the Carlovingians
ii		1	Visigoth monarchy in Spain
		2	Defeat of the Visigoths by the Saracens
	8	3	Leaders of the Saracen kingdom
		4	The court of Abd ar-Rahmān
		5	Ostrogothic kingdom in Italy under Theodoric; and its demise
	9	6	Foundation and location of the Lombard kingdom in Italy
		7	Government of the rest of Italy
		8	Lombard laws
		9	The Pope's appeal for French protection
	10	10	Pepin's conquests in Italy
		11	Roman withdrawal from Britain
		12	Saxon support for Britain
	11	13	Saxon leaders
		14	Saxon kingdoms in Britain
	12	15	Areas where Britons took refuge from the Saxons
		16	Unification of the Saxon kingdoms
		17	Conversion of the Saxons to Christianity
	13	18	Slow rise of feudalism in England

[2] Lesson 7 covers the last question of Lecture i and the first two questions of Lecture ii.

		19	Saxon Witenagemot
		20	Social classes under the Saxons
		21	Anglo-Saxon government
		22	Anglo-Saxon criminal laws
iii	14	1	State of Germany at the accession of Charlemagne
		2	Destruction of the Lombard kingdom
		3	Charlemagne's system of government in Italy
	15	4	Conversion of Saxons in Germany to Christianity
		5	Charlemagne's armies
		6	Charlemagne in Spain
	16	7	Charlemagne's promotion of commerce
		8	Charlemagne's promotion of culture
	[17][3]	9	Charlemagne's coronation as Emperor of the West
		10	Invasion of France by the Normans
		11	French government under Charlemagne
		12	Improvements to government administration introduced by Charlemagne
	[18][4]	13	The use of capitularies in France
		14	Principal revenues of Charlemagne
	[19][5]	15	Coins used during Charlemagne's reign
		16	Charlemagne's reign and residence
		17	Charlemagne's successors
		18	Battle of Fontenoy
	[20][6]	19	System of government under the sons of Charlemagne

3 Numbered '16' in MS. 4 Numbered '17' in MS. 5 Numbered '18' in MS.
6 Numbered '19' in MS. Lesson [20] includes the last four questions of Lecture iii and the first question of Lecture iv.

		20	Actions of Pope Nicholas I
		[21][7]	Hereditary offices of Dukes and Counts
		[22][8]	Norman invasions of France
iv		1	Norman invasions of England
	21	2	Establishment of tithes in England
		3	English princes during the invasions by the Danes
		4	Alfred's victory over the Danes
	[22][9]	5	Government administration under Alfred
		6	Alfred's encouragement of culture and commerce
	[23][10]	7	Alfred's character
		8	Charles the Fat and the Norman siege of Paris
		9	Division of the French Empire after Charles the Fat
		10	Nations and rulers in Germany
	[24][11]	11	Henry the Fowler
		12	Otto the First
		13	France after Charles the Simple
		14	Method of settling the line of descent in Germany
	[25][12]	15	Power of the clergy in Germany
		16	Title of Augustus conferred on Otto
		17	Ecclesiastical elections under Otto
		18	Otto's achievements
		19	Rome and Italy under the emperors of the House of Saxony
		20	General rights of the emperors of the House of Saxony

[7] Numbered '20' in MS. [8] Numbered '21' in MS. [9] Numbered '21' in MS.
[10] Numbered '22' in MS. [11] Numbered '23' in MS. [12] Numbered '24' in MS.

The fact that these notes on history are entitled 'Lectures', and the fact that they are arranged in a didactic manner with a numbered series of questions and answers, strongly suggest that they were given as lectures at the East India College. If that was indeed the case, it is remarkable that Malthus and/or the College authorities should have thought that European history of the period from the fifth to the tenth century was an appropriate subject for inclusion in the curriculum for young men about to enter the service of the East India Company in India. However, it must be recognised that, to our knowledge, there is as yet no textual or contextual proof that this material was *actually delivered* as lectures at the College. The only history examination paper known to have survived from Malthus' period at the College is concerned with 'Modern History' and contains no questions relating to the subject matter of these lectures.

The following authorities and sources were referred to by Malthus in these questions and answers:[13] Bede, Butler, Caesar, Centaines, Du Bos, Gibbon, Hallam, Henry, Hincmar, Hume, Leibniz, Mably, Millar, Millot, Montesquieu, Robertson, Russell, Voltaire and Whitaker.

The writing is, as usual, in ink, but some additional material has been added in pencil. On the front cover, 'History 1' is written in pencil; on the back cover there are the words 'Mr Jackson' and 'Jackson' written upside down in the bottom left-hand corner, and both deleted.

LECTURE I

[Lesson] 1

1. What rendered the Roman provinces which had formerly been filled with warlike inhabitants an easy prey to the first Barbarous invader, after the retreat of the Imperial forces?

Their long subjection to the Roman yoke and to the constant plunder [by] the Roman Governors had broken their spirit; and[14] from the[15] habit of relying entirely upon the Roman legions for their defence, they had entirely lost their martial spirit.

[16] A martial spirit and great bodily vigour were probably more necessary before the present art of war [was] introduced.

[13] For further details, see footnotes below. The most frequently cited were Montesquieu, Millar, Robertson, Mably and Gibbon. The fact that Malthus usually gave precise page references for these five authors indicates that he was reading and citing directly from their works. It is not certain that direct citation was the case with all the other sources in this list. Some may have been cited indirectly from citations in other works.

[14] 'Their long subjection ... their spirit; and' is ins. [15] 'constant' is del. [16] 'Possess' is del.

2. What were the chief moral and political causes which contributed to the destruction of the Roman Empire in the West?

1. No rival after the destruction of Carthage and conquest of the Gauls, and the[17] Change of manners introduced by the luxury of Asia.[18]

2. Want of discipline in the army, and the power and luxuriousness of the Praetorian bands first conspicuous on occasion of some disputed successions & increased by the immense domain in which they ...[19]

3. The employment of Barbarians in the service of the Empire and above all their being taught the Roman discipline.

4. The Removal of the seat of Empire to Constantinople, which weakened the Western frontiers.

To which may be added the continually increasing[20] habit of employing slaves by which the number of Roman citizens was continually diminishing.

The poorer citizens were latterly supported almost entirely by largesses, being deprived of all independant* means of support.

3. What was the character of the people with whom the Romans had to contend, and what was the original form of government under which they had lived according to Tacitus?

Of great vigour of body and delighting in war. Remarkable for their chastity, hospitality and detestation of falsehood.[21] The government under which they lived seemed to be a kind of military democracy, under a general or chieftain who had [22] the title of king, but whose power was extremely limited. Even their attendance in war[23] according to Caesar[24] was voluntary; but[25] though with regard to any particular expedition proposed by individual chiefs, the joining in it was perfectly voluntary: yet there can be little doubt, though [26] it has not been expressly stated by Caesar or[27] Tacitus that, in a national war, or war of defence, all would be under the obligation of attending.

Ubi quis ex prin[c]ipibus in concilio dixit se ducem fore, qui sequi velint profiteantur. Consurgunt ii qui et causam et hominem probant, suumque auxilium pollicentur.[28] Caesar[29]

[17] 'and conquest of the Gauls, and the' is ins. Before 'Change', '2' is del. and the numbers 2, 3 and 4 that follow have been altered from 3, 4 and 5.

[18] 'immense donations. Disputed successions' is del. [19] Words unclear.

[20] 'continually increasing' is ins.

[21] 'Remarkable for their chastity, hospitality and detestation of falsehood.' is ins.

[22] 'generally' is del. [23] 'in war' is ins. [24] 'Tacitus' is del. and 'Caesar' is ins.

[25] 'but' is ins. [26] 'the fact' is del. [27] 'Caesar or' is ins.

[28] Caesar, *De Bello Gallico*, V.i. 23.7: When one of the leading men in the council has said that he would be leader, all those who are willing to follow say so. Those who approve both the cause and the man stand up and promise their assistance.

[29] 'Caesar' is in pencil.

Nec regibus infinata aut libera potestas, et duces exemplo potius quam imperio ... praesunt.[30]

De minoribus rebus principes consultant, de maioribus omnes.[31] Tacitus[32]

[Lesson] 2

4. How were the principal nations of Barbarians settled towards the end of the 5th century?

Visigoths in Spain, Franks in Gaul, Saxons in the Roman provinces of South Britain, the Huns in Pannonia, the Ostrogoths in Italy, [33] the Burgundians in the South Eastern parts of France and the Vandals in Africa.

5. How far did the government which the Northern Invaders introduced at first[34] into the countries they conquered, differ from the form under which they had before lived, and to what system did it give rise?

It only gave rise to this system after the lapse of some time.

The word fundum[35] does not recur in any charter till the 11th century.

Henry[36] inclines too much to the opinion that the feudal system was introduced first.[37]

Victorious army cantoned out and arranged under its proper officers. Russel*[38]

Robertson[39] says that nothing bearing any resemblance to the feudal tenure was observed among the Barbarians, in the state of property before their

[30] Tacitus, *Germania* 7.1: Nor do kings have unlimited and free power, and leaders exercise authority by example rather than by command.

[31] Tacitus, *Germania* 11.1: On minor matters the leaders consult one another, on greater matters all the citizens are consulted.

We are grateful to Alan Treloar for identifying the sources of these quotations from Caesar and Tacitus, and providing a translation.

[32] 'Tacitus' is in pencil. [33] 'and' is del. [34] 'at first' is ins.

[35] 'fundus' (Latin), a piece of land, a farm or an estate.

[36] Robert Henry (1718–90), *The History of Great Britain from the First Invasion of it by the Romans under Julius Caesar*. First published 1771–93, 6 vols. The Malthus Library has the 4th edn, 1799–1805, 12 vols.

[37] 'The word ... introduced first' is in pencil.

[38] Probably, William Russell (1741–93), *The History of Modern Europe. With an Account of the Decline and Fall of the Roman Empire, and a View of the Progress of Society from the Rise of Modern Kingdoms to the Peace of Paris, in 1763. In a Series of Letters from a Nobleman to His Son*, New edition enlarged, 5 vols., London, 1786; or a later edition (*DNB*).

[39] William Robertson, DD, *The History of the Reign of the Emperor Charles V. With a View of the Progress of Society in Europe, from the Subversion of the Roman Empire to the Beginning of the Sixteenth Century*, 1769. The Malthus Library has a 1782 edition.

conquests. And if the laws by which they were governed in the earliest period of their settlement in Gaul[40] be examined, it will be found that they experienced no further variation,[41] than what necessarily arose from property in land becoming fixed. [42] These laws were the Salic and Ripuarian Codes by which the Franks were governed; while the Roman provincials in all civil matters were allowed to be governed by the Roman law.

6. What were the Salic and Ripuarian laws, and about what time are they supposed to have been reduced to writing? Montesquieu Book 28.[43]

The Salic laws coincide very nearly with all the customs mentioned by Tacitus.[44]

The Salii are supposed to have been a tribe of Franks who inhabited the country on the confines of Brabant and Hainault, and the Repuarians* another tribe of the same nation which occupied the country upon the Rhine, the Meuse and the Schelde. They are supposed to have joined under Clovis; and the Salic laws or the customs of the tribe of the Salii, were soon after written in Latin and published as the laws by which the Franks were to be governed in their new territories.[45] The Ripuarian laws which are rather more severe were collected and published some time after by a king of Austrasia, in a part of the country near the original seat of the Repuarians.*

It appears[46] in these codes, particularly in the Salic which was earlier reduced to writing,[47] that almost all property was at first allodial; and the mere obligation on every free man to serve the state cannot be considered as any part of the feudal system as such an obligation is almost universal.

The feudal system arose in time from the new circumstances in which the Barbarians were placed by their territorial conquests, but cannot with any propriety be said to have been[48] established at first. See Montesquieu Books 28 & 30.[49]

[40] 'in Gaul' is ins. [41] 'from what they were before' is del.

[42] 'The mere obligation on every free man to serve the state cannot be considered as any part of the feudal system as such an obligation is almost universal. This feudal system arose indeed in time, from the new circumstances in which the Barbarians were placed, but cannot with any propriety be said to have been established at first.' is del. and transposed (with minor alterations) to the end of the next answer.

[43] Montesquieu, Charles Secondat, Baron de (1689–1750). *De l'Esprit des Loix*, 1748. The Malthus Library has the following works by Montesquieu: *Lettres Turques*, 1748; *Œuvres*, 5 vols., 1796; and *Œuvres Posthumes*, 1798.
Book XXVIII is entitled, 'Of the Origin and Revolutions of the Civil Laws Among the French' (*The Spirit of the Laws*, transl. T. Nugent, Hafner, New York, 1949).

[44] This sentence is in pencil.

[45] 'as the laws by which the Franks were to be governed in their new territories' is ins.

[46] 'by' is del. [47] 'particularly in the Salic which was [first] earlier reduced to writing' is ins.

[48] 'to be' is del. and 'to have been' is ins.

[49] Book XXX, 'Theory of the Feudal Laws among the Franks, in the Relation They Bear to the Establishment of the Monarchy' (Montesquieu 1949).

[Lesson] 3

7. To what three sources has the feudal system been ascribed, and which seems to be the true one?

Three opinions seem to have prevailed respecting the origin of the feudal system. 1st. That it was brought directly from Germany. 2. That it was an improvement by the Goths of the manner in which lands were granted to the milites limitanei[50] of the latter* Roman Emperors. And the third, the one just mentioned.[51]

In answer to the first it may be observed that as the feudal system was not complete till after the commencement of the third race of the kings of France, it cannot rationally be supposed to have been brought directly from the woods of Germany.

To the second, it may be said that the mere grant of land on condition of military service or the defence of frontiers is very different from that complicated obligation which forms the essence of the feudal system.

The last opinion is the one I am inclined to adopt.

8. What was the main object of the feudal system according to the different views of Robertson and Millar?[52] and which view appears to be most correct?

The great object of the feudal policy according to Dr Robertson was defence; but probably this would have been sufficiently and indeed better attained by the simple obligation of every free man to appear in arms on the summons of his sovereign. But this obligation was established on the first conquest of the Roman provinces and forms no part of what may be peculiarly denominated the feudal system. The real object was probably that stated by Millar – security from those violences which the weakness of the central government had not power to prevent.[53]

The opposite statement to that of Dr Robertson with regard to defence and internal government seems to be the true one.

[50] 'soldiers of the frontier' (AT).

[51] This is apparently the opinion mentioned at the end of the answer to question 6, i.e. that the feudal system arose because of the new circumstances in which the Barbarians were placed by their territorial conquests.

[52] John Millar, *An Historical View of the English Government, from the Settlement of the Saxons in Britain to the Revolution in 1688*, 4 vols., London, 1803. A copy is held in the Malthus Library at Jesus College.

[53] The following paragraph is del.: 'The great extent of the kingdoms that were formed upon the ruins of the Western Empire together with the rudeness of the people by whom they were established, and the consequent weakness of the civil government, occasioned the necessity of those associations, which terminated in the regular feudal tenure'.

9. To what circumstances do Robertson and Millar ascribe that uniformity in the appearance of the feudal system observable[54] in all the different countries of Europe, in which[55] it was established?

Robertson ascribes it to the similar state of society and manners to which all those Northern conquerors[56] were accustomed in their native countries, and to the similar situation in which they found themselves on taking possession of their new domains.

Millar attributes this uniformity principally to the subjection of a more civilized people with whom the conquerors were at length completely incorporated[57] and to the extent of the kingdoms the Barbarians were enabled to form so much disproportioned to the[58] strength of their civil government, from which he thinks arose, their peculiar state of mixed barbarism and civilization, their peculiar system of feudal tenures by which their policy was distinguished, and the customs of duelling, chivalry and Romantic gallantry.[59]

[Lesson] 4

10. On what condition did every free man,[60] according to Robertson, hold the lands which he possessed under the new government established by the Barbarians in the countries which they had conquered? Vol i p 16.

On condition of appearing in arms when called upon by his Sovereign under a considerable penalty (p.16)[61] – a herebannum or fine of 60 crowns[62] was established, which did not amount to confiscation of property.

According to a capitulary[63] of Charlemagne, those who possessed five mansi[64] (about 60 acres) were obliged to attend in person. The Herebannum was levied with great vigour.

[54] 'which was established' is del. and 'observable' is ins.

[55] 'where' is del. and 'in which' is ins.

[56] 'they' is del. and 'all those Northern conquerors' is ins.

[57] Millar, p.57: 'The settlement of the barbarous nations ... was effected by the gradual subjection of a more civilized people, with whom the conquerors were at length completely incorporated'.

[58] 'extent' is del.

[59] Millar (pp.74–83) discusses at length the customs of duelling, chivalry, romantic love and gallantry.

[60] 'hold' is del. [61] 'But this may be doubted; because a regular fine' is del.

[62] 'or fine of 60 crowns' is ins. A herebannum was a fine imposed on free men (landholders) who did not appear in arms when called upon (Robertson 1832, p.197).

[63] A capitulary is a 'collection of ordinances ... especially those made on their own authority by the Frankish kings' (*OED*).

[64] Malthus' statement that a mansus was about 12 acres probably came from Robertson 1832, p.196, Note 8. Malthus repeated this in the answer to Question 5 in Lecture iii, below. However, Davis 1972, p.142, n.1, states that a mansus was the amount of land required to support a family, and that the size of a mansus varied, but was usually 30–35 acres of arable land.

11. What were the four successive changes which property in land seemed to go through among the barbarous nations which settled in the provinces of the Roman Empire? Robertson.

1. Property in land not fixed 2. [65] Allodial. 3. Benefices during pleasure;[66] and 4. for life and[67] in perpetuity. p.254[68]

[69]

12. In what manner according to Millar was the extent of the kingdoms erected by the Barbarous nations in Europe affected by the state and extent of each Roman Province?

Each Roman province formed a distinct society influenced by national views, and directed by a seperate* interest, and were* consequently disposed to admit the authority of a single person, and remain in that state of Union and subordination to which they were accustomed. The conqueror also was generally in a condition to avail himself of that authority however declining, which the Roman government had continued to maintain. Particular chiefs having occupied the remaining towns belonging to a Roman province were of course masters of the adjacent territory: and he who had set himself at the head of the most powerful district, was in a fair way of becoming sovereign of the whole. From these causes the boundaries of a modern kingdom often came to be the same in extent as those of an antient* Roman province.[70]

13. What causes probably made Italy fall more easily into a number of independent states than the other countries of Europe?

Italy was early subject to a more rigorous police and divided into smaller districts than the rest of the Roman Empire. It was distributed by Augustus into eleven regions; and in the time of the Emperor Adrian*[71] it included together with Sicily and Sardinia no less than seventeen divisions.

[65] 'during pleasure' is del. [66] 'for life' is del. and 'Benefices during pleasure' is ins.

[67] 'for life and' is ins. [68] Presumably a page reference to Robertson 1769.

[69] At this point the following paragraph is del.: 'According to the Abbe* Mably, Charles Martel first introduced the practice of granting beneficia for life; and Louis the debonnaire was among the first that rendered them hereditary'. Malthus was presumably referring to *Observations sur les Romains*, 1751, by Gabriel Bonnot de Mably (1709–85). The Malthus Library has Mably's *Des droits et des devoirs des citoyens*, 2 vols., Paris, 1793, but not his *Observations*.
A 'beneficium' (Latin) is a benefit, favour, kindness, benefice, etc.

[70] The whole of this answer to question 12 is a collation of passages taken almost verbatim from Millar, pp.64–6.

[71] i.e. Emperor Hadrian.

[Lesson] 5

14. Who is generally considered as the founder of the French Monarchy; and by what victory did he crush the remaining power of the Romans in Gaul? 486[72]

Clovis the grandson of Meroveus first established himself in Gaul by his victory over the Roman general[73] Syagrius near Soissons.

Syagrius was the son of Agidius. The city and diocese of Soissons was his paternal estate; and Rheims,* Troyes, Beauvais and Amiens submitted to him as patrician.

The Abbé Dubos[74]considers Clovis not in the light of a conqueror; but as succeeding to the Roman power in Gaul with the consent both of the people and the Emperors.

Dr Robertson does not explain sufficiently the state of the Roman provincials after the conquest of Clovis. This is best done, and satisfactory authorities quoted, by Montesquieu. Book 30

The distinction of ranks seems to have been principally marked by the different fines established for manslaughter. In general throughout all ranks, the fine for killing a Franck* was double that for killing a Roman; a circumstance which makes strongly against the Abbé Dubos system.

The composition[75] for a noble Frank or guest[76] of the King was 600 solidi [or] sous[77] A noble Roman 300. A common Frank 200. A Roman of same condition 100. These were however all personal distinctions and according to Mably there was no hereditary rank till fiefs became hereditary.

15. When and on what occasion did the French nation become Christian; and what advantage did Clovis derive from his new profession of faith?[78]

After a victory over the Alemanni at Tolbiac,[79] which he attributed to the God of his wife Clotilda. He was baptized by St Remigius, bishop of Rheims,* and almost the whole of the French nation followed his example.

[72] The date of Clovis' victory over Syagrius. [73] 'the Roman general' is ins.

[74] Abbé Jean-Baptiste Du Bos (1670–1742), *Histoire critique de l'établissement de la monarchie françoise* dans les Gaules*, 3 vols., Amsterdam, 1734.

[75] A 'composition' is 'An agreement for the payment (or the payment by agreement) of a sum of money, in lieu of the discharge of some other obligation ...' (*OED*). The amounts for these compositions appear to have been taken from Montesquieu 1949, Vol. II, pp.95–6.

[76] 'vassal' is del. and 'guest' is ins.

[77] 'solidi' is ins. The Roman coin known in Latin as the 'solidus' became in French the 'sou'. It was 1/20th of the libre (Latin) or livre (French).

[78] The following is written in pencil after question 15: 'The support of the clergy tended greatly to establish his power. 496.' It was presumably intended as part of the answer to question 15. The rest of the answer is written on the opposite recto.

[79] The Battle of Tolbiac (Latin: Tolbiacum; now, Zülpich near Euskirchen, in Germany) in 496.

The Gauls being zealous Catholics, and Clovis being the only catholic king among the Barbarians, he derived prodigious advantage from this conversion. The clergy had considerable power in Gaul before the conquest of Clovis, and of course as soon as he became Christian, their influence greatly contributed to [80] strengthen his authority, and establish it[81] on a firm foundation.

The Armoricans situated between the Seine and the Loire yielded to Clovis without resistance.

The Visigoths and Burgundians were Arians.[82]

16. How was France divided on the death of Clovis?

Austrasia, Orleans, Paris and Soissons

Thierry the eldest[83] had Austrasia, and Theodebert his son distinguished himself by his superior abilities. He was principally instrumental in the conquest of Burgundy, a very important addition to the monarchy which he divided with two of his uncles. He entered into a treaty with the Eastern Emperor to expel the Goths from Italy.

17. Who remained sole king of France after the second division among the sons of Clotaire; and what were the general consequences of these divisions?

Clotaire ii. Such a state of violence, and such weakness in the central government as to occasion great numbers of freemen to become [84] vassals and serfs, vassals by voluntary association for their security; and serfs from the continued exercise of the rights of conquest, by which the inhabitants of entire cities and districts became slaves.

It was [85] during these convulsions that seigneuries began to be formed. Opposite opinions of Montesquieu and Mably on the mode of their formation, and the right of administring* justice.

[86]

[80] 'establish his government and' is del. [81] 'his authority' is del. and 'it' is ins.

[82] i.e. followers of Arius of Alexandria (256–336) who denied the divinity of Christ.

[83] i.e. the eldest son of Clovis. After Clovis' death, his kingdom was divided between his four sons – Thierry (or Theuderic), Clodomir (or Chlodomer), Childebert and Clotaire (or Chlothar).

[84] 'serfs' is del. [85] 'probably' is del.

[86] At the foot of the page, in pencil, there is the following, perhaps incomplete, statement: 'If he had had the disposal of all the fiefs on the first conquest of Gaul, he would have been so'. It presumably refers to Clotaire ii, but its meaning is not obvious.

18. What was the reason according to Montesquieu that though at the commencement of the first race of French kings, there were every where great numbers of free men, both Franks and Romans, and the cities were filled with free citizens and burgesses; yet [87] at the beginning of the third race nothing was to be found but the Seigneur and his serfs?

At the beginning of the first race of French kings, there were every where vast numbers of freemen, both Franks and Roman provincials. At the beginning of the third race almost all the labourers on the land, and most of the inhabitants of the towns were serfs. At the beginning of the first race there was in the towns the same kind of administration as formerly among the Romans, a body of burgesses, a Senate and courts of judicature, while at the beginning of the third race there was only the seigneur and his serfs.

The causes of this great change were the constant wars and internal commotions[88] which took place in France during the interval; which by the usual exercise of the acknowledged laws of war among the Barbarians naturally produced such a crowd of slaves. L XXX CXI p55.[89]

Montesquieu thinks that servitude was more general in France than in other countries, and that this was one of the causes of[90] the difference of the French laws, and the laws of Italy and Spain respecting the rights of Seigneurs.

19. Under what Prince and on what occasion did the power of the Mayors of the Palace commence in France; and who were the most distinguished among them and on what account?

Clotaire ii, son of Chelperic*[91] & Fredegonda[92] on being left sole king of such [93] extensive [94] territories committed the government of the provinces of Austrasia and Burgundy to the mayors of the palace of those kingdoms.

The most celebrated of them were* Pepin d'Heristal*[95] who governed the kingdom with great vigour for 28 years at the end of the 7th and beginning of the 8th centuries.

[87] 'before' is del.

[88] 'wars and internal commotions' is first del. on verso, and then rewritten on the following recto.

[89] Montesquieu, *Esprit des Lois*, Book XXX, Ch.XI. [90] 'between' is del. and 'of' is ins.

[91] i.e. Chilpéric I (523–584), grandson of Clovis. [92] 'son of Chelperic* & Fredegonda' is ins.

[93] 'an' is del. [94] 'country' is del. [95] i.e. Héristal, or Herstal, near Liège.

[Lesson] 7

20. By whom and where was the Merovingian race excluded from the throne of France; and by what authority was the commencement of the new dynasty sanctioned? 752[96]

Charles Martel, his natural son,[97] who stopped the Saracen tide of conquest by a celebrated victory near Tours 733;[98] and his Son, Pepin the Short, who assumed the title as he had long possessed the power of king in 752,[99] and the act was sanctioned by the Pope. Zachary.[100]

Conc: The reason why the Salic Law obtained a complete superiority over the Roman Law in France was that it offered very superior advantages. This was not the case in Spain and the Roman Law there maintained its authority. Montesquieu ii 543.[101]

The Burgundian Laws were of the same nature and made no distinction between the Romans and Barbarians. All laws at first personal.[102]

LECTURE II

103

1. What was the state of the monarchy of the Visigoths in Spain at its earliest period; and when was it at its height?

It was early distinguished by the great power of the Clergy. Gibbon contrasts the conduct of the French clergy with that of the Spanish, and says that the former towards the end of the Merovengian* race had become fighting and hunting Barbarians; while the latter were cautious in their conduct, and being[104] more united among themselves,[105] were more respected by the public, and had the chief influence in all national councils. The vacancy of the throne

[96] '752' is in pencil.

[97] Charles Martel was the natural son of Pepin d'Heristal. Pepin the Short was the son of Charles Martel.

[98] '733' is ins. [99] 'in 752' is ins.

[100] Pope Zachary, or Zacharias (741–752).

[101] See Montesquieu 1949, Vol. II, Book XXVIII, Sect. 4: 'In what manner the Roman Law came to be lost in the Country subject to the Franks, and preserved in that subject to the Goths and Burgundians', pp.97–9.

[102] 'All laws at first personal' is ins.

[103] Written in pencil above the first question there are several indistinct words, followed by: 'Picture given by Russel* of lives & work. Different opinions of Gibbon & Montesquieu on the code of the Visigoths.'

[104] 'being' is ins.

[105] 'with each other' is del. and 'among themselves' is ins.

was supplied by the choice of the Bishops and Palatines. Gibbon VI, 376[106]

The Visigothic monarchy was perhaps the most powerful under Euric, the father of Alaric; but the monarchy of the Visigoths in Spain was at its height under Sirebert*[107] [at] the end of the 6th and during the[108] seventh centuries.

The power of the Clergy in Spain affected very much the Visigothic laws and ultimately[109] gave rise to the inquisition.

From the reign of Recared the first Catholic king to that of Witiza, the immediate predecessor of the unfortunate Roderic, 16 national Councils were held. Six Metropolitans[110] funded.

2. When and by whom was the Empire of the Visigoths in Spain put an end to, and what exception occurred to the general submission of the country?

By the Saracens, in the decisive battle of Xeres. 714.*[111] They are said to have been invited by Count Julian whose daughter Roderic had dishonoured. Mousa,[112] Viceroy of Africa under the Kalif Walid, came over to finish the conquest. The empire of the Saracens extended its conquests prodigiously under Walid. Pelagius of the blood royal retired to the mountains of Asturias, and there laid the foundations of the future Christian Mony[113] of Spain.

[Lesson] 8

3. On what occasion, and by whom, was an independent Saracen kingdom founded in Spain?

When the Khalifate passed from the house of Ommiady[114] to the Abassides,[115] Abdelrahman,*[116] a prince of the dispossessed family, escaped the general massacre, and founded an independent kingdom in Spain [117] The

[106] Edward Gibbon, *The History of the Decline and Fall of the Roman Empire*, first published in six volumes, 1776–88. The Malthus Library has a twelve-volume edition, 1783–90. On 17 April 1788 Malthus wrote to his father saying that he had been 'lately reading Gibbon's decline of the Roman Empire'. The comments in that letter suggest that Malthus' interest in the 'dark period' covered in these questions and answers was largely inspired by his reading of Gibbon. See Vol. I, p.53.

[107] i.e. Sigebert I (535–575), king of the Eastern Franks in Austrasia.

[108] 'beginning of' is del. and 'during the' is ins. [109] 'and ultimately' is ins.

[110] A 'metropolitan', in the ecclesiastical sense, is a 'bishop having the oversight of the bishops of a province; in the early church his see was in the metropolis of the province. In the West the term is now approximately co-extensive with *archbishop*; in the Greek church the metropolitan ranks above an archbishop and below a patriarch' (*OED*).

[111] 'Under' is del. The date of the battle of Xeres (now spelt Jerez) is given as 711 in *EB*.

[112] Musā ibn Nusayr (*EB*). [113] i.e. Monarchy. [114] The Umayyad (or Omayyad) dynasty (*EB*).

[115] The Abbāsids dynasty, founded by Abū al-'Abbās as-Saffah (*EB*).

[116] Abd ar-Rahmān I (*EB*); also spelt (by Malthus) Abdalrahman.

[117] 'fixing his residence at Cordova*' is del.

Ommiades were descended from Moavia,[118] the friend and relation of Othman, the third in succession to Mahomet. After the death of Othman, Ali the husband of Fatima succeded,* and after his assassination Moavia, a victorious general, seized the Khalifate from his son. Both the factions of Abbas the cousin of Mahomet, and of Ali the husband of Fatima, were oppressed and obliged to fly.

There were 14 princes of the house of Ommiyah and the house of Abbas succeded* in 750. 3 families contended for the Khalifate.

4. Where did Abderrahmen* fix his court and what was the character and policy of his reign?

757. His court was at Cordova,* and it was soon distinguished as[119] the seat of arts and magnificence. His policy was, without a persecution [120] of the christians, to give every possible encouragement [121] to their conversion by the distribution of honours and offices; and in this policy he was very successful.

It was the 3rd[122] and as Gibbon calls him the greatest Abdalrahman* that built the celebrated city palace and gardens of Zera[123] at the expence* of 3 millions sterling.

5. What was the state and character of the Ostrogothic kingdom of Italy, and by whom, and at what period was it put an end to?

The Ostrogoths in Italy under the celebrated Theodoric were distinguished by the mildness and humanity as well as the vigour and ability of their government. The Romans were allowed still to retain two thirds of their land and[124] possessions, and were governed by[125] their own[126] laws and their own[127] magistrates, the principal military employments only being reserved for the Goths. Italy was in a most flourishing state. Iron mines were opened in Dalmatia, a gold mine in Bruttium, and the Pontine marshes, and those of Spoleto were drained by private undertakers. A gallon of wine was sold for 3 farthings, and a

[118] Mu'āwiyah I or Moawiyah (*EB*). [119] 'became' is del. and 'was soon distinguished as' is ins.
[120] 'to give' is del. [121] 'by' is del. [122] 'Abdal' is del.
[123] The palace-city of Madmat-az-Zahrā, three miles from Cordova (Montgomery Watt 1977, p.77). Spelt 'Zehra' by Gibbon.
[124] 'their' is del. and 'two thirds of their land and' is ins. [125] 'were governed by' is ins.
[126] 'own' is ins. [127] 'own' is ins.

quarter of wheat for 5 shillings and sixpence. Great care was taken of the public buildings & a large sum allowd* for their repair. Gibbn* V.vii.35

It was put an end to by Belesarius*[128] and Narses in the 6th ceny under Justinian.[129]

The Burgundians possessed ⅔ of the land where they were settled.

Theodoric paid a kind of nominal allegiance to the Emperor Anastasius.

[Lesson] 9

6. By whom was the kingdom of the Lombards founded, what country did they possess and where was the seat of government?

By Alboin in 568. All the North of Italy [130] with Tuscany, and the Dukedoms of Tivoli, Spoleto, and Beneventum. The seat of government was Pavia.

The Lombards are said to have been invited by Narses in consequence of the affront he received from the Empress.

The Lombards were supposed to be Scandinavians and were first heard of in the times of Augustus and Trajan between the Elbe and the Oder. They were called[131] by Justinian [132] to take possession of the country between the Danube and the Alps which the Goths had evacuated, and to oppose the Gepidae.

7. How was that part of Italy which remained subject to the [133] Eastern Emperors governed during the existence of the kingdom of the Lombards?

By Exarchs[134] whose residence was at Ravenna. [135] Narses [136] was the first exarch and under him[137] a duke was appointed[138] to the government of each of the principal cities. Rome was thus[139] reduced to a city of the second rank. The Lombards continued the same kind of government.

128 i.e. Belisarius (c. 505–565). 129 From 'It was put' to 'Justinian.' is ins. 130 'from the Alps' is del.
131 'employed' is del. and 'called' is ins. 132 'under Narses in his wars with the Goths' is del.
133 'kingdom of the Lo' is del.
134 'Exarchate' is altered to 'Exarchs'. An exarch was 'Under Byzantine emperors, the governor of a distant province, as Africa or Italy; in the latter case with title "Exarch of Ravenna"' (*OED*).
135 'Rome was governed by a Duke dependent on the Exarchate.' is del. 136 'who' is del.
137 'and under him' is ins. and 'appointed' is del. 138 'was appointed' is ins.
139 'thus' is repeated.

8. By whom and when were written laws first given to the Lombards, and what was the character of the Lombard code?

By Rotharis*[140] in 643, about the middle of the 7th century. No ancient code of law[141] is more famous than that of the Lombards. It discovers strong traces of the feudal system, which is probably owing to its having been reduced to writing later than any other of the Barbarian codes. The Lombards had the advantage of receiving instruction both from the Gothic and Roman laws.

The Lombard laws on this account lasted a long while.

They are said to be in force even now in some parts of Italy. Ultimately yielded to Roman Law.

9. On what occasion was the first application made by the Pope to the French to become protectors of the Church, and what was the great object of the Pope in this application?[142]

On occasion of the severe edict against images by the Emperor Leo the Isaurian, and the advantage taken by Liutprand, king of the Lombards, of the discontent it occasioned, to seize Ravenna. Ravenna was however retaken by the Exarch, the Pope & the Venetians.[143]

The object of the Pope was to withdraw his allegiance from the Emperor of the East, without giving himself a master in so near a neighbour as the king of the Lombards. Gregory ii

[Lesson] 10

10. Through whose means and under what circumstances did the Popes first acquire temporal sovereignty?

Through the means of Pepin, the first king of France of the Carlovingian race, who in consequence of having undertaken the protection of the Catholic church, marched an army into Italy at the request of the Pope, saved Rome from the attacks of the Lombards under Astelphus, took the Exarchate, and presented it to the church.

Pope Zachary had formerly determined the question respecting the crown of France in favour of Pepin; and in this instance he appears to have been amply grateful to his successor Steven iii.[144]

[140] Rothari, king of the Lombards (636–652). [141] 'of law' is ins.

[142] Below this question, in pencil: 'Charles Martel'. [143] 'Ravenna ... Venetians.' is ins.

[144] 'iii' is ins. in pencil. There is some confusion as to whether the Steven (or Stephen) who in 752 succeeded Pope Zachary (or St Zacharias), pope from 741 to 752, should be named Steven II or Steven III. See Duffy 1997, p.295.

Pepin was the first of the French kings at whose elevation to the throne[145] the Jewish ceremony of consecration was introduced.

11. When was Britain evacuated by the Romans, and by what irruptions was it immediately infected?

Britain was ivacuated* in 420 by the Romans after they had been masters of the Southern and most fertile part of it above three centuries.

When the Roman troops were withdrawn they were soon attacked by the Scots and Picts. The Picts are[146] supposed to have been[147] painted Britons who had retired to the North on the conquest of the Southern part of the island by the Romans. [148] Controverted by Pinkerton[149] But supported in Chalmers Caledonia[150] (Bede) A people in the South of Norway were called ...[151]

12. Why were the Britons unable to defend themselves, and what people did they call to their assistance on the refusal of the Romans to send them succours?

Having been for so long a period entirely dependent for their defence on Roman legions, they were totally unused to arms. They called the Saxons to their assistance; by a regular Embassy[152] according to some,[153] but Gibbon is of opinion, that Vortigern only made use of the accidental arrival on a predatory incursion of [154] a few Saxon vessels and their crews.

[Lesson] 11

13. Who were the Saxon leaders that came to the assistance of the Britons, and what was the consequence of their interference?

Hengist* and Horsa, from Jutland in 449.[155] The natural consequence of their interference was, their taking advantage of the weakness of the Britons, to settle themselves in the fertile country which they had defended from the picts.

[145] 'coronation' is del. and 'elevation to the throne' is ins.

[146] 'have been sometimes' is del. and 'are' is ins. [147] 'to be' is del. and 'to have been' is ins.

[148] 'but they are now generally supposed to be of Scandinavian origins.' is del. and 'Controverted by ... (Bede)' is ins. See Bede ('The Venerable Bede') (673–735), *Ecclesiastical History of the English Nation.* A Latin edition (Antverpiæ, 1550) is held in the Malthus Library.

[149] John Pinkerton (1758–1826), *A Dissertation on the Origin and Progress of the Scythians or Goths*, 1787.

[150] George Chalmers (1742–1825), *Caledonia: or an Account of North Britain*, 3 vols., 1807–24.

[151] Word indistinct; possibly 'Peokti'.

[152] 'Embassy' appears to be used here in the sense of 'the sending of ambassadors' or 'the message delivered by an ambassador', rather than in the sense of 'the body of persons sent' or 'the official residence of the ambassador' (*OED*).

[153] 'to some' is ins. in pencil. [154] 'the Sa' is del. [155] 'in 449' is ins.

It is remarked however that Britain made a longer and more determined resistance[156] against their invaders than any other of the Roman provinces. This was probably owing to the mode in which they were attacked – in comparatively small numbers and by successive parties by sea, which gave an opportunity to the Britons to recover their martial habits, and contest every inch of ground. France, Spain and Italy were conquered by greater numbers and much more rapidly.

14. What was the nature of the revolution effected by the Saxons, and what kingdoms did they gradually establish?

They became masters of the country and introduced their own laws and manners, but it is by no means probable that they exterpated* the inhabitants, as some historians have intimated. It is not probable indeed that all were reduced to Slavery, but after every contest were left to enjoy the lands of which they were actually in possession. It is supposed [157] that in some parts a similar division to that adopted by the Burgundians may have taken place. But those Britons[158] who maintained their independence after one contest often became slaves in the next. The conquerors of course made use of those improvements in the country which had taken place under the Romans. In the course of [159] near a century seven kingdoms were established in the following order: Kent Sussex Essex Wessex Mercia East Anglia and Northumberland. Millar Vol I ch 3.

We know of no permission[160] to use the Roman Law. 9000 celtic words have been found by Mr Whitaker in the English language, a proof that the Britons were not exterpated.*[161]

[156] 'tha' is del. [157] 'indeed' is del. [158] 'Britons' is ins. [159] A second 'of' is del.

[160] 'permission' is here used in the sense of 'abandonment', i.e. they continued to use Roman law.

[161] Millar disputes the view that all the Britons either became captives or escaped to Armorica, adding that Mr Whitaker, 'an acute and industrious antiquary, ... has lately shown, I think in a satisfactory manner, that this extraordinary supposition is without any solid foundation' (p.45). Millar also states that in 'the language which grew up in Britain after the settlement of the Saxons ... a large proportion of the *British* and *Latin* tongues were incorporated with the Saxon'.

In *The History of Manchester*, Vol. II, 1775, John Whitaker stated that 'the English [language] retains to this day such a collection of Celtick* terms, as nothing but a collation of the languages could induce us to believe' and that 'there remains a large catalogue of three thousand British terms, discoverable even now in the English [language]' (p.238). In a section entitled 'A Specimen of an English-British Dictionary', he provided an 87-page account (pp.240–326) of the influence of British and Celtic words on the English language, for the first three letters of the alphabet.

In Vol. I of *The History of Manchester*, 1771, Whitaker argued: 'It is one of the most singular events in the Roman annals, and reflects a peculiar honour upon the bravery of the Britons, that in the long course of more than three centuries the Romans could never make an entire conquest of the island. This was the only country in the world in which the Romans reduced the greatest part of the natives, and yet were for ever beat off by the small remainder of them' (p.417).

[Lesson] 12

15. Whither did many of the Britons retire and to what part of France did they give a name?

The Britons maintained their independance* in the Western parts of the island, and erected 4 principalities – Cornwall, South Wales, North Wales and Cumberland. Millar.

Many retired to[162] that part of France formerly called Armorica, and gave it the name of Britanny.

16. By whom and at what period were the seven Saxon kingdoms united?

By Egbert king of Wessex, or of the West Saxons, in 827. Different princes had occasionally been placed at the head of the confederacy, when any of the 7 kingdoms acted in concert against the Britons or foreign invaders.[163] The most powerful of the states were Wessex, Mercia and Northumberland, to which the rest were gradually reduced into a kind of subordination, till at length they were all brought under subjection by Egbert, partly from his superior bravery and accomplishments (having been brought up in the court of Charlemagne) and partly from the accidental circumstance of the failure of the linear heirs in the other states.

Edward the Elder first took the title of Rex Anglorium* on his coins.

17. When was Christianity first introduced among the Saxons, and what character did it assume?

By Gregory the great at the end of the 6th century, who sent over the monk A[u]gustine with 40 assistants. Bertha the wife of Ethelbert, king of Kent, and daughter of a king of the Franks, being a christian made an open profession of her religion; and this circumstance it is said suggested to Gregory the idea of converting the Saxons; but there seems to be no doubt that [164] the Xtian religion had continued to be exercised by the Britons after the Saxon conquest, and probably some of the Saxons had adopted the religion of the people they had conquered. The mission of Augustine cannot be considered as a new plantation of the gospel. The character it assumed was that of the grossest superstition, and of the most abject obedience to the See of Rome.

[162] 'Ar' is del. [163] 'against the Britons or foreign invaders' is ins. [164] 'Xtianity' is del.

[Lesson] 13

18. In what respects[165] did the government of the Saxons in England differ from that of the other German nations settled in different parts of Europe? Millar Vol I ch 4.

Chiefly in the slowness of the rise of the feudal system in England; occasioned probably by the smallness of the kingdoms first established,[166] and the consequent strength of the central government compared with the extent of territory.

19. What was the nature of the Saxon Wittenagemote*[167] and who[168] were its constituent[169] members [170]? Millar Vol 1 ch 7

The Saxon Wittanagemote,* was the general assembly of the nation possessing the supreme legislative power, and a great part of the executive power. It provided for the defence of the state, [171] determined the principal military operations, and the question of peace or war.[172] It took cognisance of all abuses that had been committed in the government and provided the proper remedies. It directed and controlled the exercise of the Royal prerogative, regulated the coinage and superintended in some sort the demesne lands of the crown. It had authority in the government of the church as well as state, sanctioned the establishment of monasteries, called the sovereign to account for the abuses of his administration, and was at length erected into the supreme tribunal of Justice.

The members are supposed to have been all the[173] allodial proprietors, though many authors have supposed that 40 hides[174] of land were necessary as a qualification; but this seems by no means probable in the early periods of the Saxon government, whatever[175] might be the case[176] afterwards.

The term [177] Wite in its original signification means[178] a man of valour

[165] 'In what respects' is repeated, and the first version is del. [166] Cf. Millar, pp.67–8.

[167] The Witenagemot was the 'assembly of the Witan, the national council of Anglo-Saxon times' (*OED*). Malthus' spelling of 'Wittenagemote' is as in Millar, p.297.

[168] 'of whom' is del. and 'who' is ins. [169] 'constituent' is ins. [170] 'composed' is del.

[171] 'and' is del. [172] ', as the supreme court of justice' is del. [173] 'the' is ins.

[174] A 'hide' was a 'measure of land in old English times ... varying in extent with the nature of the ground, etc.: primarily, the amount considered adequate for the support of one free family with its dependants; at an early date defined as being as much land as could be tilled with one plough in a year. ... The question of the extent of the *hide* has been much controverted. The general conclusion appears to be that it was normally equal to 120 acres; but the size of the acre itself varied' (*OED*). See Millar, p.85.

[175] 'however it' is del. and 'whatever' is ins. [176] 'the case' is ins. [177] 'white' is del.

[178] 'signifies in Saxon' is del. and 'in its original signification means' is ins.

or military prowess.[179] All the persons who held lands in their own right were considered as Warriors and nobles.

20. Into what orders of men were the Saxons divided? Millar Vol 1 ch 5.

Millar divides them into the Thanes or nobles; the Clergy; and the ceorls.[180] He is of opinion that the ceorls were originally slaves who cultivated the outland of the nobles, and became gradually independent. It is not indeed probable that any of the free Saxon conquerors should so soon have lost their rank and warlike habits, and betaken themselves exclusively to agriculture. Possibly many of the remaining Britons might become ceorls. The slaves were very numerous from the constant wars and the multitude of captives taken.

21. What was the nature of the tythings,* hundreds and counties into which the Anglosaxon* kingdoms were divided? Millar Vol i.c 6.

The tythings* were divisions, not merely of ten families as some have supposed, but of villages[181] with a tything* man or bors holder[182] at their head, to lead the inhabitants to war, and with the assistance of the principal heads of families, to determine disputes in peace. The hundred was a larger division of the same kind containing about ten[183] villages and its commanding officer was a Centeninus*[184] or hundreder. The members of the different hundreds were also associated for their common defence and fell under the direction of a greater officer called a heretoch,[185] which in the Saxon language is synonimous* with that of Duke. These districts were called shires and at a later period of the Anglo Saxon government the officer who presided over them seems to have changed his title for that of *earl* or *alderman*.[186] From the decision of the tithing there lay

[179] *OED* defines 'wite' as 'a wise man, sage; a councillor; one of the witan'. Malthus' definition of 'wite' is from Millar, p.138: 'The term wite signifies, primarily, a man of valour, or military prowess'. Millar adds that, 'in a rude age', military skill is equated with wisdom and high rank.

[180] A 'ceorl' or 'churl' in Old English times was 'a freeman of the lowest class opposed on one side to a thane or nobleman, on the other to the servile classes'. The three degrees of freemen were: earl, thane and churl (*OED*).

[181] 'and their village' is del.

[182] The Anglo-Saxons divided their villages into ten wards or tithings. A tithingman or borsholder (also: bosholder) was the head man of a tithing (Millar, p.113). Millar also uses the term 'decennary' ('decennaries') to refer to tithing (tithings), and the term 'decanus' to refer to the head man of a tithing. Malthus' statement 'not merely of ten families as some have supposed' is probably a reference to Millar's argument on pp.118–19 where he doubts the view that tithings were groups of ten families and hundreds were groups of one hundred families.

[183] 'a hundred' is del. and 'ten' is ins.

[184] The term used by Millar was 'centenarius' (Book I, Chapter VI, p.117 in the 1787 edition).

[185] A heretoch, or heretoga, was 'the leader of an army; the commander of the militia of a shire or district' (*OED*).

[186] From 'The members of the different hundreds' to 'for that of *earl* or *alderman*' is taken almost verbatim from Millar, p.117.

an appeal to the hundred and the sentences of this latter tribunal were revised[187] in the greater meetings of the Shire.[188]

According to Millar the assessors taken to assist the president, were[189] the origin of Juries.[190] These divisions took place before the time of Alfred, and the[191] decencirs and centencirs were known in France and other countries.

Montesquieu says that hundreds were established in France by Clotaire and Childebert in order to make each district answerable for the robberies committed in it. Liv. XXX c 17.

The divisions into counties existed long before Alfred.

Not equal evidence as to the antiquity of the minor divisions. Hundreds I think are first mentioned in a[192] law of Edgar and tithings in one of Canute: Hallam

Doubt whether the Tithingman ever possessed any Judicial magistracy. Hallam

22. What was the character of the criminal laws of the Anglo saxons and the nature of their proofs? Henry Vol iii ch.3. sectn 3.

The character of the criminal laws of the Anglo Saxons like those of most Barbarians was certainly that of great levity; and their object was evidently that of compensation to the offended person or his friends.[193] The prevention of crimes, which is the great object of modern laws does not seem to have been much in their contemplation. The proofs admitted were characteristic of their total want of power to obtain and to judge of proper evidence. Ordeal, water, Iron.[194] According to Montesquieu, it was in those countries the laws of which allowed an accused person to clear himself by compurgators[195] that duels were permitted, on account of the frequency of false oaths. The Salic law did not at first admit the judicial combat, [196] because compurgators were not allowed. But afterwards from the difficulty of proofs, it was found necessary to admit it – Burgundian code.

[187] 'by' is del.

[188] 'From the decision ... meetings of the Shire' is taken almost verbatim from Millar, p.123.

[189] 'became' is del. and 'were' is ins. [190] See Millar, p.123. [191] 'the' is ins.

[192] 'a' is repeated. 'Hallam' is presumably a reference to Henry Hallam, *View of the State of Europe during the Middle Ages*, 1818. A copy is in the Malthus Library at Jesus College. The date of this work indicates that Malthus' interest in early European history was active at a time when his published works suggest that his dominant interest was political economy.

[193] 'They seemed' is del. [194] 'Ordeal, water, Iron.' is ins.

[195] A term used by modern historians for 'the "oath-helpers" whom a person on trial was allowed to call in to swear that, to their belief, as neighbours of the accused and acquainted with his character, he was speaking truth in making oath of his innocence' (*OED*).

[196] 'but it was afterwards' is del.

LECTURE III

[Lesson] 14

1. What was the state of Germany at the time of the accession of Charlemagne to the crown of France?

Possessed by a number of free and independent nations who had never been entirely subdued by the Romans, and were still pagans. These different nations were occasionally united [197] for purposes of conquest or defence under one of their most distinguished princes; and at the time we are speaking of[198] Witikand*[199] was their great leader, and maintained[200] for a considerable time a very obstinate contest with Charlemagne, though he was at length conquered and converted to christianity.

It is the opinion of the celebrated Leibnitz* that these german princes maintained their independence notwithstanding the conquest of Charlemagne, and became the Dukes and counts of the future Empire. Butler.[201]

The wars of Charlemagne with the Saxons lasted thirty years.

2. By whom, and on what occasion was the kingdom of the Lombards, destroyed and how long had it lasted?

By Charlemagne, in 774, on occasion of the application of Pope Adrian i*[202] to deliver him from the arms of Desiderius, king of the Lombards, who had ravaged the papal territories, and threatened Rome.[203] The kingdom had lasted 206 years.

Charlemagne had been further incensed against Desiderius on account of his having[204] encouraged his nephews, and attempted to disturb the peace of his kingdom.

3. What was the nature of the government which Charlemagne established in Italy; and how did the title of Marquis originate?

He continued the government nearly on the same footing as it was under the Lombards, only obliging the Dukes and Counts to swear that they would be faithful[205] to him as a vassal to his[206] Lord and Sovereign. This kind of oath[207] it is supposed was first introduced by Charles Martel, and might be

[197] '[under] under' is del. [198] 'of Charlemagne' is del. and 'we are speaking of' is ins.
[199] i.e. Widukind. [200] 'continued' is del. and 'maintained' is ins.
[201] Possibly, Charles Butler, *The Philological and Biographical Works of Charles Butler*, 5 vols., 1817. Vol. II, *German Empire*. The Malthus Library has Butler's *Horæ Biblicæ*, 2nd edn, vol. 2, 1807.
[202] Hadrian I, pope 772–795. [203] 'who had ravaged ... Rome.' is ins. [204] 'having' is ins.
[205] 'fealty' is del. and 'that they would be faithful' is ins.
[206] 'their' is del. and 'a vassal to his' is ins. [207] 'had' is del.

considered as the commencement of the proper feudal obligation.[208] The title of Marquis originated from the boundaries being called marches, and those who had the care of them, Counts of the marches or marquisses. Charlemagne added in Italy the order of ecclesiastics to that of nobles, which among the Lombards had been the sole. R.

[Lesson] 15

4. [209] When and by what means were the Saxons in Germany[210] converted to Christianity?

Towards the end of the 8th century; principally by the force of the arms of Charlemagne. One of his professed objects in his wars with the Saxons was to convert them to christianity[211] and perhaps the greatest blot in his character was the cruelty that he exercised in pursuit of this object. 4500 saxons were once massacred in cold blood after an unsuccessful revolt, because they would not deliver up their leader.[212] Witikind* however was at last obliged to submit, and he converted. He remained ever after faithful. R.

He obliged the Saxons under pain of death to receive Baptism, and condemned to the severest punishments the breakers of lent. R.

5. What was the nature of the armies of Charlemagne?

The free men were collected and[213] led by the Counts, [214] and the vassals by their particular lords, whether Leudes[215] or Ecclesiastics, though by a concession of Chalemagne* the Bishops and Clergy were exempted from the obligation of leading their vassals themselves, and this was generally done by officers called avoués of the church. Centaines.[216]

Every free man who had four mansi of land was obliged to attend in person and those who had less[217] united together and sent a man between them, one[218] for every 4 mansi.

The king himself probably led the leudes, and sometimes selected

[208] Malthus added a footnote at this point: 'The word vassal before was only applied to domestic servants'.

[209] 'What was one of Charlemagne's principal objects in his wars with [the] Saxons' is del.

[210] 'in Germany' is ins. [211] 'to christianity' is ins.

[212] 'leader' is ins. [213] 'collected and' is ins. [214] 'and Dukes' is del.

[215] Leude: 'Chez les germains et les Francs, Grand vassal attaché à la personne du chef, du roi' (Robert 1970).

[216] At the time of Charlemagne, a 'centaine' was a territorial division of a county ('comté') administered by a centenier, from the Latin 'centenarius'. In the Roman empire a centenarius (or centurian) was an officer in charge of a hundred men (*Nouveau Larousse Illustré*, Vol. II, p.609).

[217] 'clubbed to' is del. [218] 'between them, one' is ins.

one of the leudes to lead the vassals of the church. Army dissolved in winter. Montesquieu Liv xxx c17. A mansus was about 12 acres.

3 sorts of soldiery. The vassals and armies; vassals of the king, the vassals of the clergy, and the free men led by the Counts. Dispersed after campaign.

6. On what occasion did some of the Northern provinces of Spain become subject to Charlemagne?[219]

On the application of some Moorish governors under Abdelrahmen,* who offered to acknowledge Charlemagne as their sovereign. He took Pampeluna*[220] and Saragossa and established the Moorish governors under his protection. Roland[221]

[Lesson] 16

7. What famous project did Charlemagne attempt which indicated his [222] **attention to the interests of commerce?**

A project of uniting the Danube and the Rhine, which would have opened a communication between the German ocean and the Black sea. The project failed in the execution on account of the low state of the arts, but the conception proves his great attention to the interests of commerce.

8. [223] **What proofs are recorded of Charlemagnes love of letters? And who were the most distinguished literary characters at his court?**[224]

[225]

His collection of the old French poems and historical ballads with a view to illustrate the history of France. His general establishment of schools in different part[s] of the kingdom, and his care to examine frequently whether the pupils had been well taught. His frequent correspondence with his bishops on the subject of Theology, morals, history[226] and education, and his exertions to make them acquire proper information[227] by proposing various questions to them. His general encouragement[228] of learned men from all quarters. Alcuin[229]

[219] Below this question, in pencil: 'Gbn' [? Gibbon]. [220] i.e. Pamplona.

[221] Presumably, *La Chanson de Roland*, considered by some scholars to have been written about 1100. It contains an account of Charlemagne's Spanish campaign and his capture of Saragossa in 778.

[222] 'commercial' is del. [223] 'In what man' is del.

[224] 'was at the head of his Royal Academy' is del. and 'were ... court' is ins.

[225] 'How did Charlemagne conduct himself as protector of the Church, and what part did he take in the question relating to the worship of images?' is del.

[226] 'history' is ins. [227] 'do their duty' is del. and 'acquire proper information' is ins. [228] 'from' is del.

[229] Alcuin, born about 735 in England, in Northumbria; appointed by Charlemagne master of the palace school at Aachen in 782; died 804 (*New Catholic Encyclopedia*, 1967, Vol. I, pp.279–80).

from England, Clement[230] from Ireland, and Eigenhard*[231] from Germany who wrote his life, were greatly distinguished at his court.

[Lesson 17][232]

9. When and on what occasion was Charlemagne crowned Emperor of the West, and what part of Italy and its dependencies[233] still remained under the dominion of the Greeks[234] when the limits of the two Empires were settled? R.

[235] Pope Leo III had been accused and attacked in the public streets by two of the relations of the late Pope.[236] He escaped to France and [237] applied to Charlemagne for assistance, who sent him back properly attended, and afterwards came to Rome himself, where having heard and [in] a manner tryed* the accusation[238] and acquitted the Pope, he was on Xmas day while saying mass hailed by the Pope as Augustus and[239] Emperor of the Romans, and was afterwards regularly invested with the Imperial mantle, and received all the honours which had been usually paid to the Roman Emperors. This took place in the year 800.

Calabria, Cicily,* the Coast of Naples,[240] and Venice were to continue under the dominion of the Greek Emperor.

Commencement of modern history according to some.[241]

10. By what formidable invasion was France threatened towards the latter end of the reign of Charlemagne, and how did it terminate?

By an invasion of the Normans, or North men under Godfrey, who had made a descent in Friesland with such an army as even[242] to threaten [243] the safety of Charlemagne's Empire. The two armies were preparing for a decisive battle when the event was determined by the death[244] of Godfrey who was assassinated by one of his Kinsmen. The Normans [had] been for some time harassing the coasts of France, and Charlemagne had been obliged to create a

[230] Clement of Ireland, saint; born in Ireland about the middle of the eighth century; master of the palace school under Charlemagne, succeeding Alcuin; died on the Continent after 818 (*New Catholic Encyclopedia*, Vol. III, pp.944–5).

[231] Einhard or Eginhard (770? – 840?), a Frankish noble, brought by Charlemagne to France (*OCEL*).

[232] Numbered '16' in MS. [233] 'and its dependencies' is ins. [234] 'Greek Empire' is altered to 'Greeks'.

[235] 'After hearing, and in a manner trying an accusation against' is del.

[236] 'of the late Pope' is ins. Pope Leo III (796–816) succeeded Pope Hadrian I (772–795).

[237] 'escaped to France and' is ins. [238] At this point the reader is directed to a nonexistent footnote.

[239] 'Augustus and' is ins. [240] 'Dalmatia' is del. in pencil. [241] This phrase is in pencil.

[242] 'even' is ins. [243] 'even' is del. [244] 'assassination' is del. and 'death' is ins.

powerful marine to repel their ravages. He was heard to declare that if it was so difficult for him in the [245] plenitude of his power to repress their incursions, what would it be for his descendants.

Some of these Normans are supposed with some probability to have been Saxons, who had retired to the North from the conquests of Charlemagne.[246]

11. [247] Where was[248] the Legislative power of the French Monarchy [249] during the reign of Charlemagne, and what was the nature of the national council and how often did it meet?[250]

The genuine[251] national assemblies of France or champ's* de Mar's*[252] according to their original constitution had grown[253] entirely into disuse under the latter princes of the Merovingian race. They were restored in part by Pepin who regularly [254] convoked the Bishops, Abbots and principal nobility once a year in May. But it was left to Charlemagne to give them nearly their original constitution, and allow[255] them to exercise the supreme legislative power. A national council[256] was convoked twice a year. That which met in May consisted besides the clergy and nobility[257] of 12 representatives from each county chosen from the class of Rackenbourghs[258] or from the principal citizens, and accompanied by the Avoués[259] of the church, who were at that time not noble. 3 chambers sometimes united, sometimes separated. Mably takes principally from Hincmar.[260]

The assembly that met in Autumn consisted only of those among the clergy and nobility who were most experienced in public affairs.

There is considerable difficulty in distinguishing those capitularies which were really laws of the realm and enacted by the supreme legislative power, and those which were merely of the nature of Royal proclamations, though they were generally obeyed as laws. Mably Liv ii ch2.

[245] 'full' is del. [246] A question mark occurs here in MS.

[247] 'How long did the reign of Charlemagne last, what was the extent of his Empire and [what improvements] in what manner did he intervene in the French Government' is del. and 'In what part of government' is written over the deletion in pencil.

[248] 'did' is del. and 'was' is ins. [249] 'reside' is del.

[250] Below this question, in pencil: 'Progress of the feudal system suspended'.

[251] 'original and proper' is del. and 'genuine' is ins.

[252] Champ de Mars, from the Latin 'campus martius', a field outside the gates of Rome where addresses to the army, army exercises and manoeuvres, and assemblies of citizens took place; from Mars, the god of war (AT).

[253] 'almost' is del. [254] 'called' is del. [255] 'allowing' is altered to 'allow'. [256] 'conv' is del.

[257] 'besides the clergy and nobility' is ins.

[258] The function of the rackenbourghs was to advise on matters of law and on the appropriate method of proof, and to fix the amount of the composition.

[259] The 'avoués', from the Latin 'advocatus', were ministerial officers who had the right to represent plaintiffs in courts of law.

[260] Presumably, Hincmar (c. 806–882), archbishop of Reims, *Opusculum LV capitulorum* (*A Brief Tract of 55 Chapters*) (*EB*).

12. What improvement did Charlemagne introduce in the administration of Justice throughout his kingdom? [261] **Mably Liv ii ch2**

He divided his kingdom into different legations or districts each consisting of many counties, and instead of putting a Duke at their head as formerly, he confided them to the superintandence* of 3 or 4 officers chosen among the prelates and nobles, called envoyés royaux, Missi Dominici,[262] royal commissioners, who were obliged to visit their legations regularly every three months. Their office was to hold assizes, and in an assembly called by them of the Bishops, counts, Seigneurs, centencirs, rackenbourghs &c: to consult on all the affairs of the province, to hear appeals, review the conduct of magistrates, punish the guilty, provide proper remedies for abuses and make a general report of the state of the province to the prince.

[Lesson 18][263]

13. What laws gradually superseded in France the use of the Salic and Ripuarian codes? Montesquieu Liv XXVIII ch 9

The Salic and Ripuarian laws were gradually superseded by the capitularies which were published by the princes of the first and second race with the sanction of their councils[264] of Bishops and nobles. During the gradual rise of the feudal system, the original and simple laws of the Franks required of course many modifications and additions which they received in the capitularies;[265] and afterwards when the feudal system was completely established, even these capitularies fell into disuse, and the whole of the South of France[266] was governed by what was called customary law.

Capitulary is a generic term and signifies anything that is written in chapters.

14. What were the principal sources of the revenues of Charlemagne? Montesquieu Liv XXX ch 13

The principal sources of the Revenues of Charlemagne were, first, his domains which were considerable and which he cultivated with great care, giving orders that even the eggs and garden stuff of his farms which were not all consumed should be regularly sold. Secondly, the freda or that part of the fines of

261 'What were the principal sources of the Revenues of Charlemagne?' is del.

262 'Missi Dominici' is ins. They were 'Agents créés par Charlemagne, qui allaient deux par deux, un clerc et un laïc, pour inspecter les provinces' (*Petit Larousse*).

263 Numbered '17' in MS.

264 'in assemblies' is altered to 'with the sanction of their councils'.

265 'which they received in the capitularies' is ins.

266 'country by' is del. and 'of the South of France' is ins.

delinquents which was awarded to the Prince amounting in general to about one third or ¼. Sometimes these were paid to the counts.[267] And thirdly, the presents which he regularly received from his nobles at the autumnal meeting.

[Lesson 19][268]

15. In what money were accounts kept during the reign of Charlemagne; and what was the value of the principal coins? Millot[269]

In livres, sous, and deniers. The livre in silver weighed a pound troy. The sous* or solidus was a 20th part of the pound, and worth about 3 shillings sterling. The golden sous* or solidus in which most of the fines were estimated was 1/75 part of a pound of gold, but as it was mixed with nearly a third of alloy, it has been calculated by some as only worth 6 shillings. Gibbon says about ten, which I should think nearer the truth. The Denier or Denarius was 1/12 of a Sous* or Solidus and[270] worth about 3[271] pence.

Millot says that the quantity of specie in circulation has been calculated at 2 times less than at present.

It appears from the capitulari[e]s that[272] a Denier or denarius purchased 24 loaves of white bread, and Voltaire is of opinion that there was a pound of bread in each. Interest 40 per cent. Fine for stealing milch cow 35 s. Horse 35. War horse 60

16. How long did Charlemagne reign and where was his principal residence?

Charlemagne reigned 47 years, and died in 814. He kept his court principally at Aix la Chapelle, where he was afterwards buried.

17. Who succeeded to the throne of Charlemagne and to what causes were the disorders in the kingdom which followed principally to be attributed?

He was succeeded by Louis the 1st the Debonnaire.[273] The causes of the disorders which followed were principally [274] the weak and superstitious

[267] 'or ¼' and 'Sometimes these were paid to the counts.' are ins. According to *The Cambridge Illustrated History of the Middle Ages*, Vol. I, p.431, the freda amounted to two-thirds of the legal fine.

[268] Numbered '18' in MS.

[269] Claude François Xavier Millot, *Elémens d'histoire générale*, 11 vols., Paris, 1772–1811. The Malthus Library has *Elements of General History*, transl., Pt. I, *Ancient History*, 2 vols., London, 1778. Millot also wrote *Elémens d'histoire d'Angleterre*, 3 vols., Paris, 1769 and *Elémens d'histoire de France*, 3 vols., Paris, 1770.

[270] 'is supposed to have been' is del. and 'was 1/12 of a Sous or Solidus and' is ins.

[271] '[a penny] a farthing or two' is del. and '3' is ins. [272] 'It appears from the capitulari[e]s that' is ins.

[273] i.e. Louis the Pious (778–840), Emperor 814. [274] 'owing to' is del.

character of Louis, and[275] the division of his kingdom [276] among his sons, [277] which afterwards occasioned so many civil wars.

The vigour of the first [278] Carlovingian Princes had checked the progress of the[279] feudal system, and restored the legitimate power of the crown which had been falling fast to decay under the Merovingian race;[280] but the reigns of Pepin and Charlemagne had not been sufficiently long to fix the government on its new foundations; and on the accession of a weak prince, it began immediately[281] to relapse into the same course, which had been for a time interrupted.

18. On what occasion was the famous battle of Fontenai*[282] fought and what was its result? Montesquieu Liv XXXI ch 25.

On occasion of the attempt of Lothaire* to make himself master of the whole Empire after his fathers death, regardless of the rights of his brothers Louis and Charles. The result of the battle was a victory on the part of Louis and Charles; but 200,000 men[283] fell on the spot, a loss which has been considered by some historians as the cause of the sudden weakness of the monarchy. The loss of 200,000 men could not probably produce such an effect; but as this loss gave rise to the regulations which afterwards took place at Messen,*[284] it may be said greatly to have impaired the strength of the state.

[Lesson 20][285]

19. What association did the three Sons of Louis le debonnaire enter into at Messen,* and what regulations did they agree to adopt which tended to weaken the power of their crowns? ibid

To prevent another civil war which was about to take place, the three brothers entered in an association, in which the complete independence of each division of the Empire was established; and they agreed at the same time that the Crown Vassals should no longer be obliged to follow the king except in general wars or foreign invasions, and that each free man should be [286] at liberty to choose [287] whether he would be the vassal of the king or a subject.

[275] 'to' is del. [276] 'which he made' is del. [277] 'a division' is del. [278] 'of the' is del.
[279] 'the' is ins. [280] 'race' is ins. [281] 'rapidly' is del. and 'immediately' is ins.
[282] i.e. the battle of Fontenoy in 841 in which Lothair was defeated by his brothers, Charles II (the Bald) and Louis II (the German).
[283] 'were' is del.
[284] 'Messin' was the name of an area around Metz. The partition agreed upon by the sons of Louis le Debonnaire (viz. Louis II the German, Charles II the Bald and Lothair I) is known as the Treaty of Verdun (843). Metz is about 25 miles east of Verdun.
[285] Numbered '19' in MS. [286] 'obliged' is del. [287] 'his' is del.

These regulations necessarily gave great independence to the Crown Vassals and nobles, and weakened the civil government.

The confusion of the state at this time made it necessary for every free man of moderate property to choose a protector.

20. What pope first began to exercise that extensive power which afterwards became so formidable under Gregory 7th, & what claims did he assert? 863

Nicholas i. He[288] deposed the Bishops of Treves and Cologne who in a council at Mentz[289] had[290] confirmed the divorce of Lothaire* king of Lorraine and obliged Lothaire* to take his wife again.[291] He asserted a general dominion over the French clergy by reestablishing a bishop who had be[en] deposed, by a provincial council;[292] and received appeals from all ecclesiastics who were dissatisfied with their bishops. He gave orders for the succession to the kingdom of Provence, and spoke of it as held in virtue of the confirmation of the holy see &c. The Bishops of Treves and Cologne accused him of making himself Emperor of the world.

[21][293] When did the offices of Counts and Dukes in France become hereditary, and what effect did this change produce in the government? 877. Mably Liv ii ch 5.

In the reign of Charles the bald;[294] who having no more [295] benefices to give his greedy courtiers, converted the offices of Dukes and Counts into fiefs. This was the last great step in the progress[296] of the feudal system, and the commencement of the regular feudal government. It was at this time that the inhabitants of the towns lost all their remaining liberty, the counts now beginning to oppress them in the same manner as the [297] people in the country were oppressed under the [298] different seigneuries.

The country was after this divided into a number of small principalities each possessing the full rights of sovereignty, and acknowledging no more than a nominal dependance* on the king.

[288] 'who' is del. and 'He' is ins. [289] i.e. Metz. [290] 'had' is ins.
[291] 'and obliged Lothaire* to take his wife again' is ins. [292] 'by a provincial council' is ins.
[293] Numbered '20' in MS. The number '21' is added in pencil alongside '20', presumably after the error was realised.
[294] 'end of the 9th cent^{y}' is del. [295] 'fiefs' is del. [296] 'in the progress' is ins. [297] 'diff' is del.
[298] 'seigneuries' is del.

[22][299] What was the nature of the Norman irruptions and when and in what manner did they establish themselves in France?

The Norman irruptions were made by sea in light vessels, which sailed up the rivers and penetrated into almost [every] quarter. They laid waste the coasts, and marked their steps with blood & fire. If they any where met with too formidable an opposition they suddenly withdrew, and returned again with new forces. Under Louis the Debonnaire they spread a great alarm in France, and under Charles the bald [300] committed the most dreadful ravages.

Twice they pillaged Rouen, surprised and burnt Paris in 845, and[301] laid waste Aquitaine with fire and sword. Under Charles the fat the siege of Paris by the Normans, and its defence by Eudes, Count of Paris, have been highly celebrated. The siege lasted two years, and the enemy was at last bribed by Charles the fat to retire, and was allowed to march into Burgundy to wait for the payment of the money.

Under Charles the Simple France was again invaded by another body of Normans headed by Rollo who made himself so formidable that[302] Charles offered him his daughter in marriage, and a settlement in Normandy and Britanny,* on condition of his becoming a christian, and acknowledging the king of France as his feudal superior. This happened in 912, and was the era of the regular establishment of the Normans in France. R.

The Scandinavians are supposed to have emigrated from the country near the sea of Azoff* under their leader Odin at the time of the conquests of Pompey over Mithradates.* Odin, or Woden as called by the Saxons, established several of his sons in different parts of the North,* and reigned himself in Denmark and Sweden. He may be considered as the Mahomet of the North.

[303]Russia, Saxony and Westfalia. Most of the Saxon princes boasted of their descent from Odin.

L[ECTURE] IV

1. By what irruptions was the kingdom of Egbert disturbed after the reduction of the Heptarchy and with what success did he oppose them? Charmouth & Hengerdown*[304]

By the irruptions of the Danes, or Normans as they were called in France. They made no difference between the French and English kingdoms, and became the terror not only of all the coasts of the two countries, but of

[299] Numbered '21' in MS. [300] '[committed the mo] and Charles the fat' is del.
[301] 'and' is ins. [302] 'that' is repeated. [303] These two lines were in a footnote in MS.
[304] 'Charmouth & Hengerdown' is in pencil. 'Hengerdown' is presumably Hemerdon in Devonshire.

the inland provinces, into which they penetrated by means of their light barks, which sailed up the rivers.

[305] Soon after the union of the Heptarchy Egbert was attacked by these pirates, and opposed them with success in two bloody battles, one at Charmouth in Dorsetshire, and the other at Hengerdown* in Devonshire. In the latter they had united with the Britons of Cornwel,* but were totally defeated.

The first appearance of the Normans in England was in 787 during the Heptarchy when Bathric*[306] reigned in Wessex.

[Lesson] 21[307]

2. When, and under what Prince was the important grant of tithes first made to the English Clergy?[308]

Under Ethelwolf,*[309] the son of Egbert, who it is said had been originally intended for the church, and, who, when he came to the throne did not forget those who were to have been his fellow labourers. The property of the church [310] arising from the grants of kings and other piously disposed persons, had suffered much from the ravages of the Danes; and it was in part to recompence* them for their losses, that this important gift[311] was made, for which the clergy were obliged to celebrate additional masses &c.

It is supposed that the tenth of everything as the proportion settled by the Levitical law had very early been claimed[312] by the ministers of religion in all the different countries of Europe; but it required a long time and many laws to make the claim effectual. It is a matter of doubt whether a legal grant of tithes was made by Charlemagne, or whether he only encouraged contributions of this kind. Great battle of Ockley[313] against the Danes under Ethelwolf.*

3. How many princes intervened between Egbert and Alfred, and in what state was the kingdom when it came to the latter?

Four. Ethelwolf* and his three elder[314] sons: none of them princes of great vigour and ability so that the country was continually exposed to the ravages of the Danes and[315] the churches and monasteries in particular[316] had

[305] 'They came' is del. [306] i.e. Brihtric.

[307] This '21' re-establishes the correct sequence of lesson numbers; the previous lesson was incorrectly numbered '19', instead of '20'. But the correct sequence of lesson numbers is broken again in the next lesson, which is also numbered 21 (in error).

[308] 'about middle of 9th century' is added in another hand. [309] i.e. Ethelwulf (d. 858).

[310] 'had suffered much' is del. [311] 'grant' is del. and 'gift' is ins. [312] 'claimed' is ins.

[313] Aclea (Surrey). [314] 'eldest' is del. and 'elder' ins.

[315] 'and most particularly' is del. and 'was continually exposed to the ravages of the Danes and' is ins.

[316] 'in particular' is ins.

suffered most[317] dreadfully. [318] On the death of Ethered*[319] the Danes were in such force in the interior of the kingdom, that notwith[standing] the great and sometimes successful exertions of Alfred after his accession, the nation was quite disheartened, and he was obliged to give up the ensigns of Royalty and conceal himself in a peasants dress.

4. By what means did Alfred ultimately succeed in subduing the Danes, and how did he secure his kingdom against their future inroads?

By waiting in his retreat in the island of Athelney till the Danes had become careless, personally examining their camp, and afterwards taking a favourable opportunity of discovering himself to his subjects, and surprising the enemy when least prepared to expect him. He secured his kingdom from the future inroads of the Danes, by establishing a regular militia and a considerable naval force which though they could not prevent some subsequent formidable[320] attacks were sufficient when directed by the vigour and abilities of Alfred entirely to repel them.

Odduni,[321] Governer of Devonshire, had killed Hubba.[322]

In 893 a formidable armament consisting of 330 ships landed in England under the famous leader Hastings.*[323]

[Lesson 22][324]

5. What civil institutions is he said to have established for the internal government of the country and the better administration of Justice? Hume[325] Vol i

Hume seems at first to attribute[326] the regular[327] division of the country into tythings,* hundreds and counties to Alfred; but afterwards observes that as these institutions have a strong resemblance to the customs of the ancient Germans, and to the Saxon laws during the Heptarchy, Alfred ought rather to

317 'most' is ins.

318 'from the Danes' and 'Soon after the accession of Alfred' are del.

319 Presumably, Ethelred (or Aethelred) I (d. 871); king (865/6–871) of Wessex and of Kent; son of Ethelwulf of Wessex; brother of Alfred the Great (*EB*).

320 'all future' is del. and 'some subsequent formidable' is ins.

321 i.e. Odda, ealderman of Devon. 322 i.e. Ubbe (or Ubba, or Ubbi).

323 'Hasting ... chef viking danois ... A la suite d'une expedition sur la Somme (889), il se rendit en Angleterre, où il fut contraint de se faire la paix et de baptiser ses deux fils (893)' (*Grand Larousse Encyclopédique*, 1960–64, Vol. 5). Also spelt 'Haesten'.

324 Numbered '21' in MS.

325 David Hume, *The History of England, from the Invasion of Julius Caesar to the Revolution in 1688*. The Malthus Library has the edition of 1786 in 8 vols.

326 'at first attributes' is altered to 'seems at first to attribute'. 327 'regular' is del., then ins.

be considered as the reformer and improver of this plan of government than the author; and this opinion agrees exactly with that of Millar. Both Hume and Millar[328] are of opinion that the 12 assessors who were chosen to assist the hundreder and the president of the county court in their decisions, may be considered as the origin of Juries.[329] Henry thinks that these assessors which were the same as the scabini[330] and rackenburgi[331] of the Franks and Germans were only[332] law men or lawyers chosen [333] for the purpose of assisting the Judges with their legal knowledge. He thinks that Juries were introduced by Willm 1st. (not probable)

A Shiregerieve* or Sheriff was generally appointed to exercise the office of Judge in the county court, instead of the Earl or Alderman, who being [334] taken from among the greatest thanes,[335] might[336] probably be better qualified for the exercise of arms than the administration of justice and had besides often an office at court which required his attendance.

6. How did he encourage literature and the arts,[337] and provide for the education of his [338] subjects?

Invited the most celebrated scholars from all parts of Europe, repaired the University of Oxford and endowed it with many privileges, established schools, and enjoined by law all freeholders possessed of two hides of land to send their children to them. Example. Composed Poems, fables, translated those of Esop,* and the histories of Orosius[339] and[340] Bede, and the Consolation of philosophy by Boethius.

Introduced and encouraged manufactures of all kinds, and suffered no inventor or improver of any useful art to go unrewarded. The elegancies* of life came to him from the Mediterranean and the Indies, and gave his subjects a taste for commerce.

Said to have fought 56 battles in person by sea and land.

[328] 'and Millar' is ins.

[329] A repetition of an earlier statement (see above, Lecture ii, answer to question 21).

[330] i.e. court officials chosen by the count (See Barraclough 1947, p.10, n.1).

[331] See rackenbourghs, Lecture iii, Question 11, above.

[332] 'only' is ins. [333] 'with' is del. [334] 'generally' is del.

[335] In Anglo-Saxon times a thane was one who 'held lands of the king or other superior by military service'; later, a term of rank, below that of earl and above that of ceorl (*OED*).

[336] 'was' is del. before 'might'. [337] 'and the arts' is ins. [338] 'people' is del.

[339] Spanish priest, *fl.* AD 500, disciple of St Augustine and friend of St Jerome, author of *Historia adversus Paganos* (*OCEL*).

[340] 'and' is ins.

[Lesson 23][341]

7. How long did Alfred reign, and what character does Hume give of him?

29 years. [342] Died at the age of 53 in 901. Hume speaks of him as the complete model of that perfect character which under the denomination of a sage or truely* wise man, philosophers have been so fond of delineating without the hope of ever seeing it realized.

8. [343] When, and under whom were the divided dominions of Charlemagne again united,[344] and on what accounts was the Prince who held them deposed?

Under Charles the fat, the Son of Louis the German (894),[345] in preference to Charles the simple, son of Louis the Stammerer, who should have succeeded his brothers Louis and Carloman, but was rejected on account of his extreme youth.

Charles the fat had governed his own dominions with tolerable judgement; but was found totally incapable of bearing the weight of the Empire of Charlemagne; and was deposed on account of his incapacity, and his cowardly and treacherous conduct towards the Normans.

Bribed them and murdered their king at a conference – before the siege of Paris.

He wished to restore the offices of Dukes and Counts to their former state and prevent them from being hereditary, which offended his nobility.

It was under Charles the fat that the famous siege of Paris by the Normans took place, in which Count Eudes[346] and his brother Robert and Bishop Gosselin*[347] so much distinguished themselves.

Charles marched with an army to relieve[348] Paris but [349] afraid to encounter the Normans, [350] he [351] bribed them to retire and allowed them to winter in Burgundy.

[341] Numbered '22' in MS. [342] 'Hume' is del.
[343] 'Who reunited in his person, the Empire all the dominions of Charlemagne, and on what account' is del.
[344] 'reunited' is altered to 'united'. [345] '(894)' is ins. [346] Eudes, or Odo.
[347] Joscelin, bishop of Paris, died 886 (Logan 1991, pp.120–32).
[348] 'leave' is del. and 'relieve' is ins. [349] 'was' is del.
[350] 'the Norman army' is altered to 'the Normans'. [351] 'was' is del.

9. How was the French Empire divided on the deposition of Charles the fat?[352]

Into Germany, [353] France, Italy and two Burgundies. Arnold,[354] a bastard son of Carloman, king of Bavaria and Grandson of Louis the German, had Germany. Count Eudes was chosen king of France. Italy was divided between Berengarius and Guido,[355] Dukes of Friuli and Spoleto, both of the family of Charlemagne by the mothers side, and appointed Dukes by Charles the bald. Count Rodolph*[356] of the family of the Empress Judith[357] established a kingdom in Transjurane Burgundy, and Louis, the son of Boson, was confirmed in the kingdom of Arles, or Cisjurane Burgundy.[358]

10. When did the scepter* of Germany pass out of the family of Charlemagne and who was chosen King?[359]

On the death of Louis IV, son of Arnold.* The lineal male heir of Charlemagne was Louis the simple, rejected on account of the weakness of his character. Germany was at this time composed of two principal nations. The first called by Historians the nation of Franks, consisted of the states bordering on the Rhine and Franconia, at this time governed by the Duke Conrad, the states of Bavaria governed by the Duke Arnold,* and the States of Swabia governed by the Duke Burkard. The second principal nation consisted of the united people of Saxony and Thuringia, and was governed by the famous Duke Otho.*[360] All these Chiefs except Burkard were[361] descended in the female line from Charlemagne. The crown was first offered to Otho* who rejected it and recommended Conrad of Franconia. This election out of the regular line gave great power to the [362] states of Germany, and the Dukes and Counts soon after[363] took the opportunity of rendering their offices hereditary. It was [364] Arnold* that restored the original power of the Dukes after they had been almost superseded by the Missi[365] of Charlemagne.

[352] 'and under whom and on what conditions did the Normans settle themselves in Normandy and Britany*' is del.

[353] 'Italy' is del. [354] i.e. Arnulf. [355] Guido (or Guy) of Spoleto.

[356] Rodolphe 1[er] (Rudolf I), founder and first king (888–912) of the kingdom of Jurane (Upper) Burgundy (*EB*).

[357] '[great grandson] nephew of the Empress Judith' is del. and 'of the family of the Empress Judith' is ins.

[358] In pencil: 'into 5'. [359] 'Emperor' is del. and 'King' is ins. '912' is written in pencil at this point.

[360] Usually spelt 'Otto'. [361] 'were' is ins. [362] 'Duke and was' is del. [363] 'soon after' is ins.

[364] 'the Emperor' is del. [365] i.e. Missi Dominici. See above, Lecture 3, answer to question 12.

[Lesson 24][366]

11. Who was the first prince of the house of Saxony that was raised to the throne of Germany, and[367] what important services did he render to the Empire?

Henry the fowler, son[368] of the great Duke Otho* of Saxony. He entirely defeated the Hungarians and rescued Germany from the ignominious Tax[369] which it had been obliged to pay to them, and to which even Conrad had consented. Laid the foundation of that power which his son afterwards carried to so great a height.

Henry the fowler was reckoned the ablest prince of his time.

Surrounded his kingdom with fortresses, [370] established numerous walled towns, and obliged a ninth part of the nobility of the adjoining territory to people[371] them, with the same proportion of the free inhabitants. The Germans had a great dislike to Walled cities.

12. Of what house or family[372] were the Otho's* who swayed[373] the German scepter* with so much vigour, in what century did they [374] flourish, and who was the most distinguished of them?

Of the house of Saxony. They flourished principally in the tenth century. Otho* i was elected in 936, and Otho* iii died in 1002.

Otho* the first [375] distinguished by the addition of the Kingdom of Italy and the title of Emperor and Augustus, besides his other conquests, and great qualities as a prince.

13. [376] What was the state of France after the death of Charles the simple, and what family obtained the principal power in the kingdom?

The nobles and Seigneurs became almost entirely independent and exercised all the rights of sovereignty.

The Crown fell [377] into the power of Hugh the great or the Abbot, who declined however placing it on his own head, but allowed first Rodolph* Duke of Burgundy, and afterwards Louis Outremer[378] to wear it.

366 Numbered '23' in MS. 367 'by what name' is del. and 'and' is repeated.

368 As Malthus indicates later in this paragraph, Henry the Fowler was the father, not the son, of Duke Otto of Saxony (Otto the Great), who became king of Germany in 936 on the death of his father.

369 'Tax' is ins. 370 'and' is del. 371 'inhabit' is del. and 'people' is ins.

372 'or family' is ins. 373 Here used in the sense of 'to rule' or 'to govern'.

374 'principally' is del. 375 '[[was the] adde] possessd* the kingdom of' is del.

376 'After the death of Charles the simple what family' is del. 377 'almost wholly' is del.

378 i.e. Louis d'Outremer.

Soon after the death of Louis Outremer* who left a shadow of royal power to his Son Lothaire, Hugh the Great died, and was succeeded in his influence by Hugh Capet.

14. [379] How[380] was the line of hereditary descent settled in Germany and by what kind of decision?

It was settled according to the present custom. The question was determined by battle or duel, between an equal number of combatants in favour of the grandson in preference to the Uncle.

[Lesson 25][381]

15. What was the principal cause of the great temporal power of the clergy in Germany?

Charlemagne had established some great bishoprics in Germany thinking them safer on the frontiers than Dukedoms and counties. [382] But the principal cause of the[383] very great temporal dominion of the clergy in Germany[384] was the policy of Otho* i who fearing the increasing power of the Dukes was willing to remove large districts from under their authority, by granting them to the[385] church, and governing them by Avoués of his own appointment. But the policy failed. The office of Avoués was soon united to the churches; and the Bishops afterwards became as formidable as the Dukes.

16. When 962[386] and on what occasion was[387] the title of Augustus conferred on the German Emperors?

On occasion of the application of Pope John the 12th to rescue him from the Arms of Berengarius. Otho* was of course happy to take such an opportunity of extending his Empire, marched into Italy with a large army, was crowned king of Lombardy at Milan, and[388] Emperor, and Augustus at Rome. Berenger had fled, and was afterwards pursued, taken, and imprisoned by Otho.*

The transaction very similar to that which occurred in the case of Charlemagne being made Emperor of the West.[389]

379 'At what period probably was the greatest part of the allodial property' is del.
380 'In what manner' is del. and 'How' is ins. 381 Numbered '24' in MS. 382 'Otho* i' is del.
383 'their' is altered to 'the'. 384 'power' is del. and 'dominion of the clergy in Germany' is ins.
385 'the' is ins. 386 '962' is ins. 387 'did' is del. and 'was' is ins. 388 'Milan, and' is ins.
389 '864' is del.

17. What were the rights of the Emperors of the house of Saxony respecting the election of Popes and the investiture of Bishops, and on what occasion were these rights first established and acknowledged?[390]

The power of choosing a successor to the Empire, of naming the Pope, and of giving investiture to Bishops. These rights Otho* obliged Leo VIII and the Roman people to acknowledge, on his second return to Rome after having deposed John the 12th, who had rebelled, and Benedict V, another pope chosen by the same party.

The kings of Germany had before a right to invest bishops and confirm canonical elections.

On his third return to Rome Otho* banished the Consuls, hanged the tribunes and caused the prefect of Rome to be whipped.

18. How long did Otho* the first reign, and why was he called the great?

He reigned 36 years. He had delivered Germany from the scourge of the Hungarians, punished and introduced Christianity among the rebellious Bohemians, established his power among the vassals of the Empire, conquered Italy from Berengarius. He acquired the title of Augustus, and showed himself master of the Pope.

19. What were the state and temper of the Roman people during the reign of the Othos,* and in what manner did they occasionally shew* their attachment to the principles of liberty, and to[391] their old forms of government?

During the last Emperors of the Carlovingian race the Romans had been nearly independent; and when John the 12th was compelled by the tyranny of Berengarius to supplicate the assistance of Otho,* he soon repented of having given himself and the Roman people a master. [392] Three visits to Rome were necessary on the part of Otho* to repress the discontents of his new subjects. Under Otho* the 2nd an attempt was made to restore the old Consular government; and again under Otho* the[393] 3rd. Crescentius, the prefect, acquired such power [394] with the people and against the authority of the Pope[395] that the greatest severity was necessary to repress it.

But though Italy during the reign of the Emperors of the house of Saxony was in a constant state of rebellion, yet we always find them victorious and able to assert their rights.

[390] 'Had been lost under descendants of Charlemagne' is added in pencil.
[391] 'to' is ins. [392] 'and' is del. [393] 'the' is repeated. [394] 'in Rome' is del.
[395] 'with the people and against the authority of the Pope' is ins.

20. Who was the last Emperor of the house of Saxony, and what were the general rights of the Emperors of Germany during the reign of that house?

Henry ii, Duke[396] of Bavaria, second cousin of Otho* the third and great grandson of Henry the fowler. He died in[397] 1024. The Authority of the States of Germany increased greatly during his reign.

The general rights of the Emperors of the house of Saxony were: Robtn Note XLII

In their principalities
In virtue of their state.
The right to make alliances with each other and with foreign [398] princes.

To make war and build fortresses
To send ambassadors to foreign courts
To transmit their fiefs to their sons
To assemble their Provincial states and to judge their vassals in them.

By the privilege of the Emperors
The right

To coin money
To establish fairs
To receive Jews
To exercise supreme justice and to possess gold mines
To nominate to all the greater benefices
To dispose of the Holy See
To convoke councils and direct their deliberations
To give the title of king to their vassals (Bonaparte)
To confer vacant fiefs
To receive the revenues of the Empire consisting of the produce of the domain ...[399] gold and silver mines, capitation taxes of the Jews, and the tributes of the[400] Slavonic nations.
To exercise an unlimited sovereignty over Italy
To establish fairs, and towns, and [401] confer the rights of citizenship
To convoke diets, and fix the duration of their sittings
To coin money and confer the right of coining on the[402] States.
To administer[403] supreme justice in the territories of the States.

396 'Duke' is ins. 397 'in' is repeated. 398 'states' is del. 399 Word unclear.
400 'tributes of the' is ins. 401 'give the' is del. 402 'on other' is del. and 'on the' is ins.
403 'exercise' is del. and 'administer' is ins.

And in general to exercise all the rights of sovereignty in which the States could not concur.

The rights of the States were
In the Diets

> To elect the kings of Germany – future Emperors
> To appoint their guardians
> To make laws
> To authorize [404] alienations of the Domaine*
> To concur in the establishment of new Principalities
> To make war and peace
> To judge and to condemn those States accused of the crime of revolt.

[404] 'the' is del.

7 Harriet Malthus' diary of a family tour of Scotland in 1826

INTRODUCTION

In the summer of 1826 Malthus took a holiday in Scotland accompanied by his wife (Harriet), daughter (Emily) and son (Henry, or Hal). His diaries of the Scottish tour and of tours to Northern Europe in 1799, to Scotland in (probably) 1810, and to Europe in 1825 were made available to researchers by Robert Malthus in 1961 and published in 1966, edited by Patricia James; but it was not until the discovery of the manuscripts in the estate of Robert Malthus that it was realised that Malthus' wife had also kept a diary of the Scottish tour. For most days her diary entries are more detailed than Malthus' – the exception being when Malthus gives information on local economic conditions – and provide a fuller picture of people met and places visited. Harriet's diary also contains ten ink sketches (some incomplete) of Scottish scenes. Harriet's artistic leanings are also evident in the drawings (including one thought to be of her future husband) contained in her journal of the European tour of 1802 (see Hashimoto 1990).

The editing and publication of Harriet Malthus' diary have been greatly assisted by the introduction and notes made by Patricia James in her 1966 edition of Malthus' diary, here republished beside Harriet's to facilitate comparison. The map in James' edition (p.259) showing the route of the Scottish tour is also reproduced below.

The two diaries begin, probably by agreement, on the same day (17 June) when they were leaving Hollin Hall, the home near Ripon of Harriet's

7 *Harriet Malthus' diary of a family tour of Scotland in 1826*

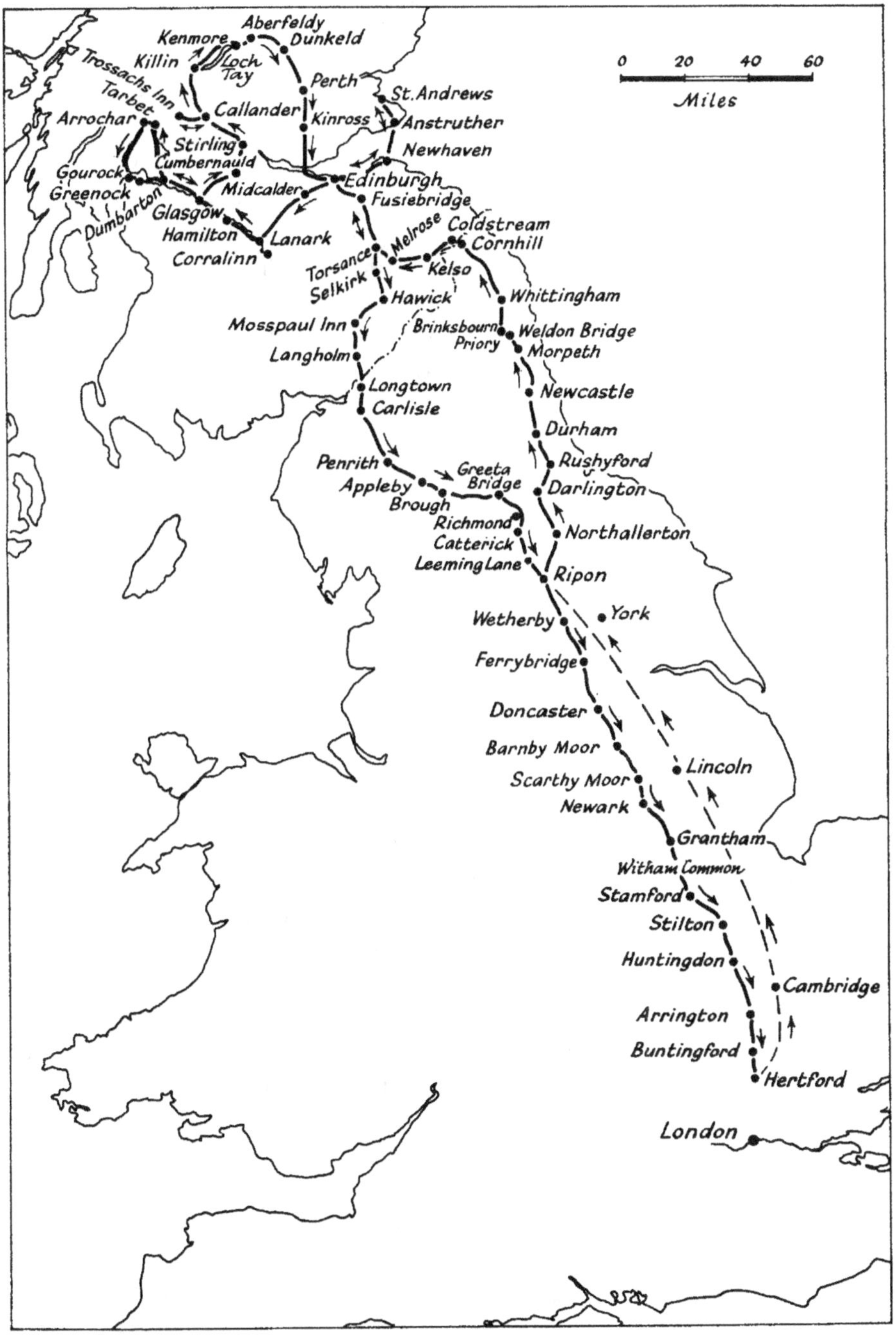

sister, Anne Eliza, and brother-in-law, Henry Wood. There are no entries in Harriet's diary for the journey from their home at the East India College, Haileybury, to Hollin Hall.[1]

They left Hollin Hall, travelling in their own carriage and hiring horses and a boy at successive stages. It took them four days to reach Edinburgh, stopping to admire the sights and scenery on the way, especially Brinkburn Priory and Melrose Abbey. On the first night they slept at Durham, on the second at Weldon Bridge, the third at Melrose, arriving in Edinburgh on 20 June where they were guests of Francis Jeffrey, first at his home in the centre of the city and then at his country house, 'Craig Crook', outside the city. Jeffrey had previously visited the Malthuses at Haileybury and in a letter of 6 January 1826 had invited them to stay with him 'next summer' in Edinburgh (Malthus 1966, p.253).

The first three days in Edinburgh, from 21 June to 23 June, were spent sightseeing, meeting guests invited by Jeffrey, and being invited to the houses of others. On 24 June they were taken by Jeffrey to 'Craig Crook', where the round of sightseeing and social engagements continued for another five days until 27 June. The distinguished members of Edinburgh's literary, judicial and academic circles whom they met during their stay in Edinburgh included Sir Walter Scott, Leonard Horner, Henry Cockburn, George Cranstoun (Lord Corehouse), David Cathcart (Lord Alloway), John Ramsay McCulloch, Henry Mackenzie, and Sir William Hamilton.[2] As neither Malthus nor his wife was a diarist in the mould of Samuel Pepys or Maria Edgeworth, we can only speculate on the conversations that transpired.

On 28 June they left Edinburgh to visit Thomas Chalmers and Thomas Jackson at St Andrews University, travelling by steamboat across the Firth of Forth to Anstruther and by road to St Andrews. Malthus had previously corresponded with Chalmers. The Malthuses appear to have slept at Anstruther on 28 June and at St Andrews on 29 June, returning to Edinburgh on 30 June, presumably sleeping that night at Craig Crook.

The following day (1 July) they set out on a thirteen-day trip to the lochs and mountains. At first they travelled in their own carriage, hiring horses along the way (and a boy to return the horses). Presumably Malthus drove, as his 'Cash Account' makes no mention of a driver's fee. They slept at Lanark on the first night (1 July) and at Glasgow the next (2 July). On 3 July, leaving their carriage and half their luggage at the inn in Glasgow, they took a steamboat to Dumbarton, hired a post chaise (and boy) to drive to Luss on the bank of Loch Lomond, rowed on the loch in the afternoon and slept at Luss.

[1] The 'Cash Account' included in Malthus' diary (see Malthus 1966, pp.268–72) begins when they left the East India College at Haileybury on 12 June, and indicates roughly the route between Haileybury and Hollin Hall.

[2] Further details can be found in the footnotes that follow.

The following day (4 July) they took a steamboat up Loch Lomond to Tarbet at the north end of the loch, landing on the way to view Rob Roy's cave, and slept at Tarbet. On 5 July they hired a cart and boy to go on to Arrochar on Loch Long where they slept the night, and on 6 July embarked on a steamboat at Arrochar and returned to Glasgow.

The next day (7 July), after replenishing their finances with a £25 draft on their London bank (Hoare's), they journeyed north from Glasgow (in their own carriage with hired horses and a driver) via Cumbernauld and Stirling to Callander, where they slept that night. On 8 July they visited the Trossachs, spent most of the day boating on Lake Katrine, and stayed that night at the Trossachs Inn. Returning the next day (9 July) to Callander for breakfast, they drove on to Loch Earn, staying the night at Lochearnhead, and proceeded on 10 July to Killin and Loch Tay, sleeping at Kenmore. After visiting Taymouth Castle on the morning of 11 July, they arrived at Aberfeldy for dinner and went on to Inver, near Dunkeld, for the night.

On 12 July, after a tour of the environs of Dunkeld, they spent the night at Perth, and on the final day of this thirteen-day tour (from 1 July to 13 July), they drove from Perth to Loch Leven and Kinross, where they discharged the horses and driver they had hired seven days earlier (on 7 July) at Glasgow, paying £1.12.0 per day or £11.4.0 for the horses and 5 shillings per day or £1.15.0 to the driver, and proceeded by post horses to Queensferry, crossing the Forth to Edinburgh (with their carriage) by steamboat and arriving back at Craig Crook at 2 p.m.

The following day (14 July) appears (understandably) to have been a rest day. They stayed at Craig Crook and went for a walk in the woods and admired the views. On 15 July they went to the court in Edinburgh to hear Jeffrey defend (unsuccessfully) a newspaper publisher charged with damaging the reputation of a professor of St Andrews. Jeffrey's opponent, Henry Cockburn, dined with them later at Craig Crook.

On Sunday, 16 July, they went to church in Edinburgh to hear Dr Robert Gordon, a celebrated preacher, but were 'a little disappointed'. They returned to Craig Crook for dinner. Monday, 17 July, involved more sightseeing in Edinburgh – including Arthur's Seat, Holyroodhouse, and the Observatory – and visits to the Lord Mayor of Edinburgh and Alexander Nasmyth ('a great oil Painter'). They dined at the home of Sir John Archibald Murray, where one of the guests was J.R. McCulloch.

The next day, 18 July, was spent quietly in the vicinity of Craig Crook. They walked to the village of Corstorphine, made a social call, and met several visitors to Craig Crook. On 19 July, their second last day in Edinburgh, Malthus and his son and daughter went into Edinburgh, but Harriet again spent the day quietly at Craig Crook.

They left Edinburgh on 20 July, hiring horses and a boy at each stage, passing through Fusiebridge and Torsplance as on the journey north to Edinburgh, but then taking a different route south to Ripon, via Selkirk (where they slept that night) and Penrith (for the night of 21 July),[3] arriving at Hollin Hall at 8.30 p.m. on 22 July. They stayed there for two days, leaving on 25 July via Wetherby, Barnby Moor and overnight at Grantham, arriving back at Haileybury on the evening of 26 July having been away from home for 45 days. Malthus' 'Cash Account' shows that the expenses of the tour amounted to over £147, or about 30 per cent of his annual salary (£500) from the East India College. Their expenses for 45 days would have been greater if they had not been guests of the Woods at Hollin Hall and of Jeffrey for thirteen days in Edinburgh.

TEXT

1826

June 17

Left Hollin,[4] dined at Darlington[5] went into a Quaker bookseller's shop by name Tom's – the Lady show'd us many curious book's such as old editions &c – and seemed very learned in these things – Slept at Durham – admired the wooded rocky glen over which the Cathedral stands – fine view of it from one of the bridges

[6]

Hollin. June 17.

To Northallerton 20.m. Darlington 16.m. dined. Rushyford 9. Durham 9. slept.

[3] Harriet's diary continues to 26 July at Haileybury. Malthus' diary ends at Penrith on 21 July but his 'Cash Account' provides additional details of their journey from Penrith to Haileybury.

[4] Hollin Hall, near Ripon, the home of Harriet Malthus' sister, Anne Eliza (1790–1875), who had married Henry Wood, the heir of Hollin Hall, in 1810. The Malthuses stayed at Hollin Hall on other occasions (see James 1979), and the Woods accompanied Harriet Malthus' parents on a tour of the Lake District in 1825 (see below, Ch. 8).

[5] The distances between successive locations are given by Malthus in his diary, as noted below. Further information on the distances travelled is given in these footnotes to Harriet Malthus' diary only where Malthus omitted to state them, or where the distances he gave appear to be incorrect.

[6] The entries in the right-hand column are reproduced from Malthus' diary of this Scottish tour, published in Malthus 1966, pp.253–72. The star (*) indicating misspellings and orthographic errors, has not been added to these reproduced entries.

Sunday 18 –
Went to Mass 11 am cathedral service – music very good – prevented by the elections from going by Alnwick, slept at Weldon Bridge – before tea had a very pretty walk to Brinkburn priory, an old abby* on the little river Coquet.

June 18.
Cathedral. Walks. College. Newcastle 15.m. dined. Morpeth 15. Weldon Bridge 10.m. Brinksbourn Priory. River Coquet. – slept.

Monday 19 –
Entered Scotland by Kelso[7] pretty country by banks of the Tweed. Slept at Melrose – admired the Abby* before tea – carv'd work remarkably fine – an artist show'd the ruin's and repeated Walter Scott's Lay.[8]

June 19.
Whittingham 10.m. breakfasted. Cornhill. 12.m. crossed the Tweed Scotland Coldstream. Kelso. Melrose. 16. Abbey moonlight, Eildon Hills. slept.

Tuesday 20 –
Went a beautiful road by the Gala water, last stage – ...[9] Bridge to Edinburgh[10] – arrived by dinner time at M[r]. Jeffrey's[11]

June 20.
Torsonce 12. banks of Tweed. Gala water. Fusie Bridge. Edinburgh. Dinner. Mr L Horner.

[7] Kelso is nine miles south-west of Cornhill-on-Tweed and Coldstream. Malthus gave the distance from Whittingham to Cornhill as 12 miles, but it would be closer to 25 miles.

[8] Sir Walter Scott (1771–1832), 'The Lay of the Last Minstrel' (1805), Introduction, Stanza XXI: 'And far beneath, in lustre wan, / Old Melros' rose, and fair Tweed ran: / Like some tall rock with lichens grey, / Seem'd dimly huge the dark Abbaye.'; and Canto Second, Stanza I: 'If thou would'st view fair Melrose aright, / Go visit it by the pale moonlight; / For the gay beams of lightsome day / Gild, but to flout, the ruins grey. / When the broken arches are black in night, / And each shafted oriel glimmers white; / When the cold light's uncertain shower / Streams on the ruin'd central tower; / When buttress and buttress, alternately, / Seem fram'd of ebon and ivory; / When silver edges the imagery, / And the scrolls that teach thee to live and die; / When distant Tweed is heard to rave, / And the owlet to hoot o'er the dead man's grave, / Then go – but go alone the while – / Then view St. David's ruin'd pile; / And, home returning, soothly swear, / Was never scene so sad and fair!' (*The Poetical Works of Sir Walter Scott*, ed. J. Logie Robertson, Humphrey Milford, Oxford University Press, 1921).

[9] Word unclear, probably 'Fushey', i.e. Fusiebridge.

[10] Edinburgh is about 25 miles north-west of Torsance.

[11] Francis Jeffrey (1773–1850), later Lord Jeffrey, co-founder and editor of the *Edinburgh Review*. As Patricia James noted (Malthus 1966, pp.253–4), a letter from Jeffrey to Malthus of 6 January 1826, inviting the Malthuses to visit them 'next summer' at his home, Craig Crook Castle, near Edinburgh, probably influenced Malthus to take this Scottish holiday. The reference to 'Mr L. Horner' in Malthus' diary for June 20 led Patricia James to state that the 'first person the Malthuses met in Edinburgh was not Jeffrey, but Leonard Horner' (Malthus 1996, p.254), but this entry for 20 June in Harriet Malthus' diary suggests that they went directly to stay with Jeffrey, and met Leonard Horner there. At that time Jeffrey and his wife Charlotte were living at 92 George Street, Edinburgh (*DNB*). As the diary states, the Malthuses did not go to Craig Crook Castle until 24 June.

Wednesday 21.
Went into the courts of law – found nothing going on, proceeded to the college[12] which is not quite completed – saw museum – and in the Even[g]. walk'd in Prince's* St. gardens from whence climb'd to the castle[13] by a zig zag walk, admired the fine rock on which it is built –

June 21.
Courts. Advocates Library. Writer's Library. College. Musaeum. Dinner Mr Murray and Mr Rutherforth.

Thursday 22.
Went into the courts again, heard nothing – but saw Sir Walter Scott, M[r]. Cranstoun,[14] M[r]. Mackenzie,[15] L[d] Alloway[16] – dined at M[r]. Jeffrey's – we Ladies walk'd before tea on the Calton Hill[17]

June 22.
Courts. Sir Walter Scott. Dinner Lord Alloway Mr Mackenzie. Mr. Cranstoun. Mr Cobourn evening.

Friday 23
Went to see Holyrood house[18] – the antient* chapel – the little [19]... boudoir hardly 3 feet wide & 5 ft long where Mary[20] was at supper with her Maid and Rizzio when he was suddenly attack'd from a little back staircase that opens into the bedroom – a large gallery of bad portraits – in the Even[g]. supped at M[r]. Horner's – after which made a party to see the Sun–rise

June 23.
Ruthvens presses. Holyrood House Dinner Mr & Mrs Rutherforth. Mr Horner's in the evening. Calton Hill ½ past two next morning.

[12] i.e. Edinburgh University. On the use of the term 'college' and on the date of completion of the building, see Malthus 1996, p.258, n.1, n.2.

[13] i.e. Edinburgh Castle, on Castle Rock.

[14] George Cranstoun, Lord Corehouse, d. 1850. Scottish judge (*DNB*).

[15] Henry Mackenzie (1748–1831); author of *The Man of Feeling* (1771) and other literary works; comptroller of taxes for Scotland. (*OCEL*; Joyce 1951, pp.182–3; Malthus 1966, pp.254–5).

[16] David Cathcart, Lord Alloway, d. 1829, lord of session (1813) and lord of justiciary (1826) (*DNB*).

[17] At the east end of Princes Street.

[18] Palace of Holyroodhouse, the chief royal palace of Scotland. [19] Word unclear.

[20] Mary Stuart (1542–87), queen of Scots. Her Italian Secretary and favourite, Rizzio (or David Riccio) (1533?–66) was assassinated in the vestibule of her audience chamber in Holyrood Palace on the order of her husband, Lord Darnley and a group of Scottish lords. See above, Ch. 5, Essay on Mary, Queen of Scots.

from the Calton hill – Mr. Mrs. ...[21] the Jeffrey's, Mr Cockburn[22] and ourselves – fine clear mild morning – light at ½ past 2 – Sun rose ½ past 3 from out the Forth – fine effect on the old Town and Castle –

Saturday 24

Went to bed after sunrise – got up late and went to craig crook[23] – pleasant party to dinner – drank wine on the green –

June 24.

Craig Crook. Bowls. Dinner. Mr Cobourn. Mr Mackenzie. Mr Rutherforth. Count Flahaut. Mr Craig. Mr Murray.

Sunday 25th

Had a Coach from Edinburgh to go to church – did not hear Dr Thompson[24] – a young man delivered a good practical sermon – returnd to Craig–Crook – Mr. Maculloch[25] dined – a long walk after tea with splendid view of the fine ...[26] city – in returning were pursued by a herd of wild Bulls –

June 25 Sunday.

St Georges Church. Dinner Mr Maculloch.

[21] Name unclear. The entry in Malthus' diary for 23 June mentions a 'Mr and Mrs Rutherforth'.

[22] Henry Cockburn (1779–1854), a lifelong friend of Jeffrey, 'shared with Jeffrey the leadership of the Scottish bar' (*DNB* and Malthus 1996, p.255).

[23] i.e. Craig Crook Castle, near Corstorphine Hill, about three miles west of Edinburgh Castle, had been owned by Jeffrey since 1815. See *DNB* and Malthus 1966, pp.255, 258.

[24] Andrew Mitchell Thomson (1779–1831), Scottish divine. After several appointments he was transferred in 1814 to St George's Church, Edinburgh, at the time of its opening. He became one of the most powerful of the Edinburgh preachers and was keenly interested in social questions. His successor was Dr Chalmers, whom the Malthuses visited in St Andrews on 29 June. Thomson received the degree of D.D. from Aberdeen University in 1823 (*DNB*).

[25] John Ramsay McCulloch (1789–1864), whom Malthus had previously met at the Political Economy Club and who generally supported Ricardo against Malthus. In letters to Ricardo in 1819 and 1820 McCulloch had been very critical of Malthus. He considered Malthus' reputation as an economist 'to be very much overrated' and said that Malthus' forthcoming *Principles of Political Economy* 'deserves to be very roughly handled' (Ricardo, *Works*, VIII, pp.139, 167); and in *The Literature of Political Economy*, 1845, he said of Malthus' *Principles*: 'Though frequently learned and ingenious, the reasonings are, for the most part, perplexed and inconclusive' (p.18).

[26] Word unclear.

Monday 26

Saw M^r^. Wood's[27] school with which we were very much interested. He produces an extraordinary quickness in the little ragged boys – then the new school, Dr William's – afterwards dined at Ld Alloways – [28]

June 26.

Courts. Mr Wood. Sessional School. New Academy. Dined at Lord Alloway's. Mrs Laing widow of the Historian. Sir Wm Hamilton. Lord Mackensie. Dr Coventry. Professor of Agriculture.

Tuesday 27

P^d^ visits –

June 27.

Visits. Courts. No company at Dinner.

Wednesday 28

Rose early and set out in the Steam boat for Anstruther[29] at 6 – fine day, no one sick, arrived to breakfast at the River by ten – ugly country but in a drive of five miles went through some Gentleman's grounds that were prettier than could be expected – particularly about Elie[30] –

June 28.

To Anstruther. Mr & Mrs Bruce. Drive in Carriage. Mr & Mrs Smith. Dr Jackson.

[27] The extra information on Mr Wood contained in this entry in Harriet Malthus' diary indicates that the 'Mr Wood' in Malthus' diary could not have been the John Philip Wood referred to by Patricia James in Malthus 1966, p.256.

[28] Harriet Malthus' diary for 26 June does not refer to the other five dinner guests of Lord Alloway mentioned in Malthus' diary, viz. Mrs Laing, widow of the historian Malcolm Laing (1762–1818); Sir William Hamilton (1788–1856), at that time Professor of Modern History at Edinburgh University, later Professor of Logic and Metaphysics; Lord Mackenzie (see n.15 above) and Dr Andrew Coventry (1764–1832), Professor of Agriculture from 1790 to 1831. (See James, in Malthus 1966, p.256.) It would be interesting to speculate on the nature of the dinner conversation. Did Malthus discuss with Sir William Hamilton the topics in modern history he had been teaching at the East India College? Did Dr Coventry raise with Malthus the possibility of agricultural production increasing in more than arithmetical progression every 25 years?

[29] About 25 miles north-east of Edinburgh, on the north side of the Firth of Forth. They appear to have stayed at Anstruther on the night of 28 June, before proceeding on 29 June to St Andrews, and returning to Edinburgh on 30 June.

[30] Five miles south-west of Anstruther, on the Firth of Forth.

Thursday 29
To S^t^. Andrews[31] to breakfast with Professor Jackson[32] – Dr Chalmers[33] met us there – went to see the antient* cathedral – the old college, old looking lecture rooms, altogether a curious old Town, being the old metropolitan see – it is worth going to – very ugly corn country in the way to it

June 29.
Breakfasted at St Andrews with Dr Jackson Dr. Chalmers. Cathedral. Square Tower. Dinner. Mrs Douglas and Sister.

Friday 30 –
Set out at ½ past 2 in the Steam boat which is caught at Anstruther in its way from Aberdeen – quite calm, beautiful view of the Town of Edinburgh off Newhaven.[34]

June 30.
Returned to Edinburgh.

Saturday July 1
Left Edinburgh after one, – chang'd horses at Mid-Calder.[35] Country from thence to old Lanark[36] bleak – arrived at 6 – dined and then proceeded to the

July 1
To Lanark. Falls of the Clyde Bonington. Corra Lynn.

31 Nine miles north-west of Anstruther.

32 Thomas Jackson was Professor of Natural and Experimental Philosophy at St Andrews University from 1809 until his death on 17 February 1837. (We are grateful to Dr Norman H. Reid, Keeper of Manuscripts, St Andrews University Library, for this and other information about Thomas Jackson.)

33 On Dr Chalmers (1780–1847), see *DNB* and Malthus 1966, p.261, n.1. Malthus and Chalmers had met at the East India College in 1822, and corresponded before and after that meeting. Seven letters from Malthus to Chalmers are held in New College Library, Edinburgh University. In his letter to Chalmers of 18 January 1827, Malthus referred to the 'two valuable presents which you were so kind as to make me, when I had the pleasure of meeting you at St Andrews, last Summer' and said that he had read the two works 'with much pleasure and instruction'.

34 A district of Edinburgh, two miles north of the city centre.

35 Midcalder, about 12 miles west of Edinburgh.

36 On the River Clyde, about 20 miles south-west of Midcalder and about 25 miles south-east of Glasgow.

falls of the clyde[37] through walks cut in the romantic woods –returned thrug* new Lanark.[38]

Sunday 2[d]

Went to the relief church at Old Lanark – long disjointed Sermon. Set out at one – at the bottom of the hill by the toll Bar got out of the carriage to see the Mouse Glen, a small thin river at the bottom of a very deep narrow valley – a Bridge of great height crosses the Glen – chang'd horses at Hamilton[39] – entered Glasgow at 6 – after dinner called on D[r] Brown[40] – walk'd with him & family about the Town – from Garden Square very fine view, tho not romantic like Edinburgh – the Town is to be much admired, handsome houses built of stone and the bridges over the clyde and Quays are very striking.

July 2

Relief Church Mr M'Farlane. Mouse River. Cartland Craigs. Bridge. Hamilton. Glasgow. Drank tea with Mr & Mrs Brown.

[37] The Falls of Clyde – a chain of waterfalls including Bonnington Linn and Corra Linn, in a wooded gorge of the river Clyde.

[38] New Lanark, a village in a gorge of the River Clyde, just south of the old town of Lanark. Richard Arkwright and David Dale established cotton mills there in the eighteenth century. Robert Owen, Dale's son-in-law, set up model employment and living conditions for its workers. It is surprising that Malthus in his diary did not mention New Lanark, and that neither Malthus nor Harriet mentioned Robert Owen's revolutionary establishment at New Lanark. The Malthuses had met Owen at the East India College in 1821 (James 1979, pp.188, 377).

[39] About 13 miles north-west of Lanark, and 11 miles south-east of Glasgow.

[40] Malthus' diary of the Scottish tour (Malthus 1966, pp.260, 262, 263) refers on 2 July to a 'Mr and Mrs Brown'; on 6 July to 'Mr and Mrs Brown and daughters'; and on 7 July to 'Dr Brown's daughter of 12 years'. James suggests that Mr and Mrs Brown were probably Dr and Mrs Thomas Brown – Mrs Brown being Marion Jeffrey, the sister of Francis Jeffrey (Malthus 1996, p.260, n.2). But Dr Thomas Brown died in 1820 (*DNB*). Another possibility would be John Brown, DD (1784–1858), but this also is unlikely as he did not receive the degree of D.D. until 1830; and because, although he was at one time a minister at Biggar, near New Lanark, in 1826 he was at Rose Street Chapel in Edinburgh (*DNB*).

Monday 3d –
At 9 set out in a Steam boat for Inverary[41] – passed steam boat after steamboat like a mail coach road – boat loaded with Women and Children. It began to rain hard and we thought we should have to remain 12 hours shut up in the cabin – therefore determind to land at Dumbarton,[42] hailed a boat & rowed to the Kings Arms – walked up to the Castle on the Rock[43] – almost all the way stone steps and iron railing – fine view of the clyde and mountains tho rainy, misty – hired an old post chaise and had a beautiful drive to Luss[44] – from the road there seemed to be a fine view of Ben Lomond[45] coming down into the Lake[46] as can be got anywhere – Luss, a small Inn, found beds, dinner – rainy* hazy weather – Ben covered with clouds ½ way down, had however a pleasant row notwithstanding some rain, landed on the Isle of 2 Moiders[47] from whence the numerous Islands are seen – it is a high rocky Isle covered with low oak wood – a small house and farm at the base – rowed round it and between another low Island – the Islands are not finely wooded like those on Killarney[48]

July 3.
Set off at 9 in the George Canning Steam boat for Inverary. Stopped at Dumbarton on account of the weather. Dumbarton Castle. Luss. Boat in the evening to highest island. Ben Lomond not free from Clouds.

[41] At the northern end of Loch Fyne.
[42] Dumbarton, on the northern shore of the River Clyde, about 11 miles north-west of Glasgow.
[43] Dumbarton Castle on Dumbarton Rock.
[44] On the western side of Loch Lomond, about ten miles north of Dumbarton.
[45] Mountain on the east shore of Loch Lomond, about six miles north of Luss.
[46] Loch Lomond, the largest lake in Great Britain.
[47] No island in Loch Lomond currently bears that name.
[48] i.e. Killarney, in County Kerry, Ireland. The largest of the three famous lakes there – Lough Leane – contains over 30 low wooded islands.

Tuesday 4th.

Fine day – walk'd a little way up a grassy hill to view the Lake – then waited for the Steam boat near a small pebbly beach from whence had a fine clear view of Ben Lomond – got on board the Boat which proceeded up the Loch – a highland piper on board to give us an idea of the bag pipe – Shores are not thickly wooded but very fine shaped mountains open upon the view – the odd shaped Ben Arthur and Ben Voirloch*[49] etc – Boat is moored close to Rob Roy's cave[50] – a board is put out to the Rocks and the whole steamboat party, old and young, fat & thin, scramble up by slippery stone & more slippery turf, a small ladder too in the way, into the mouth of the Cave and down again do.[51] without squalls or difficulty. I am sure a set of London Citizens & Citizenesses wd. never do the like – Boat turns back again by Tarbet[52] where we landed leaving Hal[53] to land at Rowerdinnan*[54] in order [to] go up Ben Lomond. Very good Inn.[55] Walk'd after dinner up part of[56] a turfy heathy mountain opposite Ben Lomond – had been burnt which made the walking on that part very disagreeable

July 4.

Hill by Turnpike before breakfast. Small hill the other way after breakfast. Down to Stoney river and wooden bridge. View of Luss & Ben Lomond. Steam boat. Rowerdennan. Tarbet. Inversnaith. Rob Roy's cave. Tarbet. Walk on a shoulder of one of the mountains in the evening.

Heard at Luss that the wages of the men who worked in the slate quarries were about 20d. a day. All had been employed, and there had been little or no fall.

In Fifeshire, from Mr Bruce the same account. Wages had risen in 1825, and had not fallen again – no want of agricultural work. In 1811, 12 and 13 the price of labour for single men had been 12s. a week. In 1823, they had fallen to 9s. and in 1825 rose to 10s. at which price they remained, June 30th 1826. For about 3 months of the year the wages are only 9s.; and during the harvest much is done by piece work.

Married men are paid by the keep of a cow, a house, potatoe & flax ground, with a certain yearly sum in money. At one period of the war unmarried ploughmen paid by the year

[49] Ben Arthur (or The Cobbler) is west of Loch Lomond. One of its twin peaks is supposed to resemble a cobbler mending a shoe. Ben Vorloch is at the northern end of Loch Lomond.

[50] Rob Roy's Cave is on the eastern side of Loch Lomond. Robert MacGregor (1671–1734), known as Rob Roy, was a celebrated Scottish outlaw; many of his exploits took place in the vicinity of Loch Lomond. Sir Walter Scott's novel, *Rob Roy*, was published in 1817.

[51] i.e. ditto. [52] On the west side of Loch Lomond, about eight miles north of Luss.

[53] i.e. their son, Henry. [54] Rowardennan, on the east side of Loch Lomond.

[55] The inn at Tarbet in 1826 had apparently greatly improved since 1822, when Dorothy Wordsworth described it as 'villainous'. (See quotation in Malthus 1966, p.262, from *Journals of Dorothy Wordsworth*, ed. E. de Selincourt, London, Macmillan, 1952, Vol. II, p.355.)

[56] 'part of' is ins.

received 18£, and 6½ bolls of meal with milk. In 1816 the money wages fell to 9£. At present. 12£. Altogether what the married men receive is worth more than the earnings of the single man. Their wages in money are about half those of the single man.

The boll of wheat is rather above 4 bushels, of barly six, of oats six.

Farms are now for the most part let in Scotland so as to vary with the price of corn. Sometimes the whole rent varies with the price of corn, and sometimes a part is reserved in Money.

The average produce is calculated according to the quality of the land and the rent is paid according to the price at the fiars.[57]

The average prices of corn at the Fiars* from 1800 to 1821 were

	s	d
Wheat per boll	41.	6
Barley	32	¾
Oats	25.	¼.

At present the price of wheat is about 30s. per boll. Lord Abercrombie's estate formerly let at 5£ per acre, that is during the high prices of the war.

At present a lease has been granted at a boll & a half of wheat, and a boll and a half of barley per acre scots.

1½ bolls of wheat at 30s.	2.	5[58]

[57] Here, and in the next line, Malthus presumably meant to write 'fairs'. [58] i.e. £2.5s.0d.

1½ bolls of barley 6 bushels at 29.	2.	3
	4.	8
In 1825.		
Wheat.	1.	16
Barley	1.	7
	3.	3

Great difference in the rent.

Wednesday 5th
Walk'd down to the landing place of Tarbet – met Hal just arriving from Rowerdinnan* – his distant view from Ben Lomond had been hazy – all the way up was clear – not a very difficult ascent – partys* *may* go very near the top – after breakfast came to Arrochar[59] – part of the way is one of the ...[60] for the purpose, the mountains round Arrochar very good, a good deal of fern about the Inn, the Cobler* and his ...[61] seen through the trees from the window – a storm of Thunder & lightning came on at 4 – followed by rain – ceased ab[ou]t ½ after 7, walk'd along the head of the Lake a little way, then up the hill to the right among the firs are magnificent views of the Mountains particularly the famous Cobler* – whose proper name is Ben Arthur –

July 5.
Mountain behind Tarbet before breakfast. Cobler, Ben Inn.[62] To Arrochar. much superior to Tarbet. Fine trees round the Inn. Rain. Dinner. Walk in the evening by steep road from Tarbet to Head of Loch Long. Mountain's looking very high and picturesque, particularly the Cobler or Ben Arthur.

59 At the northern end of Loch Long, about one mile west of Tarbet.
60 Words unclear. 61 Word unclear, possibly 'Wife'. 62 Ben Ime.

Thursday 6 –

Hard rain in the night – tops of the mountains cloudy in the morng. but cleared by two when we embarked on board the St.Catherine Steam boat – head of the Loch Long looks very grand as you go down, then adscend* the entrance of Loch Goil – one of the finest views is just [63] before you get out of Loch[64] long when the Mountains of Arran[65] are seen in the distance – the evening happened to be clear and allowed us to see all the outlines of the distant Mountains as well as the near so that we were highly satisfied with the Steam expedition – from Arrochar, cruising up the clyde first passd* Gourlock,*[66] a very pleasant bathing place, were shown the exact spot where the Comet[67] went down, then Greenock where the boat stops & passengers climb in & out and go at Port Glasgow a little further on; (they take children for nothing so that there is always plenty of all ages tossed on board) – landed about 8 and got into a Noddy[68] which took us to the George Inn where we had on Monday left the carriage with part of our luggage

July 6.

Walk before breakfast up the hill by Manse, rocky stream. Rain. Walk with party by Church and Manse and along the hill. Stations for sketching. Steam boat at ½ past 2. down Loch Long opening to Loch Goil Head. Mr and Mrs Brown and daughters. Isle of Bute. Granite mountains of Arran. fine outline. Gourlock. Raising the comet Steam boat. Rose Neath Helensburgh. Greenock. Port Glasgow. Dumbarton Castle. View of Ben Lomond. Erskine House. 100000£. Erskine Ferry. Campbell House. Swimming boys. Glasgow.

[63] 'at the entran' is del. [64] 'Loch' is ins.

[65] One of the Hebrides Islands, off the west coast of Scotland.

[66] Gourock, on the southern bank of the River Clyde.

[67] The 'Comet', said to be the first commercially successful steamboat in Europe, was built by Henry Bell at Port Glasgow and launched in 1812. It carried passengers and cargo on the River Clyde between Glasgow and Greenock. It sank in October 1825.

[68] A light two-wheeled hackney-carriage, formerly used in Ireland and Scotland (*OED*).

Friday 7
Left Glasgow after Breakfast – changed Horses at Cumbenuld*[69] and came to Stirling[70] – only stay to dinner and hired horses for the journey to Perth & Dunkeld[71] at 1£.12 pr diem – w[en]t with them as far as Callender*[72] that Eveng. – arrived late in a heavy rain –

July 7.
Ship Bank. New House. Garden Square. Number of new streets and elegant houses on the hill to the West. Exchange. Statue of King William. Trongate. High Street at right angles. College. Old, and new buildings. Cathedral. Pillar, John Knox. Dr Brown said that the introduction of Steam boating had quite altered the habits of the people of Glasgow, and given them strong locomotive propensities. This has been assisted by the Captains not charging for children, which has encouraged parents to take pleasure jaunts with all their family. Dr Brown's daughter of 12 years of age was not charged for.

The crash, and check to credit and confidence, much greater and of longer duration than was ever remembered. To Stirling by Combernald. To Callender in the evening. View back on Stirling Castle. Line of mountains to the West, Ben Ledi, Ben Venue &c: Heavy shower latter part of the way.

Saturday 8th.
Hazy and mizzling rain but pursued our plan of breakfasting at Mr. Stewarts Inn at the Trossachs[73] – cleard* up a

July 8.
To Trosachs Inn. Stuart. by Lake Vennachar. Turk Bridge, Loch Acray. Trosachs. Views of Ben Venue rising over them. The finest views of the lake

[69] Cumbernauld, about 12 miles north-east of Glasgow.
[70] On the River Forth, about 12 miles north of Cumbernauld.
[71] Perth and Dunkeld are north-east of Stirling, but the Malthuses at first proceeded north-west from Stirling to visit the Trossachs.
[72] Callander, about 14 miles north-west of Stirling.
[73] A spectacular mountainous area west of Callander.

little before we came to the Bridge of Turk*[74] (between Lochs Venachar*[75] & Achray)[76] – and continued very favourable all day, af[t]er 6pm set out walking through the Trossachs to L. ...[77] abt a mile & half – the Trossachs are high mounts of Rock & Birch over which Benvenue*[78] towers! Boats are to be had at each end of the Lake – embarked in one with provisions from the Inn – a Man, a Boy, a short oar & a long – admired much the rocky detail of the shore – landed & on climbing up among the birch & heather had fine views of the Mountains at the West end, Benvenue* in front – a winding road is cut on the right hand side of the Lake ...[79] – across the Mountain on the opposite side is most provokingly stripped of its Birch by the Duke of Montrose[80] – landed on Ellens Island[81] just at the place the old Boatman said where Ld. Ellen used to row his little skiff – there is a fine oak tree by the place – ascended to a picturesque resting shed built by Ld Gagdis, full of old armour, stags horns and skins of animals, rustic seats covered with dried heather – there are paths all round the Island which is richly wooded with birch & pine – from the higher part, views of the Lake & Trossach's – dined near the rustico[82] – then entered the boat and again landed from the Northern shore with Helens Island and a peninsular promontory in the middle distance. Much beautiful detail among the rocks and birches on the North side of the lake. The fine birches on Ben Venue were all cut by the Duke of Montrose about 8 years ago – a great loss. Dined on Helens Island and spent the greatest part of the day on the lake and its environs. The rocky & woody accompaniments to Ben Venue render the views of it more picturesque and beautiful than perhaps any other single mountain we have seen.

Labour from 9 to 12 shillings a week The Crash at Glasgow has not affected the Trosachs. Mr Stuart greatly disapproves of the poor Laws and Tithes of England.

[74] Brig o'Turk, a famous scenic spot in the Trossachs. [75] Loch Vennacher.

[76] '(between Lochs Venachar* & Achray)' is ins.

[77] Word unclear, probably 'Katrine', i.e. Loch Katrine.

[78] Ben Venue, a mountain close to Loch Katrine. [79] Words unclear.

[80] James Graham, third duke of Montrose (1755–1836); his ancestor, James Graham, the first duke of Montrose (d. 1742), harshly treated Rob Roy (Macgregor) and suffered retaliations.

[81] Ellen's Isle, at the eastern end of Loch Katrine.

[82] See below, Ch. 8, Mrs Eckersall's letter no.4, entry for 26 August.

on the same side but lower down the Loch – the winding road is there cut through a massy rock, climbed paths up the mountain – for great outline of ...[83] Ben's, Loch Lomond and Arrochar is superior but the near rock & wood close to the Lake ...[84] at Lch K.[85] – rowed to the boat house between 6 & 7 – had a beautiful walk to the Inn, going along the shore of the little river that runs into Lh Achray –

Sunday 9

Left the Trossach Inn at ½ past 7 – fine morning – a little way on a fine picturesque view of Loch Achray with the Rocks of Benvenue* behind – breakfasted at Callender* – overtook many people on the road going to the gathering [at] that place – several smart young women without shoes & stockings – a pulpit was placed near a little green mound near the Town – it was soon surrounded by numbers of people who seated themselves on raised ground on the aforesaid mound, some in a garden opposite – they assembled at eleven – the Preacher came soon after. We stood a while to hear, but the service being in Gaelic we were not likely to receive any edification – therefore R.H. and I[86] set out to see Brachlin Bridge*[87] nearly 2 miles apparently – it is over a singular rocky stream – bridge however not so alarming as represented – the rocks

July 9.

To Callender to breakfast. Fine morning. Shadows on Ben Venue. View over Loch Acray. Callender. Fine view of Benledi from the Bridge. Gaelic preaching in a field adjoining to the Town. Sacrament in the kirk. Influx of people from all quarters; a few proper highland dresses. Church overflowing, and great numbers at the Gaelic sermon sitting on the grass round a pulpit near a grassy mount. Another pulpit in the same field was occupied subsequently by a preacher in English.

Brachlin Bridge.

Pass of Leni in the road to Loch Erne Head. Waterfall. Benlidi with fine accompaniments. Trosachy. Loch Lubnaig. Further end, where an Inn was projected, and given up when half built, very picturesque, much superior to Loch Earne Head. Rain. Dined and slept at Loch Earne Head.

[83] An unclear word is del. but not replaced. [84] Word unclear.

[85] i.e. Loch Katrine. The probable meaning is that, for 'great outline', the views at Loch Lomond and at Arrochar (on Loch Long) are superior to those at Loch Katrine; but that the 'near rock & wood close to the Lake' are superior at Loch Katrine than at Loch Lomond and Loch Long.

[86] i.e. Robert, Hal and I. [87] Bracklinn Bridge is on Keltie Water, near Bracklinn Falls.

are huge & square shaped (of a slaty hue) – when half way up the hill at the other end of the vill[a]ge we could hear the Preacher's voice holding forth in Gaelic – he seemed to preach with much energy – at ½ past two when we left the Inn he was still going on – another party were then beginning to assemble round an English preacher whose pulpit was on the other side [of] the mound. The road goes by the pass of Leni*[88] – got out to view it – the glen is dark & narrow & the water that rushes among the rocks would make a fine fall when there is plenty of water – then by the small Loch Lubnaig – very pretty – a mountain comes finely down into the water. Bridge & fir trees at the end where the road turns towards Loch Earn[89] – had arrived at 2d place in the rain & the Inn's not near the Lake – from our present view of it see nothing striking, dined & slept there.

Monday 10

Before breakfast to Killin[90] by a barren pass in the Mountains – after a long descent came to a very peculiar rocky stream[91] over which two bridges are thrown – on one side of these is an old gateway leading to a mound with scotch fir – the burial place of the McNabs – a very characteristic Highland village – many cottages without chimnies* – after breakfast

July 10.

To Killin to breakfast 8 m. Mountainous road, half ascent and half descent. View back to Benvoirlick, forward to Ben More. Came into the road from Dalmally and Tyndrum. Entrance to Killin very striking Rocky river rough bridges, Mill. MacNab's burying ground. Ben Lawers. Mr & Mrs Kennedy. Walk up the hill. Fine view of the lake. Lord Glenorchy's house.

[88] Pass of Leny, about two miles north-west of Callendar, on the road to Lochearnhead.

[89] About ten miles north of Callendar.

[90] About six miles north of Loch Earn, at the western end of Loch Tay.

[91] River Dochart. See note by James in Malthus 1966, p.264, n.1.

met Mr. & Mrs. Kennedy[92] – walk'd with them up the hill to a point of view from which the lake[93] and mountains Ben More and Ben lawers are seen – walk'd to the rocky Bridge – then hired a Boat to take us 8 miles down the lake – embarking on the river close to the Inn, had a hard storm of rain, cleared up and we had a fine view of the mountains at the head of the Loch, landed on a low woody rocky[94] shore and eat our dinner spared from the wind – on getting again into the boat found the waves rather high – proceeded 2 miles more and landing at the ferry joined the carriage – the road is high above the Lake with very fine views and unguarded edges till you come to the woods through which descend to Kenmore[95] – found the Kennedies arrived and drank tea with them –

Ben Lawers. Boat to the halfway house towards Kenmore. Fine view back on the head of the lake and Ben More. Great complaints of the drought. The crops of oats and barley near Killin looking extremely ill. Wages in summer 1s. 6 – 20d. and 2s. but work not always to be had. Cottar system 2 acres of land, with keep for a cow. Rent with the house about 7 or 8£ a year. Sometimes the house is built by the tenant and no rent paid for the house for a certain term of years. Tasks for 13 or 15 yrs. Many houses without chimnies; thatched with fern. Killin a good specimen of a large highland village.

The small trades people generally rent two or three acres of land with pasture on the mountains for a cow or cows.

Dine on cold meat under a rock by the lake.

Barley and oats near the road on the side of Loch Tay after we joined the carriage looking better.

Slept at Kenmore, shared the large room with Mr & Mrs Kennedy for tea and breakfast next morning.

Landlord at Kenmore complained of the drought, the fall in the price of cattle, and the overpopulation of the country. Many small farms of 15 or 20£ a year, mountain pastures for their cattle. No great sheep farms. These prevail more to the Westward.

[92] See Malthus 1966, p.264, n.2. [93] i.e. Loch Tay. [94] 'rocky' is ins.
[95] At the northern end of Loch Tay.

Tuesday 11
All the party went together to Taymouth[96] – much admired the giltern staircase, library, dressing room very handsome, the last with satin wood doors – walk'd up to the ...[97] – were caught in a very hard highland shower & got into the carriage quite wet – quite fine when we arrived at Aberfeldy[98] – before dinner followed an old woman as guide to the falls of Moness – the Glen's singularly narrow & deep – no water in the lower fall, but were fortunate in coming to the higher to find that the Miller on the top was just letting down the water & there was a very fair summer quantity – the rocks here are very high & close together not covered with fine birch as other woods – you go through a walk cut to the falls by Ld Bredalbane* – wt on after dinner to Inver a mile from Dunkeld[99]

Dined at Aberfeldi. Falls of Moness. The labourers working at the quarries for the bridge which is building earn 20d., & 22d without victuals. The rent for two acres and a cottage generally 8£. the land apparently very indifferent.

Inn at Inver a mile from Dunkeld. Walk in the evening by the Tay.

[**July 11**: No entry.]

[96] Taymouth Castle, about one mile north-east of Kenmore, the seat of John Campbell, 5th Earl of Breadalbane and Holland (1796–1862) (*GEC*).

[97] Word unclear. [98] About five miles north-east of Kenmore.

[99] About 15 miles by road south-east of Aberfeldy.

– the walks in the Duke of Athol['s][100] are close to the Inn – wt after tea by[101] a remarkably pretty path in his grounds along the banks of the Tay – craggy looking hills covered with firs on the opposite side – slept at Inver –

Wednesday 12
Breakfasted at Dunkeld with the Kennedies – wt together to the Duke of Athols*[102] saw the old Abby* the two antient* Forests said to be the first in Scotland – the Abby's* situation very fine surround[ed] by trees and craggy hills covered with fir – along the banks of the Tay finely wooded – then crossed the Moor to the Hermitage – found a falls farther up with mirrors to reflect the fall – very little water in the rocky bed of the river – returned by Inver, dined at Dunkeld, and wt afterwards to Perth.[103]

July 12.
Breakfasted at Dunkeld with Mr and Mrs Kennedy. Dunkeld Grounds. Larches; Cathedral; Church; Walks by the River. American Garden. Ferry. Hermitage. Ossian Fall. Fine views from the hill going to Hermitage. Much might be seen from Inver without a guide. Dined at Dunkeld with Mr & Mrs K. To Perth in the evening. Mr K informed me that in Ayrshire the labourers at present earn from 6 to 9 shillings a week; average hardly more than 7. without victuals. The price of labour much affected by the influx of the Irish. Town of Perth. Tay. Hill [an illegible word] of Square.

Thursday 13
After breakfast walk'd to the banks of the River[104] – admired the handsome building erected there for a Town Hall – portico wth Grecian Column's – on leaving Perth about ½ way up the

July 13.
To Kinross. View back on Perth. Crops much burnt.
River Earn. New Bridge. Mineral Waters. Loch Leven. Kinross. N.Queens Ferry. Hill. view of

[100] John Murray, fourth duke of Atholl (1755–1830): 'was deeply interested in afforestation, is believed to have first planted larch on a large scale in Scotland, and was the author of "Observations on Larch", London, 1810'. His father, John Murray, third duke of Atholl (1729–74) was buried at Dunkeld (*DNB*, under 'John Murray, third duke of Athol').

[101] 'by' is ins.

[102] On the Duke of Atholl, the Abbey (or Cathedral), the Hermitage and the falls, see Malthus 1966, p.265, n.1–n.3.

[103] About 25 miles south-east of Dunkeld.

[104] River Tay.

hill on the going to Kinross[105] there is a grand view of the Town, Bridge and Mountains – road goes through a remarkably pretty glen[106] – Loch Lean,*[107] on the banks of which is Kinross, is low shored and bare – discharged our stirling* horses there, and wt post to Queens ferry[108] – dined and embarked with carriage on board a broad Steam boat – walk'd up, on a very pretty terrace above the Inn, a beautiful view of the Forth – arrived at Craig Crook at two –

Edinburgh & Frith* of Forth. S.Queens Ferry. Hill. Western mountain's. Craigh Crook.

Friday 14 –

Remained at Craig-crook – walk'd in its woods in the Evening to enjoy the fine view of the Forth, the castle and the Town, Arthur's seat[109] etc –

July 14.

Barley cut on the road to Edinburgh. Excellent cultivation. The farm next to Mr Jeffrey lets for a boll of wheat, a boll of barley, and £3.15. an acre. seems to have suffered but very little from the drought.

Saturday 15

Went to Edinburgh directly after breakfast, & accompanied Mr. Jeffrey to the courts – were very fortunate in hearing an amusing Jury cause, a Professor of St. Andrews,[110] prosecuting a News-paper Publisher, for putting in a Paragraph, during a time of irritation between Professor & Students about the election of a Rector, in which he said the Professors class

July 15.

Courts. Heard an excellent speech from Mr Jefferey and a good reply from Mr Colbourn. Cause – a libel on Professor Alexander of St Andrew's Insubordination in the Greek class.

[105] About 16 miles south of Perth. [106] Glen Farg. [107] Loch Leven.

[108] North Queensferry, on the River Forth, about 15 miles south of Kinross. To 'travel post' meant to obtain fresh horses for particular intervals of a journey, hiring them at one place and discharging them at a subsequent suitable place. It could also mean, as for the Malthuses, hiring a driver. The 'Cash Account' at the end of Malthus' diary of the Scottish holiday shows that they paid £1/4/0 for 'Post Horses from Kinross to Queens Ferry'.

[109] A hill of volcanic origin, a little over one mile south-east of the centre of Edinburgh.

[110] Professor Alexander. See note by James in Malthus 1966, p.266.

was in a state of insubordination – this was made a great deal of as tending to injure his character – Mr. Jeffrey made a capital and eloquent speech and shew'd* I think the nonsense of the charge and the folly of bringing the young students into court as witnesses for & against the order he kept in his lecture room – Mr. Cockburn replied – very good and very Scotch[111] tho' not equal to Mr. Jeffrey – The Judge summed up very badly and very partially for the Professor & he got 50£. damages – returned to dinner & Mr. Cockburn dined with us.

Sunday 16 –

July 16.
Dr Gordon.

Went to Edinburgh after a late breakfast, to Evening Church that we might hear Dr. Gordon,[112] reckoned one of the most celebrated of the Scotch preachers – but we were certainly a little disappointed – he's a fine looking man & his sermon very sensible & tho' he is said to be very calvinistical, there was nothing in it harsh or revolting to those not so I thought, but there was nothing striking in his manner & his sermon was assiduously read – indeed

[111] Cockburn 'retained his Scottish accent, and was fond of Scotch allusions. His manner was extremely homely, and he spoke with an air of sincerity which gave him a singular influence over Scottish juries ... [but] was more eminent in criminal than in civil cases' (*DNB*).

[112] Probably, Robert Gordon, DD (1786–1853), free church minister; 'a very popular preacher, and a man of profound piety and comprehensive learning, amiable, and conscientious in the discharge of his duties'. In 1826 he officiated at the New North Church in Edinburgh. His writings include several scientific articles in the *Edinburgh Encyclopaedia* (*DNB*).

he seemed afraid of losing his place. We returned to dinner accompanying M^rs^. Rutherford*[113] who dined at Craig crook –.

Monday 17.

Being engaged to dine at Mr. Murray's[114] we determined to go early to Edinburgh and take that opportunity of going to Arthurs seat taking a coach to Holyrood house – Mr. J.Hall[115] going with us who sd he would be our guide up the mountain – found it slippery from the deal of rain, but the wind high kept us cool[116] – the great distance hazy but all the near view fine – wt up to Ld.Anthony's ruined chapel on returning – the view of the Castle & Town very pretty from thence, got into the coach & drove to

July 17.

Captain B. Hall. Mr Hall. Arthur's Seat. Mrs Trotter, Upholsterer. Provost of Edinburgh. Tables. Cabinets. Curious Elm. Calton Hill Camera Obscura. Mr Naismith Pictures. Models of Steam Engines. Lectern. Invention for securing the safety of High Pressure Engine.

113 Presumably, Mrs Rutherfurd, the wife of Andrew Rutherfurd (1791–1854), Lord Rutherfurd (1851), Scottish judge: 'In legal acuteness and argument ... he was superior to both his friends, Cockburn and Jeffrey' (Archibald Alison, quoted *DNB*). The Rutherfurds are not mentioned by Harriet Malthus before this occasion on 16 July, but Malthus' diary notes that they met 'Mr Rutherforth' on 21 and 24 June, and 'Mr & Mrs Rutherforth' on 23 June.

114 Probably, Sir John Archibald Murray (1779–1859), Lord Murray (1839), Scottish judge, a frequent contributor to the *Edinburgh Review*: 'His hospitality was profuse and famous' (*DNB*). This dinner on 17 July is the first mention of Murray in Harriet Malthus' diary, but Malthus' diary records that they met him in Edinburgh on 21 and 24 June also.

115 James suggests (Malthus 1966, p.256) that the person referred to by Malthus as 'Mr Hall' could have been John Hall, the elder brother of Captain Basil Hall (see n.119 below), or his younger brother James. The fact that Harriet referred to him as 'M^r^. J. Hall' adds credence to this suggestion. As James notes, John Hall became the fifth baronet and an F.R.S.; and James Hall became a well-known patron of art and was an amateur painter.

116 Twenty-four years earlier, Malthus had been most impressed by the mountain-climbing ability of Miss Eckersall (the future Harriet Malthus). On 12 September 1802 he wrote from Lucerne to Monsieur Acerbi in Paris: 'In Chamouni Miss Eckersall has acquired a deathless name, and is to be handed down to posterity by the Historian of the Alpes, as the first lady that ever reached the summit of Mount Brevin, a mountain of very cons[iderable] height opposite Mont Blanc, and hitherto untrodden by female foot' (Masè-Dari 1929).

Mr Trotter[117] a great uppholdsterer* and Ld Provost ie Ld Mayor of Edinburgh – he has most beautiful Tables & cabinets of knotted elm, and oak, & other woods that can be seen – he gave us an order for the Observatory on the Calton hill – only saw the Camera Obscura,[118] which turned out to be obscure. Next to Mr. Nasmyth's[119] who is a great oil Painter whose 6 daughters are excellent Paintresses and whose 2 sons are very ingenious mechanic's – it was to see the model of a section of a Steam engine of their making that we went. Called on Mrs. Rich & then dressed to dine at Mr. Murray's – there we met Capt Basil Hall,[120] Mr. McCulloch, Mr. Fullarton & one or two more – returned to Craig Crook by ½ past ten.

[117] William Trotter, Lord Provost of Edinburgh from 1825 to 1827, usually referred to as William Trotter of Ballindean, after the estate he purchased in Perthshire before he became provost. He was head of a firm of cabinet-makers and upholsterers at 9 Princes Street. It is not clear whether the Malthuses visited him there, or at his home at 13 Abercromby Place. Trotter was also involved in a number of public and charitable organisations. He died in 1833 at the age of 61. (For this and other information on William Trotter we are indebted to Mr J. Hogg, Library Officer, Edinburgh Room, Central Library, Edinburgh.) Malthus' reference to 'Mrs Trotter' in his entry for 17 July was presumably a slip of the pen.

[118] The Observatory on Calton Hill was built in 1818, but transferred to its present site on Blackford Hill in 1896 (D. Keir, ed., *The City of Edinburgh*, 1966). The Camera Obscura (literally, 'dark room') is an optical device that projects images of the surrounding area onto a screen. It was used in the eighteenth century by illustrators and topographers, and is said to have been used as an aid to painting by Canaletto and Reynolds, although this latter view has been disputed. However, its 'principal application seems to have been for diversion, naïve wonder, and poetic inspiration', as noted by Pope, Gay and Addison (see R. Smith, 'Canaletto and the *Camera Obscura*', *Studies in the Eighteenth Century*, ed. R.F. Brissenden and J.C. Eade, Vol. IV, pp.223–34, 1979, Australian National University Press, Canberra). Little is known about the Camera Obscura seen by the Malthuses on Calton Hill in 1826. A Camera Obscura has existed on Castlehill in Edinburgh since 1853. It is situated on the rooftop terrace of a building known as the Outlook Tower, next to Edinburgh Castle. It projects 360° life-size views of the city onto a white concave wooden table by means of a system of mirrors and lenses (the present lenses were installed in 1947) rising to about 28 feet above the table and facing out through a protected opening on the roof. (We are grateful to Mr Andrew Johnson, Manager, Camera Obscura, Castlehill, Edinburgh, for information on the history and present design of the Edinburgh Camera Obscura.)

[119] On Mr Nasmyth, see Malthus 1966, pp.256–7.

[120] Captain Basil Hall (1788–1834), a naval officer who had written accounts of his naval engagements and travels (see James, in Malthus 1966, p.256; and n.115 above). See Appendix A, item 24, letter from Captain Hall.

Tuesday 18.
Had a beautiful walk to Cotersphen*[121] – called on the Moreheads and returned on the hill, met the Ld M's[122] who had been to call at Craig Crook – Mr. & Mrs. Buchan had called in the Eveng.

July 18.
Village of Costolphen. Mr Morehead.

Wednesday 19
R. H. & Emily wt to Edinburgh – Had to take a view of C.Crook & Env from the hill – had rain in the Eveng. Mrs. Gordon[123] & her little girl came –

July 19.
Waterloo Hotel. Castle. Grass Market. Leith. Newhaven

Thursday 20 –
Rain most of the day – left Craig crook & Edinburgh after dinner – same road we entered till a little past Torsplance*[124] Inn – latter part of the way to Selkirk[125] by the banks of the Tweed extremely pretty – slept at Selkirk.

July 20.
To Selkirk – Valley and banks of the Tweed. Crossed both Tweed and Ettrick.

Friday 21
Set out before breakfast – rain – took Hal inside first stage to Hawick[126] – cleared up after breakfast. Next stage, Mospaul Inn,*[127] road from thence a curious narrow pass among steep, green, bare mountains, road cut out from the side making a frightful

July 21.
To Penrith

Source of the Teviot between Hawick and Mospaul Inn. Another stream running the opposite way from the same source joins the Esk. Green mountains. Not burnt. To Langholm – same kind of country chiefly. From

[121] Presumably, Corstorphine. [122] Presumably, Lord Murray and his wife. (See n.114 above.)

[123] Possibly, Isabella Gordon, the wife of the Dr Robert Gordon mentioned in the diary entry for 16 July.

[124] Torsance. The journey north from Ripon to Torsance had been via Durham, Newcastle and Kelso. The journey south from Torsance to Ripon was via Selkirk, Carlisle and Penrith.

[125] About 35 miles from Edinburgh.

[126] About ten miles south of Selkirk. Although Hal (then aged 21 years) had been well enough to climb Ben Lomond on 4 July, this suggests that his health was a cause for concern. His younger sister, Lucy, had died of tuberculosis the previous year (1825), aged 17 years; and in the following year (1827), according to Patricia James, Hal began to show signs of the same disease. The Malthus family spent the winter of 1827–8 at Bordeaux for the sake of Hal's health (James 1979, p.412).

[127] Mosspaul Inn, about 12 miles south-west of Hawick.

unguarded precipice without the compensation of beauty – after Langholm[128] the road is uncommonly beautiful by the banks of the Esk – dined at Carlisle[129] – from thence came to Penrith[130] through heavy rain – saw nothing of the country.[131]

Langholm to Long Town. Vale of the Esk.

Saturday 22d–
Breakfasted at Appleby,[132] very small County Town – at Brough,[133] the next stage were obliged to take 4 horses[134] – to help us up to the top of Stanmoor,[135] a bleak high down over which the road passes – rainy day and the wind very high & cold on the moor – after the first 7 miles it is down hill to Greta bridge[136] – next through the rain into the grounds of Rokeby[137] by the side of the rocky river Greta to where it is joined by the Tees – then on to Catterick bridge[138] and to Hollin[139] by ½ past 8 – found all well & boys at home –

Sunday 23 –
Some of the party went to the Cathedral[140] – fine day but not warm – walk'd along the road – Capt Horn dined.

[128] About ten miles south of Mosspaul Inn. [129] About 18 miles south of Langholm.

[130] About 18 miles south-east of Carlisle. They appear to have slept that night at Penrith.

[131] The entries in Malthus' diary end at Penrith on 21 July; but his 'Cash Account' provides details of the journey from Penrith to Haileybury (Malthus 1966, p.272).

[132] About 12 miles south-east of Penrith. [133] About eight miles south-east of Appleby.

[134] The extra cost of the four horses is listed in Malthus' Cash Account. [135] Stainmore.

[136] About 19 miles east of Brough.

[137] Rokeby Hall and its grounds, Rokeby Park, which lie just north (although the text suggests south) of Greta Bridge. Sir Walter Scott had intended to visit the owner of Rokeby Hall, John B.S. Morritt, in 1825. See letters from Scott to Morritt in Lockhart 1902.

[138] About 15 miles south-east of Greta Bridge.

[139] i.e. Hollin Hall, near Ripon (where the diary begins), about 25 miles south of Catterick Bridge.

[140] Presumably, Ripon Cathedral.

Monday 24

Fine day, had a sail on the Lake – a game of cricket with the boys – Mr. & Mrs. Jamieson dined, attacked a wasp nest after tea, took leave of the Woods – and early –

Tuesday 25

Left Hollin, b.[141] at Wetherby[142] – dined at Barnby Moor,[143] and slept at Grantham,[144] arrived soon after nine –

Wednesday 26

B. at Stamford[145] – dined at Arrington,[146] walk'd in Ld Hardwicks* park[147] – arrived at Haybury*[148] a little before nine.

[141] i.e. breakfast. [142] About 16 miles south of Ripon.

[143] About 45 miles south-east of Wetherby.

[144] About 37 miles south-east of Barnby Moor. The journey on 25 July from Hollin Hall to Grantham, a distance of about 100 miles, was the longest day's travel during the tour.

[145] About 20 miles south of Grantham. [146] About 40 miles south-east of Grantham.

[147] i.e. the grounds of Wimpole Hall (near Arrington), the seat of Philip Yorke, third Earl of Hardwicke (1757–1834) (*DNB*).

[148] i.e. East India College, at Haileybury, about 26 miles south of Arrington.

8 *Letters to Harriet Malthus from her mother, Catherine Eckersall*

INTRODUCTION

The five long letters in this chapter are from Catherine Eckersall to her eldest daughter, Harriet Malthus, wife of Malthus. Catherine Eckersall wrote the letters while on a two-month holiday to the Lake District in the summer of 1825 with a large family party. As the first letter indicates, Malthus and his wife and their two surviving children (Emily and Henry) were then about to return from a holiday in Europe, following the death of their third child, Lucy, on 3 May 1825, aged 17. The letters refer to specific days and months, but not the year. However, the year (1825) is evident from the (indirect) references to the death of Lucy.

Although the letters contribute only slightly to our knowledge of Malthus himself, they are a valuable source of information about the characters and activities of his relatives, and provide an interesting insight into the lives and attitudes of an upper-middle-class English family in the 1820s.

Catherine Eckersall (1755–1837), née Wathen, was a first cousin of Malthus – a daughter of a sister of Malthus' father. She was said to be very handsome and was painted by Sir Joshua Reynolds. In 1774 she married John Eckersall (1748–1837), who was a first cousin to her (son of a sister of her mother). As Catherine Eckersall's mother and John Eckersall's mother were sisters of Malthus' father, they were both first cousins to Malthus. In 1825 Catherine and John Eckersall had a house at St Catherine (referred to in the letters as 'St. Cats'), near Bath. They appear to have been accompanied on their holiday by their two unmarried daughters Fanny and Clara; by their eldest son, George, and his wife; by a married daughter, Eliza, and her husband, Henry Wood, and at least two of their children; and by their son-in-law, Henry Wynne, and at least four of his children, his wife having died in 1821. Thus, the members of this family holiday party were:

(1) Catherine Eckersall (1755–1837), the writer of the five letters, signed 'CE'.

(2) John Eckersall (1748–1837), husband of (1); referred to as 'Mr. Eck' and 'Mr. E.'

(3) Frances (Fanny) Eckersall (1781–1861), fifth daughter of (1) and (2), unmarried.

(4) Clara Eckersall (1791–1869), eighth daughter of (1) and (2), unmarried; referred to also as 'Clara Eck'.

(5) George Eckersall (1782–1849), eldest son of (1) and (2). He is referred to as 'George' or 'G', and he and his wife are referred to as 'the GEs', 'the G Ecks', and 'Mr & Mrs G Eck'.

(6) Sarah Caroline Eckersall, née Grace (d. 1855), wife of (5), referred to as 'Caroline', 'Car', 'Mrs G', 'Mrs George', and 'Aunt George'.

(7) Revd Henry Wynne, rector of Killucan, Co. Westmeath, Ireland; third son of Rt. Hon. Owen Wynne, of Hazlewood, MP, High Sheriff of Co. Sligo 1745 and 1785; son-in-law of (1) and (2); his wife Catherine (b. 1777) (7a), the second daughter of (1) and (2), had died in 1821. They had eight children – four daughters, who were present on this holiday, see (8)–(11) below; and four sons, who were apparently not present, but who are mentioned in the letters – see (18)–(21) below (*BLGI*). He is referred to as 'Mr. W' or Mr. Wynne'.

(8) Marianne Wynne, daughter of (7) and (7a), 9 years old; also spelt Mary Anne; later married her first cousin, Edmond Wynne, a son of William Wynne, who was a brother of Henry Wynne (7); died 1877 (*BLGI*).

(9) Lucy Catherine Wynne, daughter of (7) and (7a); married (1828) Revd Edward Nixon, MA, rector of Castletown, Co. Meath; died 1883 (*BLGI*).

(10) Clara Wynne, daughter of (7) and (7a); married (1836) her first cousin, George Wynne, a son of Robert Wynne, who was a brother of Henry Wynne (7); died 1895 (*BLGI*); referred to also as Clara W.

(11) Kate [Katherine] Wynne, daughter of (7) and (7a); married Solomon Richards, of Ounavarra; died 1848 (*BLGI*).

(12) Anne Eliza Wood (1790–1875) (née Eckersall), seventh daughter of (1) and (2), referred to as 'Eliza'.

(13) Henry Richard Wood (1786–1844), husband of (12), of Hollin Hall, near Ripon; referred to as 'HW' and 'H Wood'.

(14) Frederick Wood (1811–86), son of (12) and (13), referred to as 'Fred'.

(15) Boynton Wood (1814–41), son of (12) and (13).

(16) Maria Frances Wood, daughter of (12) and (13), 9 years old.

The Woods (12) and (13), had another son, Richard John Wood (1817–53), who is not mentioned in the letters, but might have been present also.

The party also included an 'Ann' or 'Anne' who looked after the two 9-year-old cousins, Marianne Wynne and Maria Frances Wood, and who was probably a maid or governess employed by the Woods. There was also a servant (the 'new Man') of Catherine and John Eckersall, named Sergeant, who drove their barouche and who 'rowd* the Skin off both his hands'.

Catherine Eckersall's handwriting is difficult to decipher – especially the proper names – and we cannot therefore guarantee that the following transcription is completely accurate.

The biographical details given in this introduction and in the editorial footnotes have been compiled from James 1979, *BLG* (entry: Wood, with sub-entry Eckersall), *BLGI*, and Leslie 1936.

Other family members are mentioned in the letters but were apparently not present on the holiday, viz:

(17) Revd Charles Eckersall (1797–1863), eleventh and youngest child of (1) and (2), later rector of Farnborough (Hants) and of All Saints, Worcester.

(18) George Wynne, son of (7) and (7a); born 1804; married (1834) Anne, daughter of Sir Daniel Toler Osborne, 12th bart; became General George Wynne, RE.

(19) Revd Harry Wynne (1799–1847), son of (7) and (7a); rector of Ardcolm, Co. Wexford; married Marianne, daughter of Solomon Richards, of Roebuck, near Dublin.

(20) Revd John George Wynne, son of (7) and (7a); rector of Lorum, Co. Carlow; married (1831) Emily, daughter of Thomas Goold, MP, Master in Chancery; died 1854.

(21) Charly [Charles] Wynne, son of (7) and (7a); married Isabella, daughter of James Nugent, of Clonlost; became Lieutenant-Colonel Fifeshire RA; died 1893.

(22) William Wynne, barrister, MP, one of the five brothers of Henry Wynne (7).

(23) Malthus (1766–1834), referred to as 'Robert' or 'Rob'.

(24) Harriet Malthus (the addressee), wife of (23), daughter of (1) and (2). Malthus (23) and his wife (24) are also referred to as 'the Malthus'' and as 'the M's'.

(25) Henry (Hal) Malthus, son of (23) and (24).

(26) Emily Malthus, daughter of (23) and (24).

(27) Lucy Taunton (1780–1860), née Eckersall, daughter of (1) and (2), married (28) in 1805.

(28) Robert Cropp Taunton, husband of (27), rector of Ashley, Hampshire. He had officiated at the wedding of (23) and (24) in 1804.

There is also mention of two deceased members of the family:

(29) Amelia (Emily) Eckersall (1784–98), sixth daughter of (1) and (2).

(30) Caroline Eckersall, third daughter of (1) and (2), died 1797, aged 18.

LETTER 1[1]

Begun at Milnthorpe[2]
Sunday July 24
sent Wed[y].27th [1825]

My dear Harriet,

I wish to write in time for you to receive it [at] Halybury* – but I fear it will not arrive in time to be found upon yr table by the 27th [3] but I wait, to see all our folks & give you some little acc[t] of them – which I may do tomorrow if we get to Keswick. I fear you have suffer'd still more by the uncommon heat of the weather, which lasted till Wedy the 20th & since has been succeeded, by remarkably cold winds especially towards Even[g] – The papers mention the Thermometer being at 97 at Brussels [4] – it was 95 at Cheltenham,[5] where we spent a week of great suffering, for our Lodgings were on the High S[t] in the middle of the Town & our bedchambers had no Garrett* over them – so the night was worse than the day – Fanny[6] wd have benefitted by the waters in more moderate weather; as it was, the waters seemd* to agree, & took away her sick headache but she is grown thin & looks but ill for the fatigue of the journey overcomes her, but now it is[7] nearly at an end I trust she will get better – Our only amusement at Cheltenham was Fanny Twiss[8] in her new character of Saint,

[1] Addressed: 'Mrs.T.R.Malthus / E I College / Hertford'.
Postmark: KESWICK 298.

[2] Milnthorpe (Cumbria), a village seven miles south of Kendal.

[3] The return of the Malthus family from their continental tour was slightly delayed. They finally arrived at the East India College, Haileybury, some time between 5 and 9 August. Catherine Eckersall's second letter suggests that Malthus and his family were at Marlow in early August.

[4] In Malthus' diary of the continental tour the following entry can be found: '*July 18*. Cologne. ... The master of the hotel Rheinberg Cologne said that the day before the Thermometer in the shade had been as high as 27 Reaumeurs – 99 of Farenheit' (Malthus 1966, p.242).

[5] Cheltenham, about eight miles east of Gloucester, was formerly a spa. They appear to have stayed there for the sake of Fanny's health.

[6] For information on the family members mentioned in these letters, see the list of family members in the introduction to this chapter.

[7] 'is' is ins.

[8] Possibly related to Horace Twiss (1787–1849), son of Francis Twiss (1760–1827) and Frances (Fanny) Kemble (1759–1822), who was a sister of the actress Mrs Siddons (*DNB*). Horace Twiss was a friend of the Eckersall family and acted in amateur theatricals at their home in Claverton (James Archive, p.10219).

& devoted follower of M^r^. Close[9] – but she is as agreable* as ever – & as open & frank as she always was, so that we discuss'd these opinions in the most friendly manner – but she wd not introduce us to her friend – whose right hand she is become; she has prepar'd his Sermons for the Press, & there is already[10] a 2^d^ Ed^n^.; she has formd* a school for him, which she sedulously attends – M^r^. Eck read all the 9 Sermons, besides Erskine's internal Evidences –[11] I was too hot, so I only read 3 Sermons & ½ the Evidences but I lik'd the former, & thought the latter very ingenious – M^r^. Close is Evangelical – a very lively person, his countenance has more of hilarity, than of inteligence* – On Wed^y^ the 20th we saw from the walks in the even^g^. some beautifull* & strong Lightening* – which seem'd to cool the air almost immediately – & the next day[12] after breakfast, we set off & got to Birmingham[13] which the girls were anxious to see, & we thought we sh'd get all sorts of pretty things – but it was all dear & the people disagreable* – & we were faggd* with seeing the machinery etc etc & the dirt & the finery at the fine Inn were quite sickening – so we were happy to drive away from the place – but we drove into more dirt – more manufacturing Towns – salt works, Hatmaking – Potteries, Glass works, Cotton works smoking from their lofty narrow Towers – for miles & miles to be seen on all sides. It was only this morn^g^. we began to get clear of these annoyances; we slept last night at Preston,[14] & went to Church this morn^g^., & coming out fell in with George & his Wife, who had kept the Coach waiting to see us. They had spent ½ an hour with M^r^. Eck, who not being quite well, staid* away, & in the Street then met quite accidentaly* – & we hope to join them at breakfast tomorrow at Kendal,[15] where we also expect to find letters from the Wynnes & Woods, to tell us where they are, & if they have provided any lodgings for us at Keswick or else where

9 Francis Close (1797–1882), BA (1820), MA (1824), DD (1856), was curate at Cheltenham (1824–6), and perpetual curate there (1826–56). As well as being a popular evangelical preacher, he erected, or caused to be erected, five district churches, with schools, and was one of the founders of Cheltenham College. Dean Close School, Cheltenham, was founded in his memory. He was the author of upwards of seventy publications – including *A Course of Nine Sermons on the Liturgy*, first edition 1825, seventh edition 1844 – 'but few of these are of any permanent value' (*DNB*). He was dean of Carlisle (1856–81) and perpetual curate of St Mary, Carlisle (1865–8). He was bitterly opposed to the theatre, as well as to alcohol, tobacco (*Tobacco: Its Influence, Physical, Moral and Religious*, 1851), and horse racing (*The Evil Consequences of Attending the Race Course*, 1827) (Venn; *DNB*).

10 'now' is del. and 'already' is ins.

11 Thomas Erskine (1788–1870), *Remarks on the Internal Evidence for the Truth of Revealed Religion*, Edinburgh, 1820.

12 i.e. Thursday 21 July. 13 About 50 miles north-east of Cheltenham.

14 About 110 miles north-west of Birmingham. They slept at Preston on Saturday 23 July. No details are given for Friday 22 July. On Sunday 24 July, they travelled from Preston to Milnthorpe (about 28 miles north of Preston), where Mrs Eckersall began this letter. They slept at Milnthorpe on the night of 24 July, and travelled to Kendal on Monday 25 July.

15 About seven miles north of Milnthorpe.

– We had a letter from Eliza to say they were all heartily sick of Allonby[16] – a horrid bare sand, & nothing to be seen but Sea & Sand – well adieu & goodnight for the present. I shall take up my pen in yr service tomorrow[17] I hope.

Tuesday 26 – we [18] met the GEs at Kendal, M^rs^. G unwell, M^r^. Eck the same, so we agreed to get on to Bowness,[19] & take some rest & repose there – they acc[ompanie]d us in a Chaise[20] & we passd* a delightfull* day at a new Inn, the Crown, whose Garden was a *Station* N°.5 – with one of the finest views on the Lake[21] – we sent for a letter from Ambleside – which told us we were expected at Keswick where they had taken Lodgings for us – therefore after breakfast we proceeded – over tremendous hills – 22 long miles to Keswick;[22] it was near 6, & they were all on the water, but dear not little Maria gave us a most cordial reception, & for the 1st time I beheld Marianne Wynne; they are of the same age 9 years – this last *is* something like her dear Mother – the eyes, & the beautifull* brow & forehead – she is grown quite good & school has done much for her, her carriage is gracefull* – in about an hour all return'd – M^r^. Wynne the same as ever perhaps a little aged – I am sorry to find poor Lucy W does not much amend, & walks as little as possible – Clara, thinner than she was, so her figure is not improv'd – Kate grown, & a nice girl, but her face not quite so handsome as when she was at St Cats[23] – George was sent for to take his station as one of the[24] Coast surveyors & he will have an exelent* situation of it[25] – Harry is well now & beginning to add to his Rectory House – & his wife expected to lye* in in Sepr next !! – John has studied himself sick

16 Allonby (Cumbria), a seaside town on Solway Firth, five miles north-east of Maryport.

17 There is no entry for Monday 25 July, but the events of that day are recorded at the beginning of the next entry, for Tuesday 26 July.

18 'spent' is del.

19 Bowness, on the east bank of Windermere, is about eight miles west of Kendal, and about five miles south of Ambleside.

20 'Chaise' is a 'term applied to various pleasure or travelling carriages, the exact application having varied from time to time' (*OED*).

21 i.e. Windermere. The Eckersalls in 1825, like Malthus in 1795, were apparently using West's *Guide to the Lakes* – the account of 'Station V' begins on p.65 in West's description of Windermere.

22 Keswick, on Derwent Water, is about 15 miles north-west of Ambleside. From Kendal to Keswick is about '22 long miles'.

23 i.e. St Catherine's. Catherine and John Eckersall had a house at St Catherine, near Bath. They also had a house at 17 Portland Place, Bath. According to James 1979, pp.415–16, the Eckersalls lived during the summer months from 1821 onwards at St Catherine's Court, a seventeenth-century house. There is some doubt, however, whether they lived at St Catherine's Court or at St Catherine's Lodge on the estate of the Court. (We are grateful to Mr Colin Johnston, Archivist, Bath & North East Somerset, for information on St Catherine's Court and St Catherine's Lodge.) In a letter of 9 June 1830 to Wilmot-Horton Malthus wrote (and then deleted) that they were about to go to 'St Catherine's, near Bath', not 'St Catherine's Court, near Bath' as stated by James (1979, p.415).

24 'one of the' is ins.

25 There is another reference to George Wynne's appointment as a surveyor at the end of the fifth letter.

– but when it is over & he gets ordain'd, it is expected he will be well again – Charly is left among friends for his Holidays – Henry Wood tann'd as brown as Mahogany – but looking so young nobody will believe him the Father of his 2 fine boys – Fred^{k} – a very nice pretty lad of 14 – Boynton nearly as tall & much stouter – He is a little more Humaniz'd – Eliza looking very handsome – & interesting herself in every thing scientific & curious as ever – I suppose she will be a Geologist like Fanny & Clara!! who having attended Lectures at the Bath Institution are becoming adepts –

Well now having told you abt every body, I must proceed to say I was much annoy'd when George told me M^{rs}. Bray[26] had informd* him you had not heard from me – I wrote to Antwerp & to Amsterdam 2 long letters, surely you must have ere now recd* them for I made no delay – tho yr letters did not reach St Cats very expeditiously – G tells me too you call at Brighton & leave Emily there – I hope Hal will stay with you then, for you sh'd not be without one of them[27] – the G Ecks tell me too you intend coming to us at Xmas, my letters both propos'd it & we are very glad you intend it – I hear too, that you will not be at Halybury* till the 31st. so this will greet you then. We have all been invalid*ish* with Bowel complaints & the intence* heat yesterday overcame me & I was v...[28] & faint with the burning Sun[29] just as we came down the hill & burst upon the ...[30] of the Lake – we walkd* out last night, to Fryers Craig*[31] and saw the moon beams glitter in a sparkling line from our feet quite down to Lowdore;*[32] – by the bye, they lock it up for the lucre of a Shilling – Some of us saw last night some fine Northern lights & beautifull* falling coruscations – Nothing can be in greater confusion, & Hullabaloo, than the whole party at present – we cd procure nothing – not a towel to wash ourselves, no candles to light us to bed at past 12 O Clock – it is to be hoped we shall set ourselves to rights bye & bye – Lucy is Housekeeper & by my desire we dine at two, & have order'd the boat at 3; some go in M^{r}. Wynne's Car & some in Henry Woods little

26 Presumably Malthus' sister, Mary Anne Catherine Bray (1771–1852), widow of Edward Bray (died 1814). She was living in London in 1825.

27 Emily would probably have been left with one of Malthus' sisters, holidaying at Brighton.

28 Word (possibly 'vexed') partially missing because of damaged MS.

29 'with the burning Sun' is ins.

30 Word missing, possibly 'view', because of damaged MS.

31 Friars Crag.

32 Lodore.

Phaeton & Gig[33] – & we shall walk as far as[34] the Bowder Stone[35] – The Lakes are new to Clara & she got on [the] Barouche[36] Seat along side of Sergeant, our new Man, & was charm'd & delighted beyond her expectations – The G.Ecks spent a most agreable* time in London – & afterwards visited Marlow,[37] & came down in their Canoe, visiting Windsor,[38] H Court,[39] Twickenham,[40] where they found friends to visit all the way back to London – Charles fully intends calling on you & said it was always his intention – he is going afterward to make sundry visits in Hampshire. The Bishop[41] has been to visit Katherine Church & has directed Service & a Sermon to be performd* *every* Sunday, & our nice agreable* Vicar Mr. Spencer Madan[42] agrees to it with pleasure – Now they ought to make a good road, for this good man who is to attend in all weathers – The G Ecks will go on to visit Scotland, so they hope to get letters from you to some of yr friends in the ...[43] *they* have some good recommendations already – they promise to return after Xmas, & are to be establishd* at St Cats which will be a great comfort & pleasure to us – Well now, I have told you all our news, & us'd up my tea spoonful of ink in my small Patent ink bottle – & I am tolerably indifferent & have not shaken off my Invalidship – therefore with all

33 A 'phaeton' is a 'species of four-wheeled open carriage, of light construction, usually drawn by a pair of horses, and with one or (now generally) two seats facing forward ...' (*OED*). A 'gig' is a 'light two-wheeled one-horse carriage' (*OED*).

34 'to' is del. and 'as far as' is ins.

35 In Borrowdale, on the Derwent River, south of Derwent Water, about five miles south of Keswick. Catherine Eckersall (presumably with her husband, John, and perhaps also their daughter Fanny, who was unwell) seems to have taken a boat to the south end of Derwent Water and walked from there to Bowder Stone, about 1½ miles.

36 A barouche is a 'four-wheeled carriage with a half-head behind which can be raised or let down at pleasure, having a seat in front for the driver, and seats inside for two couples to sit facing each other' (*OED*).

37 Marlow (Buckinghamshire) is on the River Thames, about four miles north-west of Maidenhead.

38 In Berkshire, on the Thames, 22 miles west of London.

39 Presumably, Hampton Court Palace, on the River Thames, about ten miles south-west of London, built by Cardinal Wolsey in 1515 and presented by him to King Henry VIII.

40 A district in Middlesex, on the Thames, 10 miles south-west of London.

41 George Henry Law, bishop of Bath and Wells.

42 Spencer Madan was vicar (1824) of Batheaston (three miles north-east of Bath, on the road to St Catherine) and vicar (1825) of Twerton (a district on the western side of Bath). He was chaplain to the king from 1830 until his death in 1851 (Foster).

43 Word unclear, possibly 'K. dom' (Kingdom?).

kind love from *all* the party to my dear Robt, & yourself, Emily & Hal, & hoping & wishing & desiring you will write soon & direct to Capt Bagshaws Keswick, for here we shall stay a week at least – believe me my dear Harriet

Y^{r} ever very aff^{e} Mother
C E.

We certainly shall not stay a day after our week which ends Monday or tuesday next – but we will get yr letter forwarded to us.

LETTER 2

Ambleside
sent sunday Aug.14 [1825] – or
rather early Monday 15

My dear Charles – & my dear Harriet[44]

I got yr letter on Sat: the 6th. & we were very glad to hear from you at last, & shall begin to answer it as soon as possible – it was only 3 days on the road from Marlow to Keswick, where it found us just on the wing for Patterdale[45] – but as I mean to continue my journal in a regular way for the Malthus' & your information (if you wish it) I will take up where I left off in my last to Harriet & as you are going to Halybury* very shortly Harriet will read it to you I dare say if you desire it & so you then will hear the whole History of the whole party – as far as it goes & so will the M's if you communicate this to them. I thought you were at Halybury* by this time but as you desire me to direct to Cork St.[46] I shall, & you can take it with you; I believe they have been expecting you some time – We were all very well amus'd with the His.of y^{r} Voyage & g^{t} adventure was comical enough – I fear the exercise of rowing must have been a great exertion to you after the g^{t} trials you gave your constitution in attending hot stifling parties in London during the late uncommon hot weather – pray continue to give us your history & adventures & we shall communicate only what is proper for general information – I agree perfectly with you that these

[44] Addressed: 'Mrs.T.R.Malthus / E I College / Hertford'. When Catherine Eckersall began this letter she was addressing her son, Charles, at Cork St, London, but as she explains towards the end of the letter, she later decided to send it to her daughter, Harriet Malthus, at the East India College, where Charles would be visiting.

[45] A village situated just south of the southern end of Ullswater.

[46] Cork St., London W1, in the borough of Westminster, near Piccadilly, Savile Row and Albemarle St.

lovely scenes sh'd be view'd in much smaller parties, than This of 12!![47] & the confusion & noise is to be set against the pleasure of this otherwise agreable* family meeting – Y^{r}. Father & I are still in a grumbling sort of state – the rest quite well – Mr. Wynne is far more agreable* than I ever knew him. Lucy much improv'd – Kate as delightfull* & usefull* as ever – Clara, not strong enough to exert herself to be usefull* even if she chose to be so & puts her Aunt George sometimes in a fret with her – she never will hear, never will attend to any ones wants but her own – poor George has a return of pain – but hopes to be better for 3 pills, some potted char,[48] a sawcer* of Gooseberries, 3 sorts of sweetmeat, Honey in the Comb besides the usual articles for breakfast etc etc – Eliza is much oblig'd for yr *promise* of writing when she gets to Hollin[49] – but she has learnt not to depend upon you she says – she is in very good looks – which she had better not try to improve – & her faithfull* admirer HW. complain'd to me of this mistaken method of improving her beauty – she is very active & up to every thing that any of the party can undertake, excepting Clara Eck who goes up a Mountain & takes walks of 10 & 12 miles every day – & Fanny too, hops & skips about like a mountain Goat – well – shall I take to my journal, & you will then hear all in a regular way – I keep no other journal except a few notes in my pocket book – I sent off my letter to Harriet on Friday the 5th[50] on our return to Keswick from Buttermere[51] – We spent best part of Saturday Morn^{g} or rather F. & Cl.[52] purchasing minerals which our good natur'd Landlord, Capt Bagshaw, undertook to pack & send off to Bath – a little after 2 we set off with 4 Horses they made us take ½ way, a stage of 22 *long* miles to Patterdale – good road. The latter part very beautifull* coming down upon the centre of Ulswater*[53] Lake which we all agree to think preferable to Keswick[54] & Windermere & far more picturesque to the eye of an Artist no doubt, since most of the views exibited* are on this Lake – the drive thro Goborrow*[55] is enchanting, passing close by some towering perpendicular rocks till you come to Patterdale where the river,[56] the woods, the perpetual Cascades just now, & the green chearfull*

[47] The number '12' is puzzling. As noted in the Introduction to this chapter, the family party appears to have numbered sixteen. Catherine Eckersall's calculation must have excluded four younger children.

[48] A fish found deep in the lakes, a relative of the trout. It was the custom to prepare it in attractive pots.

[49] i.e. Hollin Hall, near Ripon, the home of Anne Eliza Wood (née Eckersall) and Henry Richard Wood.

[50] The letter of 5 August to Harriet Malthus is missing from this collection.

[51] The village of Buttermere at the northern end of the lake of that name is about 7½ miles south-west of Keswick.

[52] i.e. Fanny and Clara Eckersall. The previous letter referred to them as geologists.

[53] Ullswater. [54] i.e. Derwent Water. [55] Gowbarrow Park.

[56] Grisedale Beck flows into Goldrill Beck between Patterdale and the south end of Ullswater.

Meadows with the view of the Lake & fine Mountains are all that can be desir'd. Here is a good Inn, some part so recently added as only in March last that those rooms are perfectly damp, yet our party is so large some of them were forc'd to sleep in them the first night – but some people going away, we are all now accomodated* in safety I trust – tho without all the comforts one cou'd ...[57] & one w'd wish to dispense with the more shewy* articles for other more common comforts – Wynnes & Woods had just arriv'd – the G.Ecks d^{o} having walkd* from Ambleside 10 m – left Anne & the 2 children in comfortable Lodgings[58] – Marianne had been a source of great amusement to George – she is a very sensible & clever girl & he finds her as witty as ever – Caroline was happy he was amusd* for his disorder always makes him low spirited –

Sunday we went to the beautifull* little Church here – The *Parson* was in Corderoys* & black worsted stock^{gs} – NC.[59] dialect & a shock^{g} drawl – after C. we took a most rash unfortunate walk up the horrid Slate Mountain, Place Fell,[60] to see – nothing – a line in the clouds – the Scotch Coast, wasting our strength for no purpose – however the near views were charming as were the assemblage of Mountains – but Mr. Eck & I & George were dreadfully fagg'd –

On Monday the 8th. we were foolishly deterr'd by the rain from boating but it afterwards clear'd up & we each took our own *glad way* – some walkd* to the opp^{te}. side & view'd G'oborrow* etc & a slate quarry, a walk I was able to undertake.

Tuesday 9 – with our luncheon on board, we seated ourselves in *one* large boat, 13 inc Boatman – & when the wind ruffled the water & a few Horses heads appear'd we thought ourselves too large a Crew – landed on an Island,[61] with a fine view – Then past M^{r}. Askew's Lodge, a green retreat among fine rocky scenery close to the Lake[62] next Lyulphs Tower[63] – M^{r}. Howards[64] – where we landed & walkd* up to Airy*[65] Force – a grand & beautifull* Waterfall with 2 Alpine bridges – inspiring – we kept some of the party waiting in the boat 2 hours & ½ & then proceeded further to Yew Craig*[66] – a fine rocky promontory &

[57] 'wish' is del. and a word, possibly 'crave', is ins.

[58] Anne was possibly a maid or governess – there is a reference to the Woods' maid in the entry for Wednesday 3 September, in letter 4. The two children were probably the nine-year-old cousins, Marianne Wynne and Maria Frances Wood. There is a reference to 'Ann & the 2 little Girls' in the entry for Friday 26 August, in Letter 4.

[59] North country.

[60] A mountain of 2154 feet, about one mile east of the south end of Ullswater. It is understandable that Catherine Eckersall and her husband were 'dreadfully fagg'd' after walking up Place Fell. They were respectively 70 and 77 years of age in 1825.

[61] Possibly, Norfolk Island. [62] 'close to the Lake' is ins.

[63] Lyulph's Tower – 'a singular building which serves as a hunting-seat for the duke of Norfolk' (Robert Southey, *Letters from England*, p.234).

[64] Bernard Edward Howard, Duke of Norfolk, 1765–1842 (*GEC*).

[65] Aira Force. [66] Yew Crag is about one mile east-north-east of Lyulph's Tower.

then being ab^{t} ½ way down the Lake we turn'd round, some walking occasionally thro' Goborrow* & M^{r}. Askews to dinner at ½ past 6 – we stay here till Saturday – just one week & are boarded at 35^{s}.& 6^{d}. p^{r}. week exclusive of Wine & Spirits. Keswick & this will be expensive enough – still more probably as we are not in Lodgings here & there is no other Inn in the place & it is cramm* full – We are looking for Lodgings at Ambleside where we stay a week at least – The Weather is uncommonly favorable* to us, raining in the night only just to fill the Waterfalls & clearing away at 12 O Clock –

[Wednesday 10] – in the Eveng* – in the Eveng* of yesterday 9 we had the Cannon fir'd on the rock behind the house, & poor Lucy was carried up & we all stood behind – but instead of 17 Echo's !![67] we had only one fine reverberated sound for ab^{t} a q^{r} of a minute – This morn^{g} Wed^{y} 10 – is *not* so favorable* & a party to Helvelyn* is put off – Eliza, Clara & Kate Wynne[68] were to have ascended to the top –

Thursday 11 – we spent the whole day on the water coasting at first the rocky & wooded shores of Placefell,* that same Placefell* that looks so barren & we execrated on my Sunday walk – some walk'd up to a curious waterfall under Blaburn knob*[69] – we lunchd* on bread & cheese among rocks that had we slip'd* we shoud* have fallen many a fathom deep in the water – we went on two reaches of this 9 mile Lake till we got a view of Dunmallet & Pooley Bridge – & then turnd* about & at Lyulphs Tower M^{r}. E.& I & M^{r}. G. got into M^{r}. Wynnes Car & drove home – this was a day of great enjoyment without any fatigue. This Lake we agree to think superior to all the others – for it only grows tamer at the 3$^{'d}$ reach – every walk, every step here is lovely in the Detail & the sketches taken are innumerable by M^{r}. Wynne & Lucy, who is even more inspir'd than her Father – she is much improv'd in manners & is a very amiable girl – It is decided now that they do not go to Hollin – all this travelling she is sensible is injurious to her – so they will after they have seen all the ...[70] return & spend all the remaining Autumn at Arklow[71] for Sea air & Bathing – this place

[67] It was the custom to fire a cannon so that visitors could listen to the echoes. Catherine Eckersall's expectation of 17 echoes probably came from a misreading of West [1778] 1799, p.157: '... the report [of the cannon] is reverberated from rock to rock, promontory, cavern, and hill, with every variety of sound; now dying away upon the ear, and again returning like peals of thunder, and thus re-echoed seven times distinctly'.

[68] Presumably Eliza Wood, Clara Eckersall and Kate Wynne.

[69] Probably, Bleaberry Knott, on the eastern side of the lake, about 500 metres high, and about 1.25 kilometres north of Place Fell. Its slopes are very steep, and the lake at that point is 60 metres deep.

[70] Word(s) missing.

[71] Arklow, in Co. Wicklow, is on the Irish Sea, 14 miles south-south-west of Wicklow, in south-east Ireland.

will be near John's Living, who finds it difficult to get ordain'd, but thro' some Bishops influence it will be all settled[72] – Harry and his wife go to Dublin on the 1st of Septr to prepare for her acouchment* –

Friday 12 was showery – hitherto the rain had not prevented us on any excursion but falling in the morn^g. derang'd all our plans. [T]herefore M^r. Eck & I & M^r. Wynne & Lucy & Eliza walk'd & sketch'd only – the rest wa[l]ked 3 miles up the lovely[73] Vale of Glen-ridding, to see a Lead mine, all went in, but Fanny & Clara – the 1st for fear of the wet, the last for fear of being in the dark – they brot* home specimens of pure Ore mix'd with Christalizations,* – at ½ past 2 George & Caroline set off in M^r. Wynne's Car, 4 miles on their way to Ambleside, the rest they performd* on foot – these two chargd* with many commission[s], had much to do – & on [74] their exertions we chiefly depend for our establishment – we have engagd* Lodgings that will just hold us, that a Lady C[75] ...[76] has just quitted – the rest *hope* to be accomodated* – & M^rs. G. is to buy in provisions for us all for 3 days – there will be no general sitting room – we intend to invite alternately to Tea & ... & ...[77] –

here comes Saturday 13 – a very wet day, & little prospect of its clearing away – the 4 Horses are arriv'd – nobody drives away from this place with less.

Sunday 14 – after waiting in vain till ½ past 5 for the weather to remit a little of its wrath we orded* out the Horses & set off – the Wynnes & Woods thought best to stay & take the chance of a better day as they had not 4 horses to pay for – before we got ½ a mile, it was discoverd* one of the leaders had lost a shoe, & they wanted to go back – but Sergeant gave them a sal...[78] for their negligence – & we proceeded close[79] by the side of a roaring stream ...[80] had the hood up so cd see little & the rain threw all the mountains into ...t[81] tho it increased their height. Torrents were rushing down all their sides – we passed close along the small Lake of Broader water or Brotherwater*[82] from two brothers having been droun'd* in it – immediately after, we began to ascend Kirkstone M^tn., 3 miles in ascent & as many in the descent,[83] it was lucky for me I cd see but little – a precipice on one side to which we were at one Time y^r Father said within a few inches – never was there so wild a scene – he declar'd he had never witnessd* such – & Clara even was nervous & began to shake her head – dont tell

[72] The reason why John Wynne was finding it difficult to get ordained is not explained. His future living had obviously been settled.

[73] 'lovely' is ins. [74] 'from' is del. and 'on' is ins. [75] 'C' is ins.

[76] Word unclear, probably 'Mordaunt'. See n.92 below. [77] Words unclear.

[78] Word partly missing, probably 'salvo'; MS damaged here and below. [79] 'close' is ins.

[80] Word missing, probably '– we'. [81] Word partly missing, probably 'mist'.

[82] Brothers Water, about 1½ miles south of Patterdale. [83] i.e. Kirkstone Pass.

her of it – 9 or 10 torrents were seen at once & ...[84] of them all the way – when we arrivd* at the top, they took off the lea[ders] & we draggd* down – steep,[85] almost perpendicular, the descent w[as] more formidable than the ascent, except that there appeard* no precipices – we cd see little of the beauties of Ambleside[86] in the rain, which continued to pour & arrriv'd at our nice & very comfortable lodgings soon after & George & Caroline ready to receive us with an exelent* fire to dry our wet garments – Clara obligd* to change every thing as Car brot* her a complete change from their lodgings close by – oh how happy we found ourselves, after being at a dirty Inn for a week, where we had not a drawer or scarce one article of comfort – & in the common sitting room you had to part yr way thro clothes & shoes, & drawing books that the Wynne girls & M^r^. W. himself left lying about in "confusion worse confounded".[87] We had a delightfull* dish of tea & some fine Honey, Car had supplied us with – she is to continue her office of provider, so I shall be quite in clover, without care – we found a letter from Miss Bedford, a large sheet most agreably* & curiously fill'd, which Clara read out to us – she is return'd from Tenby, where she went in the Steam Packet, a passage of 13 hours & sufferd* most severely – wd have thankd* any one if they had push'd her overboard – she has been since to Cheddar cliffs with the Brandrams, who have just left Elmhurst[88] – she says she is very glad to hear Charles has got Bedford Chapel, as she shall see him in Town in Octr. but I fancy she is mistaken by what you tell us in yr letter – she has been to the Bagman's to see & kiss Clara's child i.e. the white Kitten – who she says is well worth her maternal cares – This morn^g^. we went to Church – & after walkd* to see the two children[89] – who are looking very well & as wild as Hares – George wd not let them acc[ompan]y us to Stockgill Force,[90] as we shd not see it in any comfort if

[84] MS damaged here and below. [85] MS has 'a steep'.

[86] Ambleside, at the north end of Windermere, is about 6½ miles south of Patterdale. The Eckersalls (Catherine, her husband and two daughters) had passed through Ambleside on the way north to Keswick, but had not stopped there to explore Windermere and its environs, presumably because they had arranged to meet the Wynnes and the Woods at Keswick – the Wynnes had been holidaying at Allonby, about 18 miles north-west of Keswick – and to return south to Ambleside in company with them.

[87] John Milton, *Paradise Lost*, Book ii, lines 995–6: 'With ruin upon ruin, rout on rout,/Confusion worse confounded.'

[88] Possibly, Francis Holles Brandram (b. 1787) and his wife Maria (m. 1823), youngest daughter of William Bedford, of Birches Green, Warwick, and Elmhurst, nr. Bath (*BLG*, 18th edn, Vol. II, p.62). The 'Miss Bedford', writer of the 'curiously fill'd' letter, was presumably another relative of William Bedford; and possibly the 'Sophia Bedford' who advised the Eckersall's servants of their impending return (letter of 21 August, below).

[89] Presumably, Marianne Wynne and Maria Wood, who had been left at Ambleside while the party were at Patterdale.

[90] Stockgill (or Stockghyll) Force is a waterfall about one kilometre east of Ambleside on Stock Gill (or Ghyll) – a river running from Kirkstone to Ambleside.

we had to look after them – it was in high beauty so well fill'd & the Salutation[91] Landlord has made a walk of great accomodation* to it – but the people have pulld* up many of his seats & most of the Fences – on our return the first thing we saw was the 2 Carriages – Henry Wood thought little of the road, anymore than his good Horse, but Mr. Wynne said it was a very alarming road indeed & one he shd not like to take again – their Lodgings are larger, but not so pretty or comfortable as ours. Lady Mordaunt, the Widow of Sir Charles, with her 3 children have just left it – we met & spoke to her at Patterdale – she has the remains of some beauty she possessd* when Miss [Holbech][92] – the celebrated Warwickshire toast – I have been thinking my dear Charles I had better direct this to Harriet as I have been forcd* to keep it so long by me, you may have finishd* yr visit at Halybury* – Therefore it can be sent after you faster – as she will probably know where to direct to you, at least to yr lodgings when she has done with it – They all desire their love & George particularly who wishes as we do to hear the sequel of yr acquatic* tour – & if you have sold the Canoe – They are all coming to Town, & *it will* be some contrivance to accomodate* them all in the small apartment – as to our parlor,* it will scarsely* hold us 6 Ecks[93] at Dinner time – The good Lady of the house who has a Son she means to educate for a Clergyman is to dress our dinner. It is happy for her she has got the old English Set – instead of the Irish etc – Yr Father is better, & so am I – We shall stay a week here & some days at Bowness, so pray write directly or in 2 or 3 days after you get this, for it may follow us to Bowness – We shall see Coniston Lake from hence – & we are to [go] up a small Mountain[94] here from which many lakes are seen, & the Sea also – I remember going up it 45 years since – Farewell my dear Charles – Harriet – Robt, Hal & Emily, yr ever affec CE – all send their love to all.

[91] Presumably intended in the sense of a visit paid to someone, from the antiquarian meaning – 'A visit of ceremony paid to a Roman in his house' (*OED*).

[92] MS appears to have 'Holbitch'. Sir Charles Mordaunt (d. 1823) married (1807) Marianne, eldest daughter of William Holbech, of Farnborough, Warwickshire (*Burke's Peerage* 1938, p.1783).

[93] Presumably, the Eckersalls listed as (1)–(6) in the introduction to this chapter.

[94] Probably, Loughrigg. See n.112.

LETTER 3[95]

Finish'd Sunday Aug 21 – [1825]

My dear Harriet

Y[r] letter[96] which I got yesterday Morn[g] was just 4 days on the road – you were in perfect time to direct here, & so you will be for the next letter as we stay another week at these delightfull* headquarters which are also less expensive – & we can be excu[r]sive from hence to many places – I am enabled this morn[g] only to give you our plans, as they have been agitating some time, & seem just now settled to everyones satisfaction – but before I proceed, let me thank you for your care of Charles, who I am sorry to hear has got a Cough, & the G Ecks said he had a sort of cough in Town – & no wonder, as he tried his constitution in hot rooms & often walkd* home in the rain etc – he had better make a breastwork[97] of fine flannel – & also tell him not to over fatigue himself if he goes to Ashley to shoot, & then sit 7 or 8 hours over Taunton's Port wine[98] – who can stand that? Neither Charles or Hal Malthus I shd think – George continues to complain of his side, & I shd not wonder, if as his Father suspects, his Liver may not be affected in some degree, as most hard livers, I mean drinkers, are apt to be after a course of it – pray do you or Charles write to me very soon after you receive this as I shall be uneasy ab[t] this same cough if it remains – I am glad Robt has got a horse he likes, is it one that he is to drive as well as ride? for I think a few drives will be of service to you – I am sorry to hear you object to seeing y[r] neighbors* & I hope you will feel able sooner than you expect to conquer your reluctance – you that was always so socially despos'd* – *Well* – as they say here – Henry Wood calld* here this morn[g] – & gave in a written acc't of their intentions, he having kindly agreed, as well as M[r]. Eck to prolong their stay – & M[r]. Wynne poor man felt so rejoic'd yesterday after he had succeed'd in perswading[99] those two that he actually *sung** as he drove us in the Car down to Waterhead[100] – I never saw a Man enjoy himself so much & his Girls say – the day *the moment* he gets back to Killucan he is miserable, sick, & unhappy – but what is so delightfull* to him is doubtless *very* injurious to poor Lucy – I gave him yr message but tho he thanks you kindly – the Dublin Surgeons are quite competent indeed, if she *can* but be quiet that is

[95] Addressed: 'Mrs.T.R.Malthus / E I College / Hertford'. Postmark: KENDAL PENNY POST.

[96] Harriet Malthus' letter to her mother is not held in this collection.

[97] The context suggests some kind of garment or poultice to be applied to his chest as a remedy for his ailment – a meaning not found in *OED*.

[98] Revd Robert Cropp Taunton, rector of Ashley (Hampshire), who had married (1805) Lucy Eckersall (1780–1840), fourth daughter of Catherine and John Eckersall.

[99] 'perswading'* is changed from 'perswaded'*.

[100] At the north end of Windermere, just south of Ambleside.

all that is necessary – & poor girl she is perfectly sensible of this necessity – & a fortnight hence I trust will see her safely deposited by the Sea side at Arklow – but to return to Henry Woods document – Wynnes & Woods to Coniston Friday the 26th, leave it on Monday 29 /ie/ Woods – who proceed to Hollin & hope to arrive there on the 1st of Sepr where we shall follow them abt the 4th or 5th of that same month – & stay till the 12th the day they set out for the York Festival[101] & during their absence of 4 days, we shall take the opportunity of seeing Bolton Abbey[102] & remaining at the pretty Inn there – to see every thing. It is possible Clara may acc[ompan]y them to York – & Fanny has receiv'd an invitation to stay at Hollin 2 or 3 months – which she is happy to accept – I wish I cd [do] more for Clara – but indeed, we shd be quite undone, without *one* at home – If Fanny returns Via London, she will be happy to be set down at the College gates to stay a little time with you, & if before Xmas, will return with you to Bath – We shall go to Coniston from hence & return the same day – it is only 8 miles,[103] & if Mr. Eck will agree to breakfast there we can go on the Lake & see a good deal of the stile* of country – Mr. Wynne, Eliza, Fanny & Clara, & Kate, are all stark wild – the more danger & fatigue, the more delight & they will pursue a Mountain or a boggy Tarn at all events & every risk [&] run away with poor Henry Woods Horse which they put into Mr. Wynnes horrid heavy rough outside daunting Car – leave him fishing – & forget to call for him – Mr. Wynnes Mare has been very ill & is only just now recovering – but I shall proceed more regularly from where I left off in my last on Monday the 15th – I walkd* before breakfast to Brathey*[104] bridge – After with the party to The Falls at Rydal which were in perfection – & a walk is now made with Seats at every pri[n]cipal point of view – we return'd by a ...[105] route, & were all dreadfully fatigued, myself *almost* knockd* up & indeed I have never quite recover'd it on the first walk up the horrid Mountain Place Fell – We drink tea

101 Hollin Hall is about 25 miles north-west of York. The Second Yorkshire Musical Festival was held in York on 13–16 September, 1825. The First was in 1823; subsequent festivals were held in 1828 and 1835. Funds raised by the Second Festival were for the York County Hospital and for the general infirmaries of Leeds, Hull and Sheffield. Morning concerts of sacred music were held in York Minster, and evening concerts in the 'Concert Room', which had been built 'for the purpose of such musical festivals as may be held for the benefit of charities', and which was opened with the 'First Grand Concert' on the evening of Tuesday 13 September. The concert began with Beethoven's Symphony No.2 in D Major, Op.36. Handel's 'Messiah' was performed on the second morning, 14 September. We are grateful to Mr R. Geoffrey Bowling, Acting Local Studies Librarian, York Library, for the above information and for providing copies of the concert programmes.

102 The remains of the twelfth-century Bolton Priory are about 20 miles south-west of Ripon.

103 The village of Coniston, at the north end of Coniston Water, is about six miles south-west of Ambleside.

104 The river Brathay flows from the west into the north end of Windermere. The bridge is about one mile from the centre of Ambleside.

105 Word(s) unclear, possibly 'very rugged'.

alternately at each others Lodgings – very hot & squeezy – some play at Whist with Baby cards – others draw – the younger play at Pope Joan[106] – and then we call for Lucys Chairmen[107] & Lantern to light us home –

Tuesday 16 – went on the Water rowing round the Head of the Lake – thought it appeard* *very* tame after Ulswater* – after dinner, we walk'd a mile to see what they call Nooks* end[108] – a romantic rocky river & bridge, surrounded by those fine Mountains, & their green cultivated Vales at their feet –

Wedy 17 – being rainy we pass'd a large portion of the day at Mr. Greens exhibition of his Voluminous Sketches & finishd drawings – We purchas'd a set of Etchings, some of which Mr. W. & Lucy & Kate are shading for us, they are very good & 60 in number for 24s – in the Eveng we subscrib'd for the Band to play to us –

Thursday – while they were on the water – it being a fine day – Mr. E. & I took the Car onto Skelwith bridge,[109] saw the Fall,[110] which is not much of one – then walkd* on to Lochrigg* Tarn[111] a mile – it has some pretty scenes on its banks – our walk home again tir'd us – The wild party went up the Mountain of Lochrigg[112] & saw 6 lakes – & retd* still more tird* than ourselves –

Yesterday Friday 19 – The wild set, having first as usual[113] taken Lucy & her Sisters & the 2 children down to a boat that a Capt Watson an acquaintance of Mr. Wynnes has lent him – set off in the Car on a 19 mile expedition to a wretched boggy Tarn call'd Blen* Tarn[114] but the scene was wild & grand on to & even beyond Langdale Pikes[115] & did not return till ½ past 6, to fetch poor Lucy – who however had inducd* her Aunt Clara to stay with her & row her about after Sergeant was obligd* to return to wait on us, who has rowd* the Skin off both his hands – All were pretty well faggd,* but I dare wd have been ready for another expedition to day, only that Henry Wood wd not let them have the Horse – Fanny is as enterprising as any one – & what is wonderfull* can do as much as any one of them – when it is what she likes – I had got into

106 'A card-game played by three or more persons, with a pack from which the eight of diamonds has been removed, and a tray or board having eight compartments for holding the stakes, these being won by the players who play out certain cards' (*OED*).

107 Lucy Wynne was apparently too ill to walk. She appears, however, to have later recuperated from her illness. She married in 1828 and lived until 1883.

108 Nook End, north of Ambleside. The bridge is over Scandale Beck.

109 Skelwith Bridge, a village about two miles west of Ambleside, on the River Brathay.

110 Skelwith Force, a waterfall just west of Skelwith Bridge.

111 i.e. Loughrigg Tarn, to the north of Skelwith Bridge.

112 Loughrigg is about 2½ miles north-west of Ambleside. From its peak (1099 feet) it is possible on a clear day to see seven lakes – Windermere, Rydal Water, Grasmere, Elterwater, Blea Tarn, Coniston Water and Esthwaite Water.

113 'as usual' is ins. 114 Blea Tarn, a small lake, three miles west of Skelwith Bridge.

115 A series of jagged peaks at the summit of Langdale Fall, the highest being 2403 feet.

the boat, but got out again – to walk with M^r^. Eck to Low Wood*[116] – & we found our way thro the woods to Troutbeck[117] & back, a very delightful walk – but still all these walks, seem to encrease* the pains in my limbs & feet, & I must give it up I believe for a season, & see if I can recover the effects of so much fagging – Nothing can be had here that is convenient & comfortable to go in – Yesterday some of our party, landing, saw a fine 6 oard* boat come up in gallant stile* with dressd* boatmen, from which landed M^r^. Canning[118] in a white hat, looking very pale, & a handsome old lame Lord – & a M^r^. Barber, who has a beautifull* Cottage in capital good taste in Grassmere,*[119] which we are going to see, he was their guide – & they all went off together in Carriages which met them on the shore – We are going, some of us, on the water, that want repose, & I am writing in the mean time, it is very difficult to find time for this operation & still worse, eyesight, for ...[120] fagging days are as hurtfull* to a mans eyes as to a horse. I rather apprehend, we shall now be able to return to St Cats by the end of Sep^r^. – & we have given notice, thro Sophia Bedford to our Servants that they may expect us, & I shall write to M^rs^. Nutcombe too, that we shall visit her much sooner than I had led her to expect – In this place are inumerable* little pretty Cottages, where you might live delightfully & at very small expence* – The Inns however here & at Low Wood,* are extravagant beyond even that at Raines bridge – & in consequence people get only Lodgings – or only stay one night, seeing every *thing* in the most rapid manner – they will

116 Lowwood.

117 Troutbeck Bridge, a village on the eastern shore of Windermere, is at the foot of Troutbeckdale and about 1½ miles south-east of Lowwood.

118 George Canning (1770–1827), statesman. On 24 July 1825, Canning invited Sir Walter Scott to visit him at Windermere: 'You would find me (from about the 10th of August) and Charles Ellis at my friend Mr. Bolton's, on the Banks of Windermere' (Lockhart 1902, Vol. VIII, p.27; and *DNB*). Scott accepted the invitation and, in a letter of 2 September 1825, also commented on Canning's poor state of health (Lockhart 1902, VIII, p.49). Charles Rose Ellis (1771–1845) was nominated for a peerage by Canning, but could not have been the 'handsome old lame lord' in this boating party; he was not created first Baron Seaford until 1826 (*DNB*). According to Lockhart, Mr Bolton was 'a plain English merchant, wholly the architect of his own fortunes'. Canning appears to have arrived at Bolton's seat on 25 August 1825, together with a large group of guests (including Wordsworth), assembled in Canning's honour. Lockhart gives a vivid account of the proceedings: 'There was "high discourse", intermingled with as gay flashings of courtly wit as ever Canning displayed; and a plentiful allowance, on all sides, of those airy transient pleasantries, in which the fancy of poets, however wise and grave, delights to run riot when they are sure not to be misunderstood. There were beautiful and accomplished women to adorn and enjoy this circle. The weather was as Elysian as the scenery. There were brilliant cavalcades through the woods in the mornings, and delicious boatings on the Lake by moonlight' (Lockhart 1902, VIII, p.46).

The visit of Canning and Scott to Mr Bolton's ended with 'one of the most splendid regattas that ever enlivened Windermere' (Lockhart 1902, VIII, p.47).

119 Grasmere. The southern end of the lake is about 2½ miles north of Ambleside; the village of Grasmere, about 4 miles.

120 MS damaged here and below; word(s) obscured.

find their folly, as ...[121] breaking & ruining them selves & their finery as fast as possible – *Well* I shall put up my paper & repose a little – & finish & send it off just before we meet at ten at our house this Even[g] –

Here they all are this hot Eveng in our little Stuffy – after a most laborious Morn[g]. walking round Grassmere* – and not content with that Clara Eck strided* over Loughrigg* Fell to see the 7 Lakes, & came home first of the party – Fatigue seems to agree with her, if she can but get her dinner as soon as she comes home, & M[r]. Wynne declard* she cried before it c'd be set before her – George was of the party & is greatly tir'd & says he will walk no more – & that as Fanny came thro the Village he was asham'd of her for her Face was the color* of a Brickbat – I contented myself with a row on the Lake with H Wood, Eliza & Clara Wynne – M[r]. Eck spent the Morng* in Stock gill Force* & here we are all alive again – have had the Band to play us a few tunes in their way to a Jews House – & are going to play our small cards, for they are Too tir'd to do anything else – M[r]. Canning is at a M[r]. Boltons in this neighborhood,* & is very fond of this Country – he was in one Lodgings 3 years ago – It is uncommonly hot to day – & it is supposd* we shall have Thunder, or an Earthquake – If you write in a day or two after you get this it will be time enough, [122] or we can have them sent after us – here comes Eliza & she can fill up the corner she says tho in a hurry to get to Pope Joan – Good night my dear good people.

Yrs in great haste aff[y]

CE

My dear Harriet: I have long owed you a letter which I should have payed* you with pleasure long ago but did not know at all where to find you till I joined the lake party & then I found my mother and Fanny in such frequent correspondance* with you that I have put off writing to you till after we are all dispersed again which will not be I hope till near the end of September when the Ecks[123] leave Hollin, when I hope our correspondance* will commence again. Your very affte sister AEW.[124]

[125] I recollect M[r]. Bruce perfectly well & so ought you, for he was a great admirer of yours & you may remember yr dear little sister Emily[126] comparing his face, to "an old halfpenny" – I do not so well remember the Ball I gave

[121] Words missing, possibly 'they go'. [122] 'tho' is del.

[123] i.e. Eliza's parents (Catherine and John Eckersall) and her sisters, Fanny and Clara.

[124] Anne Eliza Wood, in her hand. [125] In the hand of Catherine Eckersall.

[126] Amelia (Emily) Eckersall (1784–98), the sixth daughter of Catherine and John Eckersall.

because we had one generally every year – The G Ecks will like much to have a letter sent to him, *M^r^. Bruce*, as they might not know where to find him in Edinburgh – they cannot yet say when they shall be there – G. is low about his side, which he thinks the worse for his long walk yesterday. This is Sunday, I kept the letter as there is new regulations at the Post Office.

LETTER 4[127]

Hollin Hall
Begun – Friday 2 – sent to
the Post at Ripon –
Tuesday the 6th.[Sept. 1825]

My dear Harriet

It may be full time to begin another Epistle to you, tho I doubt not Lucy has forwarded one I wrote to Charles at Ashley dated the 25th with the continuation of our History so I shall go on from that date to the present which will include 9 days, or more, as I find time or not – You will perceive you had plenty of time to direct another letter to Ambleside, as we only left it *this* day after staying there 3 weeks all but one day – we w'd gladly have left it a week sooner – but our party was too large to find accomodation* altogether either at Coniston Water head,[128] or the Ferry House[129] – at both of these places we wd have made some stay, but cou'd not for the above reason – else we were rather tird* & sick of Ambleside, its closeness, stenches, & publicity – our Lodgings were just upon the bridge,[130] the Gossiping place & resort of Men & boys – who watch'd all our proceedings & made their comments in our hearing without any reserve – We cou'd only spend a day at each of the above mentiond* places, as you shall hear in course – for I will not anticipate – only observing what glorious weather we have had, it rain'd only on the *nights* of the 28th 29th & 30th ! & since then seems fairly set in for another series of fine weather, as if it had only just begin* – people say here, they never remember such a Summer – there are & have been of late however heavy clouds upon the Mountains

[127] Addressed: 'Mrs.T.R.Malthus / E I College / Hertford'.
Postmark: Ripon SE6 182... 20... /

[128] Waterhead, a village at the north end of Coniston Water; cf. the village of the same name at the north end of Windermere.

[129] On the west bank of Windermere.

[130] Their lodgings were probably the building known now as Bride House, or Old Bridge House, near the bridge over Stock Ghyll.

that have increasd* their interest by the continued variety of their appearance – Alass* we have now turn'd our backs on these Majestic Falls, & taken a last leave of them –

Well – on Thursday the 25th we only walk'd with all the party to Nooks* end, enjoyd* the pretty *Beck*-bridge & Fall[131] – Eliza, Fanny, Clara & Mrs. George, attended by Henry Wood, whose civility at length got the better of his disinclination, follow'd these scrambling Ladies, over the Wall into Rydal park[132] – where after a beautifull* detour they return'd to dinner hot & foaming with fatigue & the heat of the day –

The next day, Friday, the Wynnes & Woods broke up from Ambleside – leaving Ann & the 2 little Girls in a small Lodging – & drove off in their 2 little Carriages to Coniston[133] – taking Clara with them – We 5 Eckersalls[134] that remain'd amusd* ourselves with walking a beautifull* round, for we are in the centre of these fine Mountains & their lovely rich Valleys – & nothing can compare with Rydal we said 45 years ago – & fourteen years since we said the same, & now again repeat it – that day we had a letter from Lucy who was expecting Charles & Hal with great pleasure – she had enjoyd* her Regatta at Cowes very much – & was then giving Fetes in her Rustico[135] to her neighbors*–

Saturday 27 – after an early breakfast we had horses to our Barouche & leaving Sergeant to walk the 8 m[iles] there, we took Mr. & Mrs. G.Eck in & drove to Water head,* found the party well pleasd* with their quarters – 2 Boats were in readiness to take us down the Lake,[136] which like all the others is richer in Mountains at the head – but *this* is a very inferior one, too chearfull* & pleasing; we landed at Coniston Hall,[137] a curious old ruinous Mansion, now converted into a Farm house, the Chimneys are round & high – some coverd* with Ivy, proceeded down to near the end of the Lake close to a rocky Island,[138] & then return'd in order to walk into ...[139] before dinner, reckond* a picturesque Valley – between two rocky Mountains – At Dinner we had 3 small exelent* Char – quite red – it seems in Summer they are best, but they will not rise but remain at the botton – in the winter they let them selves be caught. I suppose

[131] They had walked to Nook End on Tuesday 16th August (see Letter 3). '*Beck*-bridge & Fall' presumably refers to the bridge over Scandale Beck, and the falls below the bridge.

[132] The grounds of Rydal Hall, about one mile north of Ambleside.

[133] The village of Coniston is six miles south-west of Ambleside at the north end of Coniston Water.

[134] i.e. Catherine and John Eckersall, their daughter Fanny, and their son George and his wife Caroline.

[135] Italian for 'outhouse', 'lodge', 'labourer's cottage', etc.

[136] i.e. Coniston Water. [137] On the west bank of Coniston Water. [138] Probably, Peel Island.

[139] Word unclear, probably 'Grizedale', a village about two miles east of the mid-point of Coniston Water.

they d'ont* regard being potted –[140] There is no writing with these Inn pen's that give all their ink to yr fingers, & keep none to[141] themselves – this par parenthese. We left the G Ecks & Clara & return'd with Fanny only to Ambleside rather late –

Sunday 28 – heard a most super exelent* Sermon from the Bishop of Chester[142] – walkd* in Rydal, had the children to dinner, as we had indeed almost everyday – & nice children they are – Marianne is a very clever little girl indeed –

Monday – we amusd* ourselves with walking as usual – tho' indeed I must say, it was far from being any *amusement* to me – for having overwalkd* myself at first – I have[143] never recover'd my walking powers, but grew more & more aching & tir'd, till at last the very *proposal* of taking a walk, was pain & grief to me – yet I persisted –

Tuesday 30 – we had horses to our Barouche – & drove to see M^r^. Barbers Cottage at Grassmere* – It is unique, & in the best taste, beautifull,* & the Situation a chosen one, the Lake is seen in perfection – for all its imperfections are obscur'd, & hidden from the view – his grounds extend quite up to the top of the Mountain, Silver Howe,*[144] & he is making an easy path to the top[145] – he was at home, & shew'd* us over his place, & into one of[146] his Cottages, built without mortar or any sement* that he appropriates to his company – whenever he has any – he is himself a very disgusting conceited old quiz[147] – once a Manchester Linnen* draper – Where he had his good taste no one can account for – he put us strongly in mind of the late Tom Bowdler,[148] who us'd to call him self the "poor little hermit of St Boniface" – only that this Man Barber had not his sense or cultivation of mind – Canning makes him his Butt they say & really one might enjoy the sport, without much remorse for such an animal –

140 At this point the writing becomes almost illegibly faint, hence her comment on the 'Inn pen's'.

141 'for' is del. and 'to' is ins.

142 Charles James Blomfield, bishop of Chester (1824–8). Ambleside was then in the diocese of Chester. As noted in Ch. 2 above, Malthus was confirmed by a previous bishop of Chester at Kendal in 1795.

143 'have' is ins.

144 Silver How, a mountain about one mile west of the town of Grasmere, north-west of the lake.

145 'to the top' is ins. 146 'one of' is ins.

147 A 'quiz' is an 'odd or eccentric person, in character or appearance' (*OED*).

148 Thomas Bowdler (1754–1825), famous for his bowdlerisations of Shakespeare and Gibbon. Between 1800 and 1810 he lived at St Boniface on the Isle of Wight (*DNB*). The tone of Catherine Eckersall's remarks suggests that Bowdler was a personal friend of the Eckersalls. Bowdler had connections with Bath, having been born at Ashley, near St Catherine, and having attended the school conducted by Richard Graves at Claverton, near Bath – the same school that Malthus later attended. When the school closed following the death of Graves, the Eckersalls lived at Claverton before moving to Bath and St Catherine.

Wed^y the 3^d.[149] Sergeant row'd us 3[150] down the Lake to the Ferry house, & [151] when reaching it were met by some of the party in the large boat with Flags flying & a Bugle horn sounding trying to awaken the Echo's – they had been sailing with young Curwen & another friend of his, both tall dissipated drunken young men who spend their time sailing, smoking, drinking, quite lost to all good & decent company we were given to understand – & indeed mostly by their own[152] appearance & expression – We Ecks saw nothing of them – The party had amusd* them selves very well at Coniston – the G Ecks, Eliza & Clara & Kate went after Church assisted by a Shandry (a Cart with a slung bench in it)[153] up to the top of the Old Man Mountain[154] – saw a curious Tarn call'd ...[155] Tarn that had a[156] complete [157] Volcanic shape – had a fine very extensive view with an assemblage of Mountains surrounding them – M^rs. Smith & her daughter reside close upon Coniston Lake – We brought an immense store of cold provisions & with some additions for the good of the Ferry house, who by the bye poison'd us all & every one that partook of 2 bottles of Devon Cyder* – & landing on one of the most beautifull* of the Islands we took our parting farewell dinner – at least it was a parting between us Ecks & the Wynnes – for the Woods went on with them first to[158] Bowness to pick up the Children & their maid, & then proceeded alltogether* to Kendal, where they slept & breakfasted the next morning, the Wynnes taking the road to Liverpool, & the Woods to Hollin – I long to hear how Lucy has borne the journey;[159] she appears to have recoverd* pretty well from her late shaking excursions, but more relapses w'd be dangerous indeed – It occurrs* to me now that poor Clara W. resembles in some degree my poor Caroline[160] – her head is confus'd, & oppress'd, as if by a severe cold, & she herself poor Girl, when her Aunt George reminded her of restoring something she had borrowd* of the Chambermaid, exclaim'd "Oh bother I don't think I have 3 wits left" – Rest & quiet [161] if they can get it at Arklow with Sea bathing may do much for her as well as Lucy – & Kate has done too much for so young a Girl I fear – We had a delightfull* row back, the G Ecks & Clara assisted poor Sergeant – & we enjoy'd our tea at our small quarters – Just before we sat down, George calld* me out to get a Stare at M^r.

[149] This should of course be the 31st. [150] '3' is ins. [151] 'a few' is del.

[152] 'mostly' and 'own' are ins. The 'young Curwen' was presumably a descendant of John Christian Curwen.

[153] Shandry – a 'light cart or trap on springs' (*OED*). See also later in this letter, Friday 2 September.

[154] i.e. the mountain known as the 'Old Man of Coniston'.

[155] Line drawn in MS., presumably to be filled in later with a name – probably, Low Water, just north of the Old Man of Coniston.

[156] 'the' is del. and 'a' is ins. [157] 'app' is del. [158] 'to' is repeated.

[159] Catherine Eckersall was clearly concerned about the effect on the health of her granddaughter, Lucy Wynne, of the return journey from the Lake District to Ireland.

[160] Catherine Eckersall's third daughter, Caroline (1779–97). [161] 'at' is del.

Canning in his open Barouche, changing Horses to go on to *Stores**[162] – Col Boltons, so call'd from his ...[163] India situation & property, M[rs]. Canning[164] & Ld.C.Somerset[165] ...[166] him –

Thursday Sep. 1st – spent in walking & packing.

Friday 2 – The G.Ecks after breakfast set off with their trunk in a Shandry, which I w'd have you to know is a very fashionable mode of conveyance employ'd by Bishops, Ladies etc etc, for Penrith 24 miles – whence they expect to find various means of conveyance to Scotland – I am happy to tell you Georges side is much better partly in consequence perhaps of the warm plaister,* he put on some days since – & his good spirits had return'd – We took an early dinner & then drove, or rather rattled on at a furious rate to Kendal 14 miles – for they drive here among these Mountains & Valleys, as if the D-L was behind them –

Saturday 3 – we rattled on by Sedburgh* & Hawes to Leyburn in all 45.M. – passd* [167] beautiful Wensley Dale – & Asgarth[168] [169]

At Leyburn, Sunday the 4th we walkd* near 2m to Westwick Church,[170] & back, & after to a Ledge of Rocks abt a mile from L. on to the Queens' Gap – where our Landlord informd* us poor Mary tried to escape, but was overtaken & carried back to Bolton Castle – at 3 O Clock we drove to Masham[171] 12 miles, when we had a sumptuous cold Luncheon – & then 12m further to Hollin Hall, where we found our worthy Hosts taking their tea after walking to meet us & giving us up for that Eveng – they had arriv'd only the day before by 12 O Clock at noon – We find the place much grown & improv'd since we saw it – & [a] most comfortable & enjoyable place it is –

[162] i.e. Mr Bolton's seat, 'Storrs', on the eastern side of Windermere, just south of Bowness.

[163] Word obscured by seal.

[164] 'On 8 July 1800 Canning married Joan, daughter of Major-general John Scott, a young lady with £100,000 ... This made him independent'. She was created Viscountess Canning in 1828, and died in 1837 (*DNB*).

[165] Edward Adolphe Somerset (1775–1855), 11th Duke of Somerset. The 'handsome old lame lord' mentioned in the entry for Friday 19 in Letter 3 was presumably not the eleventh duke. He was only 50 years old in 1825.

[166] Words obscured by seal, probably 'were with'. [167] 'the' is del. [168] Aysgarth.

[169] Sedbergh is about nine miles east of Kendal. Hawes is about 15 miles east of Sedbergh. Aysgarth is about eight miles east of Hawes. Leyburn is about seven miles east of Aysgarth. The total distance travelled on Saturday 3 September, from Kendal to Leyburn, would have been about 40 miles.

[170] Possibly the church at Wensley (just over a mile west-south-west of Leyburn) or West Witton (about 3 miles west-south-west of Leyburn).

[171] South-east of Leyburn.

We have not yet visited the Lake[172] as yesterday, Monday, 5, Eliza was obligd* to[173] Ripon to prepare her dresses for this grand Festival at York that takes place next week – I went as well as Fanny & Clara for repairs, after all[174] this wear & tear –

Here comes Tuesday, 6, & as you perceive I have only just now, after breakfast, found a moments time for writing – we calld* yesterday on M[rs] Wood[175] & her daughters all looking much the same as ever – excepting poor Eliza, who is a pale Specke* of disease & *famine* – this warm relaxing Summer has kept her alive – it is expected when Cold weather comes & contracts her poor digestive powers that she must entirely fail – yet she & all the family are in high preparation for this Festival. The Horses for miles round the Country are engagd* for the whole week & can scarse* be had at enormous prices & as a favor* besides for the common purposes of travelling – that as Henry says, we had better compose ourselves to remain quiet at Hollin & not attempt a digression to Bolton Abby* as we had purpos'd – I believe Clara is going with them. They wd have taken Fanny likewise – but she is quite incapable of the exertion, heat & fatigue of such a thing – tho they will take it more favorably* than others, as it is to a most Comfortable Mansion & Farm of Horses they go at 4 miles distance from York[176] – & he has scrambled together another p[r] of Horses so that with M[rs]. Woods Carriage & their own, they will manage capitally to go & return – Why have you not written to me here my dear Harriet ? I am looking out for a letter every day – This should go to night* by the return of some of the Woods to Ripon – No letter yet from the Wynnes – I will write again soon, when I have news to tell & have heard from you as I hope to do. I answerd* Charles letter directly & wrote to Ashley – which letter you have seen I dare say – Fanny has had two attacks of bile – this last I fancy brt* on by too great indulgence among their fine fruit trees in the garden & at table also – the greatest profusion of Vegetables, Peas etc etc – she is in bed & getting better – I believe I told you we leave her here – & that if it is worth while & there is time

172 A lake in the grounds. Hollin Hall is about 2½ miles south of Ripon.

173 'to' is repeated; 'to go to' was presumably intended. 174 'all' is ins.

175 Mrs Delia Wood (died 1849), mother of Henry Richard Wood. Her husband, Richard Wood, had died in 1815. She had four daughters – Eliza (who, despite the ominous prognosis given here, lived until 1840, aged 63), Delia Maria (1779–1824), Louisa Frances (1784–1868) and Emma Juliana (1798–1885). The last two are mentioned in the following letter.

176 As indicated in the next letter, Henry Wood had arranged for them to stay with the tenants of his property at Copmanthorpe, which being only four miles from York would have been very convenient for attending the festival. As also indicated in the next letter, he had another tenant in York, where their horses could wait.

she might spend a few weeks with you on her return – She had a great mind to go to York – but this Billious* attack has quite settled that matter – Nothing w'd tempt me to such an undertaking – I can go too with *such ease* to hear sacred Music at our own Abbey[177] – I was quite delighted there last year – I shd like you to come when there is another performance – All loves attend you – CE

LETTER 5[178]

Hollin Hall
begun the 12th.[Sept.1825]
sent off Sunday [18th]

My dear Harriet

I had yours dated the 5th or the 7th following & notwithstanding you have since rec'd as I doubt not, one I wrote on the 8th [179] I will proceed with another, which may or may not be the last I shall send you before we reach our own home – but here we are *now* in the utmost charm of "retired leisure" & I may add, "which in trim gardens takes his pleasure"[180] – for after all my fatigues, it is very pleasant to me to stroll about sans Chapeau in this very pretty & luxuriant Garden – & such a *termination* too as it possesses, a Garden full of the finest ripest fruit – into which we are often decoy'd to eat & transgress by the Fair Eve of the domain – This same fair Eve with her sposo[181] and our Clara, are this morng the 12th [182] departed after an early breakfast for York & its festivities – which are expected to exceed every other description of Festivity that ever was propos'd with an Arch Bishop*[183] at the head, who is the grand promoter – & he actually [184] is to hold up the signal of office wether* of Stick or of Scroll that will set all the 600 Instruments going & produce the *crash* that is to electrify the whole multitude assembled in this immense Building – It seems the Town has been filling for the week past & Lodgings engagd* for 6 months

177 Bath Abbey.

178 Addressed: 'Mrs.T.R.Malthus / E I College / Hertford'. Postmark: RIPON SE18 1825 208. On a blank part of the letter, in another hand, there is a list of fourteen items of expenditure and their amounts.

179 There is no letter from Catherine Eckersall dated 8 September in this collection. It is possible that she had mistaken the dates, and that the letter she thought she wrote on the 8th was in fact letter No. 4 above, posted on the 6th.

180 John Milton, *Il Penseroso*, lines 49–50: 'And adde to these retired Leasure;/That in trim Gardens takes his pleasure'.

181 Italian for 'husband', i.e. Henry Wood, husband of Anne Eliza (the 'Fair Eve of the domain').

182 'the 12th' is ins.

183 Edward Venables Vernon (surnamed Harcourt from 1831), archbishop of York (1807/8–47).

184 'is actually' is del.

[185] at ruinous prices – The Woods have managd* uncommonly well – by going to Tenants houses at Copmanthorpe[186] 4 miles from York, where they will have exelent* accomodation* in an old large[187] Mansion – Henry has musterd* 4 horses for his own & his Mothers Carriages – & has engagd* he hopes a Tenant at York to give them & the Horses accomodation,* while in waiting during the performances so that I hope they will enjoy it with as little expence* & trouble as possible – The Tickets for 14 Concerts for each individual are 3£ – Eliza will be very splendid, & Clara what with buying & begging very smart – They resist every perswasion* however to attend the Fancy Ball so only Louisa & Emma Wood will partake of that amusement, having found friends to give them beds at York – Hugh Wood[188] is also of the party so poor Henry will have an adjutant to assist him besides his white wand in quality of one of the 24 Stewards, & all the Constables who are directed to carry off with all due order & silence any Lady that may faint, or otherwise be affected out of the Minster – We 3 had proposd* a visit to Bolton Abbey during their absence, & we may yet put it in practice if the weather sh'd be favorable,* which has now since Friday night the 9th. evinc'd great disposition to change – & there has actually fallen Torrents of rain, with high winds [189] ever since, tho cheifly* in the night-time – here as I told you before they had none those days on which we had it at Ambleside – the dust blew thro all the plantations by the road side – so that we avoided walking by the Lodge, which is now pass'd & repass'd 16 times by 8 Coaches every day – All the Horses around are engag'd so that we c'd only procure them by engaging them some days before & that you know is too decided a measure for us to adopt – so unless we get weary of the place, we shall probably make no exertions to quit it during the 5 days absence of our hosts – for we all yet feel our mountain exertions in our feet & limbs – & enjoy the process of repose not a little – Miss Schalk*[190] is coming to stay here during these 5 days – & I suppose we shall now & then see her Future to whom she will soon be united as a small house is taken [191] by them near the Bridge – he has good prospects of a living – which reminds me of yr. question concerning John Wynne whose living *is* in the Co. Wicklow, & more agreably* situated than his brother Harry's – he is just ordaind* – just before we parted Mr. Wynne inform'd us all, hope of the Newtown ...[192] Estate being judgd* in his favor* was at end & the favorable* opinions he had before rec'd were now all revers'd !! this appears strange – but so it is – He has since written a short letter to Eliza, informing her of their safe arrival

[185] 'past' is del. [186] South-south-west of York. [187] 'large' is ins.
[188] Hugh Wood (born 1800) was a first cousin of Henry Wood. Their fathers were brothers.
[189] 'every' is del.
[190] Presumably a relative of Henry Wood. His mother was the daughter of a Captain Thomas Schaak.
[191] 'for' is del. [192] Word unclear.

in Dublin after 16 hours disagreable* passage, from Liverpool. He had not then seen Harry or John[193] – Lucy bore the journey & Voyage very well – if going to Arklow sh'd be given up, they will take Lodgings by the Sea side in or close to Dublin – Poor M^r^. W. complaind* of his health & bad spirits so very soon after his Landing in his own Country ! I believe the rest of the family wd prefer going directly to Killucan – for Lucy is convincd* that repose *only* is necessary for her complaint – they met the W.Wynnes[194] he said which was a fortunate thing for them he said – Harry & John, he expected to see eve[ry] moment – but he wd not wait a moment after he had procurd* a Frank[195] to inclose* a beautifull* Moravian workd* Frill Eliza had desir'd him to procure her – Since I wrote to you on the 6th. we have been twice to Studley Gardens & taken our fill of the Abbey[196] & all the beauties of the Garden – in our first visit we met Sir James Mackintosh, with M^r^. ...[197] & after encounterd* Miss M[198] – we gave her a cordial invitation to come & spend a day or two at Hollin, & she said she wou'd but I believe if it shd be the plan to go on to the Lakes she might not find leisure for the visit – her Father is much benefitted by the Harrogate waters[199] – in the last excursion to Studley[200] an old Woman, in an old straw bonnet, stopp'd me to ask if I recollected her – it was the Baroness De Rolles,[201] with the Key of the Gardens on her finger, priviledgd* as an Inmate to traverse the place without a ½ crown guide attending – which indignity her old neighbors* are rather

193 Two of the four sons of Henry and Catherine Wynne.

194 Probably the family of William Wynne, barrister-at-law, MP, one of the five brothers of Henry Wynne. William Wynne's daughter, Catherine, married Euseby Cleaver. See Vol. I, Ch. 3, n.7.

195 A letter or envelope bearing the superscribed signature of a person entitled to send letters without charge (*OED*).

196 Fountains Abbey, the ruins of a Cistercian Abbey founded in 1132, about two miles south-west of Ripon and two miles north-west of Hollin Hall. The Fountains Abbey Gardens were created in the early eighteenth century by John Aislabie, Chancellor of the Exchequer in the Walpole government. The nearby Studley Gardens, with its lakes, temples and statues, belonged to Aislabie's house, Studley Royal, destroyed by fire in 1945.

197 Name unclear.

198 Sir James Mackintosh (1765–1832) was a colleague and friend of Malthus at the East India College from 1818 to 1824 (*DNB*). 'Miss M' was probably one of his two daughters, Fanny and Elizabeth, from his second marriage.

199 Harrogate, a spa town in North Yorkshire, about 15 miles east of Bolton Abbey, and about ten miles south of Ripon.

200 'to Studley' is ins.

201 John Rolle (1756–1842) was created (1796) Baron Rolle of Stevenstone. A footnote to 'Rolle' in *The Complete Peerage* states that 'venal heralds' sold the Rolle arms 'to a family named Rolls, which had no connection with that of Rolle having been founded by a dairy farmer, "who had acquired a large fortune as a cow-keeper" in Camberwell and Peckham Rye (Manning and Bray (1804–14) 1974, Vol. III, p. 403, note)' (*GEC*, Vol. XI, p. 76, note). The son of Mr Rolls spent a great sum completing the house built by his father, and then pulled it down in 1812, selling the materials in lots (Manning and Bray (1804–14) 1974, Vol. III, p.403n.) Where and when the Eckersalls were neighbours of Baroness de Rolles is not stated. The Eckersalls formerly lived in Surrey, in a house called 'Burford Lodge', near Dorking.

disposd* to resent – but the poor old Lady, growing more & more contracted, both in body & mind, will not make any sort of distinction – or discrimination – whatever – I am going to write to M[rs]. Nutcombe, & settle, if possible, when we can come to her & spend just 3 days, that is one whole one between arrival & departure – & probably with all exertions we may not reach home before the end,[202] or very beginning of Oct[r] – I hope we may find Charles there awaiting our arrival – & in better health – I want to recommend to him – The Syrop* of Sassaparilla[203] – as a sweetener of the blood – sh'd you have communication with him, do mention it – I find by a letter from Miss Bedford that Sancho has been sent for – it was hardly worth while I think for the poor old fat beast to travel so far – I am glad Hal found his dog & that his first efforts are crownd* with such success – I expected as much – they say Partridges are scarse* but we have them at table every day – there are plenty of Perch & Pike in the Lake so they might live on their own produce altogether if they chose it & fare sumptuously every day – There is some idea of their coming to Bath this winter or rather towards the Spring, & after they have been to Hartlepool – so we shall have a pleasing succession of married Children, Malthus's, Tauntons & Woods – not to mention the probable return at that Season of the G Ecks from Scotland – I believe as you suggest that they conclude M[r]. Bruce is living at Edinburgh – so you must inform them thro me where they do reside – probably I shall keep my letter open till I hear from them as they talk'd of writing in about a week & when they had reach'd Glasgow –

Well – here is a very long interval indeed for this is Friday the 16th. – & I will scribble a little just to say I have this morn[g] only got a letter from George, they missd* a good opportunity of sending a letter & were forcd* to await another – It seems they got to Glasgow Saturday the 3[d]. the day after they set off from Ambleside in their Shandry – which shook them heartily, & they sought their repose in the Glasgow Coach where they were fortunately alone. As I hope to find some opportunity of sending you his letter I will only mention, they have steam'd & coach'd & walk'd to several Lakes, more pleas'd with the Archipelago of Islands in Loch Lomond ...[204] they have yet seen – Heavy rains & wind, that came on [as] they did with us Friday 9 – & *continued* some days after *with them*, has made them give up, or rather doubt, concerning going on the Caledonian Canal – "rather too much of a good thing" he says – so he is now returnd* to Iverary*[205] – & thinks they may go on to Edinburgh. The weather is too stormy to visit Staffa[206] & the scotch Islands – he does not tell

[202] i.e. before the end of September. [203] An obsolete spelling of 'sarsaparilla'.
[204] Several words unclear, probably 'than any thing else'.
[205] Inverary, on the west shore of Loch Fyne.
[206] An uninhabited island, of the Inner Hebrides group, six miles north of Iona.

me where to write, so I shall expect another letter when I get back to St Cats – I shall not send off this till our folk's return tomorrow, from the Festival – we expect them to dinner – Miss Schaach* – better known as Matilda – has been here ever since & is a very agreable* addition to our small party, she plays & sings very delightfully – We amuse ourselves very much rowing & fishing on the Lake & with the Swans who are uncommonly tame & a wild Duck, who is a very amusing person, taking the food out of their clumsy bills for which he gets a pretty severe ducking, that he does not regard much, for he sails after them & plucks their tails, which he seems to think a very good joke – the Lake is a great resort for wild as well as tame ducks, geese & water hens – & in winter is often coverd* with them – I have written to M^rs^. Nutcombe in answer to a letter[207] she venturd* to send at Keswick – to say she & her Neice* Kitty were going on a small tour into Derbyshire for a few days – & I have settled with her to come to Inchbrooke[208] either on the 29th, 30th or even on the 1st of Oct^r^ – therefore we propose leaving Hollin on Tuesday the 27th – how many miles we have to travel to her I know not – No other letter from M^r^. Wynne yet – another Frank came with some workd* cuffs – & a print of the Menai bridge – but not a word of inteligence* –

Sunday – No Church, for the Horses are all dead tir'd, so are the Folk who returnd* yesterday the 17th – but highly delighted with the Festival – Clara was so unsatiable* that she walkd* into York – with Hugh Wood on Wed^y^ to hear the Messiah – then din'd with the Dixons & after went to the Concert with the rest of the party 4000 odd hundreds[209] in this fine new room – the receipts have been so great for all the performances, that besides being able to give *largely* to all the Hospitals round in York – they can pay for the buildg* of this new Room – more then 20,000£ it is supposd* will be collected. Henry Wood is in bed with a cold & fever but is getting better fast – the others went through all the squeezing, pushing, nervous watch^g^ etc etc wonderfully. We have got a great deal to do this week – to see ...[210] etc. The Masons to dinner on Wed^y^ – & Clara now petitions to stay over the 1st Ripon Ball, next Tuesday, so we cannot set off till Wed^y^. – Henry & M^r^. Mason are Stewards – The ...[211] are abroad – Henrys Library is rather an amasing* one, & I have read till my poor old eyes turn'd

[207] 'one' is del. and 'a letter' is ins.

[208] Later in this letter Inchbrooke is said to be in Warwick. The reason for visiting Inchbrooke is not stated, but could possibly have been to visit the Brandrams – Maria Brandram's father, William Bedford, lived in Warwick. It would appear that the journey from Hollin Hall to Warwick was to be undertaken by Catherine and John Eckersall, and their two daughters, Fanny and Clara – accompanied no doubt by Sergeant. The Woods were to remain at home at Hollin Hall, the Wynnes had returned to Ireland, and George and Caroline Eckersall were travelling in Scotland.

[209] Presumably means '4000 plus odd hundreds'.

[210] Two words unclear. [211] Name unclear, possibly 'Granthams'.

round in my head – as has M[r]. Eck – & Fanny of course who lives upon reading – she has returns of bile frequently – I believe the weather to be very relaxing – we have had Fog often but no rain all last week excepting some on Thursday the 15th. & that cheifly* in the night – every thing damp, & our hair never in curl – Why have you not written to me? – pray direct a letter to Inchbrooke, Warwick – Lucy has not written, neither has Charles – Did I ever tell you that George Wynne is one on[212] the surveying list & will get 2 or 300 pr ann – We shall walk to Ripon Minister for 2 o'Clock service & send This into the Post Office & return in M[rs]. Woods little Carriage perhaps – I must conclude this dull Epistle at last with kindest loves to you & Robert & Emily – & Hal if return'd in which M[r].E., Fanny & Eliza join with yr ever very aff[te] Mother CE –

[212] 'of' is del. and 'on' is ins.

9 *Eight brief miscellaneous items*

1. AN ESSAY ON THE ADVANTAGES OF COLONIES[1]

Colonies properly regulated, do not tend to weaken the mother country, but only draw off her exuberant population.

An attempt to prove the general utility of colonies to the mother country, after the very recent loss of our settlements in America, may perhaps appear presumtuous;* yet I persuade myself if the subject be impartially, & not too precipitately judged, it will be found that under proper regulations, they are a source of great strength & power to the country which gave them birth.

The fixing settlements in distant regions for the sake of commerce has been a measure almost universally adopted by the wisest & most intelligent nations of antient* times; & indeed if we may credit the accounts we have received of the early ages, most of those nations which have made so conspicuous a figure in the historical page will appear to have received their chief support from establishments of this kind. Athens, justly the most celebrated of all the grecian states, derived that strength which made her the terror of surrounding nations from the correspondence she maintained with her numerous colonies in different parts of the world – The country in itself barren & uncultivated, deprived of the support[2] it received from without, instead of holding the highest station, must inevitably have sunk to the lowest in Greece.

The sentiments of the Ancients with regard to this custom are incontestably evident from their practice. Had it not been considered as a measure replete with the most solid & permanent advantages, it would not have met with the constant approbation of those who, we have reason to think, acted from maxims of the soundest policy & prudence. It has been urged however that colonies in general must operate to the detriment of the mother country, &

[1] The tone suggests a student essay, and the reference to 'the very recent loss of our settlements in America' suggests a date of composition not long after 3 September 1783, when Great Britain signed the final treaty recognizing the independence of her thirteen American colonies.

[2] 'instead of holding' is del.

in time become the source of gradual depopulation: but I fear that those who make this an argument against their utility, have not well considered, of what people colonies are chiefly composed.

They afford a retreat to the unhappy – a comfortable assylum* to those who by losses in trade are reduced to the hard necessity of quitting their native land – & a safe refuge to those who, could they not have found such a retirement,[3] from various causes which cannot fail to happen in every nation, would have emigrated to some other country & been obliged perhaps to lend their unwilling assistance to a natural enemy.

Far therefore from being a source of depopulation they are quite the contrary. They preserve those subjects which otherwise would have been for ever lost, & not only preserve them, but render them more useful to their country. Men who from their situation at home, were prevented from pursuing that line of life in which [4] they had been educated have here an open field for the exercise of their ab[i]lities. Without the painful reflection that the unhappy circumstances in their life are known to those who surround them, they are here at liberty to form their schemes, & adopt the plans best suited to their disposition.

The commercial advantages that must result from an amicable correspondence between countrymen in different parts of the world, are too obvious to need much explanation. By mutually exchanging the produce of each climate, a new & very great source of industry is opened, which by affording employment to multitudes cannot but have an effect in augmenting the numbers, as well as greatly conducing to the ease & happiness of the people at home. Besides as these communications are carried on by sea, they must extend the navigation & encrease* the shipping of the mother country. At the same time the rising & subsi[s]ting[5] numbers of experienced seamen must evidently contribute to the support of the naval power.

With regard to America, I cannot but think, nor do I believe it is an opinion adopted only by a few, that some mismanagement, & not entirely the strength & flourishing state of the [6] settlements occasioned that rupture, the consequences of which have been so fatal to this country.

Colonies by their nature require ease & freedom. When once these are infringed, there is no answering for the consequences. Sprung from the same stock, they are no doubt actuated by the same spirit as Englishmen, & it is not the peculiar characteristic of those who have a title to this appellation, patiently to see the violation of their natural rights & privileges.

[3] 'could they not have found such a retirement' is ins. [4] 'they were ed' is del.

[5] i.e. 'abiding', 'lasting' (now obsolete) (*OED*). [6] 'colonies' is del.

Had such however been the situation of our settlements, such their spirit, that independance* alone was the mark at which they aimed, if instead of entering into a long & painful war with our fellow countrymen we had freely given up the independance* they asked. [7]

[8] 2. NOTES ON TAXATION

Object to be aimed at in Taxation.
General rules of Smith.
Preliminary question whether there is a fund on which taxes on consump[n] fall.
The general rule applicable to the determination of prices, applicable also in taxation.
The causes on which the force of those who are taxed depends, and which determine[9] where a tax will finally rest.
[10]

Of Taxes on Strict Monopolies
Of Taxes on partial monopolies, or on the Rents and Profits of land
Of Taxes on profits of stock where the competition is free[11]
Of taxes on the interest of money
Of taxes on the wages of labour
Of taxes on consumption
Of Direct taxes on Income

What is wanted in order to prevent taxes from being felt is an annual accumulation of capital which would have gone to the lowering the rate of [12] profits and interest and which, instead, goes to supply loans.

And a power of imposing taxes which will affect only the least necessary expenditure of individuals and not interfere [13] with the annual accumulation.

[7] MS ends here.

[8] The second of these three leaves has an 1811 watermark. It is possible that these notes were intended by Malthus to be the basis of a new segment on taxation to be included in the revised, second edition of his *Principles of Political Economy*. The manuscript annotations he made to the Table of Contents in his copy of the first edition included a new heading 'On Taxation', and in a letter of 5 October 1827 to his publisher, John Murray, he stated that in the proposed new edition of the *Principles* there would be 'much new matter relating to Taxation' and other subjects. However, the proposed new segment on taxation did not appear in the (posthumous) second edition. See Malthus 1989b, II, pp. 251, 430–1.

[9] 'determines' is altered to 'determine'. [10] 'Taxes on the rent and produce of land' is del.

[11] 'and interest of money' is del. and 'of stock where the competition is free' is ins.

[12] 'interest' is del. [13] 'either' is del.

The great source of accumulation being the profits of capital, and the profits of capital being greatest during a war, it may frequently happen that, after the first disturbance which the war occasions, the annual accumulation may be more than adequate to supply the annual loans.

Resemblance of the laws by which capital in increased and the laws by which population is increased. Capital [14] as well as population is more easily recovered than added to.

Comparative merits of the funding system and of raising the supplies within the year.

Quite clear that it would be very impolitic to impose such heavy taxes [15] in raising the supplies within the year, as to make it necessary for individuals to borrow. Government can borrow [16] upon much better terms than individuals without capitals. Nothing has a tendency to raise the rate of interest but an increased rate of[17] facility in[18] obtaining the means of subsistence.

3. AN EXTRACT FROM A DRAFT LETTER TO AN UNNAMED CORRESPONDENT ON SAVING AND SPENDING

[19] for the fall of profits, which I believe you will allow usually takes place from accumulation, than that the price of produce falls compared with the expence* of production, or in other words that demand does not increase in proportion to supply.

You say also [20] in reference to [21] the will to purchase, that[22] the true question is, whether if money should retain the same value next year as at present, any man would want the will to spend half as much again, if he had it, as he now does. But this is merely asking a man whether he would not like to be half as rich again as he is now;[23] and has nothing at all to do with the difficulty [24] to which I alluded of increasing greatly the supply of produce in the *actual state of people's* fortunes[25] without losing the *effective* demand. The question really is, can you without essentially lowering profits, and diminishing or even destroying[26] the means of future accumulation, furnish to the man of 100£ or

[14] 'and' is del. [15] ', as woul' is del. [16] 'mon' is del.
[17] 'rate of' is ins. [18] 'of' is del. and 'in' is ins.
[19] MS begins here. This extract emphasises the dangers of either excessive saving or excessive expenditure, and the importance of attaining 'a mean between the two extremes of frugality and expence'*. It is yet another application of the 'doctrine of proportions' which played such a major part in Malthus' methodology (see Pullen 1982).
[20] 'that' is del. [21] 'the increase of demand or' is del. [22] 'that' is ins.
[23] 'rich rather than poor' is del. and 'half as rich again as he is now' is ins.
[24] 'of increasing' is del. [25] 'of produce in the *actual state of people's* fortunes' is ins.
[26] 'or even destroying' is ins.

5000£ a year[27] the commodities which he has been in the habit of purchasing greatly[28] *cheaper*, so as to enable him to purchase others, or furnish him with commoditis* of a different kind for the same income[29] on which he sets a higher value.

It will readily occur, that the more abundant Capital is, the more difficult this will be [30] as attempts of the kind have been constantly making. And on the other hand the more scanty capital is the more easy it will be, as the means of furnishing commodities cheaper, and a greater variety of them, do not approach towards being exhausted.

I of course agree with you intirely* in that the tendency of an increased capital is to beget an increased inclination for luxuries of all descriptions, and it is precisely this tendency which *practically* prevents the princuple* of frugality from being carried too [31] far. The difficulty of making a fortune [32] when profits are very low and the consequent discouragement to save and temptation to spend, are the natural checks to the principle of accumulation and the indefinite increase of capital. While the facility of making a fortune when profits are high and the consequent encouragement to save, and discouragement to spend are the natural checks to the principle of expence* and the [33] indefinite decrease of capital.

These [34] checks to expence*[35] are always sufficient in industrious nations, with tolerably frugal habits, to recover capital that has been destroyed by wars or other causes, in the same manner as population is rapidly recovered, under similar circumstances. But they are not sufficient always to generate an adequate[36] tendency to accumulation in nations with invetaratly* idle and expensive habits, in the same manner as even plenty of good land will not occasion an adequate increase of[37] population in a country very ill governed and without industry and exertion.

It is a mean between the two extremes of frugality and expence,* varying according to the state and natural resources of the country that tends to produce the greatest quantity of wealth in proportion to a given extent of territory. In the early period of such a country while fresh territory is in abundance the principle of frugality cannot very easily[38] be carried too far, as effective demand will be secured by a rapid increase of population. But after all or nearly all the land has been divided and cultivated, the increase of population will depend

[27] 'a year' is ins. [28] 'greatly' is ins. [29] 'for the same income' is ins.
[30] 'and the more scanty it is, the more easy it will be' is del.
[31] 'excess' is del. [32] ', and the conse' is del. [33] Second 'the' is del. [34] 'latter' is del.
[35] 'to expence'* is ins. [36] 'a sufficient' is del. and 'an adequate' is ins.
[37] 'a full' is del. and 'an adequate increase of' is ins.
[38] 'can hardly' is del. and 'cannot very easily' is ins.

intirely* upon the demand for labour, and the demand for labour will depend mainly on the demand for manufactures and the products of foreign commerrce,* and consequently a principle of frugality carried so far as essentially to diminish the demand for these articles of convenience and luxury, would [39] bring the [40] produce population and capital of the country to a stand, before the land had reached a very [41]

4. WHETHER TO PAY FOR IMPORTS BY EXPORTING EITHER PRECIOUS METALS OR COMMODITIES

If from a particular country you import more than you export, the whole mass of what you have imported and exported will undoubtedly exchange for a larger quantity of the precious metals than the whole mass of what has been imported and exported in the country with which you have been dealing; but this cannot be considered as a proof that the precious metals are redundant in your country, because the more you import the more you will increase this apparent redundancy, though in reality the precious metals will be flowing from you, and the redundancy ought to be growing less & less.

It is never meant to be said that a nation will pay a debt with the precious metals when it can pay it cheaper by the export of any other commodities; but it is meant to be distinctly asserted that it may be the interest of a nation to pay a debt with the precious metals, although the precious [metals] in the nation so paying the debt cannot in any correct sense of the term be considered as comparatively redundant or cheaper. It is surely an advantage amply sufficient to produce an exchange of two commodities and the only necessary condition of such exchange[42] that each party decidedly prefers the commodity which he receives to the commodity which he [43] parts with. If I give a shilling for a loaf, or send out bullion for corn I have derived an advantage from the exchange perfectly independent of the consideration whether money is[44] more redundant with me than [45] with the Baker, or whether bullion is on the whole more redundant in the country from which I send it than in the country to which it is sent. This is, in fact, quite a seperate* question and a comparative redundancy of this kind is[46] by no means a necessary condition of an exchange. It is true indeed that in the present state of things, no person ever thinks of sending a *commodity* abroad which sells at a higher price at home; [47] no person will send sugar to France

[39] 'very soon' is del. [40] 'population prop' is del. [41] MS ends here.
[42] 'and the only necessary condition of such exchange' is ins.
[43] 'receives to the c' is del. [44] 'on money or' is altered to 'money is'. [45] 'the' is del.
[46] 'a [such] comparative redundancy of this kind is' is ins. [47] 'but this is solely and' is del.

even in exchange for a commodity which he values much more than sugar, if sugar will sell for a higher price at home than in France: But this is precisely and exclusively because the very [48] article in which the sugar is valued in both countries is susceptible of exportation and consequently the exchange may be effected cheaper. If this were not the case, that is, if the medium in which commodities are valued were not capable of being exported; [49] and yet if we could suppose a method invented of estimating the value of commodities correctly in paper, it appears to me quite certain that commodities would sometimes be sent to a market[50] where they were not estimated so highly as at home. If I wanted corn much more than sugar, that is, if I could sell it at home at a higher price than sugar;[51] and if the country which had corn to dispose of, though it might not particularly want sugar, still preferred it to corn, that is, could sell it at a higher price than the corn, an exchange of the sugar for[52] the corn [53] would clearly be advantageous, both to the country which sent it out and the country which received it,[54] although in the country which sent it out it might have been selling for a shilling a pound and in the country to which it was exported it would only sell for eleven pence.[55] Of course the sugar could not be sent out in this case if there was either an exportable circulating medium, or any other commodity with which the corn could be obtained more advantageously. The sending out the sugar would indeed be a clear proof that the sugar was the cheapest exportable commodity for the purpose in question, and[56] that is, that there was no other [57] which purchased at the same price as the sugar at home would yield a higher price than the sugar abroad; but if the supposition just made be allowable, it is evidently no proof that the sugar was more redundant or cheaper in the country which sent it out than in the country which received it,[58]

5. REDUNDANCY OF CURRENCY

[59] would be no proof of a redundancy of currency in America. If each article for the sake of simplicity were supposed to be two shillings a pound, and each article in the foreign country 30 per cent dearer than in the home, 460 £ would in each command 1000 lb of each commodity, although there would be a regular[60]

[48] 'commodity' is del. [49] 'it appears to me quite certain that commodities;' is del.

[50] 'not unfrequently move towards markets' is altered to 'sometimes be sent to a market'.

[51] 'than sugar' is ins. [52] 'with' is del. and 'for' is ins.

[53] ', an exchange of the sugar [with] for the corn' is del. [54] 'it' is ins.

[55] 'not sell for such an additional sum as would pay the expence* of carriage' is del. and 'only sell for eleven pence' is ins.

[56] 'and a proof' is del. and 'proof that ... in question, and' is ins. [57] 'commodity' is del.

[58] MS ends. [59] The previous part of this sentence is wanting in MS. [60] 'regular' is ins.

influx of bullion into England. If the debtor country traded with others in its neighbourhood in such a way as to be able to supply itself with bullion, and the creditor country in such a way as to get rid of what was superfluous, it is clear that this traffic might continue for any length of time without our being able to say with propriety that it was occasioned by a redundancy of bullion in one country, and a comparative deficiency in the other. But if these nations were not connected with any others, then it [is] evident that the increase of currency and prices in England[61] and the[62] diminished currency & prices[63] of America [64] would either enable the latter to export some other commodity with advantage, or if the distance was too great for any other commodity to answer, would absolutely oblige her to diminish her[65] imports and proportion them to her exports.

A fall in the price of any commodity from abundance would rather lower than raise the exchange, if it did not produce the effect of[66] tempting foreigners to purchase a greater value of your commodities which it certainly will not always do.[67]

When countries are near, and trade in commodities of a similar kind, a[68] rise or fall of prices will probably always have the effect of diminishing or increasing the value of exports;[69] but when countries are distant and the commodities peculiar, the effect of a rise or fall of prices on the exchanges[70] must be very slow, and might sometimes even be in a[71] direction opposite to the usual one.[72] A rise in the price of claret or port might perhaps increase the balance to be paid to France or Portugal.

The grand leveller of the value of the precious metals is corn. [73] The only necessary condition in an exchange that the [74]

If corn has risen in price more than others have fallen in price, a rise of prices has taken place upon the whole but a rise of prices is equivalent to a redundancy of currency. The question is whether a rise of prices is the same as a redundant currency

A Redundancy of currency will always shew* itself in a rise of prices, but it may be doubted whether a rise of prices necessarily indicates redundancy of currency[75]

[61] 'the rise in the price of iron and tin' is del. and 'the increase of currency and prices in England' is ins.

[62] 'the' is ins. [63] 'power' is del. and 'currency & prices' is ins. [64] 'to purchase' is del.

[65] 'to diminish her' is ins. [66] 'of' is ins. [67] 'which it certainly will not always do' is ins.

[68] 'a' is ins. [69] 'the value of exports' is ins. [70] 'on the exchanges' is ins.

[71] 'a' is ins. [72] 'one' is ins. [73] 'That' is del.

[74] MS ends. The following seven lines are on a different sheet.

[75] On the same sheet, but upside down and apparently written at another time and without reference to the words on this sheet, there are two calculations showing that the ratio of 38:7 is approximately equal to 100:18, and the rate of 35:4 is approximately equal to 100:11.

6. AGRICULTURAL PROTECTION

by protecting duties [76] drawbacks [77] and taxes [78] on almost every kind of foreign commodity, capital is prevented from leaving those trades the prices of the products of which have been increased by domestic[79] taxation while [80] if the ports were open agriculture would be exposed to the[81] loss of capital occasioned by the competition of foreigners [82] who not being burdened by the same handicap of taxes[83] would possess the most obvious advantages in the market with our home growers
[84]

7. NOTES ON FOREIGN TRADE AND THE BULLION REPORT

[85] Account of the importation of Bullion very deficient.

Value of Gold on Continent higher than in England – Not sufficiently attended to in the report.[86]

[87] Might arise from a great balance of trade to be paid in the precious metals.

Whether possible to ascertain the market price of bullion on the continent in any other way than by comparing it with our currency that is[88] with the bills on the continent upon our merchants

What woud* happen if it became necessary to pay in specie for a considerable portion of our goods.

A great temporary effect would be produced in [the s]tate[89] of the

[76] 'and' is del. [77] 'of various kinds' is del. and 'taxes ... commodity' is ins.
[78] 'of' is del. [79] 'domestic' is ins. [80] 'under the same system of taxation' is del.
[81] 'to the' is repeated. [82] 'under the most obviously disadvantageous circumstances' is del.
[83] 'not being burdened by the same handicap of taxes' is ins.
[84] On the other side of this sheet in Malthus' hand there is the name 'Rev^{d}. Wm Thompson. Beasby. Alford.' and a long division in which Malthus incorrectly calculated that the ratio 29:24 is equal to 122.7:100, or an increase of 22.7 per cent.
[85] The following three lines are on a sheet watermarked '... 08'.
[86] On the other side of this sheet, in pencil, a calculation:

		18	6
		15	0
Edmonton		6	0
	1	19	6

[87] The sheet containing the following ten statements is watermarked '... 08'.
[88] 'that is' is ins. [89] MS torn here and below.

exchange by the circumstance of our [merch]ants giving credit, and foreign merchants requiring prompt payment.

Whether the bullion price of goods on the continent has fallen

Curious to see the manner in which the bullion trade is carried on but probably though the imports may be accurate, the exports may not be

How are the imports valued.

Whether.

The prodigious demand for bullion must arise from a temporary unfavourable balance of trade.

The Bullion price of the goods that we import greater than the bullion price of the goods we exp[ort.]

[90] Expence* of transport in times of peace

How is the silver collected for the East India Company

Country banks

8. FOUR BOOK TITLES[91]

The Principles of Exchange and Currency applied to the report from the Select Committee
by Couts*[92] Trotter Esqr
Cadell & Davies

Walkers critical and pronouncing Dictionary Abridgement[93]
price 6 boards.

On the expediency of establishing a new Chartered Bank[94]

Thoughts on the repeal of the restriction law.
David Bentic
Murray

[90] 'Amount' is del. The following three lines are written on blank space of a letter addressed to 'The Rev[d] T.R.Malthus / India College'.

[91] Presumably, the titles of books that Malthus intended to obtain or consult. They are not in the Malthus Library at Jesus College.

[92] Coutts Trotter, *The Principles of Currency and Exchanges Applied to the Report from the Select Committee of the House of Commons, Appointed to Inquire into the High Price of Gold Bullion, &c. &c.*, London, W. Winchester and Son, Dec. 1, 1810.

[93] Word del.

[94] Joseph Marryat, MP, *Thoughts on the Expediency of Establishing a New Chartered Bank, Suggested by the Application to Parliament for the Establishment of a New Chartered Marine Insurance Company, and Confirmed by the Report of the Bullion Committee*, London, J.M. Richardson and J. Hatchard, 1811.

Appendix A
Additional material contained in the collection but not reproduced[1]

1. Legal documents relating to property transactions, including one signed by John Malthus in 1581, one by Richard Malthus in 1585, and some in the name of Jane Dalton (a cousin and close companion of Malthus' father, Daniel Malthus).

2. A letter from Daniel Malthus (Malthus' father) to Sydenham Malthus (Daniel's father; Malthus' grandfather) written from Marseilles, during a holiday in France, accompanied by his wife, Harriet, and his sister Anne Hackshaw. The letter refers also to a third (unnamed) lady. The letter is dated 'Octr 30th', but the year is not given. The year must have been before 1757 (the year Daniel's father died) and after 1752 (the year of Daniel's marriage).

3. A biographical account of Rear-Admiral George Frederick Ryves (1758–1826). This document of 22 pages, on paper watermarked 'EIC [East India College?] 1825', does not appear to be in Malthus' hand. Malthus was a first cousin of the Rear-Admiral. Malthus' mother's sister, Anna Maria (née Graham) married in 1757 Thomas Ryves (1720–88), FRS. The future Rear-Admiral Ryves was their eldest son. He obtained the rank of Rear-Admiral in 1825.

[1] Volume I of this collection of manuscripts stated (p. 4, n. 9 and n. 11) that Volume II would contain a letter from Daniel Malthus to his father, and a biographical account of Rear-Admiral George Frederick Ryves. A subsequent editorial decision to restrict Volume II to Malthus' correspondence, or to material closely relevant to his life and thought, has meant that only brief summaries of these two items have been included in Volume II (see 2 and 3 below).

4. A letter from George Frederick Ryves to Lord Arundell of Wardour, Wardour Castle, Sarum, Wiltshire, giving details of various naval engagements against the French. Ryves' first wife (m. 1792), Catherine Elizabeth (née Arundell), was related to Lord Arundell of Wardour. She died in 1803 when her husband was at Naples. An indistinct post mark indicates that this letter was probably written in 1795. Ryves' second wife (m. 1806) was a first cousin, Emma, daughter of Richard Robert Graham (1735–1816), apothecary of Chelsea Hospital. She was also a first cousin of Malthus. Her father was a brother of Ryves' mother and of Malthus' mother.

5. A few brief notes on members of the Ryves family in the seventeenth century.

6. A newspaper report of the funeral of Mr George Frederick Ryves who died on 12 March 1876, age 33, at the Ryves family seat, Shroton House, near Blandford, in Dorset. He was the son of Admiral George Frederick Ryves, CB (d. 1858, aged 65); the grandson of Rear-Admiral George Frederick Ryves; and the great-grandson of Anna Maria Ryves (née Graham; Malthus' aunt). All the above are buried, with other members of the family, in the family vault at Blandford.

7. Fourteen letters relating to Malthus' nephew, Sydenham Malthus (1801–68), and his wife, Mary Anne Malthus (née White). The first letter is from Henry Tasker, Sydenham's tutor at Pembroke College, University of Cambridge. It is dated 28 November 1821 and is addressed to Sydenham's father, Sydenham (1754–1821; Malthus' elder brother; he died on 21 December 1821). It states that the young Sydenham has made very little progress in his studies, because of his poor health and because 'his taste is so little suited to Mathematical studies', and advises that any further perseverance in those studies would be hopeless.

8. Four letters from Sydenham (1801–68) to his future wife, Mary Anne White, daughter of Revd Samuel White, Vicar of Hampstead (see *DNB*). The first is written from Llyswen Cottage, in Wales, dated 26 April 1829, and addressed to 'Miss Marianne White, Montagu Drive, Hampstead, Middlesex'. It is a love letter asking her to marry him. They were married later in 1829 and had a large family, some of whom migrated to New Zealand. The Kanto Gakuen collection of Malthus manuscripts comes from the estate of their grandson, Robert Malthus (1881–1972).

9. In a letter dated 5 May 1829, also from Llyswen Cottage, Sydenham replies to a letter (not in this collection) from Mary Anne. He refers to a proposed visit of Dr White to Llyswen, and to his new brother (-in-law) 'Mr Holt'. Holt married Sydenham's sister, Jane (b. 1802) in 1828. Mary Anne had met Jane at the 'Brays', presumably the family of Malthus' sister, Mary Anne Catherine (1771–1852) who married Edward Bray (d. 1814) in 1790 (Malthus 1966).

10. In a letter, dated 14 May 1829 from Llyswen Cottage, Sydenham refers to the visit of Dr White to Llyswen Cottage; to the beauty of the Welsh countryside in spring; and to his garden and farm.

11. A letter from Sydenham at Albury Cottage to Mary Anne White on 27 June 1829, discusses preparations for their wedding, with fervent expressions of affection. It contains the following references to Malthus and his family ('the RM's'): 'as you were so good as to propose asking some of my Uncles family [to their forthcoming wedding], I think it would be paying them a compliment with which they would be pleased, particularly Mrs Malthus ... Mary [Sydenham's elder sister] went yesterday to Dorking with Aunt Maria [Malthus' sister, Eliza Maria] to spend the day with the RM's with whom she found Louisa Bray [Malthus' niece; daughter of Malthus' sister, Mary Anne Catherine Bray] – they have taken a house there for a month, and come here for a day or two on Tuesday next ...'

12. A letter from Sydenham to his wife Mary Anne ('Minny'), addressed to 'Mrs Malthus, Llyswen House, near The Hay, Brecknock Sh.', 1830.

13. A letter from Marianna Georgina Malthus (Malthus' sister-in-law) to her daughter-in-law, Mary Anne Malthus, addressed to 'Mrs Malthus, Llyswen House, Haye, Brecknockshire', 1830.

14. A letter to Mary Anne Malthus from Reginald Bray, at Great Russell Street, addressed to 'Mrs Sydenham Malthus, near The Hay, Brecknockshire', 28 October 1830. Reginald Bray was a nephew of Malthus, the son of Malthus' sister, Mary Anne Catherine Bray. He acted as the Malthus family solicitor.

15. A letter from Rev. Samuel White to his daughter, Mary Anne Malthus, 25 June 1831, after the birth of her son, Sydenham (1831–1916).

16. A letter from Isabella White to her daughter, Mary Anne Malthus, 27 May 1840.

17. A letter (in a large childish hand), 28 July 1840, to Mary Anne Malthus from her daughter, Laura.

18. A letter dated 26 November 1870 from 'H.P.M.' (Henry Percival Malthus, b. 1842; great-nephew of Malthus; brother of Colonel Sydenham Malthus and of Charles Edward Daniel Malthus) in Christchurch, New Zealand, to his mother, Mary Anne Malthus.

19. A letter dated 10 March 1871 from Charles Edward Daniel Malthus (b. 1838; great-nephew of Malthus; brother of Colonel Sydenham Malthus and Henry Percival Malthus) in Christchurch, New Zealand, to his mother, Mary Anne Malthus.

20. A letter dated April 1871 from C.E.D. Malthus in New Zealand to Mary Anne Malthus.

21. A letter of 24 September 1887 to 'My dearest Etta' (Henrietta) from her brother 'S.M.' (Colonel Sydenham Malthus).

22. A collection of eight commissions given to George Frederick Symes (1794–1851), Malthus' step-nephew and first cousin once removed, being the son of Marianna Georgina Malthus (the first cousin and wife of Malthus' brother, Sydenham) by her first husband, W.L. Symes. Also a one-page balance sheet showing debits and credits (in rupees) for the account of 'Captain G.F. Symes Artillery in account with the Military Fund'.

23. Several letters to John Watson Pringle, husband of Malthus' daughter, Emily.

24. A letter of introduction for Malthus and his family, written by Captain Basil Hall (of 8 St. Colme Street, Edinburgh) on 24 June 1826, and addressed to Mrs Walker, of Balloch Inn, near Loch Lomond. The letter also advises a suggested itinerary for a 15-day tour of Scotland. The route taken by the Malthuses appears to have been roughly that advised by Captain Hall, but there is no reference in Malthus' diary of the Scottish tour of 1826, nor in his Cash Account, nor in Harriet Malthus' diary, of their having stayed with Mrs Walker at Balloch.

25. A letter to 'My dear Bertie' (presumably, Robert Malthus (1881–1972)) from his sister, Mary, at Holywell, Bishop's Waltham, referring to her illness.

26. A letter to Robert Malthus (1881–1972) in London from his mother Henrietta (Harriet) Malthus, five years after the death of his sister Mary, and just before his marriage. Includes a copy of a marriage prayer written by his father, Sydenham Malthus (1831–1916), on the occasion of the marriage (in 1867) of Sydenham and Henrietta.

27. Three letters to Robert Malthus (1881–1972) in Ceylon from his father, Sydenham, dated 30 March 1879, 19 April 1916 and 26 April 1916.

28. A letter to Robert Malthus (1881–1972), great-great-nephew of Malthus, son of Colonel Sydenham Malthus (1813–1916), with the executors' account of the Colonel's estate.

29. A book entitled *The Lady's New-years Gift or, Advice to a Daughter, Under these following Heads: Viz. Religion, Husband, House and Family, Servants, Behaviour and Conversations, Friendships, Censure, Vanity and Affectation, Pride, Diversions, Dancing*, London, 2nd edition, 1688, 164 pp. It is inscribed on a fly-leaf: 'Harriett Symes, from her Affectionate Aunts, Mary ... [?] & Laura Matilda Ryves. March 28th 1846'. Above that inscription, there is another inscripter: 'Eliz. Williams, her Book, Oct. y22 1720' – presumably a previous owner. On three other fly-leaves there are the names of the following eighteenth-century members of the Ryves family, with dates of birth and death, and names of godparents: George Frederick Ryves, Henry Pleydell Ryves, Robert Graham Ryves, Richard Ryves, Diana Maria Ryves, Marianna Georgina Ryves, Lucy Graham Ryves, [... ?] Maria Ryves, Heneretta [... ?] Ryves.

30. 'Chronological Order of Letters': a two-page chronological list of the letters between Malthus and his father, and from Richard Graves to Daniel Malthus, as published in Vol. I of this present work. The list appears to be in the hand of James Bonar. Below the numbered list, in another hand, there is 'Daniel to Sydenham', which presumably refers to the letter (noted above in this Appendix) from Daniel Malthus (Malthus' father) to Sydenham Malthus (Daniel's father; Malthus' grandfather).

On another page, there is the statement (in another hand): 'The packet was sent to R.A(?). Leigh, Trinity College, Cambridge'.

31. A few statistics of the number of people in four broad occupational groups (location not stated), with some (perhaps unrelated) calculations. Watermark 1812.

32. A few statistics and calculations relating to Indian agricultural production and prices.

33. Report in the *Morning Chronicle* of 2 February 1810 on the bullion debate in the House of Commons.

34. A letter dated 28 July [18]34 from 'Julius m.d.' expressing thanks for a letter of introduction to Col. Paisley, and referring to a collection of ancient miniatures. There is no address and no reference to Malthus by name.

35. A list of topics relating to population.

36. A note on the population of the Batavian republic in 1796 and the population of the province of Holland in 1732.

37. A large-scale folding map of Norway, dated 1785, probably used by Malthus during his tour in 1799.

38. A copy of T.R. Malthus, *The Measure of Value Stated and Illustrated*, 1823.

39. 'The Table Shewing* the Amount of the Foreign Expenditure and the Value of Grain Imported Compared with the Rates of Exchange on Hamburgh from the Year 1793 to 1819'. (A printed set of three graphs on one large sheet. No source is indicated.)

40. 'Arbitration or Estimate of Remittances to Amsterdam ... Published as the Act directs March ..., 1806, by W.I. & J. Richardson, Cornhill'.

A one-page table showing how to compare exchange rates between different countries; for example, it shows that 'when a bill in Spain is taken in London at 39 pence p[er] dollar, and negotiated in Amsterdam at 36 grotes p[er] ducat, the remittance is effected at 32 Schellings p[er] £ sterl[ing]'.

41. 'Arbitration or Estimate of Remittances to Hamburgh* ...'

A one-page table similar to the preceding. It shows, for example, that 'when a bill in Portugal is taken in London at 65 [pence] for 1 milrec [1000 Rees], remitted to Hamburgh,* and there negotiated at 45½ grotes for 1 crusado, the remittance is effected at 36 sch[ellings] p. £1 sterling'.

Appendix B
Letters to David Ricardo [? by John Cazenove]

INTRODUCTION

Amongst the Malthus papers there are 17 pages of manuscript in the form of three letters to David Ricardo subsequent to the publication of the third edition (1821) of his *On the Principles of Political Economy and Taxation*. However, their form and tone indicate that they were probably intended not as letters to be delivered through the post, but as letters for publication, in the conventional literary genre used, for example, by J.-B. Say in his *Lettres à M. Malthus*, 1820.

The authorship and date of the three letters are uncertain. They are not in Malthus' hand. The handwriting is almost certainly that of John Cazenove, a friend and supporter of Malthus; but the letters include a number of insertions, some of which appear to be in a different hand, which might be that of Malthus. The paucity and brevity of the insertions make it difficult to be certain.

The content of the letters does not lead to any *definite* conclusion concerning their authorship. Malthus and Cazenove held similar views on many issues,[1] particularly in their criticisms of Ricardo. The views expressed in these three letters are not entirely clear, but they do not appear to be inconsistent with Malthus' writings.

[1] Writing to Thomas Chalmers on 6 February 1833, Malthus said that Cazenove was 'a particular friend, ... a very clever man, and good political economist'; but their views were not identical in all respects. In editing the posthumous second edition of Malthus' *Principles of Political Economy*, Cazenove criticised Malthus on several points. See Pullen 1978; and Introduction, pp. lxi–lxviii, in Malthus 1989b.

The dating of the letters also presents a problem. It is unlikely (but, of course, not impossible) that the author would have adopted the literary genre of letters, commencing with 'Sir' and using the personal pronoun 'you', if Ricardo were not still alive. It would seem therefore that the letters were written between 18 May 1821 (the date on which an advertisement for the publication of the third edition of Ricardo's *Principles* appeared in the *Morning Chronicle*[2]) and 11 September 1823 (the date of Ricardo's death). However, six pages in these letters have an 1833 watermark. If in fact the letters were composed and written between 1821 and 1823, why were they rewritten in or after 1833, and why was the literary genre of letters to Ricardo retained when Ricardo had been dead for ten years or more?

There are thus (at least) two authorship possibilities:

1. The letters were composed by Malthus between 1821 and 1823, and either dictated to or transcribed by Cazenove in or after 1833, with Malthus inserting some additions and/or corrections to the transcription in his own hand.

2. The letters were composed and written by Cazenove between 1821 and 1823, transcribed by him in or after 1833, and then sent to Malthus for comment.

Of the two possibilities, the latter would appear to be the more probable. It would have been very strange for Malthus to have conceived a plan to publish criticisms of Ricardo by means of the literary genre of letters when he was still in direct personal correspondence with Ricardo, and when they had both expressed a preference for private rather than public debate. In his *Principles of Political Economy* (1820), Malthus referred apologetically to the need to make public his disagreements with Ricardo.

Also, there are features of the tone and literary style of the letters that tend to exclude Malthus as author. For example, the author addresses Ricardo as if he were a complete stranger, showing no hint of the long acquaintance and close friendship that existed between Malthus and Ricardo; and the frequent use of the first person singular – 'I believe', 'I fully agree', 'I have to notice', etc. – is untypical of Malthus.

Perhaps the main argument against Malthus' authorship is that he had given a very extensive treatment of the subject material of the letters – viz. measure of value, profits and wages – in his *Principles of Political Economy*, 1820. Chapter V, 'Of the Profits of Capital', in his *Principles* included a section specifically entitled 'Remarks on Mr. Ricardo's Theory of Profits' (Section IV).

[2] See Sraffa, Introduction, in Ricardo, *Works*, I, p. liv.

Why would he have bothered to compose three brief letters on these three topics when he had recently treated them so extensively elsewhere? The absence of any references in the letters to Malthus' published writings on these topics is also significant. If in fact Malthus was the author, he would surely have referred to the fuller treatment given in his *Principles* and elsewhere.

It seems very probable therefore that the letters were composed and written by Cazenove between 1821 and 1823, and were rewritten by him in or after 1833 and sent to Malthus for comment. His friendship with Malthus would explain why Malthus had been prepared to make alterations to the text. Malthus was possibly in the process of inserting the alterations in the time leading up to his death on 29 December 1834 – which could explain why the letters remained amongst Malthus' papers and were not returned to Cazenove.

The letters are written on lined paper, and on the rectos only, with the exception of a long 'Note' written on the verso of a leaf of the second letter.

TEXT

[Letter I. On the Measure of Value][3]

Sir,

The rapidity with which your Work on the *Principles of Political Economy & Taxation* has passed through three Editions, if it proves nothing as to the correctness of its peculiar doctrines, betokens at least, on the part of the reading and intelligent Public, a higher relish for this species of study than it has heretofore shewn – *

To those who with yourself are thoroughly impressed with its importance, this cannot fail to be a source of considerable gratification: for how many absurd and pernicious regulations would probably have been avoided had the subject been more generally known and understood; and how common is it, even at the present day to meet with Gentlemen of refined & liberal education and distinguished for their talents in other respects, who are miserably deficient in this department of knowledge, and who go into the Senate to legislate upon matters relating to Trade & Agriculture, without possessing the sligh[t]est acquaintance with the principles which ought to guide them in their judgment.

It may now however be hoped that the attention which you have been so instrumental by your influence and your writings in drawing to the subject, may not only lead to its wider diffusion, but may likewise pave the way for the introduction of a more free and liberal system than that which has hitherto prevailed among the different Countries of the Commercial World.

[3] The first letter does not have a number or title in MS.

In regard to the policy which it is most desirable for a free and enlightened Community to adopt, and indeed on most other questions involving any practical regulations, there is, I believe, scarcely a difference of opinion between us; but as to the mode of explaining some of the most important doctrines, and accounting for the facts connected with them, I have the misfortune to differ from you very materially.

In your last Edition, you appear to have greatly modified some of your opinions and to have changed others – This readiness on your part to correct any error into which you may have fallen is a proof how much more you are actuated by a sincere love of the truth, than by the empty vanity of wishing to appear singular or original.

Notwithstanding however the alterations you have made, I cannot reconcile myself to the general view you have taken of the subject though I am quite ready to admit it is stated with great force and ingenuity.

You are still of opinion that Adam Smith was wrong in selecting the Labour which a commodity would command, in preference to that which it has cost, as a measure of its value – That Adam Smith has not expressed himself so guardedly and explicitly on this point as he ought to have done,[4] is certain since[5] almost all subsequent writers, and yourself (as it appears to me) among the number, have misconceived his meaning. Nevertheless as I feel fully convinced of the correctness of his doctrine in this particular I will take leave to state to you my reasons for adhering to it.

Suppose we lived in a State of Society in which every thing was produced by sheer Labour without any Capital. In that case, commodities would naturally exchange for each other in proportion to the quantities of Labour which they had respectively cost: and not only so, but they would likewise be worth or would exchange for a quantity of Labour equal to that which they had cost. If for instance, by a days labour a uniform quantity of Gold or of Silver could always be picked up, such quantity of Gold or of Silver would always command or be worth a days labour. This is distinctly stated by Adam Smith (Book 1 ch: vi) and is, I believe, fully admitted by yourself. So far then you can have no fault to find with his measure of Value, seeing it is identical with your own.

But even, in this state of things, it is probable that some commodities would occasionally be supplied more or less abundantly compared with the wants of those who were desirous of possessing them; and the produce of a days labour in one occupation would not always exactly exchange for the produce of a day's labour in another occupation. Now whenever this occurred and that

[4] 'might have been wished' is written above 'he ought to have done', possibly in Malthus' hand.

[5] 'since' is ins.

a commodity exchanged for either more or less labour than it had cost, which of the two would be the proper criterion of its value, the Labour it had *cost*, or that which it would *command*? – Undoubtedly the latter quantity – The very supposition is that the *cost* and *value* do not coincide. It would therefore be absurd to take the one as the estimate of the other; and it would be equally absurd to say that the exchangeable value of a commodity estimated in Labour is a quantity of Labour different from that for which it will exchange – Thus then it appears that in the state of things I have supposed, viz that in which Labour is the sole productive Agent, whenever the market values of commodities coincided with their natural values, your measure would be the same as Adam Smith's, and that whenever they were different, his measure would be the true one to go by, while yours would not.

Now let us pass on to the actual state of things in which Capital of every possible kind and variety and of various degrees of durability is employed conjointly with Labour in the process of production. And here it is manifest at the outset, that Commodities do exchange for very different quantities of Labour than those[6] they have cost. And why is this? Obviously because a quantity of Labour is *indirectly* worked up in them in the shape of Capital with its profits – If then in all such cases, to the *direct* Labour employed as much more[7] is added as is equivalent to that capital and those profits, the total cost, thus estimated, will be found ordinarily[8] to agree with the quantity of Labour which the commodity in question would command – Thus if to produce a particular object it took 10 days labour and capital equal to 10 other days Labour and that the profit upon the capital & the advance of wages were 10 pc^{e}, that commodity would be worth 22 days Labour and would naturally exchange with any other commodity which was the produce of 22 days *immediate* Labour. And if owing to a temporary scarcity or abundance it should exchange either for more or less than that quantity, the excess or deficiency of the Labour it would command above or below that which it had cost, would precisely measure the greater or less degree of profit, which, owing to that particular circumstance, it would yield. And furthermore, although Rent does not, according to your Theory, enter as a component part into price (which perhaps it does not except in a trifling degree) yet the value of such Agricultural Produce as does yield a Rent is equally measured by the quantity of Labour which it will command.

So far therefore from thinking that Adam Smith's selection of Labour

[6] 'those' is ins.

[7] 'more' is ins., possibly in Malthus' hand.

[8] 'ordinarily' is ins., possibly in Malthus' hand.

as the standard[9] measure of Value is an arbitrary one, it appears to me that he really had no choice in the matter. He could not take Coals or Iron, which you esteem to be as good as Labour, because a given quantity of these commodities or of any others[10] would at different times and under different circumstances, represent very different degrees of toil & trouble; and where he has adopted Corn for his measure, as in his digression on the value of Silver, it was because he esteemed it, as he himself stated (Book 1 ch v) the next best measure to Labour, to which indeed he continually refers, and of which it may be presumed he could not procure prices accurate enough to answer his purpose.

The great distinction between the measure of Adam Smith's* and your own is, that whereas he proposes to estimate the value of every thing by its total or entire cost, you are for measuring them by a part only of their cost. I am fully aware that you have not committed the error of saying that the value of commodities is *equal* to the Labour they have cost. What you have said is, that commodities will exchange with each other *in proportion* to the Labour they have cost. This however they will not do, as you yourself admit, unless they are produced under precisely the same circumstances, and if they did, your rule would serve only to shew* their mutual value or their relation to each other, but would not measure their *real* cost – the *real* sacrifice that must be made to obtain them –

It forms a necessary part of your theory of Value, or is a natural consequence of it, that a rise or fall in the general rate of profits will not affect the value of commodities, because being common to all, it will not alter the proportion in which they severally exchange with each other; but to be consistent, you ought equally to have held[11] that an increase or diminution in the quantity of Labour which they cost (provided such increase or diminution applied in an equal degree to all) would not affect their value; for it is certain that the proportion in which they exchange with each other will no more be affected by this circumstance, than it would be by the rise or fall or profits – Nevertheless, according to your doctrine, an increase or diminution in the quantity of Labour required to produce commodities always *does* increase or reduce their Value. In the first of these propositions it seems clear that you had in view only the relation subsisting between different commodities. In the latter you obviously had a reference to the relation which subsists between commodities and their cost of production –

It is the latter species of relation which Adam Smith has always had in

9 'standard' is ins.

10 'or of any others' is ins.

11 'have' is ins. and 'held' changed from 'hold'.

view and which in ordinary language is always[12] meant to be referred to.

A Commodity which does not exist cannot be had for money: but it can always (if it be within the reach of human skill or power) be obtained by labour. "Labour" says Adam Smith "was the first price, the original purchase money that was paid for all things. It was not by gold or by silver, but by Labour that all the wealth of the world was originally purchased"[13] – Whenever therefore we are desirous of ascertaining what *the value* of any commodity is, we must enquire how much of this original purchase-money it is worth – Whatever that quantity be, it is the precise measure of the sacrifice that must be made in order to procure it –

Letter II. On Profits

Sir,

The subject of Value is so intimately connected with all other questions in Political Economy especially those relating to the distribution of the Produce, that having adopted Adam Smith's measure (and I flatter myself not without good reason) I am necessarily obliged to differ from you in some essential points relating to Profits and Wages.

I fully agree, however, in the truth of your proposition, (and a most useful proposition it is) that *Profits depend upon the proportion of the whole produce that goes to the Labourer.*

Putting Rent out of the question, (which is allowed to be the extra produce of all the Soils under cultivation, excepting the least productive), all commodities, or the price of them, is[14] divided into wages and profits: consequently whatever does not fall to the share of the Labourer must belong to his[15] Employer, and the important question is, what is it, that determines where the line shall be drawn; or that fixes what the share of each shall be. But before I enter into this enquiry, I must first notice two important consequences which flow from your doctrine as above stated, and which appear to have been totally overlooked by some Writers who profess to have adopted your principles.

The first is – That inasmuch as Profits are high or low according as the proportion which the share of the Capitalist bears to that of the Labourer is great or small, they are not affected by the augmentation or diminution in the productive powers of the Capitalist or Labourer so long as the proportion

[12] 'always' is ins.

[13] Smith (1776) 1976, I.v.2.

[14] 'them, is' is ins.

[15] 'his' is ins.

remains the same. If for instance a hatter at the expiration of the year, finds that out of every *10* hats which[16] he has sold, *9* suffice to repay him for his outlay, every tenth hat will be profit to him, or his profits will consist of one in ten. If now he can produce double the number of hats at the same cost and that each hat falls to half its former price, and he sells double the quantity he did before, would his profits be increased or not? certainly not – It is true that in common with every other Consumer of hats, he might have two where he had one before, but when he came to exchange his hats for other things he would be obliged to give a double quantity of them[17] for all other things which had not varied in their relation to Labour, and if he accumulated his profits it would take double the number of hats to command the same quantity of labour as before.

This has been partially adverted to by yourself in your chapter on Profits where you say "..."[18] only it is necessary for me to observe that your remark is as applicable to the *value* of profits as it is to their *rate* whether their value be measured by your own standard, or by Adam Smiths.

The second consequence I have to notice, which is similar to the first, is, that Profits are unaffected by the rise or fall in the value of other things for which they are exchanged. If the hatter, the shoemaker, the Tailor find that every tenth hat, tenth pair of shoes & tenth suit of clothing form their profit, and that there is a glut of Tea Sugar Coffee Soap and Candles, their profits are not augmented merely because they can procure in exchange more of these cheap[19] articles – They cannot procure more of other articles which have not varied in their relation to Labour, nor can they with the larger quantity of cheap articles command more labour than before – They are benefitted as Consumers and in common with every other Consumer of those cheap commodities. Even if it were held that this constituted an augmentation of their profit, still as the Landlord with his Rent, the Labourer with his wages, and the money Annuitant with his fixed Income would participate in the benefit, it would not be true that one set of Capitalists gained all that was lost by another set of Capitalists.

It is therefore an utter mistake, and a glaring one too, to imagine that if some dealers are selling their stocks at 30 or 40 pc^{e} below their cost other dealers must be selling theirs 30 or 40 pc^{e} above the ordinary rate. The rise or fall of profit in different employments no doubt attracts Capital from those occupations in which it is[20] less advantageous, to those in which it is more so. But at the time being, every Man's profit depends upon the proportion of his

[16] 'which' is ins.

[17] 'a double quantity of them' is altered from 'double the quantity'.

[18] Space of eight lines in MS for insertion of a quotation at a later date.

[19] 'cheap' is ins.

[20] There is an ellipsis between 'is' and 'less'.

own particular Commodity which is absorbed by the[21] proportionate wages, and not upon the greater or less[22] quantity of other things which he gets in exchange for those profits. [23]

And now as to the great question what is it which determines[24] the proportion which is so absorbed? Your doctrine is that it depends altogether[25] upon the State of the Land – But suppose that this worst soil in cultivation at the present moment were of such a degree of fertility as would allow of its yielding 20 pc profit, if the Labourer's share were reduced to its minimum, I ask[26] what is it that [27] determines the profit that it would actually yield between that highest limit & the lowest at which any one would undertake to till it – I am persuaded you will at once agree with me that it is the state of the demand compared with the supply that does this; – and if so, it follows that the fertility of the Land affects profits in one direction only, and not in the other – It determines not what they shall be, but rather what they shall not be – It is a bar to their ever rising above a certain rate, but does not prevent their falling below it.

Practically, profits are scarcely ever at their *rack* rate (if I may be allowed the expression) or the highest that the Land will admit of, and consequently there is a principle in constant operation which determines them quite independently of the cause to which you refer, though subject to its controul* and within its range – This can be no other than the principle of Demand & Supply before referred to; and by demand I do not mean the offer for any Commodity of a quantity of others which have been produced under the same circumstances, since you have yourself very justly stated that the proportion in which commodities exchange with each other has nothing to do with profits; but by demand I mean the amount of sacrifice which those who are desirous of possessing a commodity are willing to make in order to obtain it; which evidently cannot be measured by any quantity

[21] 'the' is ins.

[22] 'greater or less' is ins.

[23] A mark in the text at this point refers the reader to the following note written on the preceding verso: 'Mr Mill's doctrine of the impossibility of a General Glut is founded entirely upon this false notion of every profit *below* the average, being counterbalanced by a profit *above* the average in some other quarter; as if a high profit consisted in a man's getting an unusually large quantity of cheap commodities in exchange for the same quantity of his own – How is it that Mr Mill does not see, that it is precisely because those commodities are cheaper that the man gets more of them – their value sinks in proportion to the increased quantity he receives, and consequently his profits are no greater than before, while those of the Sellers of those Commodities are less – His profits are stationary, because the proportion of his commodity which goes to the Labourer is the same as before. Theirs have fallen, because the proportion of their commodities which go [to] the Labourer has increased. –'

[24] 'the great question what is it which determines' is ins.

[25] 'altogether' is ins.

[26] 'I ask' is ins.

[27] 'would' is del.

of other things but solely by the[28] Labour which they are willing to[29] give to the seller of the Commodity the means of commanding. So necessary indeed is it to refer in this case to Labour, that it is only by comparing the Labour which commodities are worth with that which they have cost, that the dealers in them can ascertain what[30] their profits really are –

It appears then that whatever influence the state of the Land may have upon profits, their rate is in every instance determined by the state of the demand compared with the supply.

Letter III. On Wages

Sir,

In treating of the wages of Labour, you have dwelt chiefly on the proportion which they bear to the produce, and the *increase* or *diminution* of this proportion you have somewhat inappropriately termed the *rise* or *fall* of wages although you admit that in this sense of the term higher wages may sometimes be represented by a smaller quantity of food & necessaries and lower wages by a larger quantity –

It is to be regretted that you have given this new and very unusual meaning to terms, which have hitherto been always understood in a much more simple and obvious sense – In the minds of most persons the rise and fall of wages are invariably associated with an increase or diminution of their *quantity* and I suspect that by not adhering to this plain and well understood definition you have not only misled others but yourself also.

For instance, you have been led to infer that what you call high wages – i.e. the labourers receiving a large *proportion*, is the proof of a great demand for labour and therefore of the labourer's being in a prosperous condition, and low wages are of course the proof of the reverse – Your proposition, that *when wages are high profits are low, and when wages are low profits are high*, is true according to your own definition of high and low as applied to wages; but is very far from being true as these terms are commonly applied and yet you have drawn inferences from them as though you had used them in their ordinary sense.

It is a remarkable fact, and a most important and interesting one it is, that the labourer is generally worse off when his proportion is the largest and vice versâ – When such is the case profits are necessarily low (as you have

[28] 'the' is ins.

[29] 'are willing to' is ins.

[30] 'what' is ins.

yourself taken great pains to shew*) and this not only discourages production but absolutely prevents the employment of more labour – The labourer may in the first instance get a larger share of the produce but this is sure to be speedily followed by a reduction of employment, so that his total earnings are less. If he works six days in the week and earns half of what he produces, he is better off [31]

[31] This is at the end of the last line of a page in MS, but as there is no full stop after 'off', it is possible that Letter III continued on a page or pages now missing.

Bibliography

BIBLIOGRAPHY OF AUTHORS AND WORKS REFERRED TO IN THE TEXT AND EDITORIAL NOTES OF VOLUME I AND VOLUME II[1]

Aikin, J. 1795. *A Description of the Country from Thirty to Forty Miles round Manchester.*

Akenside, M. 1744. *The Pleasures of Imagination. A Poem in Three Books.*

Anon. 1747–66. *Biographica Britannica: or, the Lives of the Most Eminent Persons who Have Flourished in Great Britain and Ireland.* 6 vols.

Anon. 1833. Obituary of Bewick Bridge. *Gentleman's Magazine.* July.

Anville, J.-B. Bourguignon d'. 1768. *Atlas Antiquus Major.*

Aristotle. *Art of Rhetoric.*

Aristotle. *Politics.* 1921. tr. B. Jowett, in *Works of Aristotle*, Vol. IV, Oxford.

Barraclough, G. 1947. *The Origins of Modern Germany.* 2nd edn, Oxford: Blackwell.

Bede. *Ecclesiastical History of the English Nation.*

[? Bentic], D. *Thoughts on the Repeal of the Restriction Law.* (Work not identified – Eds).

[1] Malthus and other contemporary authors did not usually give details of date, publisher, place of publication and editions. The dates shown in this list refer to the first edition, unless otherwise stated. For some items in this list, as indicated in the editorial footnotes, the names of the authors and the titles of the publications have not been established with certainty.

Bonar, J. 1924. *Malthus and his Work*, 2nd edn. London: George Allen & Unwin.

Bonar, J. 1941. 'Life of Thomas Malthus', typescript. Rare Book Room. Urbana-Champaign: Library of the University of Illinois.

Bourne, K. and Taylor, W.B. eds. 1994. *The Horner Papers. Selections from the Letters and Miscellaneous Writings of Francis Horner, M.P. 1795–1817*. Edinburgh: Edinburgh University Press.

Bray, L. 1857. 'Recollections', typescript. Guildford: Guildford Muniment Room.

Bridge, B. 1810. *Lectures on the Elements of Algebra*. (Later editions entitled *A Treatise on the Elements of Algebra.*)

Burke, Sir B. 1912. *A Genealogical and Heraldic History of the Landed Gentry of Ireland*. Revised edition by A.C. Fox-Davies. London: Harrison & Sons. 1958. 4th edition by Sir J.B. Burke.

Burke, Sir B. 1938. *Burke's Genealogical and Heraldic History of the Peerage, Baronetage and Knightage ...* . London: Shaw Publishing Co. in conjunction with Burke's Peerage.

Burke, J. and Burke, Sir J.B. 1965–72. *Burke's Genealogical and Heraldic History of the Landed Gentry*. 18th edn, London: Burke's Peerage Limited.

Butler, C. 1817. *The Philological and Biographical Works of Charles Butler*. 5 vols.

Butler, J. 1736. *The Analogy of Religion, Natural and Revealed, to the Constitution and Course of Nature*.

Caesar. *De Bello Gallico*.

Cannon, J. ed. 1997. *The Oxford Companion to British History*. Oxford: Oxford University Press.

Carey, G.G. 1818. *A Complete System of Theoretical and Mercantile Arithmetic.*

Castley, T. 1817. *Antiquarian Speculations, Consisting of Essays and Dissertations on Various Subjects.*

Chalmers, G. 1807–24. *Caledonia: or an Account of North Britain.* 3 vols.

Christian, E. 1820. *General Observations on Provident Banks.* London.

Cicero, Marcus Tullius. *Ad Attica.*

Cicero, Marcus Tullius. *Cato Major de Senectute.*

Cicero, Marcus Tullius. *De officiis.*

Clarke, E.D.C. 1812. *A Letter to Herbert Marsh ... in Reply to Certain Observations in his Pamphlet Relative to the British and Foreign Bible Society.*

Close, Francis. 1825. *A Course of Nine Sermons on the Liturgy.*

Cockburn, Lord. 1852. *Life of Lord Jeffrey with a Selection from his Correspondence.* 2 vols.

Conolly, T.J. 1898. *List of Officers of the Corps of Royal Engineers.*

Curwen, J.F. 1900. *Kirkbie-Kendall.*

Danvers, F.C. *et al.* 1894. *Memorials of Old Haileybury College.*

Davis, R.H.C. 1972. *A History of Medieval Europe: From Constantine to Saint Louis.* London: Longman.

Diodorus Siculus. (No specific work stated.)

Du Bos, Jean-Baptiste. 1734. *Histoire critique de l'établissement de la monarchie françoise dans les Gaules.* 3 vols.

Dudley, Sir Henry Bate (formerly Bate, Henry). 1808. *A Short Address to the Most Reverend and Honourable William, Lord Primate of All Ireland.*

Duffy, E. 1997. *Saints & Sinners. A History of the Popes*. Yale: Yale University Press.

Duncan, W. 1748. *The Elements of Logick.*

Dunn (or Dun), S. 1768. *General Atlas*.

Eatwell, J., Milgate, M. and Newman, P. eds. 1987. *The New Palgrave. A Dictionary of Economics*. 4 vols. London: Macmillan; New York: Stockton Press; Tokyo: Maruzen.

Eden, Sir F.M. 1797. *The State of the Poor*. 3 vols.

Emerson, W. 1758. *The Principles of Mechanicks*.

[Empson, W.] 1837. 'Life, Writings and Character of Mr Malthus', *Edinburgh Review*, Vol. 64, pp. 469–506.

Encyclopædia Britannica, various editions.

Enfield, W. 1791. *The History of Philosophy ... Drawn up from Brucker's Historia Critica Philosophiae*.

Enfield, W. 1798. *Sermons on Practical Subjects*. 3 vols.

English Encyclopædia. 1802. 10 vols.

Erskine, Thomas. 1820. *Remarks on the Internal Evidence for the Truth of Revealed Religion.*

Euclid. *The Elements of Euclid.*

Ferguson, J. (No title stated.)

Fossier, R. ed. 1989. *The Cambridge Illustrated History of the Middle Ages.* Translated by Janet Sondheimer. Cambridge: Cambridge University Press.

Foster, J. (1887–8) 1968. *Alumni Oxonienses: The Members of the University of Oxford, 1715–1886.* Nendeln/Liechtenstein: Kraus Reprint Limited.

Franklin, B. 1761. *The Interest of Great Britain Considered, with Regard to her Colonies, and the Acquisition of Canada and Guadaloupe.* To which are Added, Observations Concerning the Increase of Mankind. Peopling of Countries, &c.*, 2nd edn, London.

G.E.C. 1910–59. *The Complete Peerage of England Scotland Ireland Great Britain and the United Kingdom.* London: St Catherine Press.

Gibbon, E. 1776–88. *The History of the Decline and Fall of the Roman Empire.* 6 vols.

Giddy (later Gilbert), D. 1811. *A Plain Statement on the Bullion Question in a Letter to a Friend.*

Gilpin, W. 1772. *Observations, Relative Chiefly to Picturesque Beauty, in Several Parts of England, Particularly the Mountains and Lakes of Cumberland and Westmoreland.*

Godwin, W. 1797. *An Enquiry Concerning Political Justice.*

Godwin, W. 1797. *The Enquirer.*

Godwin, W. 1801. *Thoughts Occasioned by the Perusal of Dr Parr's Spital Sermon.*

Godwin, W. 1820. *Of Population.*

Goldsmith, O. 1764. *An History of England in a Series of Letters from a Nobleman to his Son.* 2 vols.

Goldsmith, O. 1769. *The Roman History, from the Foundation of the City of Rome, to the Destruction of the Western Empire.* 2 vols.

Goldsmith, O. 1774. *The Grecian History, from the Earliest State to the Death of Alexander the Great*. 2 vols.

Grand Larousse Encyclopédique. 1960–4. 10 vols. Paris: Librairie Larousse.

[? Grant, R.]. 1817. 'East India College', *Quarterly Review*. Vol. 17, No. 73, April, Art. 5, pp. 107–54.

Graves, R. 1780. *Euphrosyne: or, Amusements on the Road to Life.*

Graves, R. 1788. *Recollections of Some Particulars in the Life of the Late William Shenstone, Esq.*

Graves, Richard. 1772. *The Spiritual Quixote, or the Summer's Ramble of Mr. Geoffry Wildgoose.*

Gray, Thomas. 1775. *Journal in the Lakes.*

Gunning, H. 1855. *Reminiscences of the University Town, and County of Cambridge from the Year 1780*. 2 vols.

Hallam, Henry. 1818. *View of the State of Europe during the Middle Ages*, 2 vols, London.

Hand, F.G. 1829–45. *Tursellinus, seu deu particulis Latinis commentarii.*

Harvey, Sir P. ed. 1967. *Oxford Companion to English Literature*. 4th edn, rev. D. Eagle. Oxford: Clarendon Press.

Hashimoto, H. 1990. 'Journal Kept by Harriet Eckersall (afterwards the Wife of T.R. Malthus) during her Trip to France, and Switzerland in 1802'. *KSU Economic and Business Review*, No. 17, pp. 25–70. Kyoto Sangyo University.

Haygarth, J. 1778. 'Observations on the Population and Diseases of Chester in 1774', *Philosophical Transactions*, Royal Society.

Henry, Robert. 1771–98. *The History of Great Britain from the First Invasion of it by the Romans under Julius Caesar*. 6 vols.

Herodotus. *Historia*.

Higgs, H. ed. (1925–6) 1963. *Palgrave's Dictionary of Political Economy*. 2nd edn, 3 vols. Reprinted New York: Augustus M. Kelley.

Hincmar. *Opusculum LV capitulorum*.

Hogan, C.B. ed. 1960–8. *The London Stage 1660–1800. Part 5: 1776–1800*. Southern Illinois University Press.

Home, J. 1757. *Douglas*.

Horace. (No specific work stated.)

Hume, D. 1762. *The History of England, from the Invasion of Julius Caesar to the Revolution in 1688*.

Hunter, Sir W.W. 1896. *Life of Brian Houghton Hodgson*.

Huntingford, G.I. 1778. *An Introduction to the Writing of Greek, for the use of Winchester College*.

Huskisson, W. 1810. *The Question Concerning the Depreciation of Our Currency Stated and Examined*.

Hutchinson, L. (1806) 1936. *Memoirs of the Life of Colonel Hutchinson, Governor of Nottingham Castle and Town*. Reprinted London: J.M. Dent.

James Archive. Archive of Patricia James at Kanto Gakuen University.

James, P. 1979. *Population Malthus. His Life and Times*. London: Routledge & Kegan Paul.

Jesus College (University of Cambridge) 1983. *The Malthus Library Catalogue*. New York: Pergamon Press.

Johnson, S. 1781. *Lives of the Poets*.

Keill, J. 1720. *An Introduction to Natural Philosophy*.

Keir, D. ed. 1966. *The City of Edinburgh*. Glasgow: Collins.

Kersseboom, W. 1742. *Eerste (-derde) verhandeling tot een proeve om te weeten de probable menigte des colks in de provintie van Hollandt en Westvrieslandt* ... tweede druk. 3 pt. 's Gravenhage, J. Van den Bergh.

Kippis, A. and others. 1778–93. *Biographica Britannica*. 2nd edn. Vols. I–V.

Kirwan, R. 1784. *Elements of Mineralogy*.

Langford, R. (1809) 1825. *An Introduction to Trade and Business*.

Leslie, J.B. 1936. *Ferns Clergy and Parishes*.

Lister, R. 1970. *Antique Maps and their Cartographers*. London: G. Bell and Sons.

Locke, J. 1750. *Elements of Natural Philosophy*.

Lockhart, J.G. 1902. *The Life of Sir Walter Scott*. 10 vols.

Logan, F.D. 1991. *The Vikings in History*. 2nd edn.

Long, R. *Astronomy*.

Longinus. *De sublimitate commentaries*.

Lucan. *Pharsalia, or the Civil Wars*.

Lucretius. *De rerum natura libri VI*.

Mably, Gabriel Bonnot de. 1751. *Observations sur les Romains*.

Maclaurin, C. 1748. *A Treatise of Algebra*.

Maclaurin, C. 1748. *An Account of Sir Isaac Newton's Philosophical Discoveries*.

Malthus, T.R. 1796. 'The Crisis'. An unpublished pamphlet.

Malthus, T.R. 1798. *An Essay on the Principle of Population.*

Malthus, T.R. 1799. Letter in *Monthly Magazine*, April, pp. 178–9.

Malthus, T.R. 1806. *An Essay on the Principle of Population.* 3rd edn, 2 vols.

Malthus, T.R. 1807. *A Letter to Samuel Whitbread, Esq., M.P. on his Proposed Bill for the Amendment of the Poor Laws.*

Malthus, T.R. 1808. 'Newenham and Others on the State of Ireland', *Edinburgh Review*, Vol. 12, July, pp. 336–55.

Malthus, T.R. 1809. *Essai sur le principe de population*, translated by P. Prévost. 3 vols. Paris: J.J. Paschoud. (Translation of the 4th edn of Malthus' *Essay on Population*, 1807.)

Malthus, T.R. 1811a. 'Depreciation of Paper Currency', *Edinburgh Review*. Vol. XVII, February, pp. 339–71.

Malthus, T.R. 1811b. 'Pamphlets on the bullion question', *Edinburgh Review*. Vol. XVIII, August, pp. 448–70.

Malthus, T.R. 1813. *A Letter to the Rt. Hon. Lord Grenville.*

Malthus, T.R. 1814. *Observations on the Effects of the Corn Laws.*

Malthus, T.R. 1815. *The Grounds of an Opinion on the Policy of Restricting the Importation of Foreign Corn.* London: John Murray.

Malthus, T.R. 1817. *An Essay on the Principle of Population.* 5th edn.

Malthus, T.R. 1817. *Statements Respecting the East India College.*

Malthus, T.R. 1820. *Principes de l'économie politique*, trans. F.S. Constancio.

Malthus, T.R. 1820. *Principles of Political Economy.*

Malthus, T.R. 1823. *Essai sur le principe de population*, trans. P. Prévost and G. Prévost. (Translation of the 5th edn, 1817, of Malthus' *Essay on Population.*)

Malthus, T.R. 1823. *The Measure of Value Stated and Illustrated.*

Malthus, T.R. 1824. 'Population', Supplement to the 4th, 5th and 6th editions of the *Encyclopædia Britannica* (published separately, 1823).

Malthus, T.R. 1826. *An Essay on the Principle of Population.* 6th edn.

Malthus, T.R. 1827. *Definitions in Political Economy.*

Malthus, T.R. (1926) 1966. *First Essay on Population 1798.* London: Macmillan.

Malthus, T.R. 1966. *The Travel Diaries of T.R. Malthus*, ed. P. James. Cambridge: Cambridge University Press for the Royal Economic Society.

Malthus, T.R. (1836) 1968. *Principles of Political Economy.* 2nd edn. New York: Augustus M. Kelley.

Malthus, T.R. 1986. *The Works of Thomas Robert Malthus.* 8 vols. London: William Pickering.

Malthus, T.R. 1989a. *An Essay on the Principle of Population.* Variorum edition, 2 vols., ed. Patricia James. Cambridge: Cambridge University Press for the Royal Economic Society.

Malthus, T.R. 1989b. *Principles of Political Economy.* Variorum edition, 2 vols., ed. John Pullen. Cambridge: Cambridge University Press for the Royal Economic Society.

Manning, O. and Bray, W. (1804–14) 1974. *The History and Antiquities of the County of Surrey.* 3 vols. Republished by E.P. Publishing Limited in collaboration with Surrey County Library.

Mannix and Whellan. (1847) 1974. *History, Gazetteer and Directory of Cumberland.* Beverley: W.B. Johnson. Reprinted by The Beckermet Bookshop, Cumberland: Michael Moon.

Mansel, W.L. 1813. *A Sermon Preached before the Incorporated Society for the Propagation of the Gospel in Foreign Parts.*

Map Collectors' Circle. 1964–5. Vol. 2, p.19, 'Anville'; 1966–7. Vol. 4, p.124, 'Dunn'.

Marcet, J. 1816. *Conversations on Political Economy.*

Marryat, J. 1811. *Thoughts on the Expediency of Establishing a New Chartered Bank ... Confirmed by the Report of the Bullion Committee.*

Marsh, H. 1812. *An Inquiry into the Consequences of Neglecting to Give the Prayer Book with the Bible.*

Masè-Dari, E. 1929. *Tre Lettere Inedite di R.T. [sic] Malthus.* Modena: Presso l'Università degli studi.

Millar, J. 1787. *An Historical View of the English Government, from the Settlement of the Saxons in Britain to the Revolution in 1688.* 4 vols.

Millot, C.F.X. 1772–1811. *Elémens d'histoire générale.*

Milne, J. 1815. *A Treatise on the Valuation of Annuities and Assurances in Lives and Survivorships: on the Construction of Tables of Mortality; and on the Probabilities and Expectations of Life.* 2 vols.

Milner, I. 1813. *Strictures on Some of the Publications of ... H. Marsh.*

Milton, John. *Comus.*

Milton, John. *Il Penseroso.*

Milton, John. *L'Allegro.*

Milton, John. *Paradise Lost.*

Moivre, A. de. 1718. *The Doctrine of Chances.*

Moivre, A. de. 1725. *Annuities upon Lives.*

Montesquieu, Charles Louis de Secondat. 1748. *De l'esprit des loix.*

Morgan, W. 1821. *The Principles and Doctrine of Assurances, Annuities on Lives, and Contingent Reversions, Stated and Explained.*

Morning Chronicle, 2 February 1810.

Muret, J.-L. 1766. 'Mémoire sur l'état de la population dans le pays de Vaud', *Mémoires et observations recueillies par la Société Oeconomique de Berne.*

Murphy, A. 1772. *The Grecian Daughter.*

Mushet, R. 1810. *An Enquiry into the Effects Produced on the National Currency and Rates of Exchange, by the Bank Restriction Bill.* Also, 3rd edn, 1811.

Nangle, B.C. 1934. *The Monthly Review. First Series 1749–1789.* Oxford: Clarendon Press.

New Catholic Encyclopedia. 1967. New York: McGraw-Hill.

New Palgrave, The. A Dictionary of Economics 1987, ed. John Eatwell *et al.*, 4 vols., Macmillan, London.

Newton, Sir Isaac. 1704. *Opticks.*

Newton, Sir Isaac. 1736. *Method of Fluxions and Infinite Series.*

Newton, Sir Isaac. *Philosophiae naturalis principia mathematica.*

Nouveau Larousse Illustré, n.d. Dir. Claude Augé. Paris: Librairie Larousse. 7 vols.

Otter, W. 1812a. *A Vindication of Churchmen Who Become Members of the British and Foreign Bible Society.*

Otter, W. 1812b. *An Examination of Dr Marsh's Answer to all the Arguments in Favour of the British and Foreign Bible Society.*

[Otter, William] 1968. 'Memoir of Robert Malthus', in Malthus, T.R. (1836) 1968.

Oxford English Dictionary. 1989. 2nd edn, prepared by J.A. Simpson and E.S.C. Weiner. Oxford: Clarendon Press.

Palgrave's Dictionary of Political Economy 1963. 2nd edn, ed. Henry Higgs, [1925–6], reprinted Augustus M. Kelley, New York.

Parson, W. and White, W. 1976. *A History, Directory and Gazetteer of Cumberland and Westmorland*. Beckermet (Cumbria): Michael Moon at the Beckermet Bookshop.

Paul, C. Kegan. 1876. *William Godwin: his Friends and Contemporaries*. 2 vols.

Petit Larousse. 1967. Paris: Larousse.

Pinkerton, J. 1787. *A dissertation on the Origin and Progress of the Scythians or Goths*.

Pitcher, R. and Pullen, J. 1992. 'Malthus on Classical Languages and Corporal Punishment', *History of Economics Review*, No. 18, pp. 34–45.

Polkinghorn, B.A. 1986. 'An unpublished letter from Malthus to Jane Marcet, January 22, 1833'. *American Economic Review*. 76(4), pp. 845–7.

Polybius. *General History*.

Pope, A. (1720) 1881. 'To Mr. Addison, occasioned by his dialogues on medals', in *The Works of Alexander Pope*, Moral Essays, Epistle VII. London: John Murray.

Pope, A. (1732–4) 1978. *An Essay on Man*, in *Alexander Pope: Poetical Works*, ed. H. Davis (1966) 1978. Oxford University Press.

Pope, A. (1711) 1822. *Essay on Criticism*, in *The Works of Alexander Pope*, ed. Joseph Warton.

Price, R. 1771. *Observations on Reversionary Payments*.

Pullen, J.M. 1981. 'Malthus' theological ideas and their influence on his principle of population', *History of Political Economy*, Vol. 13, No. 1, pp. 39–54.

Pullen, J.M. 1982. 'Malthus on the doctrine of proportions and the concept of the optimum', *Australian Economic Papers*, December, pp. 270–85.

Pullen, J.M. 1987a. 'Some new information on the Rev. T.R. Malthus', *History of Political Economy*, Vol. 19, No. 1, pp. 127–40.

Pullen, J.M. 1987b. 'Lord Grenville's manuscript notes on Malthus', *History of Political Economy*, 19(2), pp. 217–37.

Pullen, J.M. 1998. 'Malthus on this world and the next', *The Bulletin of Matsudaira Memorial Institute for Economics and Culture*, No. 16, December, pp. 177–200.

Quintilian. (No specific work stated.)

Rau, K.H. 1816. *Ueber das Zunftwesen und die Fölgen seiner Aufhebung.*

Rau, K.H. 1921. *Ansichten der Volkswirtschaft mit besonderer Beziehung auf Deutschland.*

Ricardo, D. 1810. *The High Price of Bullion, a Proof of the Depreciation of Bank Notes.*

Ricardo, D. 1811a. *Reply to Mr Bosanquet's Practical Observations on the Report of the Bullion Committee.*

Ricardo, D. 1811b. *The High Price of Bullion, a Proof of the Depreciation of Bank Notes, the fourth edn, corrected, to which is added, an appendix containing observations on some passages in an article in the Edinburgh Review, on the depreciation of paper currency.*

Ricardo, D. 1821. *On the Principles of Political Economy and Taxation.* 3rd edn.

Ricardo, D. 1951–73. *The Works and Correspondence of David Ricardo*, ed. P. Sraffa. Cambridge: Cambridge University Press for the Royal Economic Society.

Rickman, J. (1771–1840). (No specific work stated.)

Robert, P. 1970. *Le Petit Robert. Dictionnaire Alphabétique & Analogique de la Langue Française*. Paris: Société du Nouveau Littré.

Robertson, W. 1769. *The History of the Reign of the Emperor Charles V*.

Rose, G. 1811. *Substance of the Speech Delivered in the House of Commons by the Right Honorable George Rose ... on the Report of the Bullion Committee*.

Rose, G. 1814. *Speech ... on ... the Corn Laws*.

Rose, G. 1815. *Observations on the Poor Laws, and on the Management of the Poor in Great Britain*.

Rose, G. 1816. *Observations on Banks for Savings*.

Rousseau, J.-J. 1762. *Émile ou de l'éducation*.

Russell, W. 1786. *The History of Modern Europe*.

Rutherfurth, T. 1748. *A System of Natural Philosophy, Being a Course of Lectures in Mechanics, Optics, Hydrostatics, and Astronomy ...* . 2 vols.

Sallust (Gaius Sallustius Crispus). *Bellum Iugurthinum*.

Saunderson (or Sanderson), Nicholas. In a letter of 13 January 1786, Daniel Malthus referred to 'Sanderson's Opticks' (see above, Vol. I, p.38). This could have been a mistaken reference to Saunderson's *The Elements of Algebra*, 1740; or *The Method of Fluxions*, 1756; or *Select Parts of Professor Saunderson's Elements of Algebra*, 1756. (The dates, from the British Library Catalogue, differ from those in *DNB*.) Saunderson lectured on optics, but there is no record of his having published a work of that title.

Say, J.-B. 1820. *Lettres à M. Malthus*.

Say, J.-B. 1821. *Letters to Mr Malthus*, tr. J. Richter.

Schumpeter, J.A. 1954. *History of Economic Analysis,* ed. E.B. Schumpeter. London: George Allen & Unwin.

Scott, Sir Walter. 1921. *The Poetical Works of Sir Walter Scott*, ed. J. Logie Robertson. Humphrey Milford: Oxford University Press.

Selden, J. (No specific work stated.)

Simond, L. 1815. *Journal of the Tour and Residence in Great Britain during the Years 1810 and 1811*. 2 vols.

Simonde de Sismondi, J.C.L. 1819. *Nouveaux principes d'économie politique*. 2 vols.

Six, J. 1782. 'Account of an improved thermometer', *Philosophical Transactions*. Royal Society, Vol. 72, Part 1, X, pp. 72–81.

Six, J. 1784. 'Experiments to investigate the variation of local heat', *Philosophical Transactions*. Royal Society, Vol. 74, Part 2, XXXII, pp.428–36.

Smith, A.H. 1961–3. *The Place-Names of the West Riding of Yorkshire*. 8 vols. Cambridge: Cambridge University Press.

Smith, Adam (1776) 1976. *An Inquiry into the Nature and Causes of the Wealth of Nations*, 2 vols, eds. R.H. Campbell, A.S. Skinner, W.B. Todd, *The Glasgow Edition of the Works and Correspondence of Adam Smith*. Oxford: Clarendon Press.

Smyth, W. 1840a. *Lectures on Modern History, from the Irruption of the Northern Nations to the Close of the American Revolution*.

Smyth, W. 1840b. *Lectures on History. Second and Concluding Series. On the French Revolution*. 3 vols.

Sophocles. *Philoctetes*.

Stephen, L. and Lee, S. eds. 1937–8. *Dictionary of National Biography from the Earliest Times to 1900*. Oxford: Oxford University Press.

Stiles, E. 1761. *A Discourse on the Christian Union*.

Storch, H.F. von. 1815. *Cours d'économie politique*. 6 vols.

Storch, H.F. von. 1820. *Zusätze zu Heinrich Storch ... Cours d'économie politique*. Translated by K.H. Rau.

Süssmilch, J.P. 1765. *Die göttliche Ordnung*. 3rd edn.

Tacitus. *A Treatise on the Situation, Manner, and Inhabitants of Germany; and the Life of Agricola*.

Tanneguy, C.M. (Comte Duchatel) 1829. *La Charité dans ses rapports avec l'état moral et le bien-être des classes inférieurs de la société*.

Terence. *Hecyra*.

Theocritus. (No specific work stated.)

Thicknesse, P. 1788. *Memoirs and Anecdotes of Philip Thicknesse*.

Thomson, J. (1726–30) 1981. *The Seasons*, ed. James Sambrook. Oxford: Clarendon Press.

Thucydides. (No specific work stated.)

Thucydides. *The History of the Grecian War*.

Timbs, J. 1823. *A Picturesque Promenade round Dorking, in Surrey*. 2nd edn.

Torrens, R. 1815. *An Essay on the External Corn Trade*. (Other editions: 1820, 1826, 1827, 1829).

Torrens, R. 1821. *An Essay on the Production of Wealth*.

Trotter, C. 1810. *The Principles of Currency and Exchanges Applied to the Report from the Select Committee of the House of Commons, Appointed to Inquire into the High Price of Gold Bullion, &c. &c.*

Turgot, A.R.J. 1766. *Réflexions sur la formation et la distribution des richesses.*

Tyrwhitt, R. 1787. *Two Discourses, on the Creation of all Things by Jesus Christ; and on the Resurrection.*

Venn, J.A. 1944. *Alumni Cantabrigienses. Part II. From 1752 to 1900.* Cambridge: Cambridge University Press.

Vince, S. 1781. *The Elements of the Conic Sections as Preparatory to the reading of Sir I. Newton's Principia.*

Virgil. *Aeneid.*

Wakefield, G. 1776. *Poemata. Latiné partim scripta, partim reddita: quibus accedunt quaedam in Q. Horatium Flaccum observationes criticae.* Cambridge.

Walker, T.A. 1912. *Admissions to Peterhouse or S. Peter's College in the University of Cambridge.* Cambridge: Cambridge University Press.

Walker's Critical and Pronouncing Dictionary Abridgement. (Work not identified – Eds.)

Walsh, Sir J.B. (Lord Ormathwaite) 1830. *Poor Laws in Ireland ...* .

Wargentin, P.W. 1772. 'De l'homme; mortalité de l'homme en Suéde, comparée à celle de la femme', *Mémoires (abrégés) de l'Académie Royale des Sciences de Stockholm*, pp. 20–33.

Warton, Joseph. 1763. *The Eclogues and Georgics*, in *The Works of Virgil in English Verse.*

Watson, R. ed. 1785. *A Collection of Theological Tracts.* 6 vols.

Watson, Richard. 1817. *Anecdotes of the Life of Richard Watson, Bishop of Landaff*. London: T. Cadell and W. Davies.

Watt, W. Montgomery. 1965. *A History of Islamic Spain*. Edinburgh: Edinburgh University Press.

Watts, W. 1779–86. *The Seats of the Nobility and Gentry. In a Collection of the Most Interesting and Picturesque Views Engraved by W.W. ...* .

West, Thomas. 1778. *A Guide to the Lakes in Cumberland, Westmorland and Lancashire*.

Whitaker, J. 1771. *The History of Manchester*. Vol. I.

Whitbread, S. 1807. *Substance of a Speech on the Poor Laws: Delivered in the House of Commons, on Thursday, February 19*.

Wilmot-Horton, R.J. 1830. *An Inquiry into the Causes and Remedies of Pauperism*.

Wordsworth, William. 1977. *Guide to the Lakes*. 5th edn, ed. E. de Sélincourt. Oxford: Oxford University Press.

Xenophon. *The Retreat of the Ten Thousand*.

Young, Arthur. 1770. *Six Months' Tour Through the North of England*. 4 vols.

Zinke, G.W. 1942. 'Six Letters from Malthus to Pierre Prévost', *Journal of Economic History*, Vol. 2, pp. 174–89.

Kanto Gakuen Catalogue

The items in Volume I and Volume II have the following catalogue numbers in the library of Kanto Gakuen University:

Volume I		Kanto Gakuen Catalogue
Chapter	Item	
1	1	26
	2	27
	3	28
	4	1
	5	2
	6	3
	7	29
	8	4
	9	5
	10	30
	11	6
	12	7
	13	31
	14	8
	15	9
	16	32
2	17	10
	18	11
	19	12
	20	13
	21	14
	22	15
	23	33

Volume I		Kanto Gakuen Catalogue
Chapter	Item	
2	24	34
	25	35
	26	16
	27	36
	28	17
	29	37
	30	38
	31	18
	32	19
	33	20
	34	21
	35	39
	36	22
	37	40
	38	23
	39	41
	40	42
	41	44
	42	43
3	43	45
	44	24
	45	25
	46	73
	47	68
	48	83
4	49	46
	50	49
	51	50
	52	51
	53	52
	54	53
	55	56
	56	65
	57	57
	58	58
	59	59

Volume I		Kanto Gakuen Catalogue
Chapter	Item	
4	60	60
	61	61
	62	62
	63	100
5	64	47
	65	93
	66	63
	67	48
	68	64
	69	55
	70	54
	71	67
	72	98
	73	99
	74	69
	75	66

Volume II		Kanto Gakuen Catalogue
Chapter	Item	
1	1	71
	2	72
	3	86
	4	81
2		75
3		97
4		95
5	1	91
	2	92
	3	77

Volume II		Kanto Gakuen Catalogue
Chapter	Item	
6		90
7		87
8		103
9	1	74
	2	96
	3	84
	4	78
	5	78, 79
	6	79
	7	79
	8	76
Appendix A	1	113
	2	102
	3	85
	4	85
	5	85
	6	85
	7	104
	8	105
	9	105
	10	105
	11	105
	12	106
	13	107
	14	108
	15	109
	16	110
	17	111
	18	115
	19	115
	20	115
	21	115
	22	114
	23	112

Volume II		Kanto Gakuen Catalogue
Chapter	Item	
Appendix A	24	88
	25	115
	26	115
	27	115
	28	115
	29	116
	30	-
	31	82
	32	80
	33	93
	34	70
	35	76
	36	77
	37	101
	38	-
	39	-
	40	-
	41	-
Appendix B		89

Index

INDEX OF PERSONS IN THE TEXT AND EDITORIAL NOTES OF VOLUME I AND VOLUME II*

Abbas, **II**, 183
Abdalrahman (or Abdalrahan or Abderrahmen or Abdelrahmen or Abdalrahman), i.e. Abd ar-Rahmān, **II**, 168, 182, 183, 194
Abercrombie, Lord, **II**, 225
Abū al-'Abbās as-Saffah, **II**, 182
Acerbi, Giuseppe, **I**, 4, **II**, 237
Acheson, Eric, **II**, xvi
Aeolus, **I**, 77
Aesop (or Esop), **II**, 204
Agidius, **II**, 178
Aikin, John, MD, **I**, 43, 65
Aikin, John, DD, Revd, **I**, 43
Aislabie, John, **II**, 271
Akenside, Mark, **I**, 6
Alaric, **II**, 182
Alboin, **II**, 184
Alcaeus, **I**, 19
Alcuin, **II**, 194, 195
Alexander I, Tsar of Russia, **I**, 119
Alexander, Professor, **II**, 235
Alfred the Great, **II**, 170, 191, 203, 205
Ali, **II**, 183
Alison, Archibald, **II**, 237
Alloway, Lord. See Cathcart, David.
Anastasius, **II**, 184
Ann (or Anne), a maid or governess, **II**, 244, 253, 264
Anville, Jean-Baptiste Bourgignon d', **I**, 54
Aristotle, **I**, 20, 21, 127
Arius, of Alexandria, **II**, 179
Arnulf (or Arnold), **II**, 206
Arundell, Lord, of Wardour, **II**, 286
Askew, Mr, **II**, 253, 254
Astelphus, **II**, 185
Augustine, Saint, **II**, 188, 204

Bagshaw, Captain, **II**, 251, 252
Ball, Michael, **I**, 105, **II**, xvi
Barber, Mr, **II**, 261, 265
Barraclough, G., **II**, 204
Barry, Mrs, **I**, 12
Bathric (or Brihtric), **II**, 202
Batten, Joseph Hallet, **I**, 90, 121
Beadon, Richard, **I**, 47, 56
Beaumont, George, **II**, 36
Beddoes, Thomas (1760–1808), **I**, 72, 78, 79, 80
Beddoes, Thomas Lovell (1803–1849), son of the above, **I**, 79

* References to 'Malthus', i.e. Thomas Robert Malthus, are not indexed.

Bede (The Venerable Bede), **II**, 171, 186, 204
Bedford, Miss, **II**, 256, 272
Bedford, Sophia, **II**, 256, 261
Bedford, William, **II**, 256, 273
Beethoven, Ludwig van, **II**, 259
Belisarius, **II**, 184
Bell, Henry, **II**, 227
Bennet, Charles, Earl of Tankerville, **I**, 40, 45
Bentic, David, **II**, 284
Berengarius (or Berenger), **II**, 206, 208
Berkeley, Eliza, **I**, 13
Berkeley, George, Dr, philosopher, **I**, 13
Berkeley, George, Revd, son of the above, **I**, 13
Berkeley, George Monck, son of the above, **I**, 13
Bertha, **II**, 188
Besser, **I**, 126, 127
Blake, William, **II**, 143
Blomfield, Charles James, **II**, 265
Boaden, James, **I**, 12
Boethius, **II**, 204
Bolton, Colonel, **II**, 267
Bolton, Mr, **II**, 261, 262
Bonaparte, Napoleon, **I**, 109, **II**, 210
Bonar, James, **I**, xxii, 2, 3, 4, 8, 12, 22, 53, 77, **II**, 289
Boothroyd, Helen, **I**, 63, **II**, xvi
Bosanquet, Charles, **II**, 143, 144, 150
Bosanquet, Jacob, **I**, 120
Boson, **II**, 206
Bosse, Rudolph Heinrich Bernhard von, **I**, 126
Bothwell, Earl of, **II**, 163
Bouguer, Pierre, **I**, 38
Boulton, Matthew, **II**, 41
Bourne, K., **I**, xxii, 108
Bowdler, Thomas, **II**, 265
Bowling, R. Geoffrey, **II**, xvi, 259
Brandram, Francis Holles, **II**, 256
Brandram, Maria, née Bedford, **II**, 256, 273
Brandrams, **II**, 273
Bray, Edward, **I**, 58, **II**, 249, 287
Bray, Louisa, **I**, xxii, 10, 11, 57, 58, 65, 69, **II**, 287
Bray, Mary Anne Catherine, née Malthus, **I**, 56, 58, 70, **II**, 249, 287
Bray, Reginald, **II**, 287
Bray, William, **I**, 56, **II**, 271
Breadalbane and Holland, fifth earl of. See Campbell, John.
Bridge, Bewick, **I**, 72, 73, 74, 75, 76, 89, 90, 93, 94, 95, 96, 97, 98, 101, 102
Brinckman, Mary (b. 1872), née Malthus, sister of Robert Malthus (1881–1972), **II**, 289
Brissenden, R.F., **II**, 238
Brown, Dr, **II**, 222, 227, 228
Brown, Mrs, **II**, 222, 227
Brown, John, **II**, 222
Brown, Marion, née Jeffrey, **II**, 222
Brown, Thomas, **II**, 222
Bruce, Mr, **II**, 220, 262, 263, 272
Bruce, Mrs, **II**, 220
Bruhl, Jeremy, **I**, 35, **II**, xvi
Buchan, Mr, **II**, 239
Buchan, Mrs, **II**, 239
Buquoy-Longueval, Georg Franz, Count, **I**, 126
Burdett, Sir Francis, **I**, 103
Burkard, **II**, 206
Butler, Charles, **II**, 171, 192
Butler, Joseph, **II**, 14

Caesar, **I**, 5, **II**, 171, 172
Campbell, John, fifth Earl of Breadalbane and Holland, **II**, 233
Canning, George, **II**, 261, 262, 265, 267
Canning, Joan, née Scott, **II**, 267
Canute, **II**, 191
Carey, G.G., **II**, 63
Carloman, **II**, 205, 206
Castley, Thomas, **I**, 73, 74
Catchpole, Jane, **I**, xi
Cathcart, David, Lord Alloway, **II**, 214, 218, 220
Catulus, Quintus Lutatius, **I**, 22
Cautley, Thomas, **I**, 73, 74, 76
Cazenove, John, **II**, 292, 293, 294
Centaines, **II**, 171
Chalmers, George, **II**, 186
Chalmers, Thomas, **II**, 214, 219, 221, 292
Charlemagne, **II**, 169, 176, 192, 193, 194, 195, 196, 197, 198, 199, 202, 205, 206, 208, 209
Charles I, **II**, 159, 160, 161
Charles II, the Bald, **II**, 199, 200, 201, 206
Charles the Fat, **II**, 170, 201, 205, 206
Charles the Simple, **II**, 170, 201, 205, 207
Chigusa, Yoshindo, **I**, xiii
Childebert, **II**, 179, 191
Chilpéric (or Chelpéric) I, **II**, 180
Christ, **II**, 12, 13, 14, 17, 18
Christian, Edward, **I**, 89
Christian, John, **II**, 35
Cicero, Marcus Tullius, **I**, 7, 11, 18, 22
Clarke, Edward Daniel, **I**, 66, 67, 72, 73, 74, 75, 76, 77, 106, 107, 116, 117
Cleaver, Catherine, née Wynne, **II**, 271
Cleaver, Euseby, **I**, 63, **II**, 53, 271
Cleaver, William, **II**, 53
Clement of Ireland, **II**, 195
Clodomir (or Chlodomer), **II**, 179
Close, Francis, **II**, 247
Clotaire (or Chlothar), **II**, 179, 191
Clotaire II, **II**, 168, 179, 180
Clotilda, **II**, 178
Clovis, **II**, 167, 174, 178, 179, 180
Cockburn (or Coburn or Cobourn or Colbourn), Henry, **I**, 117, 118, **II**, 214, 215, 218, 219, 235, 236, 237
Condamine, C.L. de la, **I**, 38
Conrad, **II**, 206
Constancio, F.S., **I**, 92
Coppard, William, **I**, 28
Corehouse, Lord. See Cranstoun, George.
Coventry, Andrew, **II**, 220
Craig, Mr, **II**, 219
Cranstoun, George, Lord Corehouse, **II**, 214, 218
Crawford, Ann, **I**, 12, 14, 17, 19
Crescentius, **II**, 209
Cripps, John Marten, **I**, 66, 67, 74
Crosthwaite, Peter, **II**, 26, 46
Curwen, Isabella, **II**, 35
Curwen, John Christian, **II**, 35
Curwen, J.F., **II**, 30
Curwen, 'young Curwen', **II**, 266

Dalton, Jane, **I**, 6, 10, 57, 65, **II**, 285
Dalton, John, **II**, 46
Danvers, F.C., **I**, xxii, 108

Darnley, Lord, **II**, 163, 218
Davis, R.H.C., **II**, 176
Debrett, **I**, 62
Desiderius, **II**, 192
Diehl, Frits, **II**, xvi
Diodorus Siculus, **I**, 17, 21
Dixons, **II**, 273
Dodsley, J., **I**, 6, 68
Douglas, Mrs, **II**, 221
Drummond, Mr, **I**, 70
Du Bos, Jean-Baptiste, **II**, 171, 178
Duchatel, Comte. See Tanneguy, C.M.
Dudley, Henry Bate, formerly Henry Bate, **I**, 87
Duffy E., **II**, 185
Duncan, William, **I**, 29
Duncumb, Thomas, **I**, 55
Dunn, Samuel, **I**, 54
Duval, K.D., **I**, xi, xii

Eade, J.C., **II**, 238
Eagle, D., **I**, xxi
Eatwell, John, **I**, xxiii
Eckersall, Amelia (Emily), **II**, 245, 262
Eckersall, Anne Eliza. See Wood, Anne Eliza.
Eckersall, Caroline, **II**, 245, 266
Eckersall, Catherine, née Malthus, aunt of Malthus, **I**, 57, 62
Eckersall, Catherine (1758–1837), née Wathen, cousin and mother-in-law of Malthus, **I**, 55, 58, 62, **II**, 229, 242, 243, 244, 262, 264, 269, 273
Eckersall, Charles, **II**, 244, 250, 251, 256, 257, 258, 263, 264, 268, 272, 274
Eckersall, Clara, **II**, 242, 243, 249, 250, 252, 254, 255, 256, 259, 260, 262, 264, 265, 266, 268, 269, 270, 273
Eckersall, Frances (Fanny), **II**, 242, 243, 246, 249, 250, 252, 255, 259, 260, 262, 264, 265, 268, 273, 274
Eckersall, George, **I**, 62, **II**, 242, 243, 247, 248, 249, 252, 253, 254, 255, 256, 257, 258, 262, 263, 264, 266, 267, 272, 273
Eckersall, John, **I**, 55, 57, 62, 63, **II**, 242, 243, 244, 247, 248, 250, 253, 254, 255, 258, 259, 260, 261, 262, 264, 273, 274
Eckersall, Sarah Caroline, née Grace, **II**, 243, 248, 252, 253, 255, 256, 264, 266, 273
Ecks (i.e. Eckersalls), **II**, 257, 265
Eden, Frederick Morton, **I**, 65
Edgar, **II**, 191
Edgeworth, Maria, **II**, 214
Edward III, **I**, 130, 131
Edward the Elder, **II**, 188
Egbert, king of Wessex, **II**, 188, 201, 202
Einhard (or Eginhard), **II**, 195
Elizabeth I, **II**, 163, 164, 165
Ellen, Lord, **II**, 229
Ellis, Charles Rose (Baron Seaford), **II**, 261
Elmsly, Mr, **I**, 52
Emerson, William, **I**, 38, 39
Empson, Charlotte, née Jeffrey, **I**, 114, **II**, 2
Empson, William, **I**, xxii, 114
Enfield, William, **I**, 1, 8, 9, 10
Ermenonville, Marquis de, **I**, 68
Ethelbert, **II**, 188

Ethelred (or Aethelred or Ethered) I, **II**, 203
Ethelwolf (or Ethelwulf) of Wessex, **II**, 202, 203
Euclid, **I**, 8, 10, 36
Eudes (or Odo), Count of Paris, **II**, 201, 205, 206
Euphrasia, **I**, 14
Euphrosyne, **I**, 13
Euric, **II**, 182
Evelyn, Sir Frederick, **I**, 55

Fatima, **II**, 183
Ferguson, James, **I**, 41
Flahaut, Comte de, **II**, 219
Fleming, Daniel, **II**, 32
Fleming, George, **II**, 32
Fleming, Michael le, **II**, 32, 33, 38
Foster, Joseph, **I**, xx, 13, 35, 55
Foster, Mr, **I**, 34, 106
Fox, Charles James, **I**, 20
Franklin, Benjamin, **I**, 65
Fredegonda, **II**, 180
Frend, William, **I**, 30, 31, 32, 38, 43, 45, 46, 48, 49, 50
Frost, Colin, **I**, xi
Fullarton, Mr, **I**, 63, **II**, 238

Gagdis (?), Lord, **II**, 229
Gardner, Edward, **I**, 138
Garrick, David, **I**, 17
Gay, Rich., **I**, 106
George IV, **I**, 131
GEs or G Ecks (George and Caroline Eckersall), **II**, 248, 249, 250, 253, 258, 265, 266, 267, 272
Gibbon, Edward, **I**, 53, **II**, 171, 181, 182, 183, 184, 186, 198, 265
Giddy (later, Gilbert), Davies, **I**, 78, 79
Gilbert, Thomas, **I**, 79
Gilpin, William, **II**, 29
Glenorchy, Lord, **II**, 231
God, **II**, 4, 10, 11, 12, 15, 16, 17, 19, 20, 21, 22, 23, 24
Godfrey, **II**, 195
Godschall, Anne Catherine Lucy, née Malthus, **I**, 18, 19, 56, 58, 66, 70
Godschall, Samuel Man, **I**, 18, 56, 58, 70, **II**, 52, 53
Godwin, William, **I**, 75, 77
Goldsmith, Oliver, **I**, 7, 54
Goold, Thomas, **II**, 245
Gordon, Isabella, **II**, 239
Gordon, Robert, **II**, 215, 236, 239
Gordon, William, **II**, 45
Graham, James, first duke of Montrose, **II**, 229
Graham, James, third duke of Montrose, **II**, 229
Graham, Richard Robert, **I**, 15, 15, 37, **II**, 286
Grant, Charles, **I**, 120
Grant, Robert, **I**, 120, 121, 122, 123
Granthams, **II**, 273
Graves, Richard, **I**, 1, 2, 3, 4, 6, 13, **II**, 53, 265, 289
Gray, Thomas, **II**, 37, 42, 43, 44, 47
Gregory II, pope (Gregory the Great), **II**, 185, 188
Gregory VII, **II**, 200
Grenville, William Wyndham, Lord Grenville, **I**, 123
Grimstone, A.V., **I**, 35, **II**, xvi
Guido (or Guy), **II**, 206
Gunning, Henry, **I**, xxii, 73

Hackshaw, Anne, née Malthus, **II**, 285

Hadrian, emperor, **II**, 177
Hadrian I, pope, **II**, 192, 195
Haldimand, A.F., **I**, 91
Halifax, S., **II**, 14
Hall, Basil, **II**, 237, 238, 288
Hall, James, **II**, 237
Hall, John, **II**, 237
Hallam, Henry, **II**, 171, 191
Hallam, John, **I**, 55, 56
Halley, Edmund (or Edmond), **I**, 102
Hamilton, Alexander, **I**, 119
Hamilton, Colin, **I**, xi
Hamilton, William, **II**, 214, 220
Hand, Ferdinand Gotthelf (1786–1851), **I**, 3
Handel, George Frideric, **II**, 259
Hardwicke, third earl of. See Yorke, Philip.
Harris, William Robert, **I**, 69
Harvey, Sir Paul, **I**, xxi
Hashimoto, Hitoshi, **I**, xxii, 4, **II**, 212
Hasting (or Hastings or Haesten), Viking chief, **II**, 203
Hastings, Francis, tenth earl of Huntingdon, **I**, 35
Hatchard, J., **I**, 80, **II**, 284
Haygarth, John, **I**, 64
Heale, Mr, **I**, 77
Hegewisch, Franz Hermann, **I**, 125
Hengist, **II**, 186
Henry II, **II**, 210
Henry VIII, **II**, 159, 161, 165, 250
Henry the Fowler, **II**, 170, 207, 210
Henry, Robert, **II**, 171, 173, 191, 204
Herodotus, **I**, 13, 16, 18
Higgs, Henry, **I**, xxiv
Hincmar, **II**, 171, 196
Hodgson, Brian Houghton, **I**, 138, 139
Hodgson, Edward Legh, **I**, 139
Hodson, Francis, **I**, 116
Hodson, J., **I**, 117
Hogan, Charles Beecher, **I**, xxii, 12, 14
Hogarth, William, **I**, 15
Hogg, J., **II**, xvi, 238
Holbech, William, **II**, 257
Holt, Jane (b. 1802), née Malthus, **I**, 70, **II**, 287
Holt, Robert Fowler, **I**, 70, **II**, 287
Home, John, **I**, 12
Homes, Sir Robert, **I**, 66
Horace, **I**, 6, 11, 18
Horn, Captain, **II**, 240
Horne, Mr, **I**, 4
Horner, Francis, **I**, 108, 113, 118, **II**, 143
Horner, Leonard, **II**, 214, 217, 218
Horsa, **II**, 186
Horton, Eusebius, **I**, 103
Howard, Bernard Edward (duke of Norfolk), **II**, 253
Hubba. See Ubbe.
Huddleston, David, **II**, 36
Hufeland, Gottlieb, **I**, 126
Hugh Capet, **II**, 208
Hugh the Great, **II**, 208
Hughes Parry, Trevor, **I**, xi, xii, **II**, ix, x
Hume, David, **II**, 171, 203, 204, 205
Hume, Joseph, **I**, 120
Hunter, William Wilson, **I**, xxii, 138, 139
Huntingford, George Isaac, **I**, 17
Huskisson, William, **II**, 143, 151
Hutchinson, John, **II**, 160, 165
Hutchinson, Julius, **II**, 160

Hutchinson, Lucy, **II**, 160, 165
Hutton, Mr, **II**, 50

Jackson, Mr, **II**, 171
Jackson, Randle, **I**, 90, 120
Jackson, Thomas, **II**, 214, 220, 221
James, Patricia, **I**, xi, xxiii, xxiii, 1, 11, 13, 14, 18, 34, 35, 47, 55, 56, 57, 58, 60, 62, 64, 65, 66, 68, 69, 73, 78, 79, 80, 85, 88, 89, 98, 108, 114, 118, 120, 121, 138, **II**, 141, 142, 212, 217, 220, 222, 231, 235, 237, 238, 239, 244, 246, 248
Jamieson, Mr, **II**, 241
Jamieson, Mrs, **II**, 241
Jeffrey, Charlotte, née Wilkes, **I**, 118, **II**, 217
Jeffrey, Francis, **I**, 114, 115, 117, 118, 119, **II**, 141, 142, 143, 214, 215, 216, 217, 218, 219, 222, 235, 236, 237
Jerome, Saint, **II**, 204
Jesus, **II**, 13
Jesus Christ, **II**, 13, 17, 24
Job, **II**, 1, 8, 9
John XII, pope, **II**, 208, 209
John, Saint, **II**, 1, 2, 12, 13, 17
John the Baptist, **II**, 13
Johnson, Andrew, **II**, xvi, 238
Johnson, Dr, **I**, 3
Johnson, J., **I**, 80, 82
Johnston, Colin, **II**, xvi, 248
Jones, Alice, **II**, xvii
Jonker, Joost, **II**, xvi
Joscelin (or Gosselin), bishop of Paris, **II**, 205
Jowett, B., **I**, 127
Judith, empress, **II**, 206
Julian, Count, **II**, 182
Julius, Dr, **II**, 290
Justinian, **II**, 184
Juvenal, **I**, 6

Kaplan, Herbert, **II**, xvi
Keill, John, **I**, 28, 39
Keir, D., **II**, 238
Kemble, Frances (Fanny), **II**, 246
Kemble, John Philip, **I**, 20, 22
Kennedy, Sophia, née Romilly, **II**, 231, 232, 234
Kennedy, Thomas Francis, **II**, 231, 232, 234
Kerr, Beverley, **II**, xvii
Kersseboom, Willem, **I**, 64
Kidd, Charles, **II**, xvii
Kippis, Andrew, **I**, 53
Kirwan, Richard, **I**, 52, 53
Kitty, niece of Mrs Nutcombe, **II**, 273
Knight, Mr, **I**, 63
Knox, John, **II**, 228

Laing, Malcolm, **II**, 220
Laing, Mrs, **II**, 220
Langman, Lady, **II**, 143
Laplagne, Patrick, **I**, 140, **II**, xvii
Lavater, Johann Kaspar, **II**, 41
Law, George Henry, **II**, 250
Law, Mr, **II**, 34
le Bas, Charles Webb, **I**, 90, 94, 121, 122
Lee, S., **I**, xx
Leeves, Anna, née Wathen, **I**, 58
Leeves, William, **I**, 58
Leibniz (or Leibnitz), G.W., **II**, 171, 192
Leigh, R.A.(?), **II**, 290
Leivsey, J., **I**, 140
Leo III, pope, **II**, 195
Leo VIII, pope, **II**, 209

Leo the Isaurian, **II**, 185
Leslie, J.B., **I**, 63, **II**, 244
Lewton, Edward, **I**, 90
Lister, Raymond, **I**, xxiii
Liutprand, **II**, 185
Locke, John, **I**, 33
Lockhart, **II**, 240, 261
Logan, F.D., **II**, 205
Long, Roger, **I**, 35, 38, 49
Longinus, **I**, 8, 10
Lothair (or Lothaire), **II**, 199, 200, 208
Lotz, Johann Friedrich Eusebius, **I**, 126
Louis I, the Debonaire (or Louis the Pious), **II**, 198, 199, 201, 205
Louis II, the German, **II**, 199, 205, 206
Louis IV, **II**, 206
Louis d'Outremer (or Louis Outremer), **II**, 207, 208
Louis the Simple, **II**, 206
Louis, son of Boson. **II**, 206
Louis the Stammerer, **II**, 205
Lowndes, Mr, **I**, 90
Lucan, **I**, 5
Luke, Dr, **I**, 94
Luke, Saint, **II**, 2, 13, 16

Mably, Gabriel Bonnot de, **II**, 171, 177, 179, 196, 197
McCulloch, John Ramsay, **I**, 133, 137, **II**, 214, 215, 219, 238
McEachern, Shona, **II**, xvii
McFarlane, Mr, **II**, 222
MacGregor, Ian, **II**, 46
MacGregor, Robert (Rob Roy), **II**, 224, 229
Mackenzie, Henry, **II**, 214, 218, 219, 220
Mackintosh, Elizabeth, **II**, 271
Mackintosh, Fanny, **II**, 271
Mackintosh, James, **II**, 271
Maclaurin, Colin, **I**, 28, 33, 39
McNab, **II**, 231
Madan, Spencer, **II**, 250
Maggs Bros, **I**, xi, xii
Mahomet, **II**, 183, 201
Malthus, Anne Catherine Lucy. See Godschall.
Malthus, Charles Edward Daniel, **II**, 288
Malthus, Daniel, father of Malthus, **I**, 1, 2, 4, 6, 8, 9, 11, 12, 14, 16, 17, 18, 20, 21, 23, 24, 25, 27, 28, 29, 31, 32, 34, 35, 36, 37, 39, 40, 41, 43, 44, 45, 47, 48, 49, 50, 51, 52, 53, 54, 56, 57, 58, 59, 60, 61, 62, 63, 66, 68, **II**, 285, 289
Malthus, Eliza Maria, **I**, 14, 41, 43, 60, 63, 70, **II**, 287
Malthus, Emily. See Pringle, Emily.
Malthus, Harriet, née Eckersall, wife of Malthus, **I**, 4, 55, 58, 61, 62, 71, 90, 94, 96, 98, 101, 102, 112, 139, **II**, 212, 216, 220, 237, 242, 245, 246, 251, 252, 257, 258, 262, 263, 268, 269, 287, 288
Malthus, Henrietta (Etta), **II**, 288
Malthus, Henrietta (Harriet), sister of Malthus, **I**, 10, 11, 12, 13, 14
Malthus, Henrietta (Harriet) (1733–1800), née Graham, mother of Malthus, **I**, 7, 14, 15, **II**, 285
Malthus, Henrietta (Harriet), née Maberly, **II**, 289
Malthus, Henry (Hal), **I**, 71, 106, **II**, 25, 212, 224, 230, 239, 242, 245, 249, 251, 257, 258, 264, 272, 274

Malthus, Henry Percival, **II**, 288
Malthus, John, **II**, 285
Malthus, Laura, **II**, 287
Malthus, Lucy, **I**, 71, 90, **II**, 25, 239, 242
Malthus, Marianna Georgina, née Ryves, **I**, 4, 10, 37, 69, 70, 71, **II**, 287, 288, 289. See also, Symes, Marianna Georgina.
Malthus, Mary (1800–81), **II**, 287
Malthus, Mary Anne (or Marianne or Minny), née White, **II**, 286, 287, 288
Malthus, Mary Catherine Charlotte, **I**, 38, 50, 57, 58, 93, **II**, 42
Malthus, Richard, **II**, 285
Malthus, Robert (1881–1972), **I**, xi, **II**, 212, 286, 289
Malthus, Sophia, née Otter, **I**, 106
Malthus, Sydenham (1754–1821), brother of Malthus, **I**, xi, 4, 9, 15, 51, 57, 59, 61, 69, 70, **II**, 286, 288
Malthus, Sydenham (d. 1757), grandfather of Malthus, **II**, 285, 289
Malthus, Sydenham (1801–68), nephew of Malthus, **I**, 70, **II**, 286, 287
Malthus, Sydenham (1831–1916), great-nephew of Malthus, **I**, xx, **II**, 287, 288, 289
Malthuses (i.e. family of T.R. Malthus), **II**, 272
Malthuses, Miss, **I**, 5
Manning, Owen, **I**, 56, **II**, 271
Mannix, **II**, 35
Mansel, William Lort, **I**, 116
Marcet, Alexander John Gaspard, **I**, 72, 88, 92
Marcet, Jane (née Haldimand), **I**, 88, 91
Mark, Saint, **II**, 13, 16
Marryat, Joseph, **II**, 284
Marsh, Herbert, **I**, 116
Martel, Charles, **II**, 168, 177, 181, 185, 192
Maruzen & Co., **I**, xi
Mary, Queen of Scots, **II**, 159, 160, 162, 163, 164, 165, 218, 267
Masè-Dari, Eugenio, **I**, xxiii, 4, **II**, 237
Mason, Monck, **I**, 15
Mason, Mr, **II**, 273
Masons, **II**, 273
Matsudaira, Masahisa, **I**, xi
Matsudaira, Masatoshi, **I**, xii
Matthew, Saint, **II**, 1, 2, 4, 7, 12, 13, 16, 22
Meroveus, **II**, 178
Mill, James, **II**, 300
Millar, John, **II**, 171, 175, 176, 177, 187, 188, 189, 190, 191, 204
Millot, Claude François Xavier, **II**, 171, 198
Milne, Joshua, **I**, 98, 99, 100, 101, 102
Milner, Isaac, **I**, 117
Milton, John, **I**, 13, 37, **II**, 256, 269
Mithadites (or Mithradates), **II**, 201
Moavia, i.e. Mu'āwiyah I (or Moawiyah), **II**, 183
Moivre, Abraham de, **I**, 102
Montesquieu, Charles Secondat, Baron de, **II**, 171, 174, 178, 179, 180, 181, 191, 194, 197, 199
Montgolfier brothers, **I**, 10
Montrose, first duke of. See Graham, James.

Montrose, third duke of. See Graham, James.
Moody, Thomas, **I**, 105
Mordaunt, Charles, **II**, 255, 257
Mordaunt, Marianne, née Holbech, **II**, 255, 257
Moreau, César, **I**, 2, 140
Morehead, Mr, **II**, 239
Morgan, William, **I**, 101
Morris, Mr, **I**, 91
Morrison, General George, **I**, 58
Morrisons, **I**, 58
Morritt, John B.S., **II**, 240
Moses, **II**, 13, 19
Muret, Jean-Louis, **I**, 640
Murphy, Arthur, **I**, 14
Murray, John, third duke of Atholl, **II**, 234
Murray, John, fourth duke of Atholl, **II**, 234
Murray, John, publisher, **I**, 108, **II**, 141, 142, 144, 277
Murray, John Archibald, Lord Murray, **II**, 215, 218, 219, 237, 238, 239
Musā (or Mousa) ibn Nasayr, **II**, 182
Mushet, Robert, **I**, 109, **II**, 143

Nangle, B.C., **I**, xxiii
Napier, Macvey, **I**, 97
Narses, **II**, 184
Nasmyth, Alexander, **II**, 215, 238
Newton, Benjamin, **I**, 31
Newton, Isaac, **I**, 11, 13, 38, 39, 40, 42, 49
Nicholas I, pope, **II**, 170, 200
Nickson, Mr, **I**, 63
Nixon, Edward, **II**, 243
Norfolk, Duke of, **II**, 164
North, Brownlow, **I**, 55
Nugent, James, **II**, 245
Nugent, T., **II**, 174
Nutcombe, Mrs, **II**, 261, 272, 273

Odda (or Odduni), elderman of Devon, **II**, 203
Odin (or Woden), **II**, 201
Og, king of Bashan, **I**, 73
Ormathwaite, Lord. See Walsh, Sir J.B.
Orosius, **II**, 204
Osborne, Daniel Toler, **II**, 244
Othman, **II**, 183
Otter, William, **I**, xxiii, 2, 66, 67, 68, 106, 108, **II**, 2
Otto (or Otho) I, **II**, 170, 206, 207, 208, 209
Otto (or Otho) II, **II**, 209
Otto (or Otho) III, **II**, 207, 209, 210

Paisley, Colonel, **II**, 290
Parnell, Henry Brooke, **I**, 72, 85, 86, 87
Parry, Trevor Hughes. See Hughes Parry, Trevor.
Parson, W., **II**, 31, 32, 33, 36, 37, 38, 39, 43, 44, 47, 48, 49, 51, 55
Paschoud, J.J., **I**, 88
Patten, Mr, **I**, 10
Paul, Charles Kegan, **I**, xxiii, 77
Paul, Saint, **II**, 2, 13, 14, 17, 20, 21, 23, 24
Peachey, General, **II**, 44
Pelagius, **II**, 182
Pepin d'Heristal (or d'Héristal), **II**, 168, 180, 181, 185, 199
Pepin the Short, **II**, 168, 181
Pepys, Samuel, **II**, 214
Perthes, **I**, 126, 127
Peter, Saint, **II**, 2, 14

Peters, Mr, **I**, 69
Peters, Mrs, **I**, 37, 56, 69
Pinkerton, John, **II**, 186
Pitcher, Roger, **I**, xxiv, 68
Pitt, William, **I**, 20, 77, **II**, 26, 47, 153
Playfair, William, **I**, 119
Pocklington, Mr, **II**, 44, 45, 51
Polkinghorn, B.A., **I**, xxiv, 88
Polybius, **I**, 21
Pompey, **II**, 201
Pope, Alexander, **I**, 5, 80
Prévost, Guillaume, **I**, 91
Prévost, Pierre, **I**, 72, 88, 90, 91, 93
Price, Richard, **I**, 64, 65, 98, 99, 101
Pringle, Emily, née Malthus, **I**, 71, 90, **II**, 25, 212, 239, 242, 245, 249, 251, 257, 274, 288
Pringle, John Watson, **I**, 71, **II**, 288
Pullen, John, **I**, xii, xxiv, 47, 54, 68, 123, **II**, ix, x, 1, 159, 278, 292

Quintilian, **I**, 33

Randolph, Lady, **I**, 12, 14, 17, 19
Rau, Karl Heinrich (Charles Henry), **I**, 123, 127, 128
Recared, **II**, 182
Reid, Norman H., **II**, xvii, 221
Remigius, Saint, **II**, 178
Reynolds, Joshua, **II**, 242
Ricardo, David, **I**, 109, 128, 129, 130, 133, 135, 137, **II**, 57, 64, 79, 80, 84, 91, 92, 93, 95, 96, 97, 102, 104, 110, 141, 142, 143, 144, 145, 146, 147, 150, 151, 152, 154, 155, 219, 292, 293
Rich, Mrs, **II**, 238
Richards, Solomon, of Ounavarra, **II**, 243
Richards, Solomon, of Roebuck, **II**, 244
Richardson, J., **II**, 290
Richardson, J.M., **II**, 284
Richardson, W.I., **II**, 290
Rickman, John, **I**, 98
Rizzio (or David Riccio), **II**, 218
Robert, brother of Count Eudes, **II**, 205
Robert, P. (*Le Petit Robert*), **II**, 193
Robertson, J. Logie, **II**, 217
Robertson, William, **II**, 171, 173, 175, 176, 177
Robinson, Henry, **II**, 53
Roderic, **II**, 182
Rodolphe I (or Rodolph or Rudolf), **II**, 206, 207
Roland, **II**, 194
Rolle, John, Baron Rolle of Stevenstone, **II**, 271
Rolles, Baroness de, **II**, 271
Rollo, **II**, 201
Rolls, Mr, **II**, 271
Rose, George, **I**, 84, 89, 112, **II**, 37
Rothari (or Rotharis), **II**, 185
Rowe, Anne, **II**, xvii, 27, 30, 31, 53
Rudge, Mr, **I**, 70
Russell, William, **II**, 171, 173, 181
Rutherforth, Thomas, **I**, 16, 17, 19, 20, 38, 39, 41
Rutherfurd (or Rutherforth), Andrew, **II**, 218, 219, 237
Rutherfurd (or Rutherforth), Mrs, **II**, 218, 219, 237
Ryves, Anna Maria, née Graham, **I**, 4, 10, 15, 41, 63, **II**, 285, 286
Ryves, Catherine Elizabeth, née Arundell, **II**, 286
Ryves, Diana Maria, **II**, 289
Ryves, Emma, née Graham, **II**, 286

Ryves, George Frederick (1758–1826), rear-admiral, **I**, 4, **II**, 285, 286

Ryves, George Frederick (d. 1858), admiral, **II**, 286, 289

Ryves, George Frederick (d. 1876), **II**, 286

Ryves, Henry Pleydell, **I**, 56, **II**, 289

Ryves, Laura Matilda, **II**, 289

Ryves, Lucy Graham, **II**, 289

Ryves, Marianna Georgina. See Malthus, Marianna Georgina.

Ryves, Richard, **II**, 289

Ryves, Robert Graham, **II**, 289

Ryves, Thomas, **I**, 4, 10, 41, 52, 63, **II**, 285

Ryvess, i.e. Ryves family, **I**, 37, 41, **II**, 286, 289

Sallust (Gaius Sallustius Crispus), **I**, 7

Sambrook, James, **II**, 28

Sanderson, **I**, 38

Sappho, **I**, 19

Sartorius, Georg Friedrich, **I**, 126

Satoh, Takeo, **I**, xiii

Say, Jean-Baptiste, **I**, 123, 126, 129, **II**, 292

Scawen, Louisa, **I**, 10

Schaak (or Schaach or Schalk), Matilda, **II**, 270, 273

Schaak, Thomas, **II**, 270

Schumpeter, Joseph A., **I**, xxiv, 126, 127

Scobie, Joyce, **II**, xvii, 28

Scott, John, **II**, 267

Scott, Walter, **I**, 119, **II**, 32, 214, 217, 218, 224, 240, 261

Seaford, Baron. See Ellis, Charles Rose.

Selden, John, **I**, 43

Selincourt, E. de, **II**, 224

Senior, Nassau William, **I**, 103

Sergeant, a servant, **II**, 244, 250, 255, 260, 264, 266, 273

Shakespeare, William, **II**, 26, 50, 55, 265

Shenstone, William, **I**, 3

Shibata, Hirofumi, **II**, x

Siddons, Sarah, **I**, 12, 14, 17, 19, 20, **II**, 246

Sigebert, I., **II**, 182

Simond, Louis, **I**, 118

Simonde de Sismondi, J.C.L., **I**, 127

Six, James, **I**, 30, 31, 32, 46

Smith, Adam, **I**, 119, 123, 126, **II**, 4, 277, 295, 296, 297, 298, 299

Smith, Mr, **II**, 220

Smith, Mrs, wife of the above, **II**, 220

Smith, Mrs, presumably different from the above, **II**, 266

Smith, R., **II**, 238

Smyth, William, **I**, 85, 89, 90, 101

Soden, Friedrich Julius Heinrich Reichsgraf von, **I**, 126

Somerset, Edward Adolphe, 11th Duke of Somerset, **II**, 267

Sophocles, **I**, 18

Southey, Robert, **I**, xiii, 98

Spineto, Dr, **I**, 119

Sraffa, Piero, **II**, 143, 293

Starr, Judith, **II**, xvii

Starr, Noel, **II**, xvii

Stephen, L., **I**, xx

Steven (or Stephen) II (or III), pope, **II**, 185

Stewart (or Stuart), innkeeper, **II**, 228, 229

Stiles, Ezra, **I**, 64

Storch, Heinrich Friedrich von, **I**, 127
Summers, Anne, **I**, xii
Süssmilch, Johann Peter, **I**, 63, 64
Swann, Henry, **I**, 69
Syagrius, **II**, 178
Sydenham, Baron. See Thomson, C.E.P.
Symes, George Frederick, **II**, 288
Symes, Harriett, **II**, 289
Symes, Marianna Georgina, née Ryves. See Malthus, Marianna Georgina.
Symes, William Leigh, **I**, 4, 69, **II**, 288

Tacitus, **I**, 29, 32, **II**, 32, 172, 173, 174
Tankerville, Earl of. See Bennet, Charles.
Tanneguy, Charles Marie, Comte Duchatel, **I**, 103
Tasker, Henry, **II**, 286
Taunton, Lucy, née Eckersall, **II**, 245, 258, 264, 274
Taunton, Robert Cropp, **II**, 245, 258
Tauntons (i.e. Lucy and Robert Cropp Taunton), **II**, 272
Taylor, Mr, **I**, 7
Taylor, W.B., **I**, xxii, 108
Terence, **I**, 2, 3
Theocritus, **I**, 36, 38, 39
Theodebert, **II**, 179
Theodoric, **II**, 168, 183, 184
Thicknesse, Philip, **II**, 26, 30
Thierry (or Theuderic), **II**, 179
Thompson, William, **II**, 283
Thomson, Andrew Mitchell, **II**, 219
Thomson, Charles Edward Poulett, Baron Sydenham, **I**, 103
Thomson, James, **II**, 26, 28, 40
Thucydides, **I**, 11, 21
Timbs, John, **I**, 57
Timothy, **II**, 13, 20
Titus, **II**, 23
Torrens, Robert, **I**, 128
Torsellino, Orazio. See Tursellinus, Horatius.
Treloar, Alan, **I**, xx, 3, 5, 18, 19, 22, 58, 139, **II**, xvii, 173
Trotter, Coutts, **II**, 284
Trotter, William, **II**, 238
Tufton, Henry, **I**, 73
Turgot, A.R.J., **II**, 153, 154
Tursellinus, Horatius, **I**, 3
Twiss, Frances (Fanny), **II**, 246
Twiss, Francis, **II**, 246
Twiss, Horace, **II**, 246
Tyrwhitt, Robert, **I**, 116

Ubbe (or Ubba or Ubbi or Hubba), **II**, 203

Venn, J.A., **I**, xxi, 31, 55, 56, 73, 89, 121, **II**, 247
Vernon (surnamed Harcourt from 1831), Edward Venables, **II**, 269
Vince, Samuel, **I**, 16, 20
Virgil, **I**, 7, 10, 18, 58
Voltaire (i.e. François-Marie Arouet), **I**, 4, **II**, 171
Vortigern, **II**, 186

Wakefield, Gilbert, **I**, 1, 9, 11, 12, 14, 15, 16, 17, 18, 19, 20, 21, 23, 24, 25, 26, 33, 34, 36, 62, **II**, 53
Wakefield, Thomas, **I**, 23, 24
Walker, author, **II**, 284
Walker, Mrs, **II**, 288
Walker, T.A., **I**, xxiv, 89

Walid, **II**, 182
Walpole, Robert, **I**, 22, **II**, 271
Walsh, John Benn, first Lord Ormathwaite, **I**, 105
Wargentin, Pierre (Per Wilhelm), **I**, 64
Warton, Joseph, **I**, 7, 8
Waterman, **I**, 5
Wathen, Elizabeth, née Malthus, **I**, 34, 58
Wathen, Samuel, **I**, 34
Watson, Captain, **II**, 260
Watson, Richard, **I**, 53, **II**, 25, 34, 38
Watt, James, **II**, 41
Watt, Montgomery, **II**, 183
Watts, William, **I**, 4
West, Thomas, **II**, 34, 35, 37, 39, 42, 43, 44, 45, 46, 47, 48, 49, 50, 51, 54, 248, 254
Whellan, **II**, 35
Whitaker, John, **II**, 171, 187
Whitbread, Samuel, **I**, 72, 80, 81, 85
White, Isabella, **II**, 288
White, Samuel, **II**, 286, 287
White, W., **II**, 31, 32, 33, 36, 37, 38, 39, 43, 44, 47, 48, 49, 51, 55
Widukind (or Witikand or Witikind), **II**, 192, 193
Wilkes, John, **I**, 118, 119
William, king, **II**, 228
Williams, Dr, **II**, 220
Williams, Eliz., **II**, 289
Wilmot, Robert, **I**, 103
Wilmot-Horton, Robert John, **I**, 73, 103, **II**, 248
Winch, Donald, **I**, xii, **II**, xvii
Winchester, W., **II**, 284
Witiza, **II**, 182
Woden. See Odin.
Wollaston, Francis, **I**, 31
Wolsey, Cardinal, **II**, 250
Wood, Anne Eliza, née Eckersall, **I**, 57, **II**, 214, 216, 242, 244, 248, 249, 252, 254, 255, 259, 262, 264, 266, 268, 269, 270, 271, 274
Wood, Boynton, **II**, 244, 249
Wood, Delia, **II**, 268, 274
Wood, Delia Maria, **II**, 268, 274
Wood, Eliza, **II**, 268
Wood, Emma Juliana, **II**, 268, 270
Wood, Frederick, **II**, 244, 249
Wood, Henry Richard, **II**, 214, 216, 242, 244, 249, 252, 257, 258, 259, 260, 262, 264, 268, 269, 270, 273
Wood, Hugh, **II**, 270, 273
Wood, John Philip, **II**, 220
Wood, Louisa Frances, **II**, 268, 270
Wood, Maria Frances, **II**, 244, 248, 256
Wood, Mr, **II**, 220
Wood, Richard, **II**, 268
Wood, Richard John, **II**, 244
Woods (i.e. the family of Henry Richard and Anne Eliza Wood), **II**, 241, 247, 253, 255, 259, 272, 273
Wordsworth, Dorothy, **II**, 224
Wordsworth, William, **II**, 31, 32, 36, 44, 49, 261
Wynne, Anne, née Osborne, **II**, 244
Wynne, Catherine, née Eckersall, **I**, 62, **II**, 53, 243, 271
Wynne, Charles (Charly), **II**, 245, 249
Wynne, Clara, **II**, 243, 248, 252, 262, 266
Wynne, Edmond, **II**, 243
Wynne, Emily, née Goold, **II**, 245

Wynne, George, son of Henry and Catherine Wynne, **II**, 244, 248, 274
Wynne, George, husband of Clara Wynne, **II**, 243
Wynne, Harry, son of the following, **II**, 244, 255, 271
Wynne, Henry, **I**, 62, 63, **II**, 53, 242, 243, 245, 248, 249, 252, 254, 255, 256, 257, 258, 259, 260, 262, 270, 271, 273
Wynne, Isabella, née Nugent, **II**, 245
Wynne, John George, **II**, 245, 248, 255, 270, 271
Wynne, Kate (Katherine), **II**, 243, 248, 252, 254, 259, 260, 266
Wynne, Lucy Catherine, **II**, 243, 248, 249, 252, 254, 255, 258, 260, 266, 271
Wynne, Marianne (or Mary Ann), **II**, 243, 248, 253, 256, 265
Wynne, Marianne, née Richards, **II**, 244
Wynne, Owen, **II**, 243
Wynne, Robert, **II**, 243
Wynne, William, **II**, 243, 245, 271
Wynnes (i.e. the family of Henry Wynne), **II**, 247, 253, 255, 259, 273

Xenophon, **I**, 21, 23

Yorke, James, **I**, 47
Yorke, Philip, third Earl of Hardwicke, **II**, 241
Young, Arthur, **II**, 34, 35, 38

Zachary (or Zacharias or Saint Zacharias), pope, **II**, 181, 185
Zinke, George William, **I**, xxiv, 88, 90, 91, 92, 93

For EU product safety concerns, contact us at Calle de José Abascal, 56–1°, 28003 Madrid, Spain or eugpsr@cambridge.org.

www.ingramcontent.com/pod-product-compliance
Lightning Source LLC
LaVergne TN
LVHW050300210926
848481LV00014BA/243

* 9 7 8 0 5 2 1 1 8 4 1 0 6 *